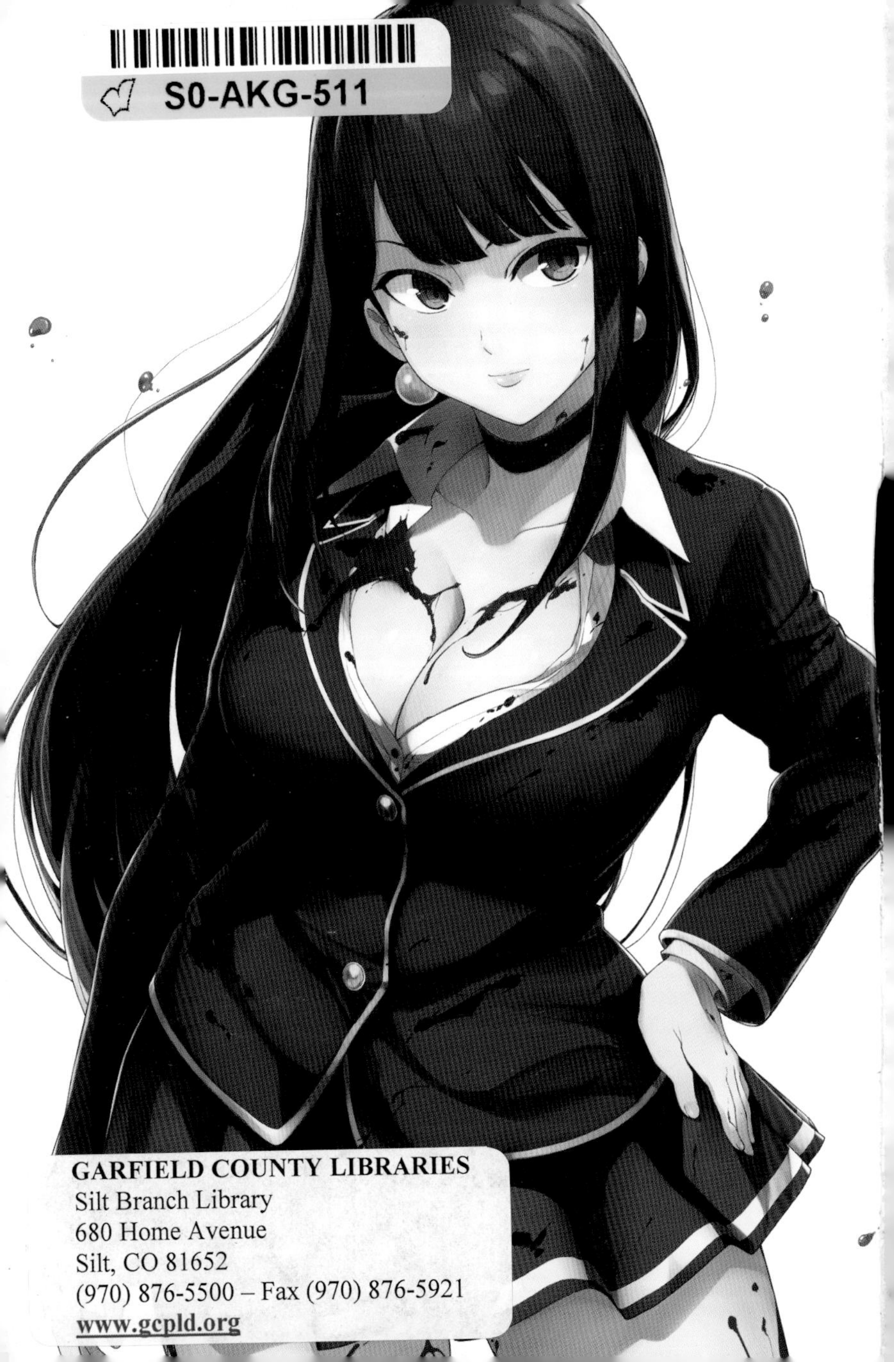

CONTENTS

THE 1ST DAY — AN UNEXPECTED ENCOUNTER — 003

THE 2ND DAY — GATHERING SUPPLIES — 055

THE 3RD DAY — RECAPTURE — 079

THE 4TH DAY — FUN AND GAMES — 113

THE 5TH DAY — SIGNAL FIRE — 137

THE 6TH DAY — MAD DASH — 159

THE 1ST DAY AN UNEXPECTED ENCOUNTER

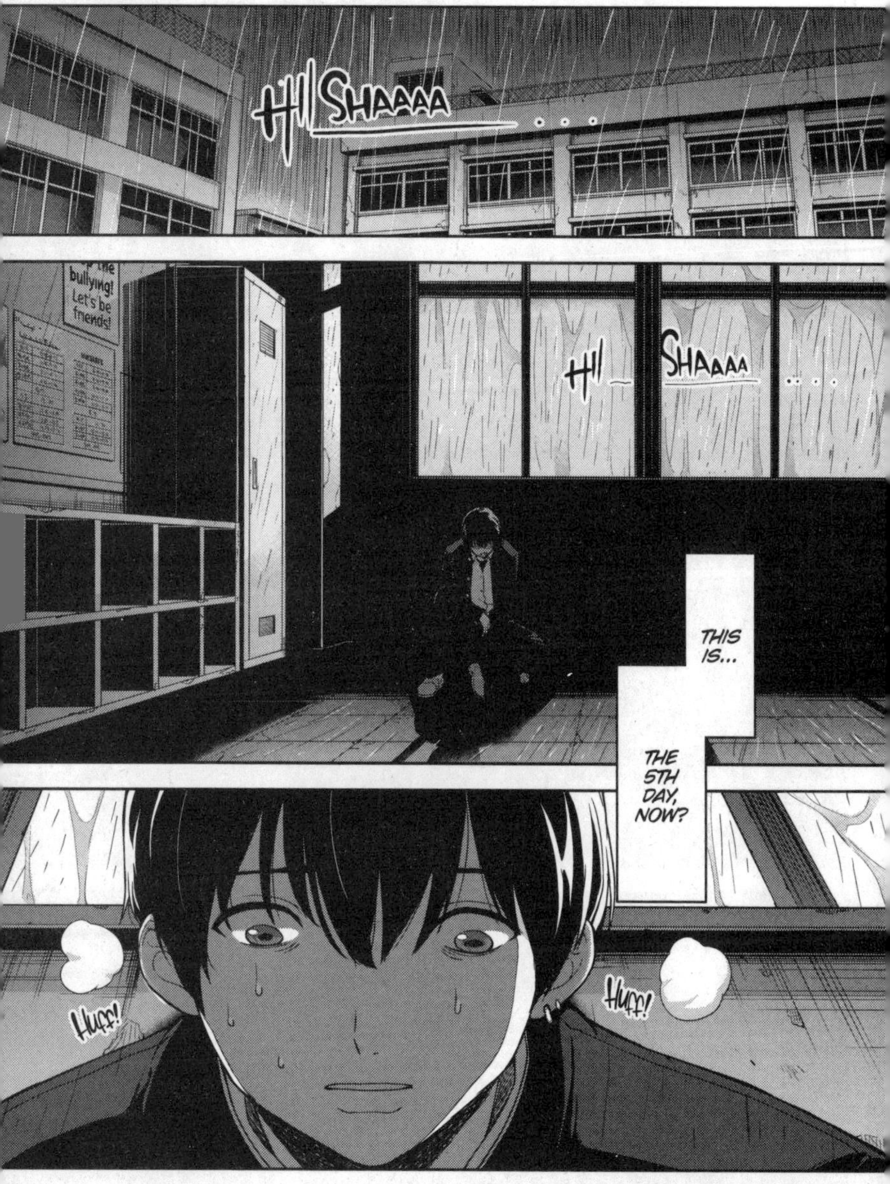
SHAAAA...
bullying! Let's be friends!
SHAAAA...
THIS IS...
THE 5TH DAY, NOW?
Huff!
Huff!

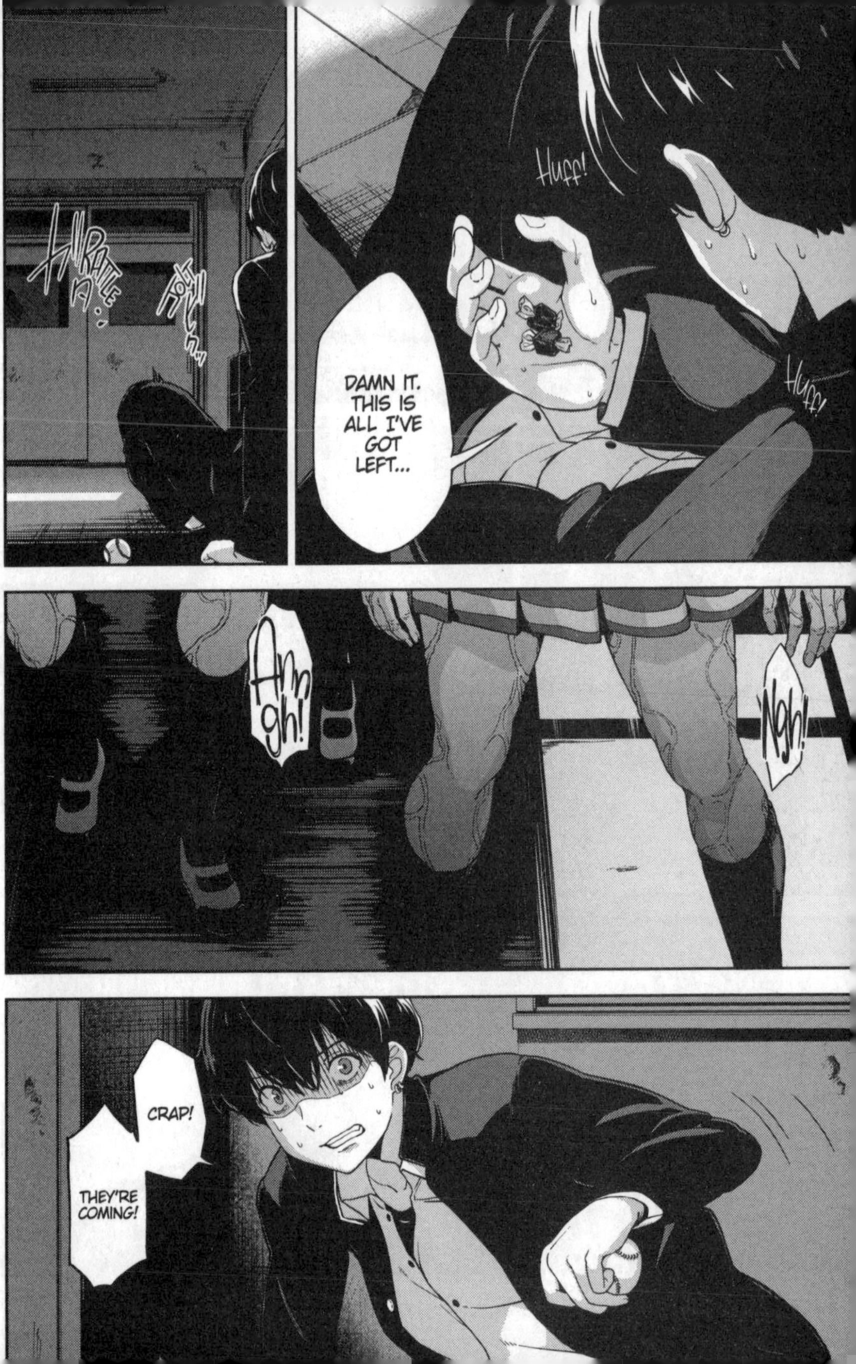
Huff!
DAMN IT. THIS IS ALL I'VE GOT LEFT...
Huff!
RATTLE
Ngh!
Anngh!
CRAP!
THEY'RE COMING!

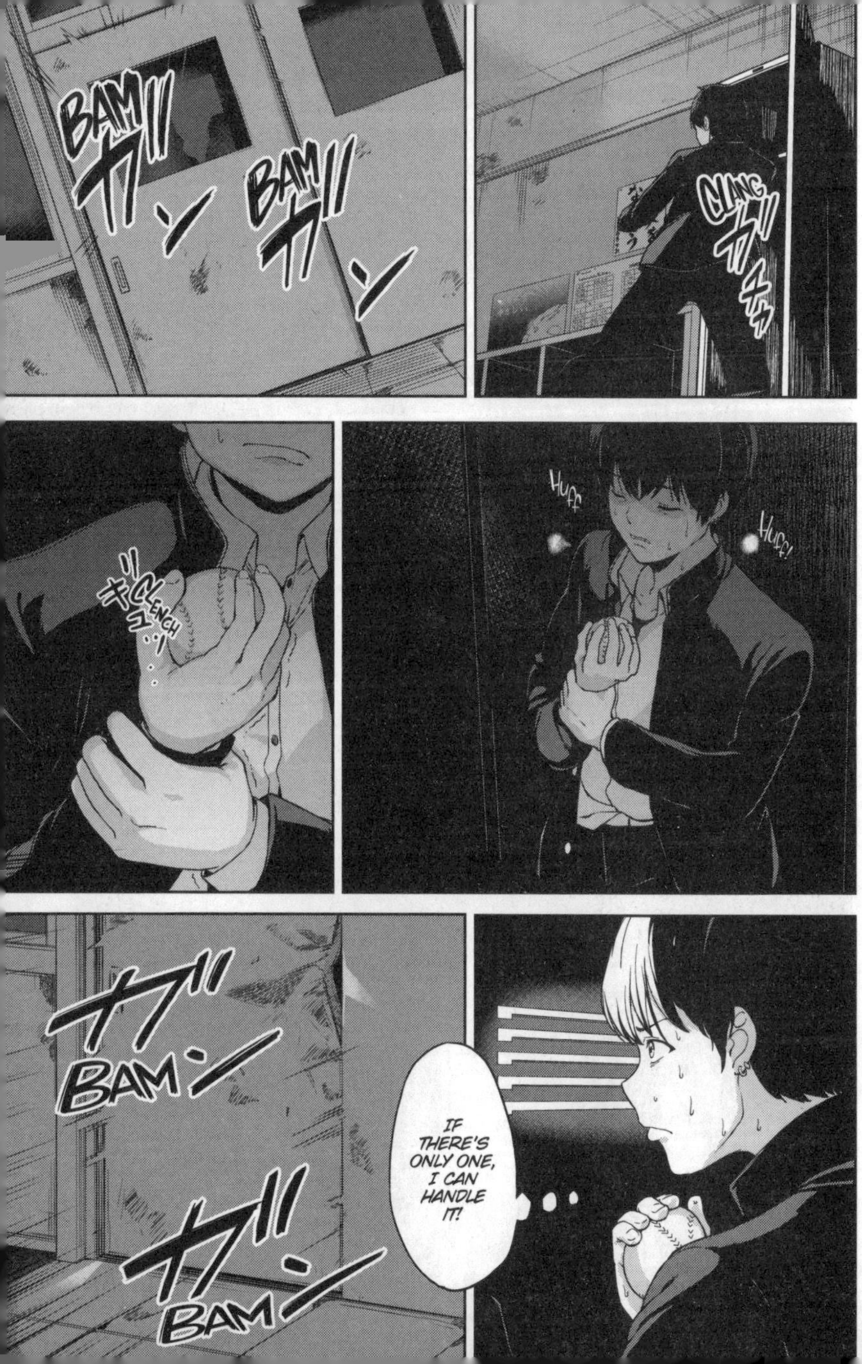

CLANG
BAM
BAM
Huff
Huff!
CLENCH
...
IF THERE'S ONLY ONE, I CAN HANDLE IT!
BAM
BAM

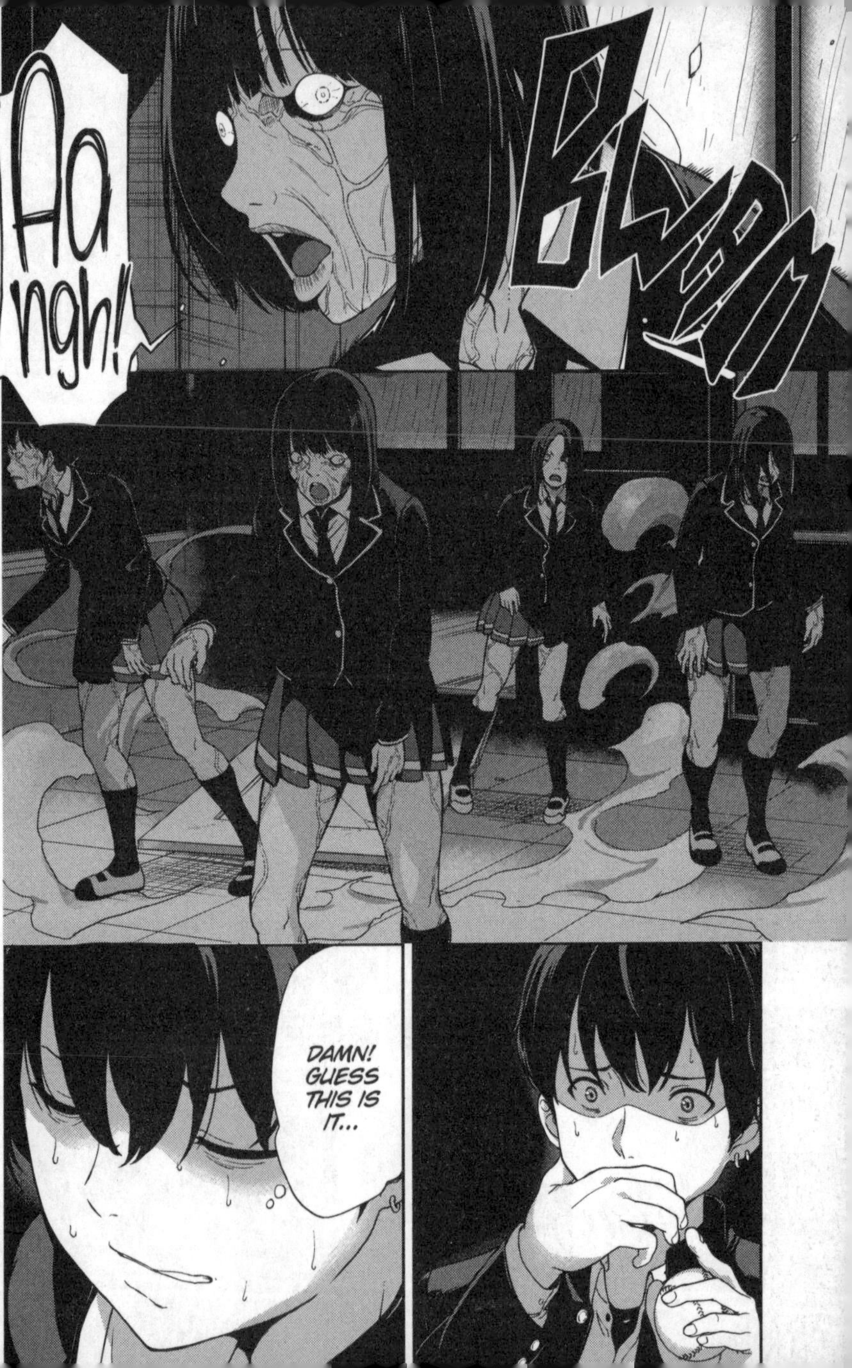
BLAM
Aa ngh!
DAMN! GUESS THIS IS IT...

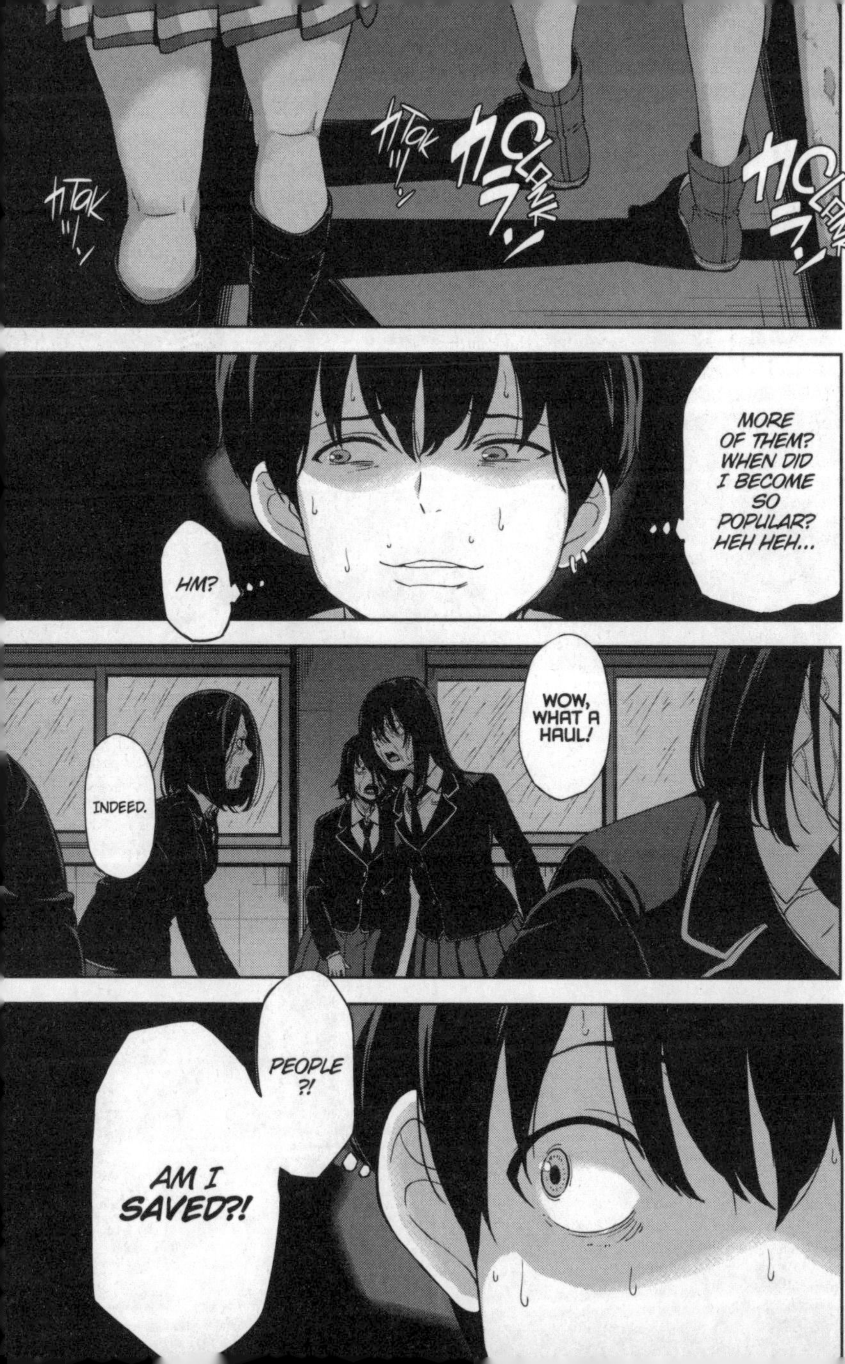
CLANK
CLANK
TAK
TAK
...MORE OF THEM? WHEN DID I BECOME SO POPULAR? HEH HEH...
HM?
WOW, WHAT A HAUL!
INDEED.
PEOPLE?!
AM I SAVED?!

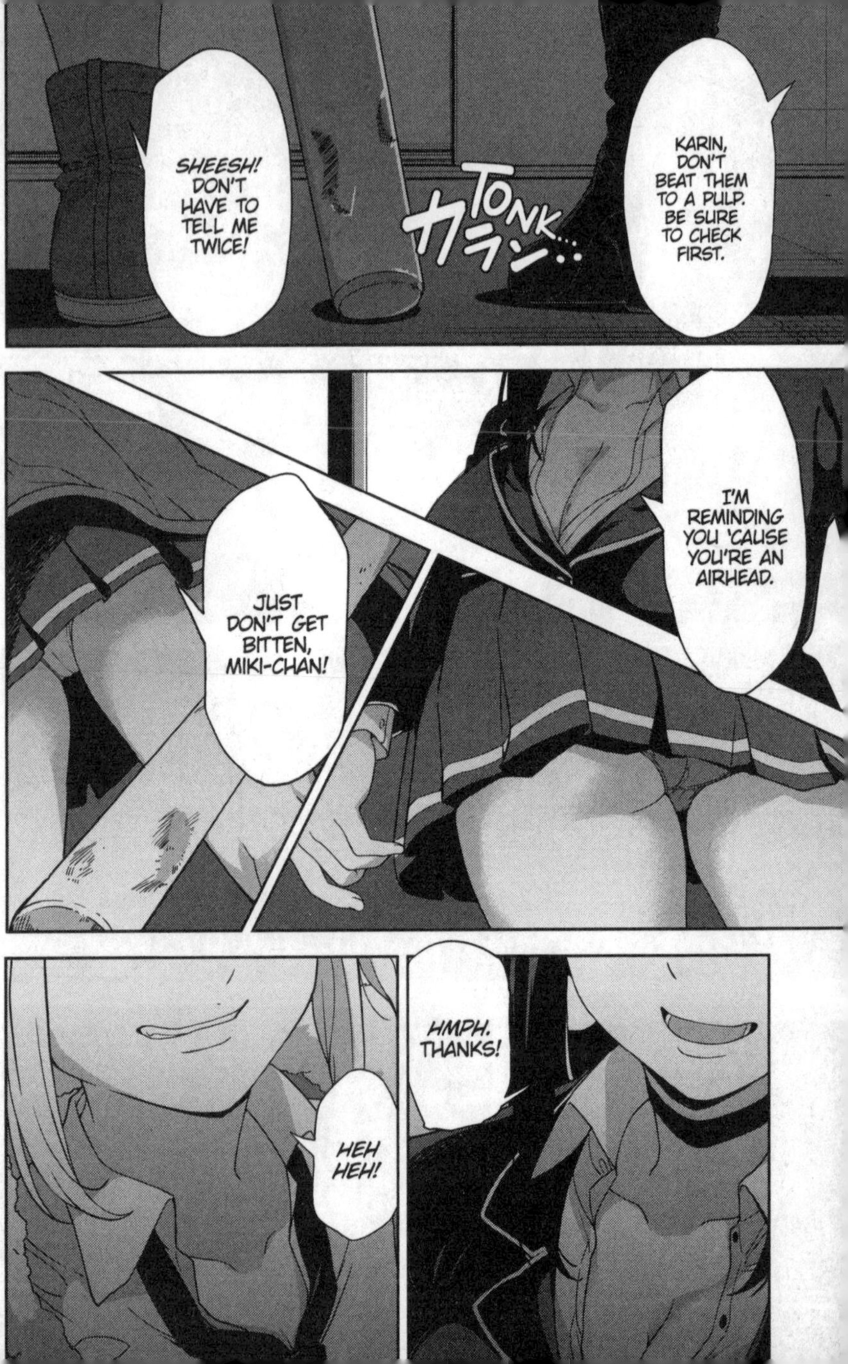
KARIN, DON'T BEAT THEM TO A PULP. BE SURE TO CHECK FIRST.
TONK...
カラン...
SHEESH! DON'T HAVE TO TELL ME TWICE!
I'M REMINDING YOU 'CAUSE YOU'RE AN AIRHEAD.
JUST DON'T GET BITTEN, MIKI-CHAN!
HMPH. THANKS!
HEH HEH!

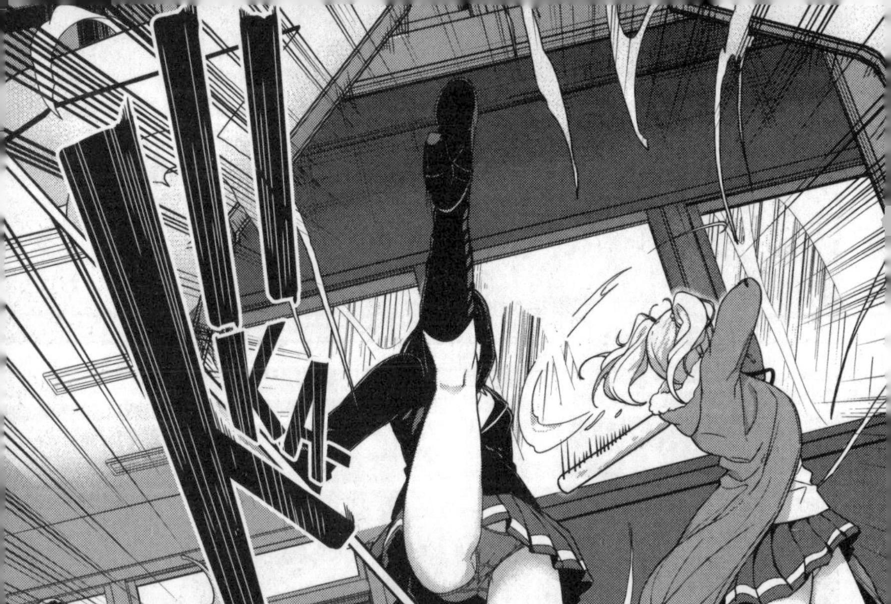
KA
THWAM
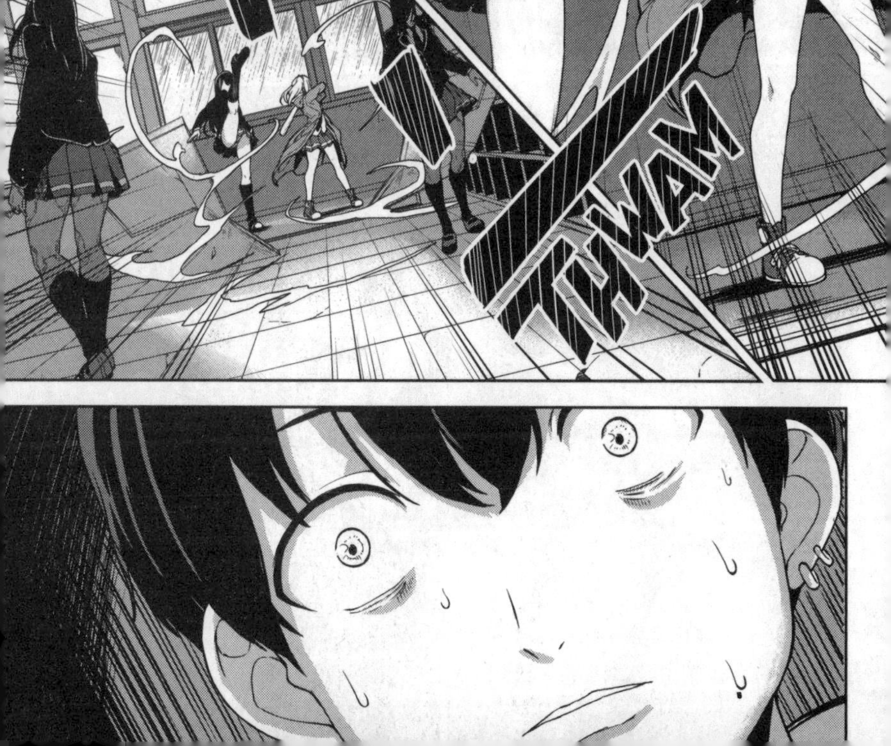

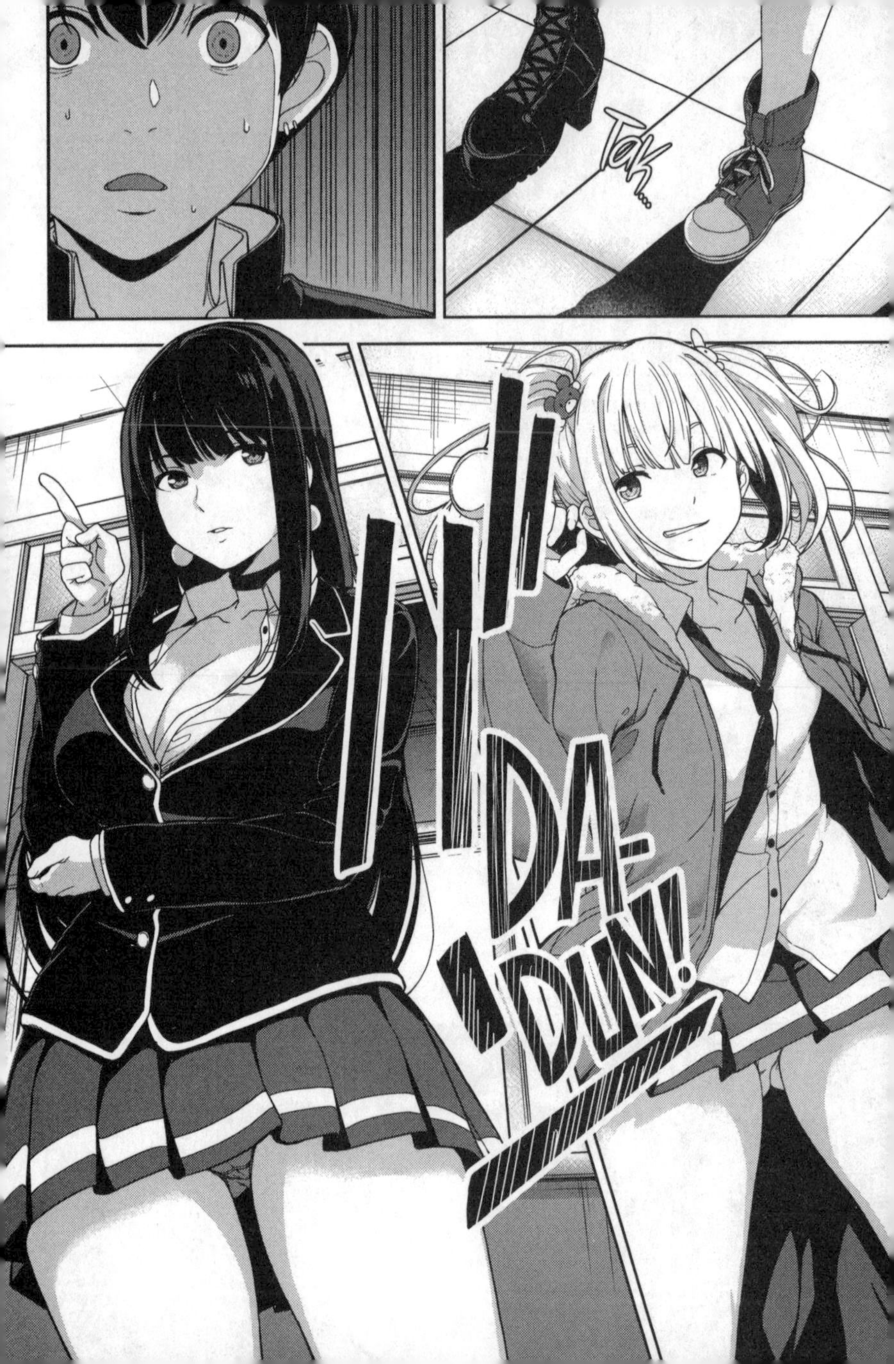
Tak...
DA-DUN!

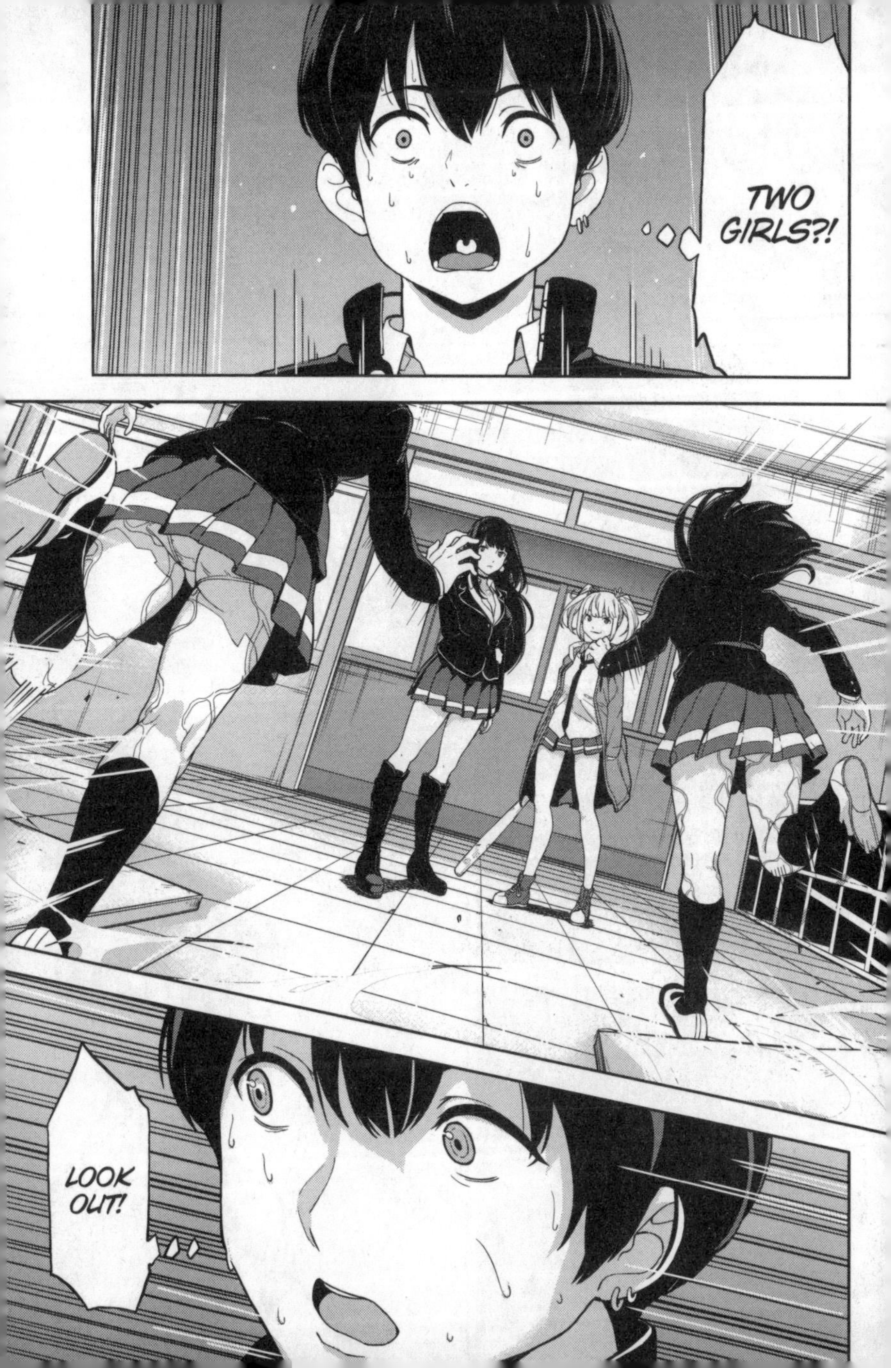
TWO GIRLS?!
LOOK OUT!

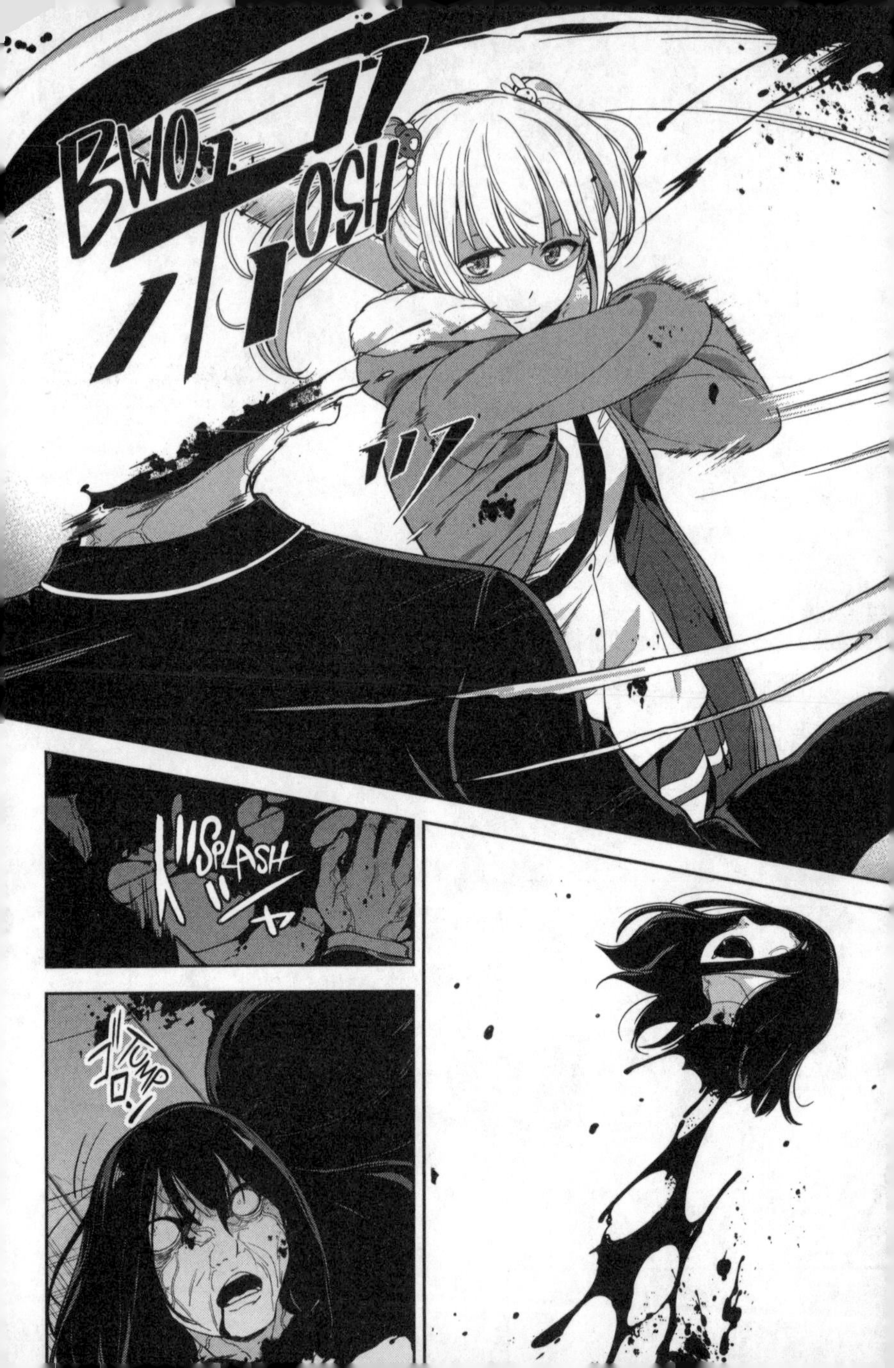
BWOOSH
SPLASH
TUMP

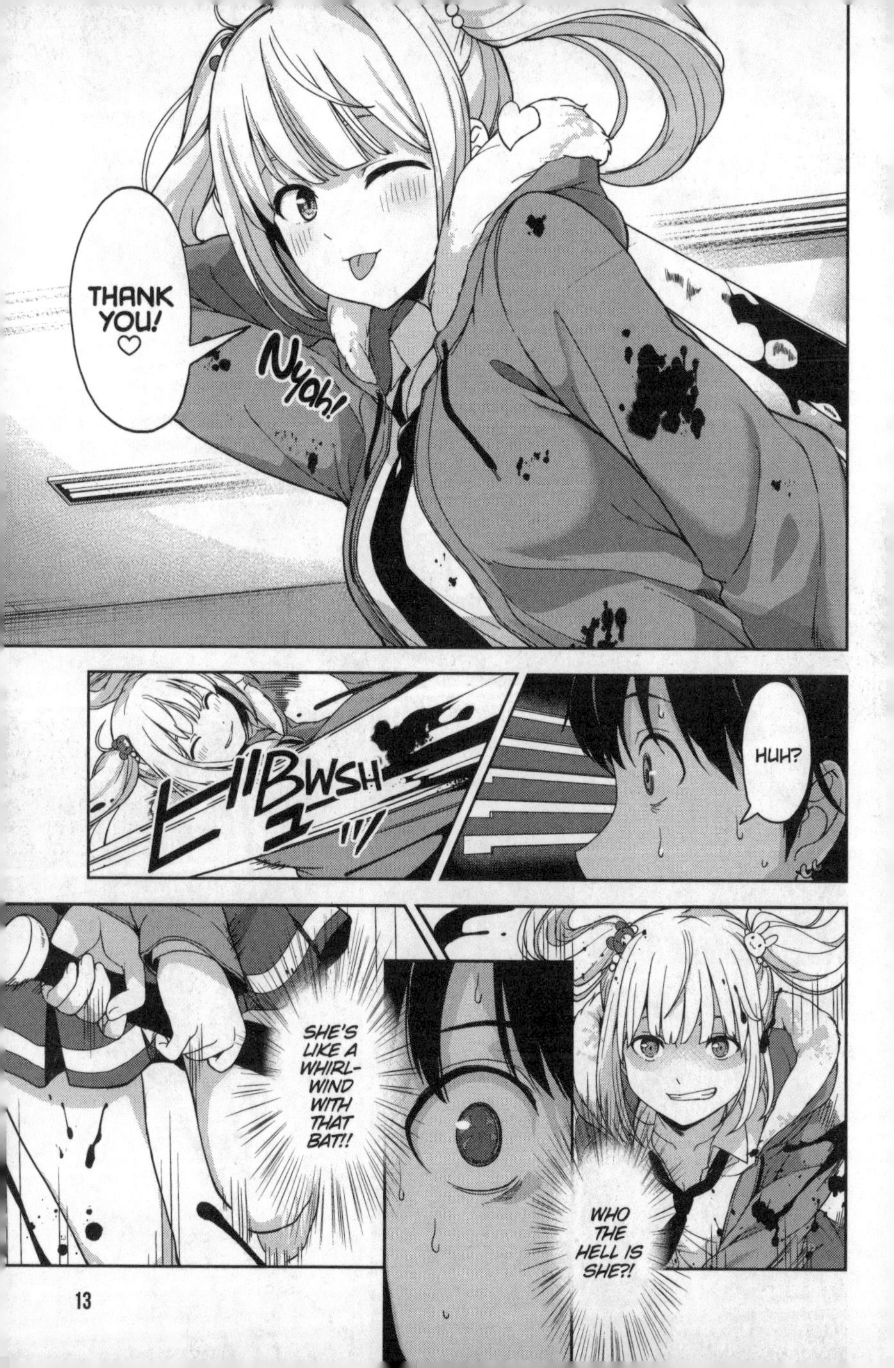
THANK YOU! ♡
Nyah!
HUH?
BWSH
ビュッ
SHE'S LIKE A WHIRLWIND WITH THAT BAT!!
WHO THE HELL IS SHE?!

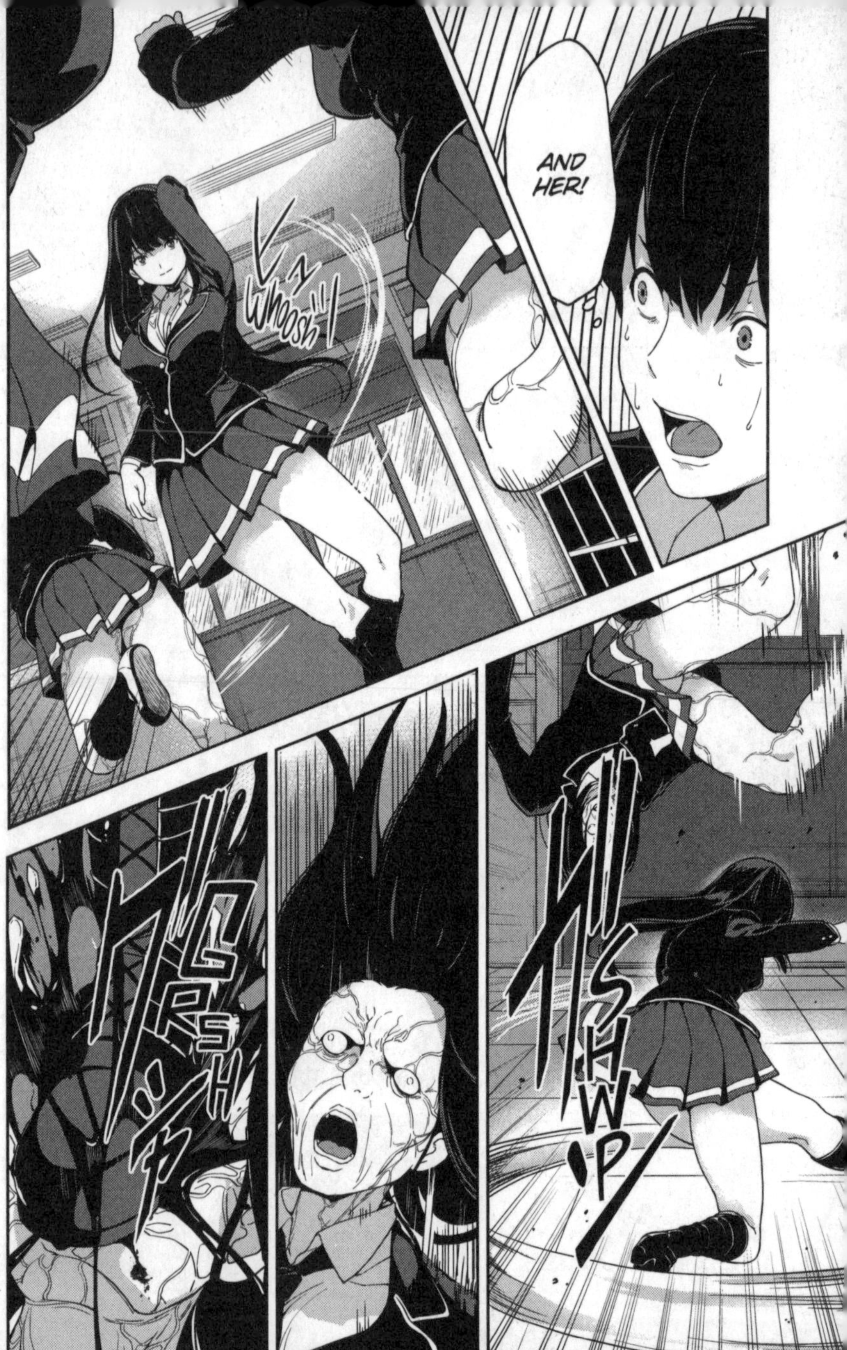
AND HER!
WHOOSH!!
SHWP!
GRSH

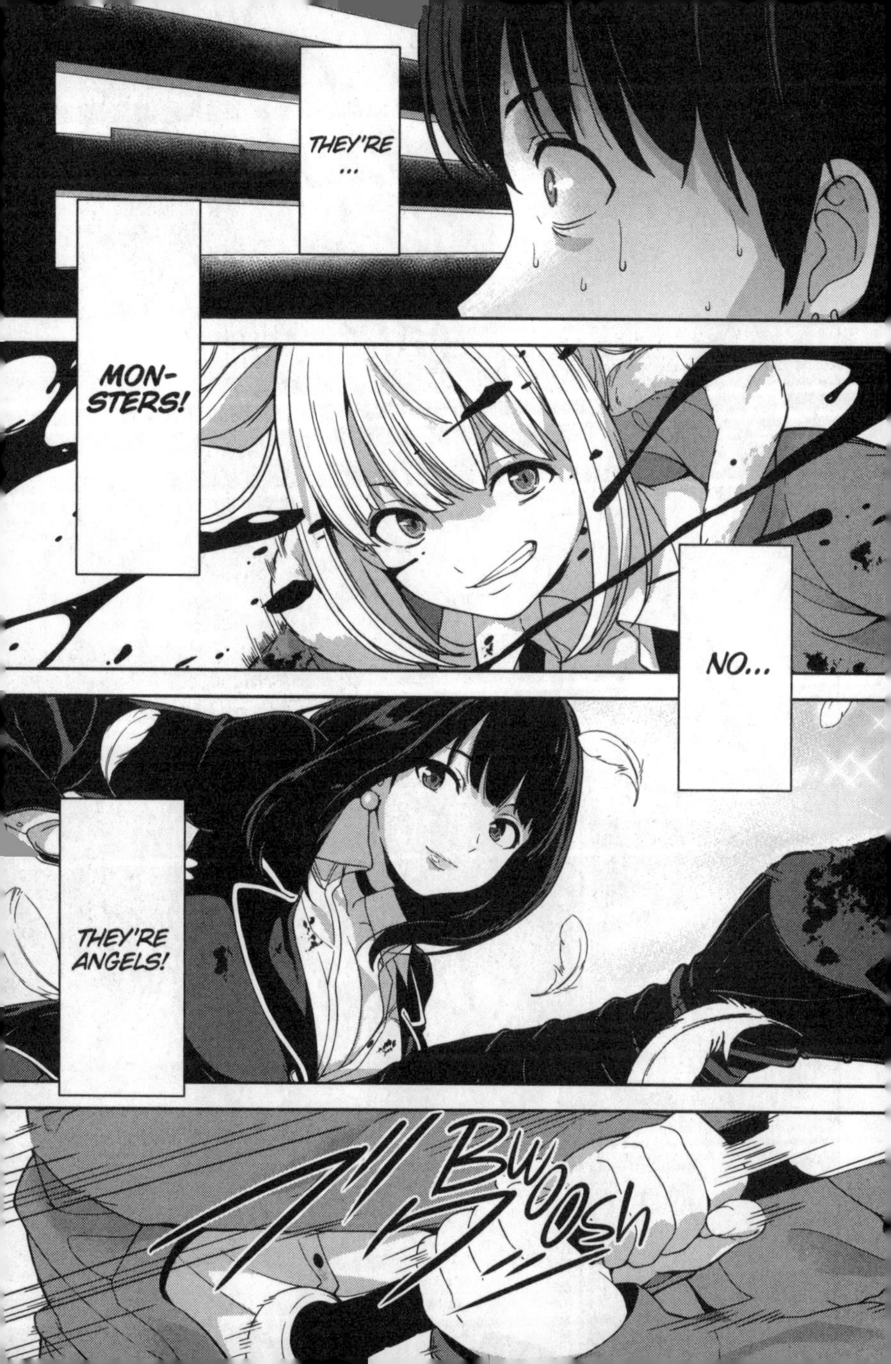
THEY'RE ...
MON-
STERS!
NO...
THEY'RE
ANGELS!
BWOOSH

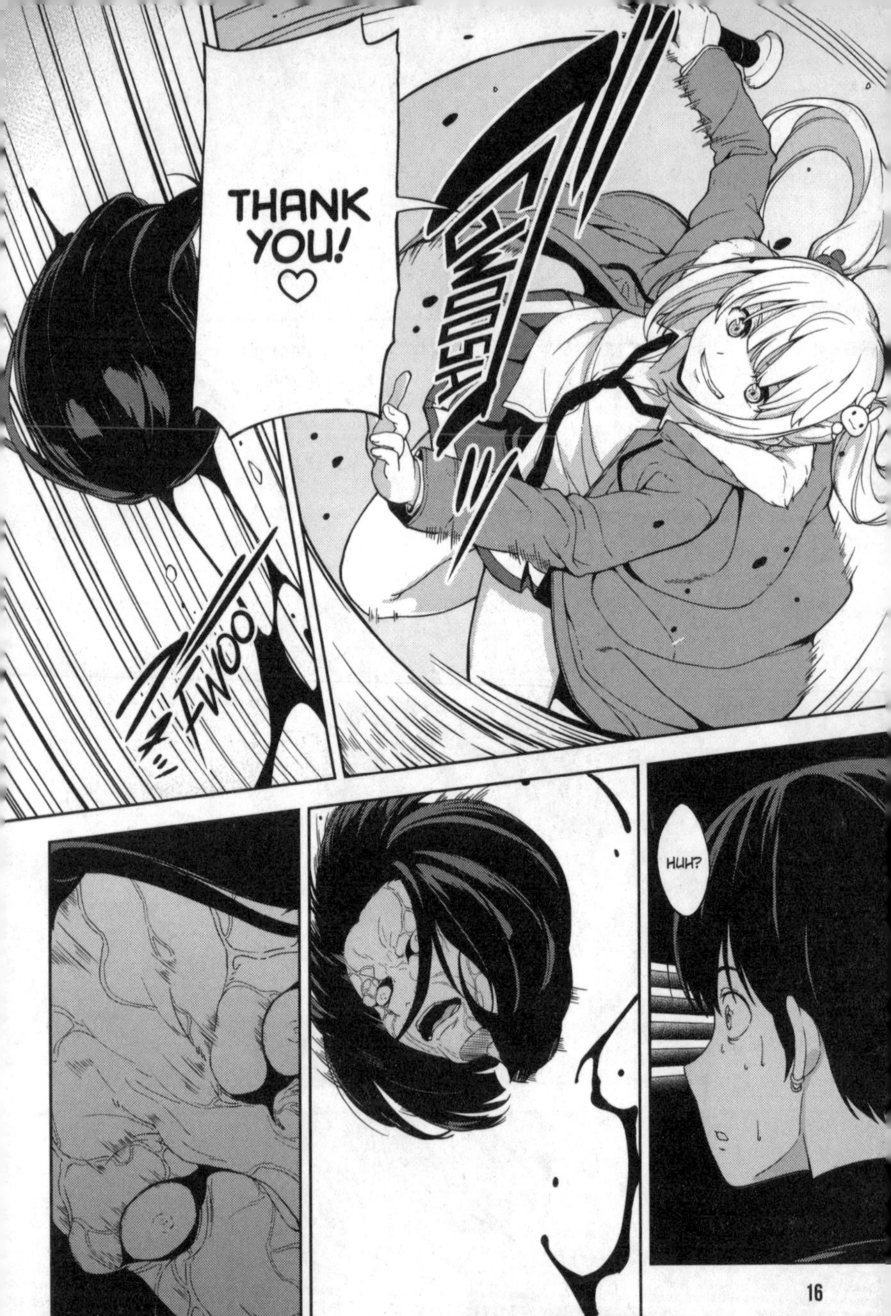
SWOOSH!
THANK YOU! ♡
FWOO
HUH?

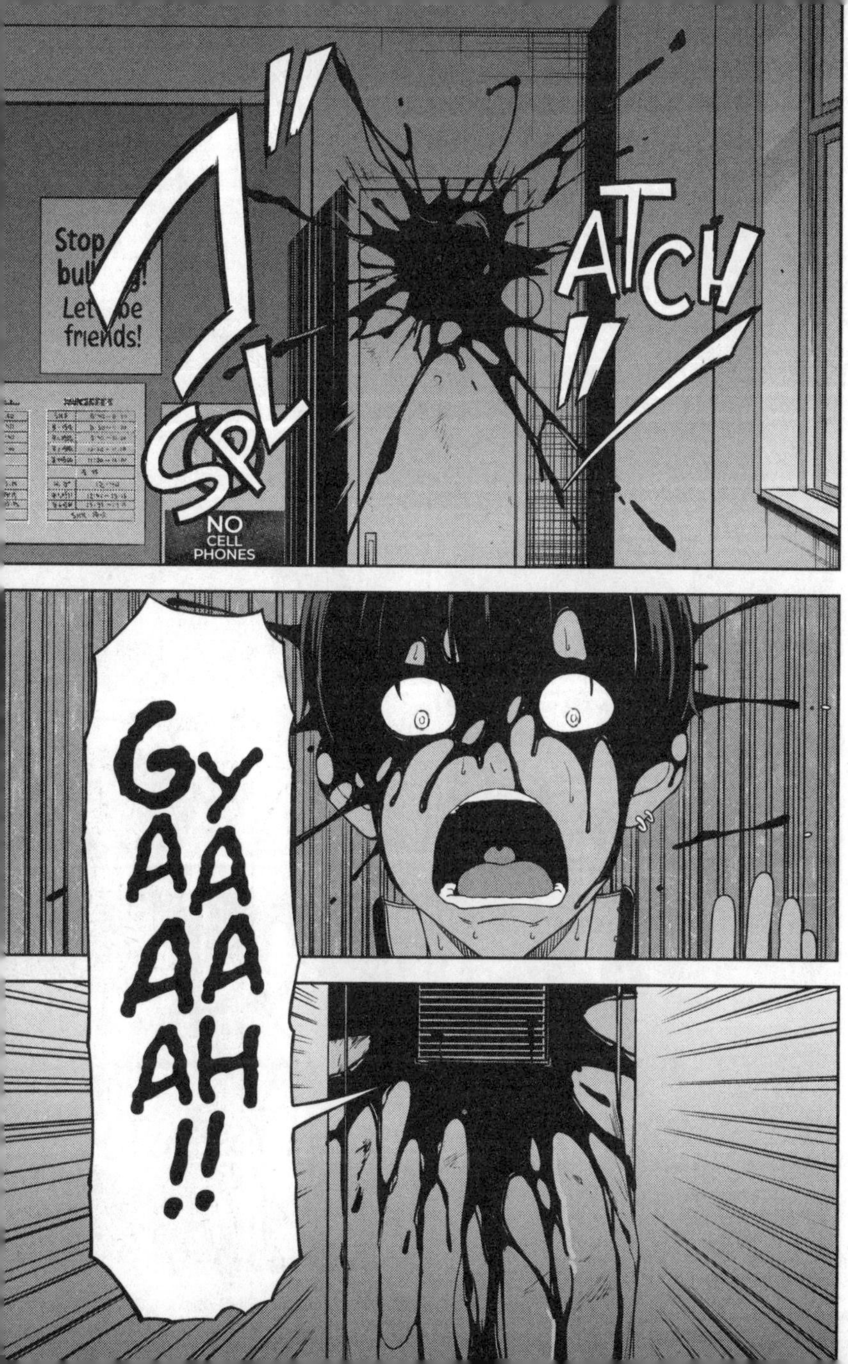
SPL
ATCH!!
Stop
bul
Let
be
friends!
NO
CELL
PHONES
GyAAAAAAH!!

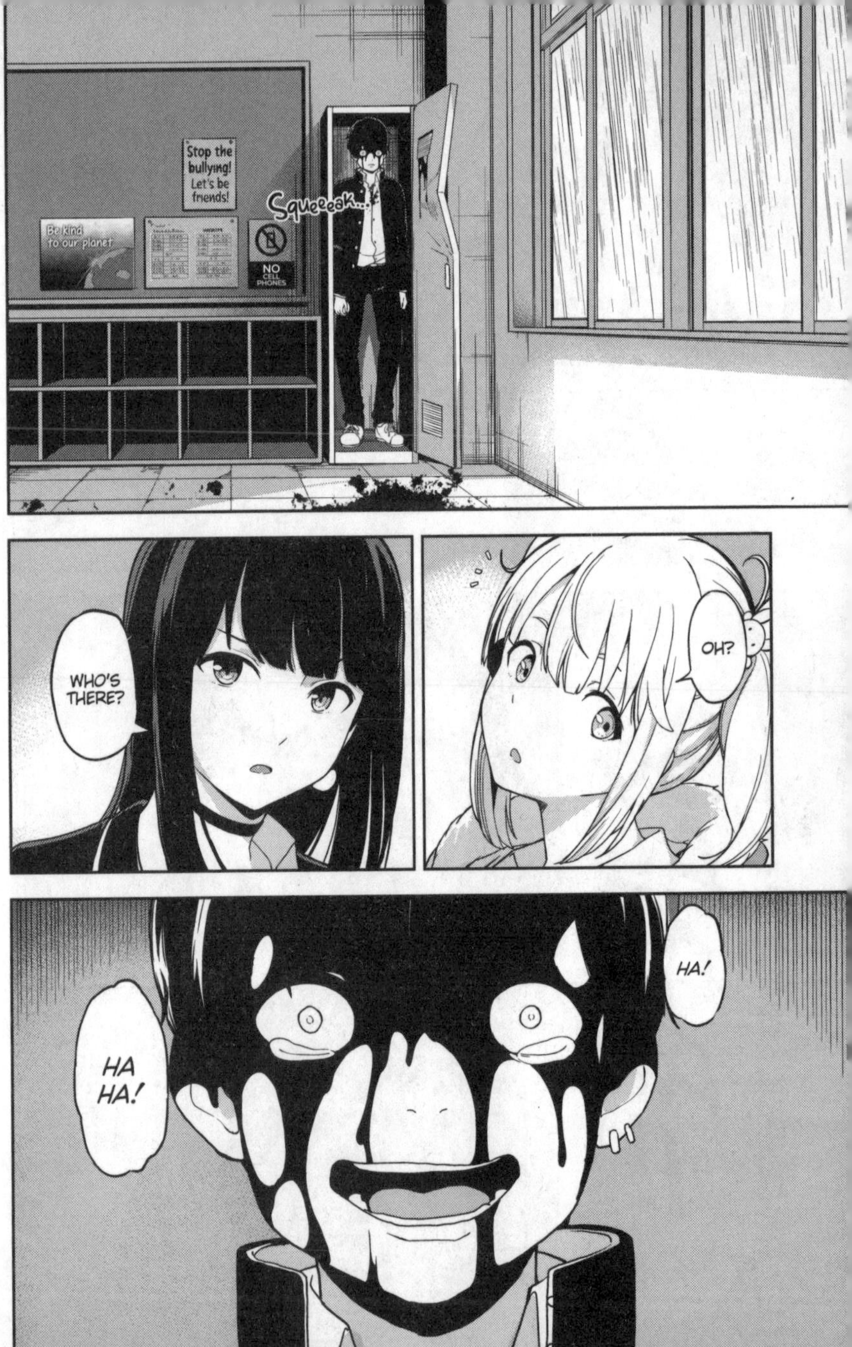
Stop the bullying! Let's be friends!
Squeeeak...
NO CELL PHONES
Be kind to our planet
OH?
WHO'S THERE?
HA!
HA HA!

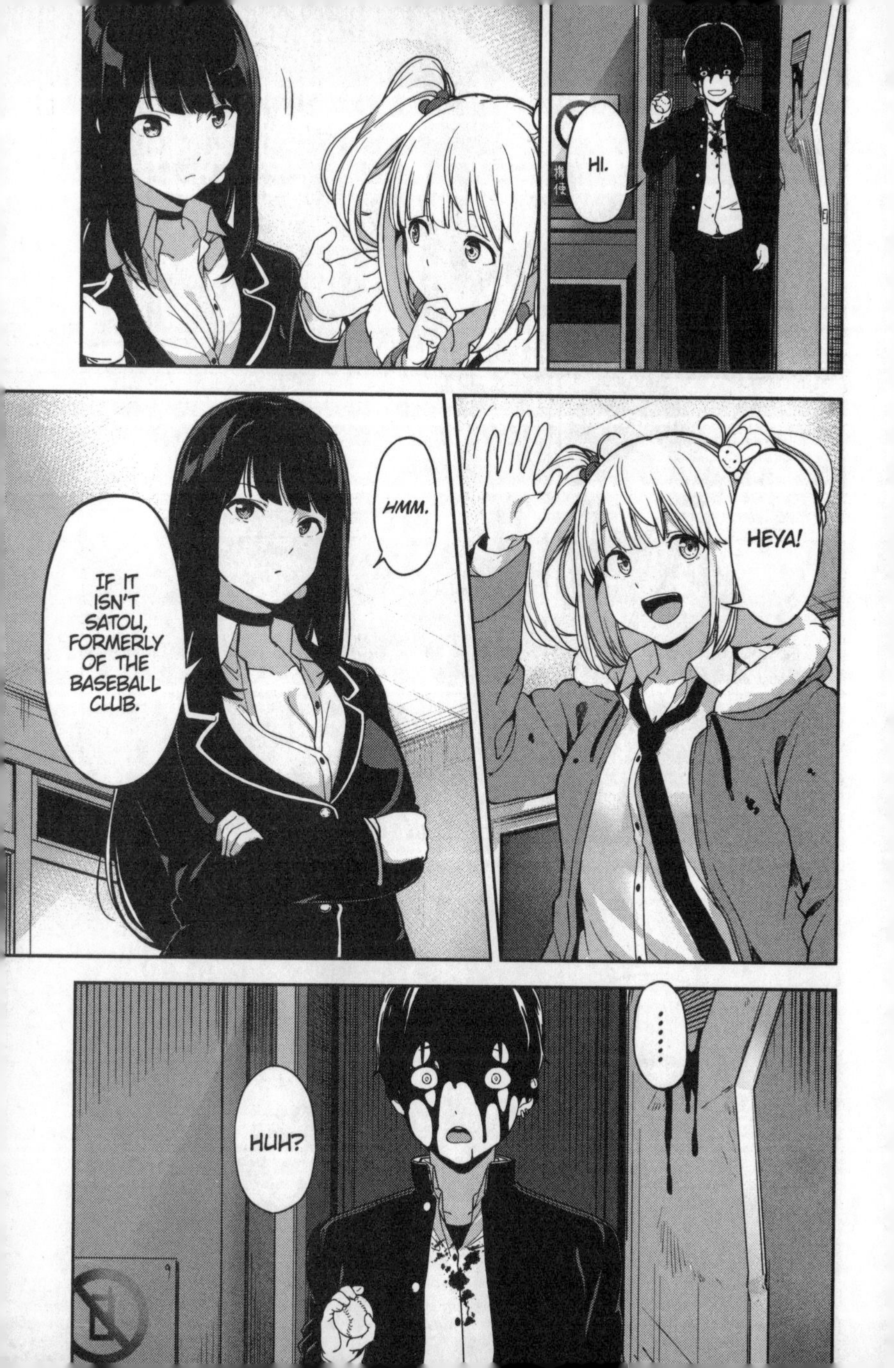
HI.
HEYA!
HMM.
IF IT ISN'T SATOU, FORMERLY OF THE BASEBALL CLUB.
......
HUH?

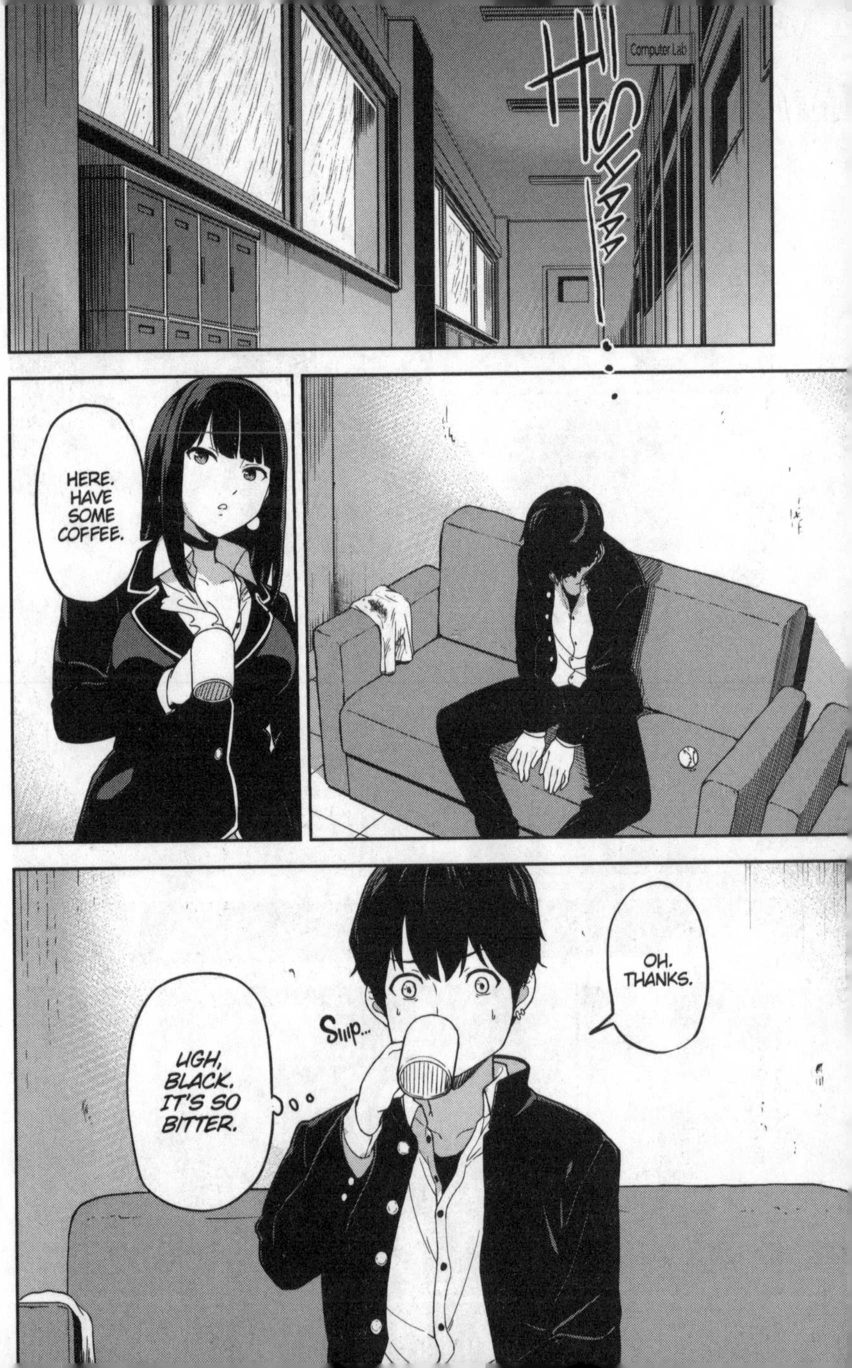
Computer Lab
HiSHAAA—...
HERE. HAVE SOME COFFEE.
OH. THANKS.
Siiip...
UGH, BLACK. IT'S SO BITTER.

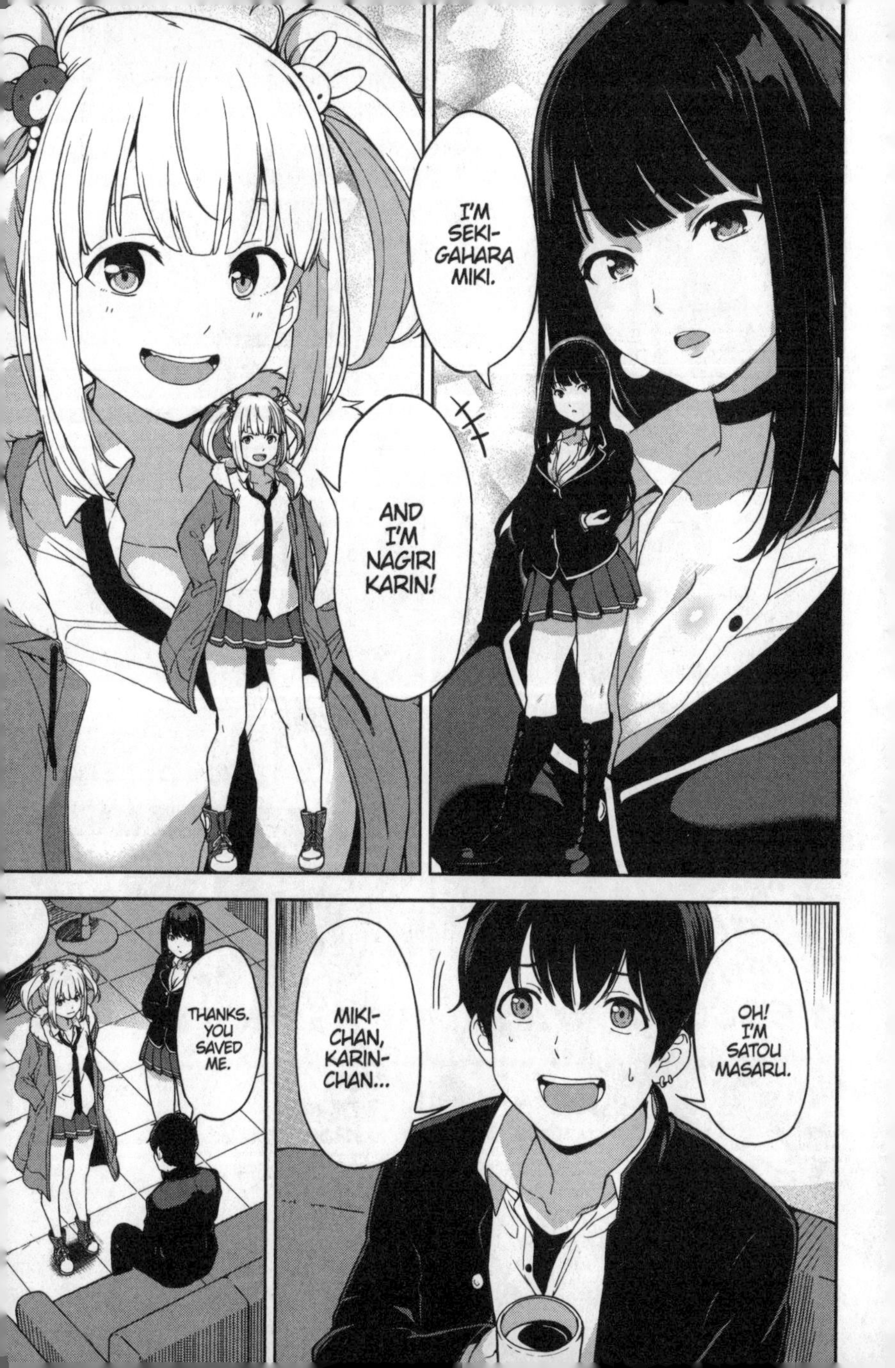
I'M SEKI-GAHARA MIKI.
AND I'M NAGIRI KARIN!
OH! I'M SATOU MASARU.
MIKI-CHAN, KARIN-CHAN...
THANKS. YOU SAVED ME.

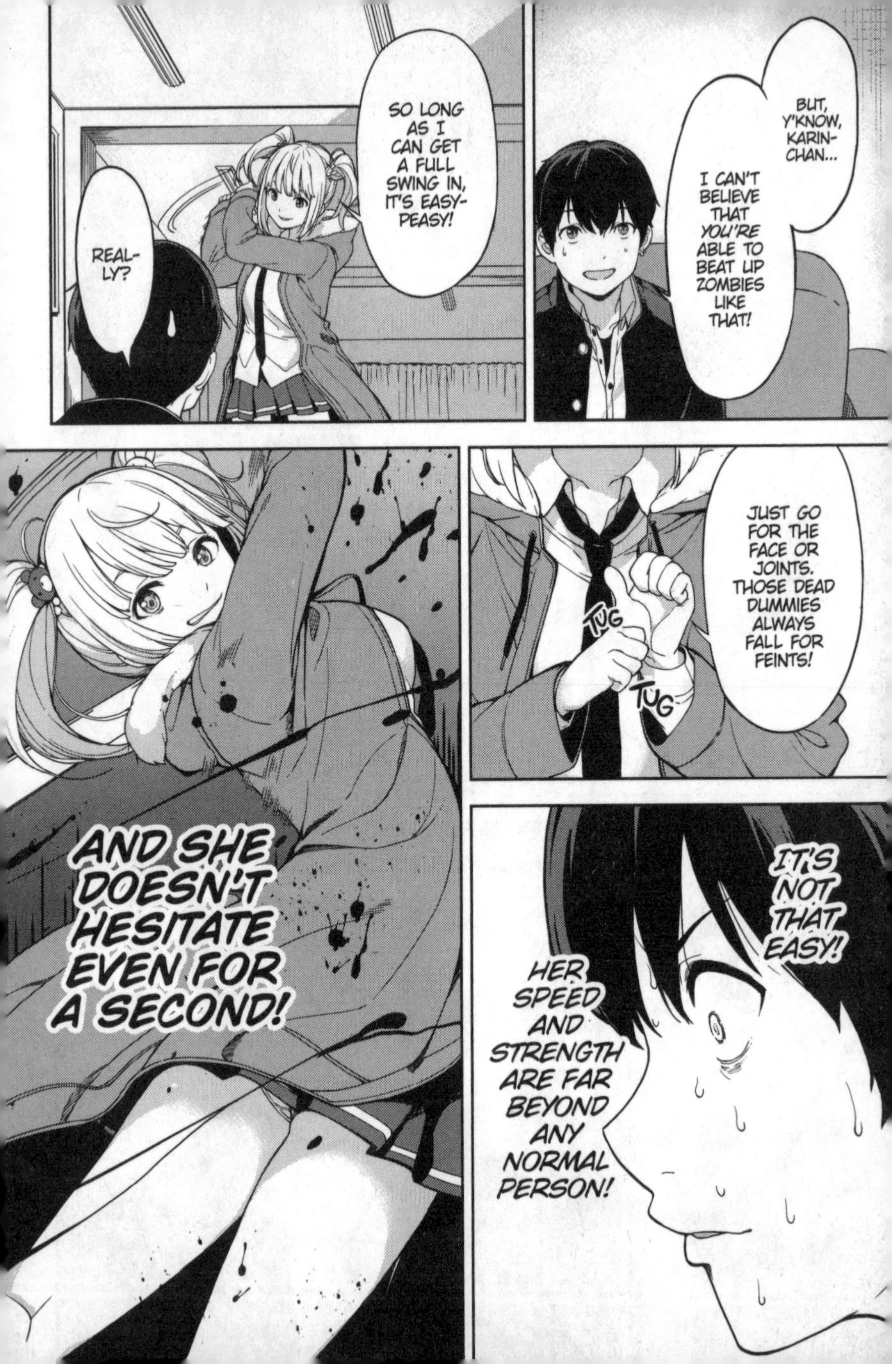
BUT, Y'KNOW, KARIN-CHAN...
I CAN'T BELIEVE THAT YOU'RE ABLE TO BEAT UP ZOMBIES LIKE THAT!
SO LONG AS I CAN GET A FULL SWING IN, IT'S EASY-PEASY!
REAL-LY?
JUST GO FOR THE FACE OR JOINTS. THOSE DEAD DUMMIES ALWAYS FALL FOR FEINTS!
TUG
TUG
IT'S NOT THAT EASY!
HER SPEED AND STRENGTH ARE FAR BEYOND ANY NORMAL PERSON!
AND SHE DOESN'T HESITATE EVEN FOR A SECOND!

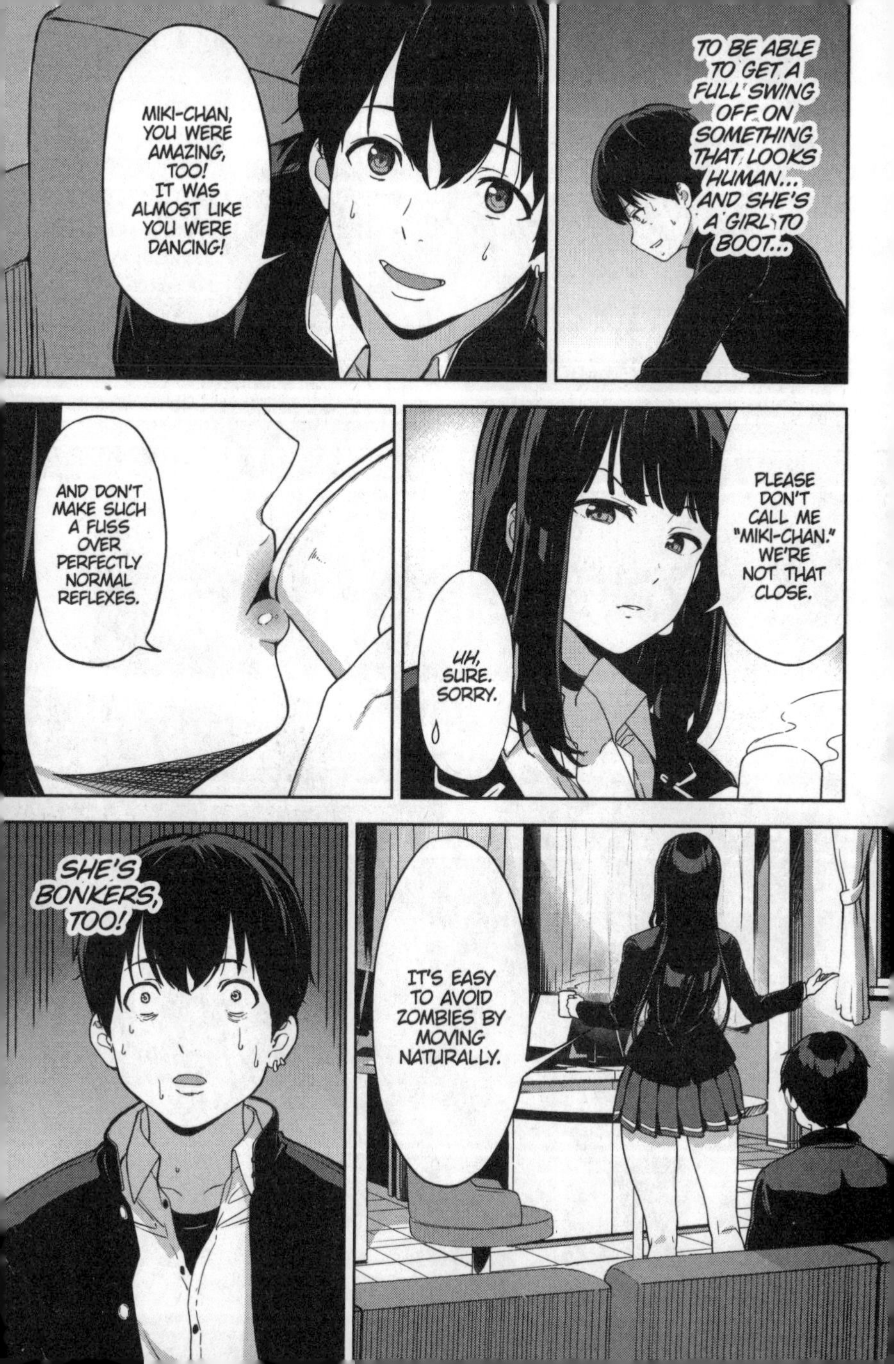
TO BE ABLE TO GET A FULL SWING OFF ON SOMETHING THAT LOOKS HUMAN... AND SHE'S A GIRL TO BOOT...
MIKI-CHAN, YOU WERE AMAZING, TOO! IT WAS ALMOST LIKE YOU WERE DANCING!
PLEASE DON'T CALL ME "MIKI-CHAN." WE'RE NOT THAT CLOSE.
UH, SURE. SORRY.
AND DON'T MAKE SUCH A FUSS OVER PERFECTLY NORMAL REFLEXES.
IT'S EASY TO AVOID ZOMBIES BY MOVING NATURALLY.
SHE'S BONKERS, TOO!

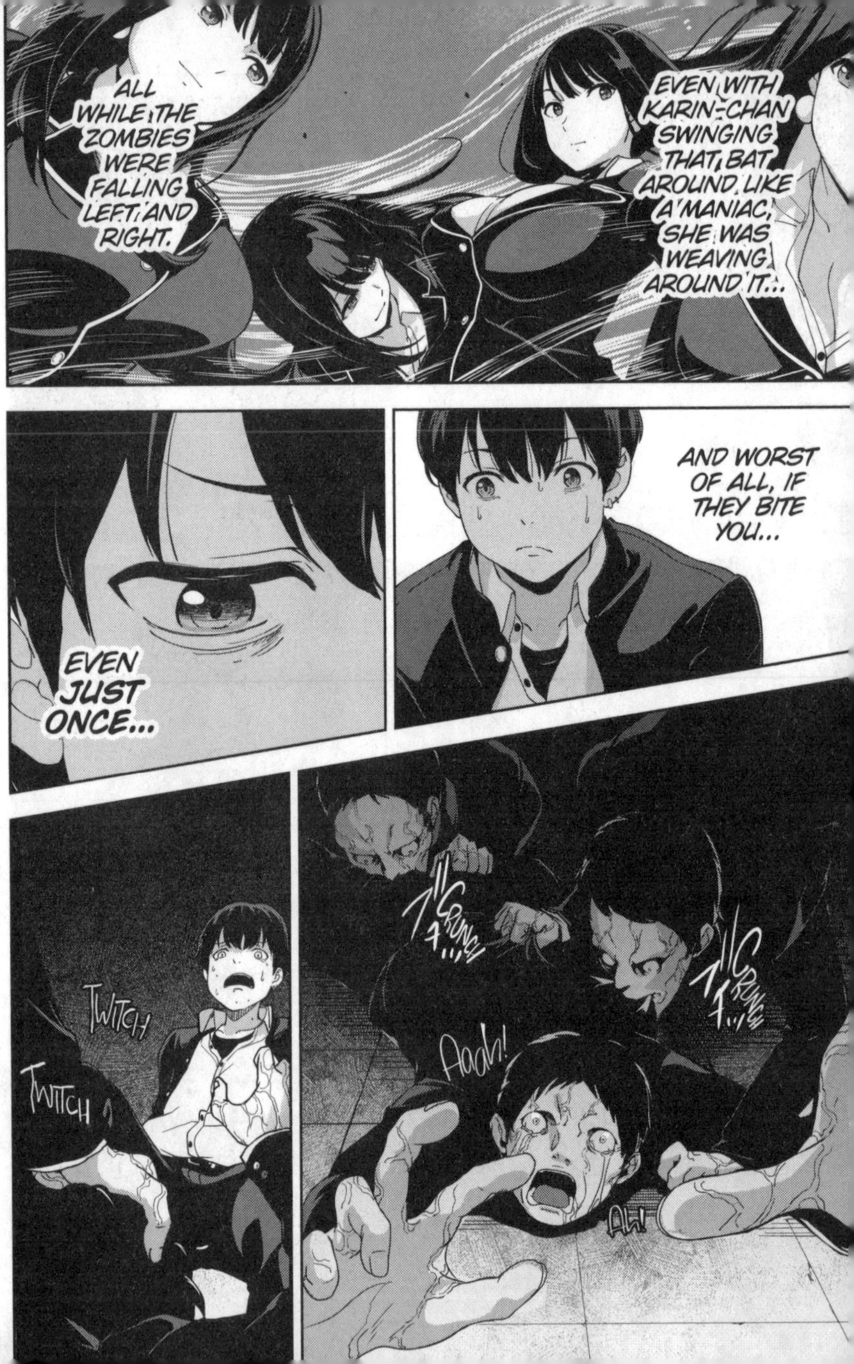
EVEN WITH KARIN-CHAN SWINGING THAT BAT AROUND LIKE A MANIAC, SHE WAS WEAVING AROUND IT...
ALL WHILE THE ZOMBIES WERE FALLING LEFT AND RIGHT.
AND WORST OF ALL, IF THEY BITE YOU...
EVEN JUST ONCE...
CRUNCH
CRUNCH
Aaah!
Ah!
TWITCH
TWITCH

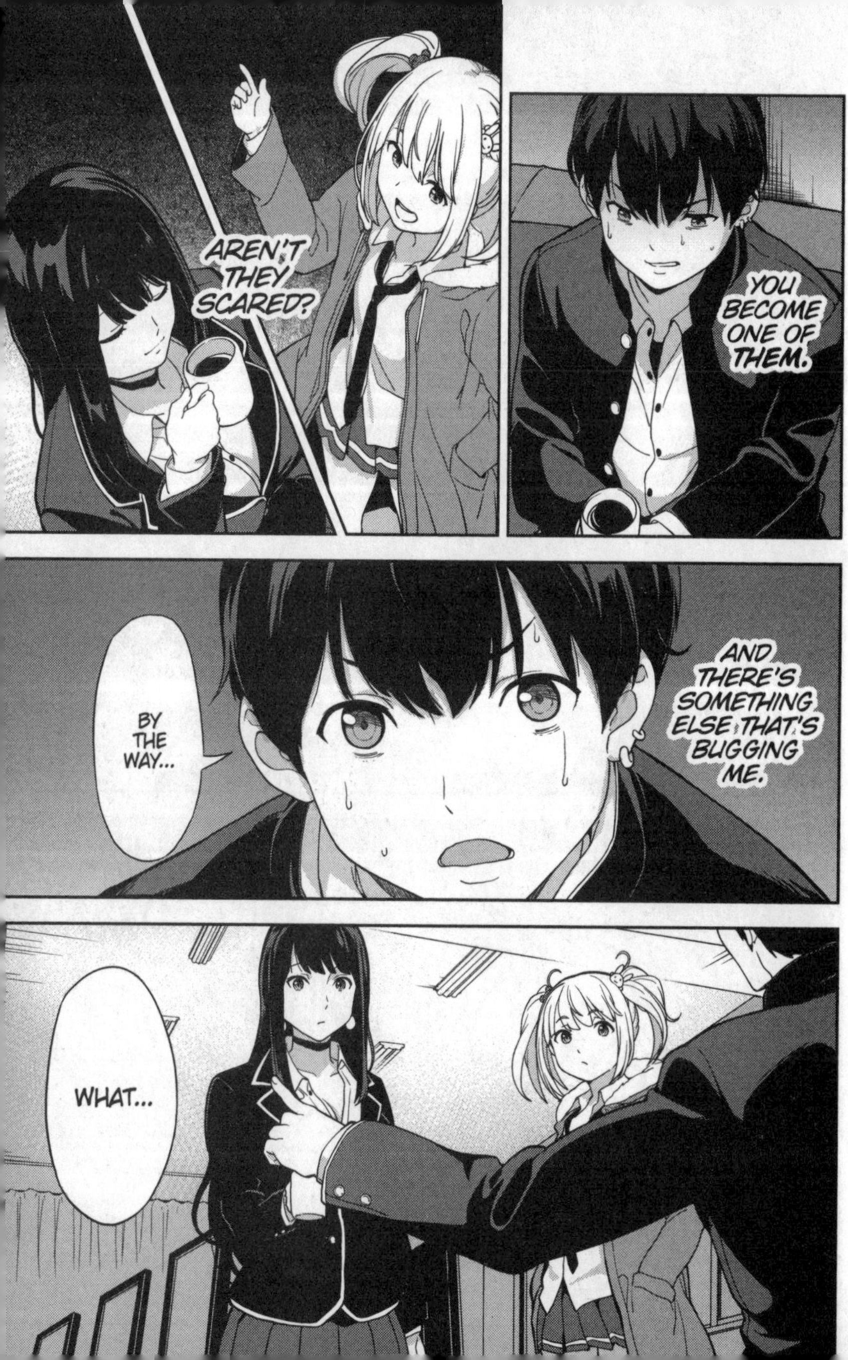
YOU BECOME ONE OF THEM.
AREN'T THEY SCARED?
AND THERE'S SOMETHING ELSE THAT'S BUGGING ME.
BY THE WAY...
WHAT...

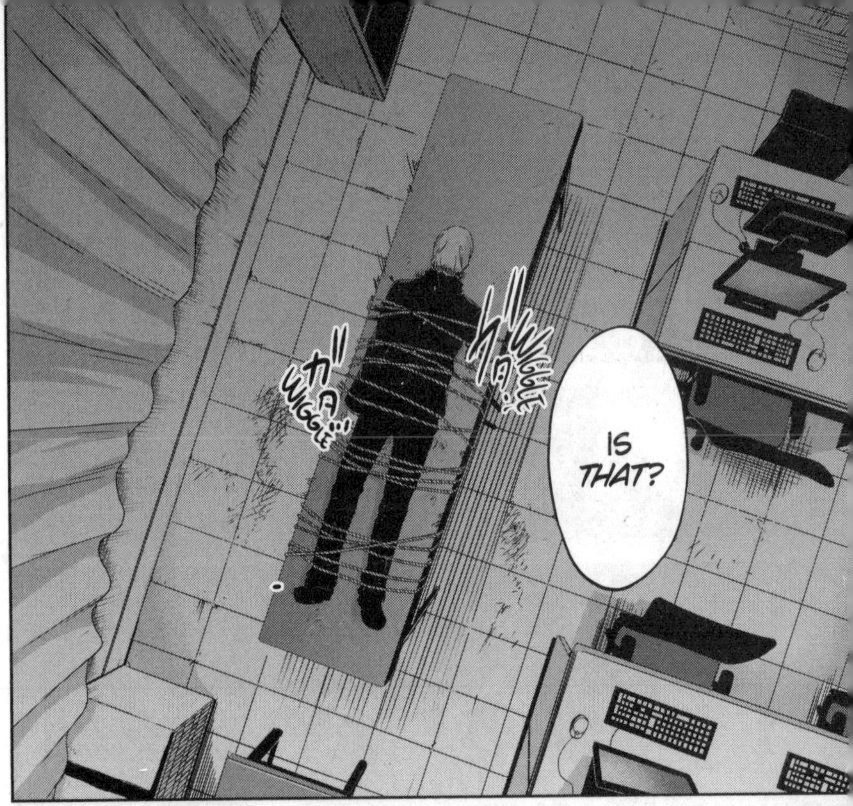
IS THAT?
WIGGLE
WIGGLE
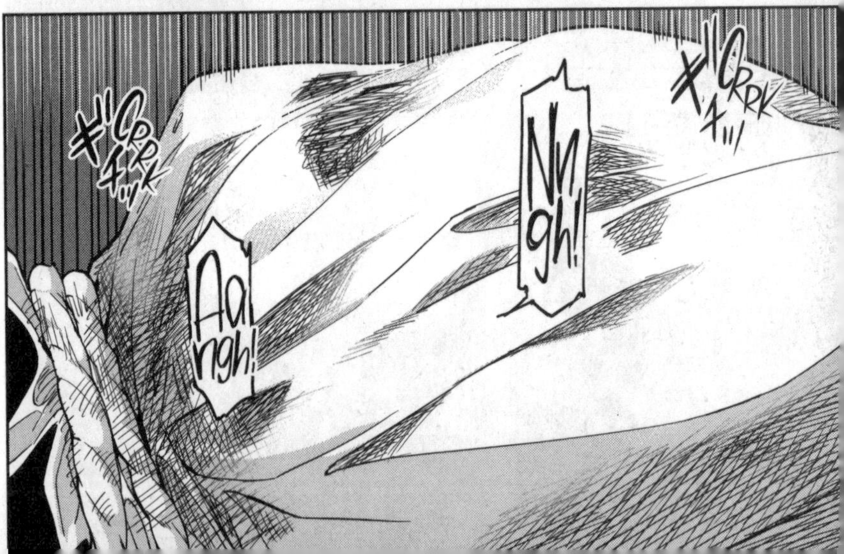
CRRK
Nngh!
Aangh!
CRRK

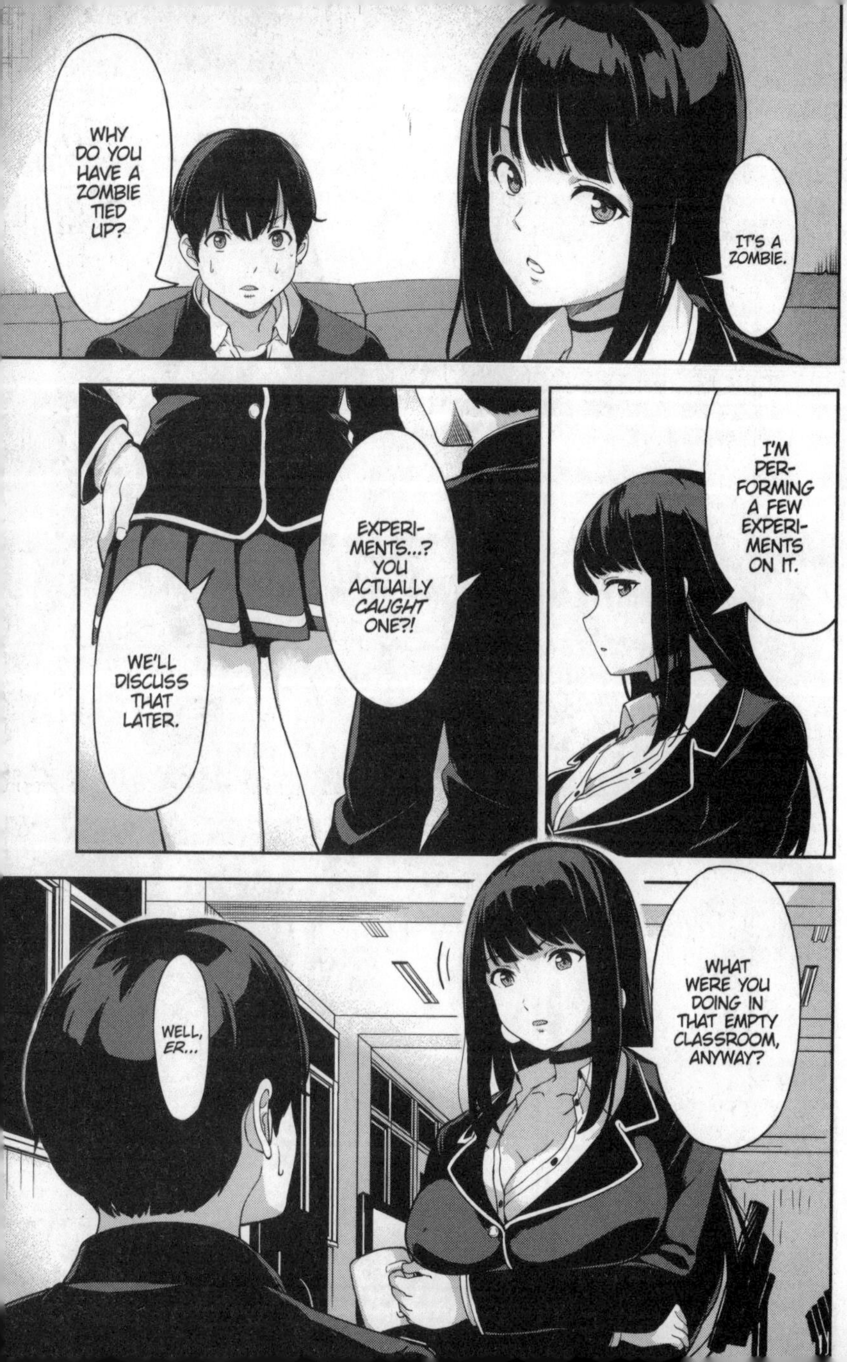
WHY DO YOU HAVE A ZOMBIE TIED UP?
IT'S A ZOMBIE.
I'M PER-FORMING A FEW EXPERI-MENTS ON IT.
EXPERI-MENTS...? YOU ACTUALLY *CAUGHT* ONE?!
WE'LL DISCUSS THAT LATER.
WHAT WERE YOU DOING IN THAT EMPTY CLASSROOM, ANYWAY?
WELL, ER...

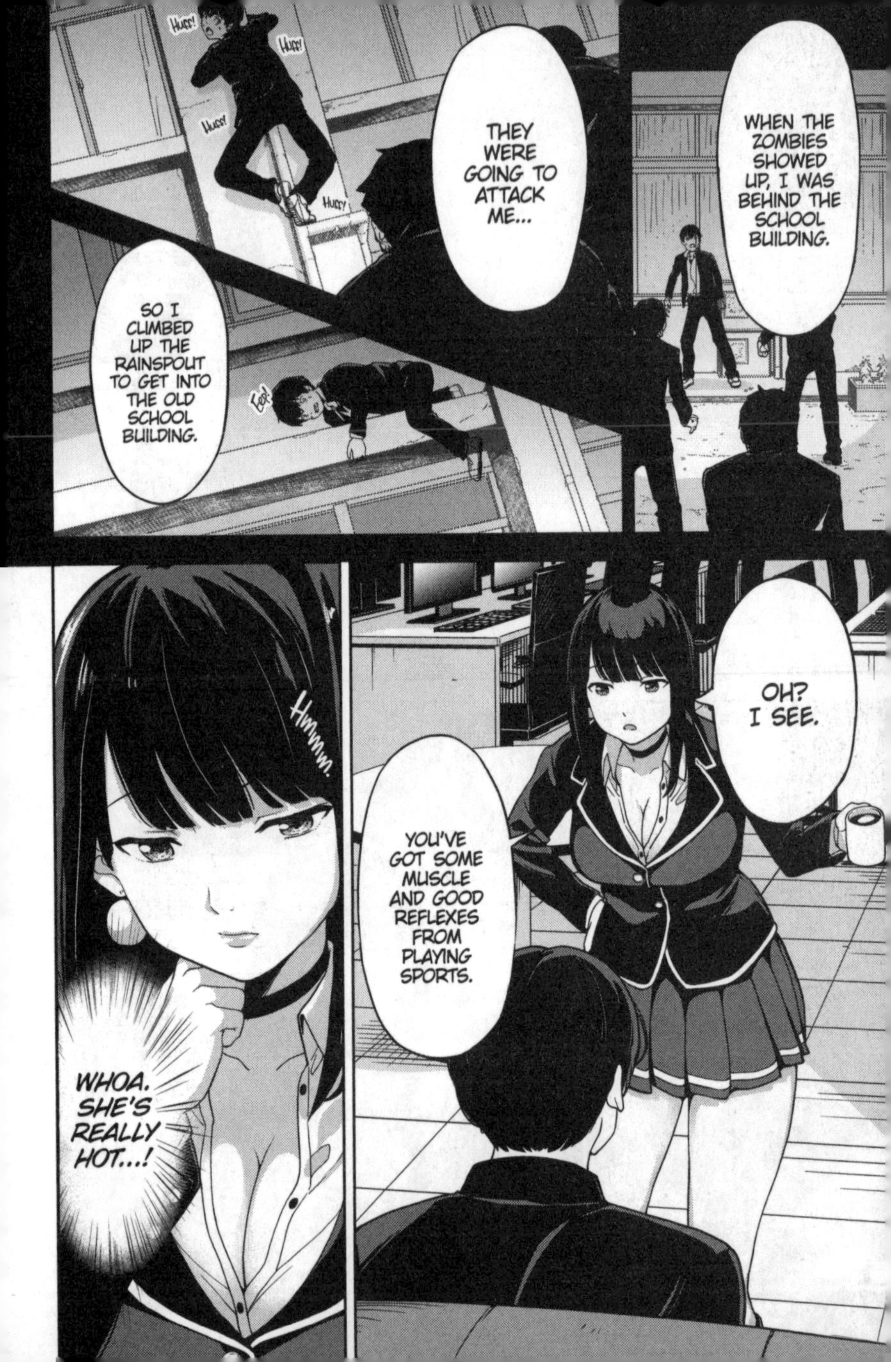
WHEN THE ZOMBIES SHOWED UP, I WAS BEHIND THE SCHOOL BUILDING.
THEY WERE GOING TO ATTACK ME...
Huff!
Huff!
Huff!
Huff!
SO I CLIMBED UP THE RAINSPOUT TO GET INTO THE OLD SCHOOL BUILDING.
Eep!
OH? I SEE.
YOU'VE GOT SOME MUSCLE AND GOOD REFLEXES FROM PLAYING SPORTS.
Hmmmm.
WHOA. SHE'S REALLY HOT...!

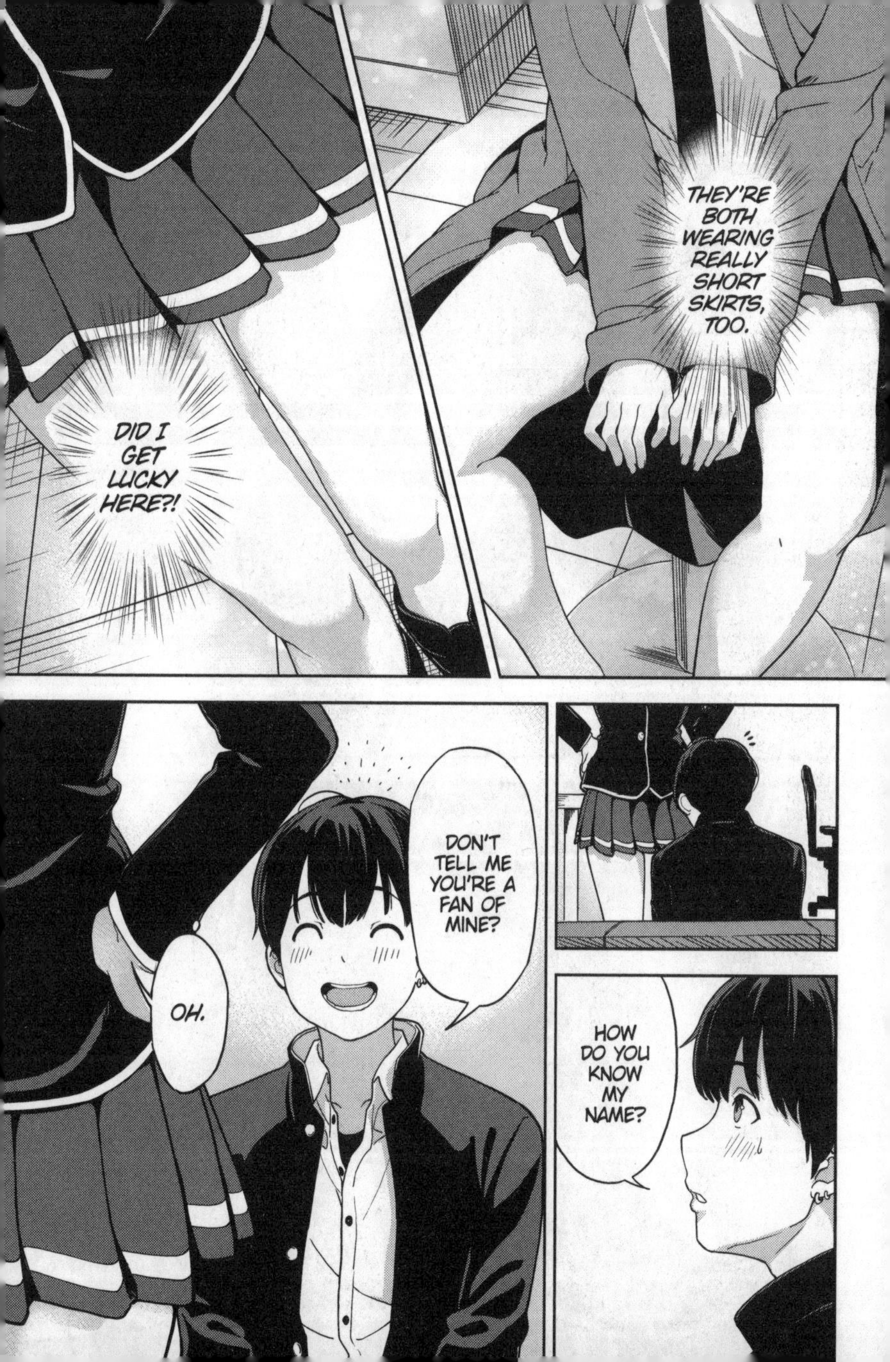
THEY'RE BOTH WEARING REALLY SHORT SKIRTS, TOO.
DID I GET LUCKY HERE?!
HOW DO YOU KNOW MY NAME?
DON'T TELL ME YOU'RE A FAN OF MINE?
OH.

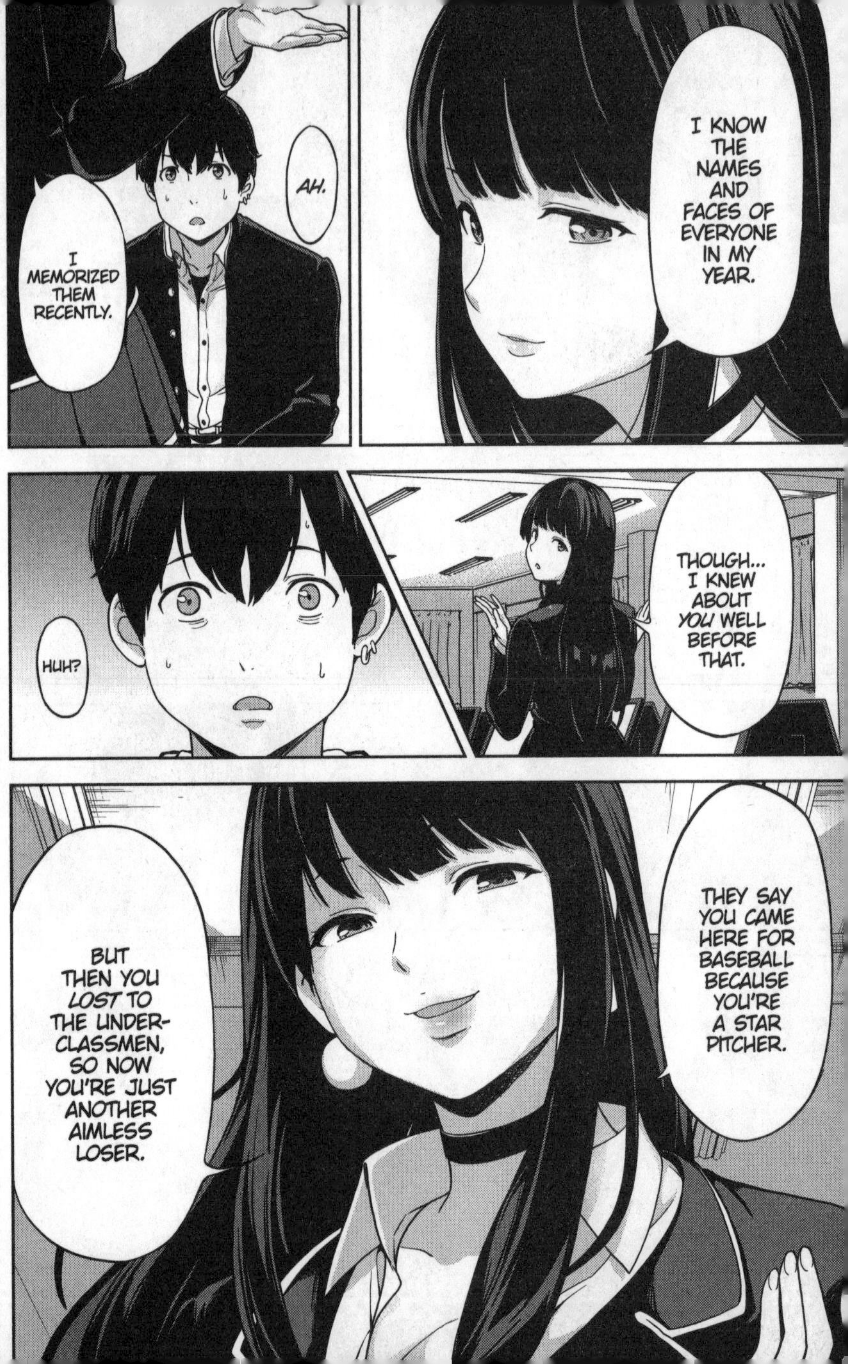
I KNOW THE NAMES AND FACES OF EVERYONE IN MY YEAR.
AH.
I MEMORIZED THEM RECENTLY.
THOUGH... I KNEW ABOUT *YOU* WELL BEFORE THAT.
HUH?
THEY SAY YOU CAME HERE FOR BASEBALL BECAUSE YOU'RE A STAR PITCHER.
BUT THEN YOU *LOST* TO THE UNDER-CLASSMEN, SO NOW YOU'RE JUST ANOTHER AIMLESS LOSER.

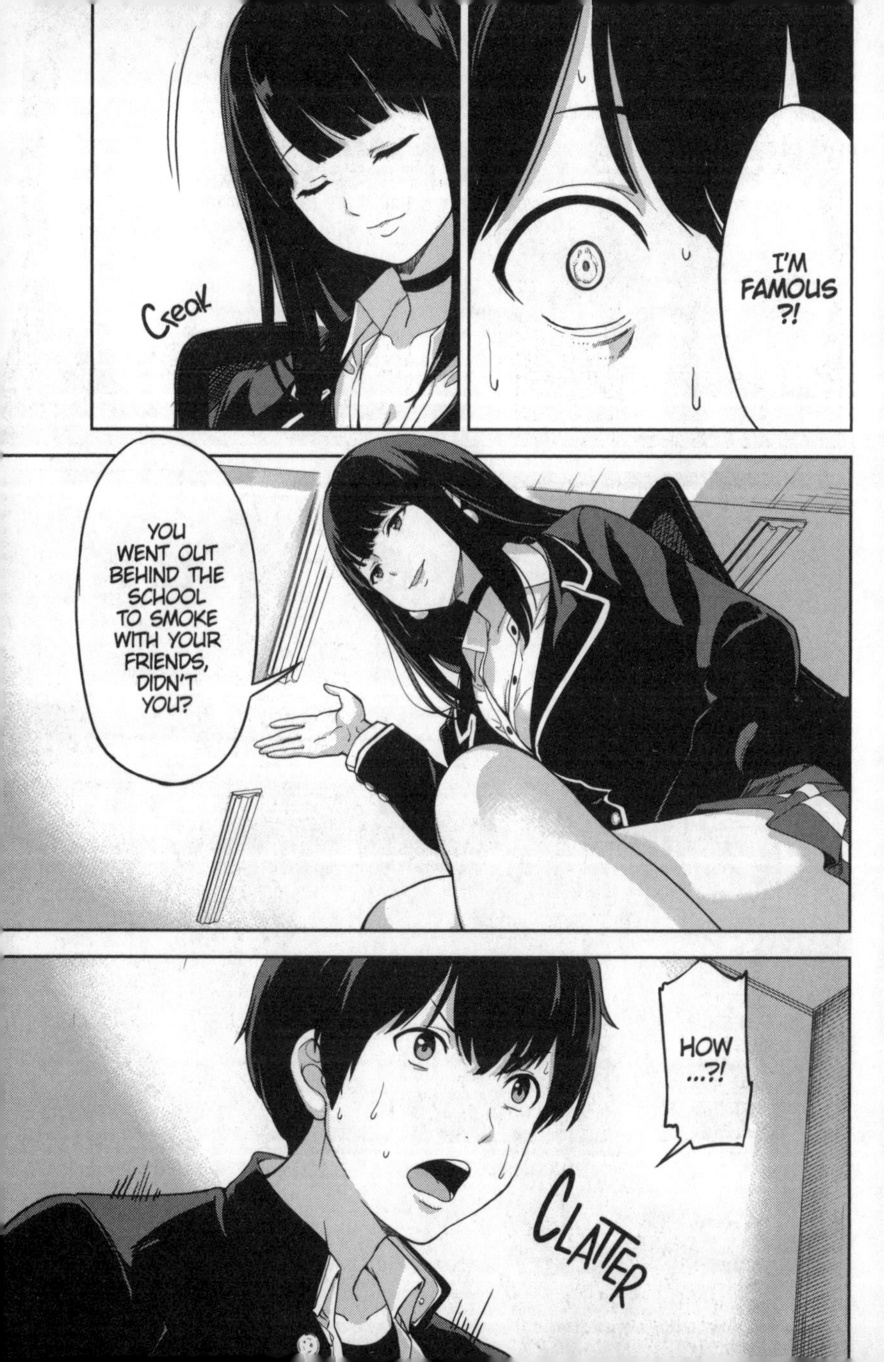
I'M FAMOUS ?!
Creak
YOU WENT OUT BEHIND THE SCHOOL TO SMOKE WITH YOUR FRIENDS, DIDN'T YOU?
HOW ...?!
CLATTER

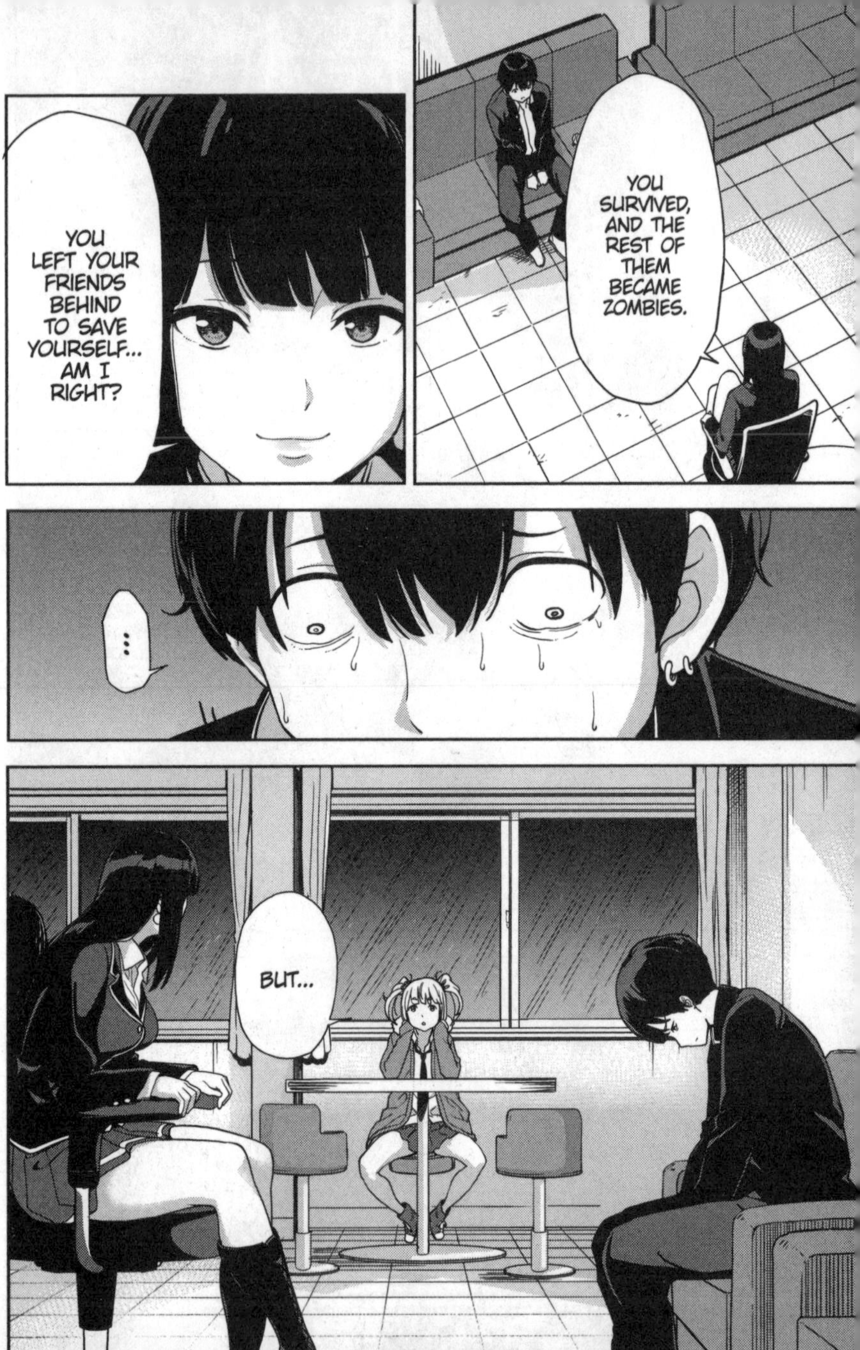
YOU SURVIVED, AND THE REST OF THEM BECAME ZOMBIES.
YOU LEFT YOUR FRIENDS BEHIND TO SAVE YOURSELF... AM I RIGHT?
...
BUT...

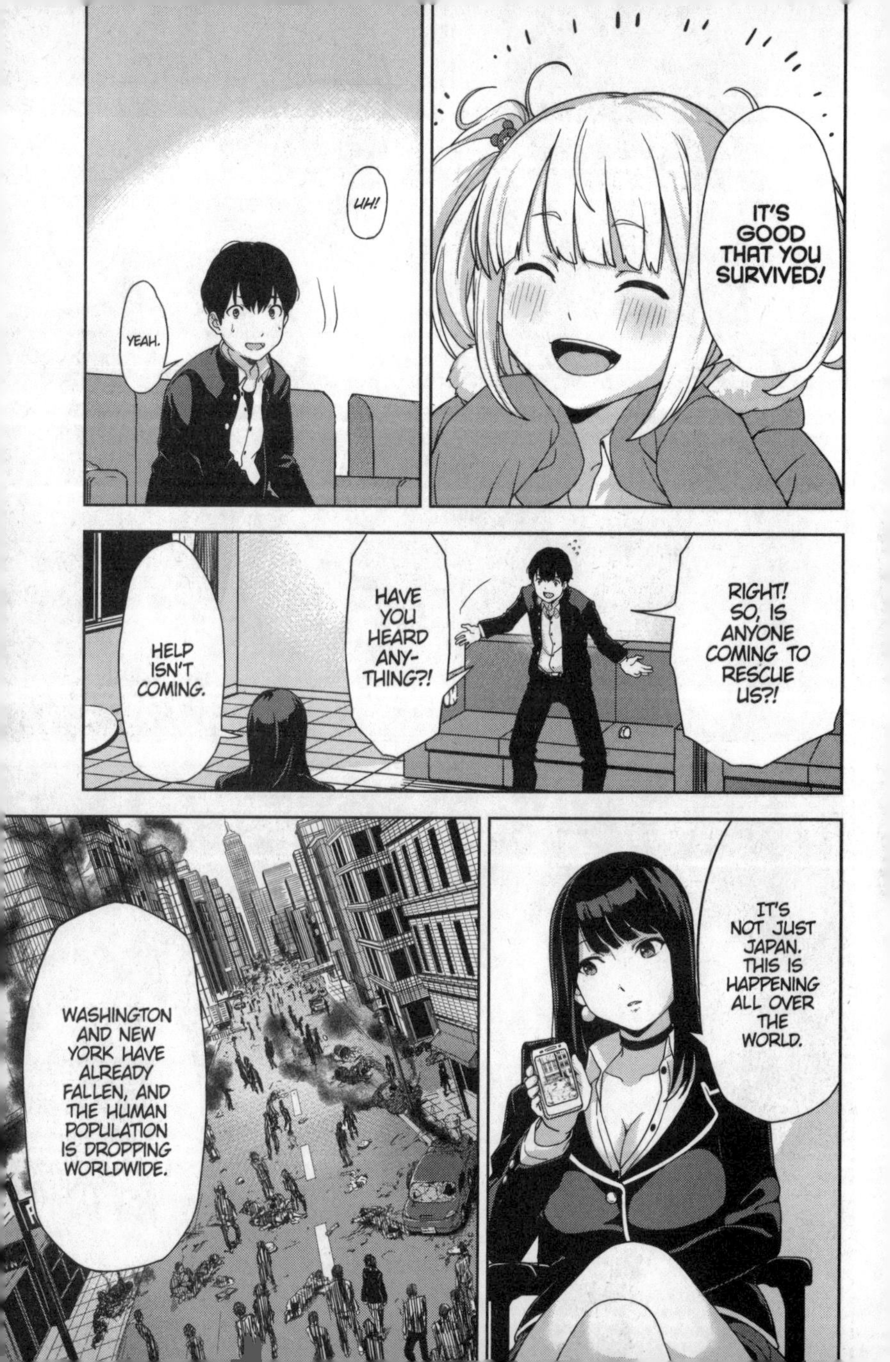
IT'S GOOD THAT YOU SURVIVED!
UH!
YEAH.
RIGHT! SO, IS ANYONE COMING TO RESCUE US?!
HAVE YOU HEARD ANYTHING?!
HELP ISN'T COMING.
IT'S NOT JUST JAPAN. THIS IS HAPPENING ALL OVER THE WORLD.
WASHINGTON AND NEW YORK HAVE ALREADY FALLEN, AND THE HUMAN POPULATION IS DROPPING WORLDWIDE.

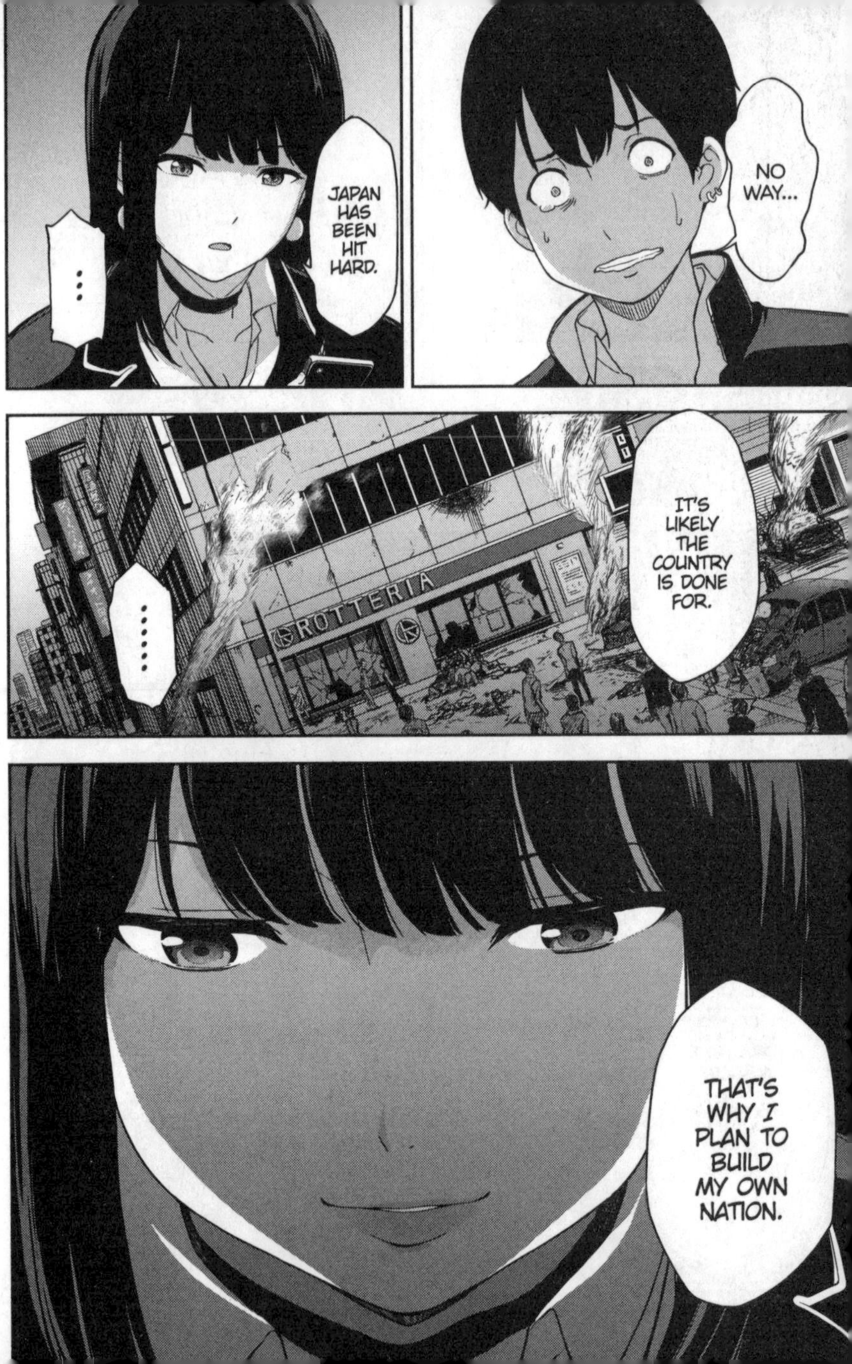
NO WAY...
JAPAN HAS BEEN HIT HARD.
...
IT'S LIKELY THE COUNTRY IS DONE FOR.
ROTTERIA
......
THAT'S WHY *I* PLAN TO BUILD MY OWN NATION.

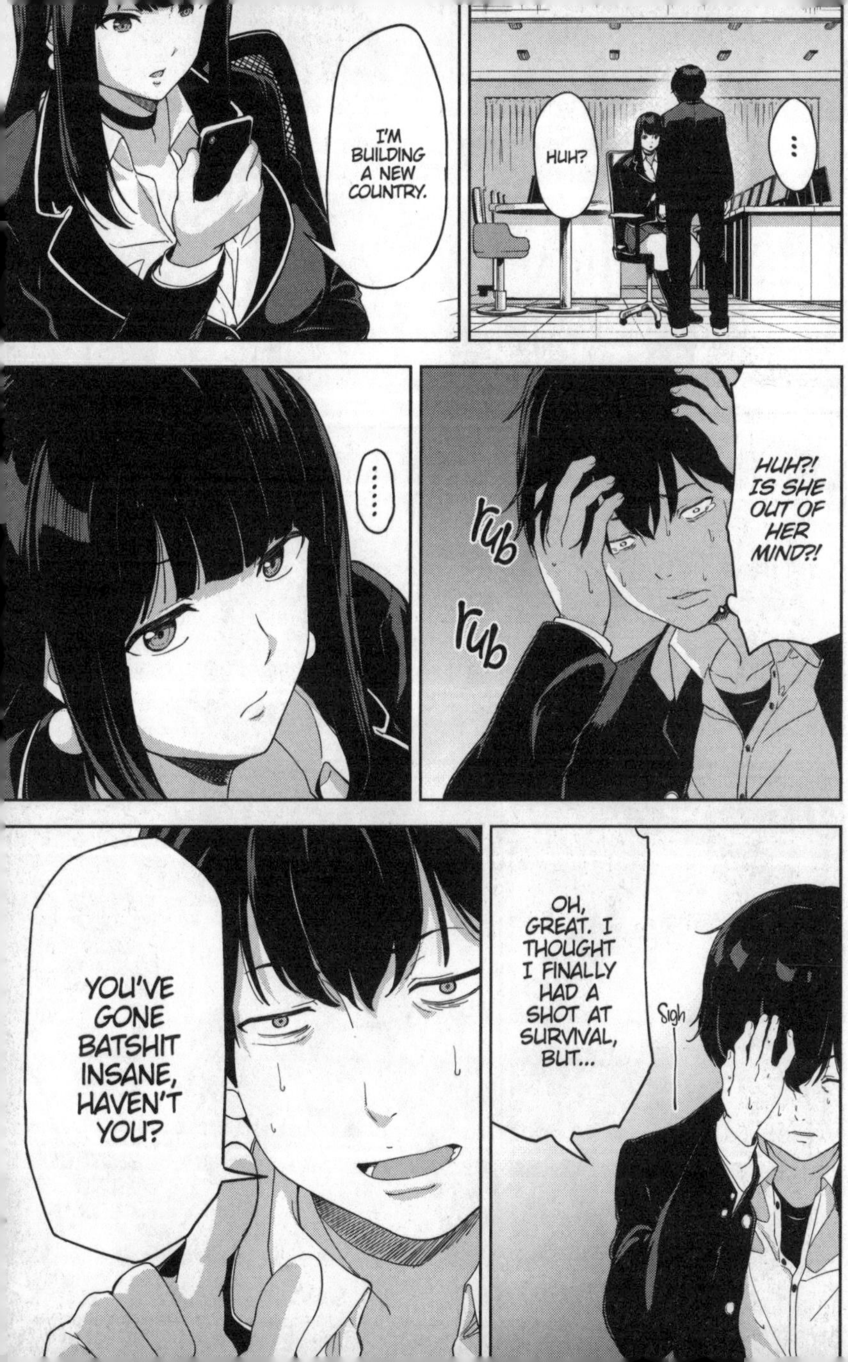

...
HUH?
I'M BUILDING A NEW COUNTRY.
HUH?! IS SHE OUT OF HER MIND?!
rub
rub
......
OH, GREAT. I THOUGHT I FINALLY HAD A SHOT AT SURVIVAL, BUT...
Sigh
YOU'VE GONE BATSHIT INSANE, HAVEN'T YOU?

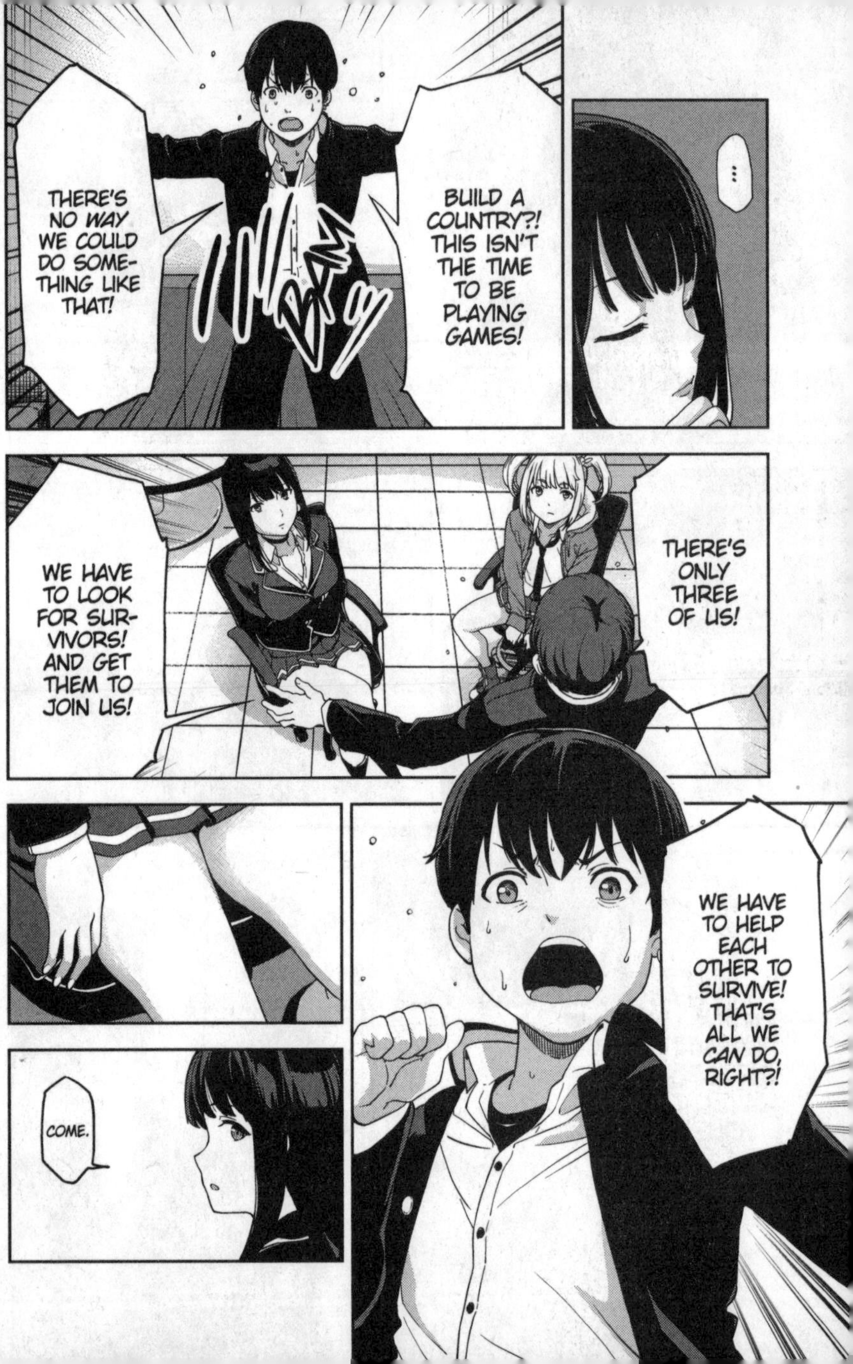
...
BUILD A COUNTRY?! THIS ISN'T THE TIME TO BE PLAYING GAMES!
THERE'S NO WAY WE COULD DO SOMETHING LIKE THAT!
THERE'S ONLY THREE OF US!
WE HAVE TO LOOK FOR SURVIVORS! AND GET THEM TO JOIN US!
WE HAVE TO HELP EACH OTHER TO SURVIVE! THAT'S ALL WE CAN DO, RIGHT?!
COME.

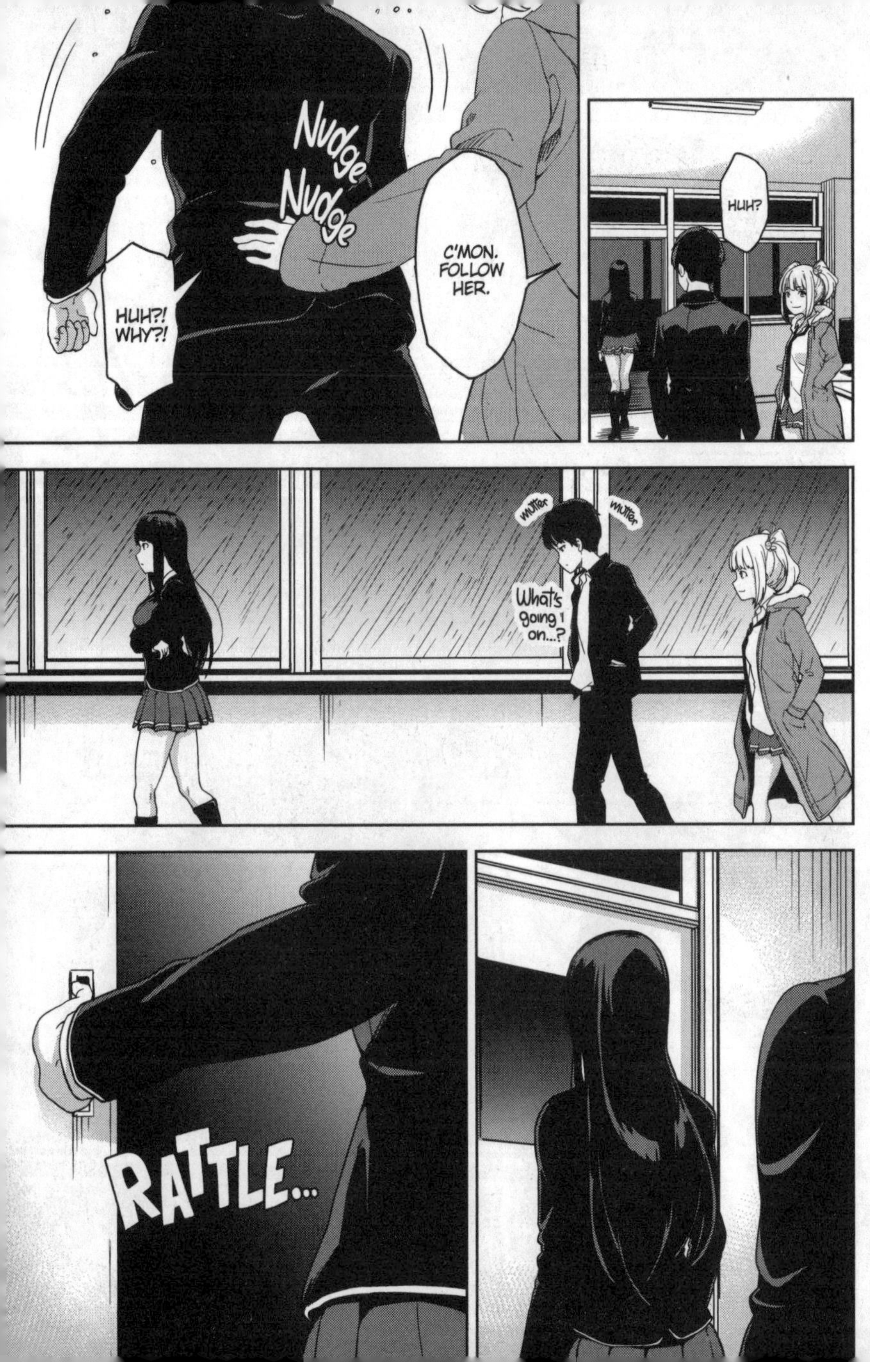
HUH?
C'MON. FOLLOW HER.
Nudge Nudge
HUH?! WHY?!
mutter
mutter
What's going on...?
RATTLE...

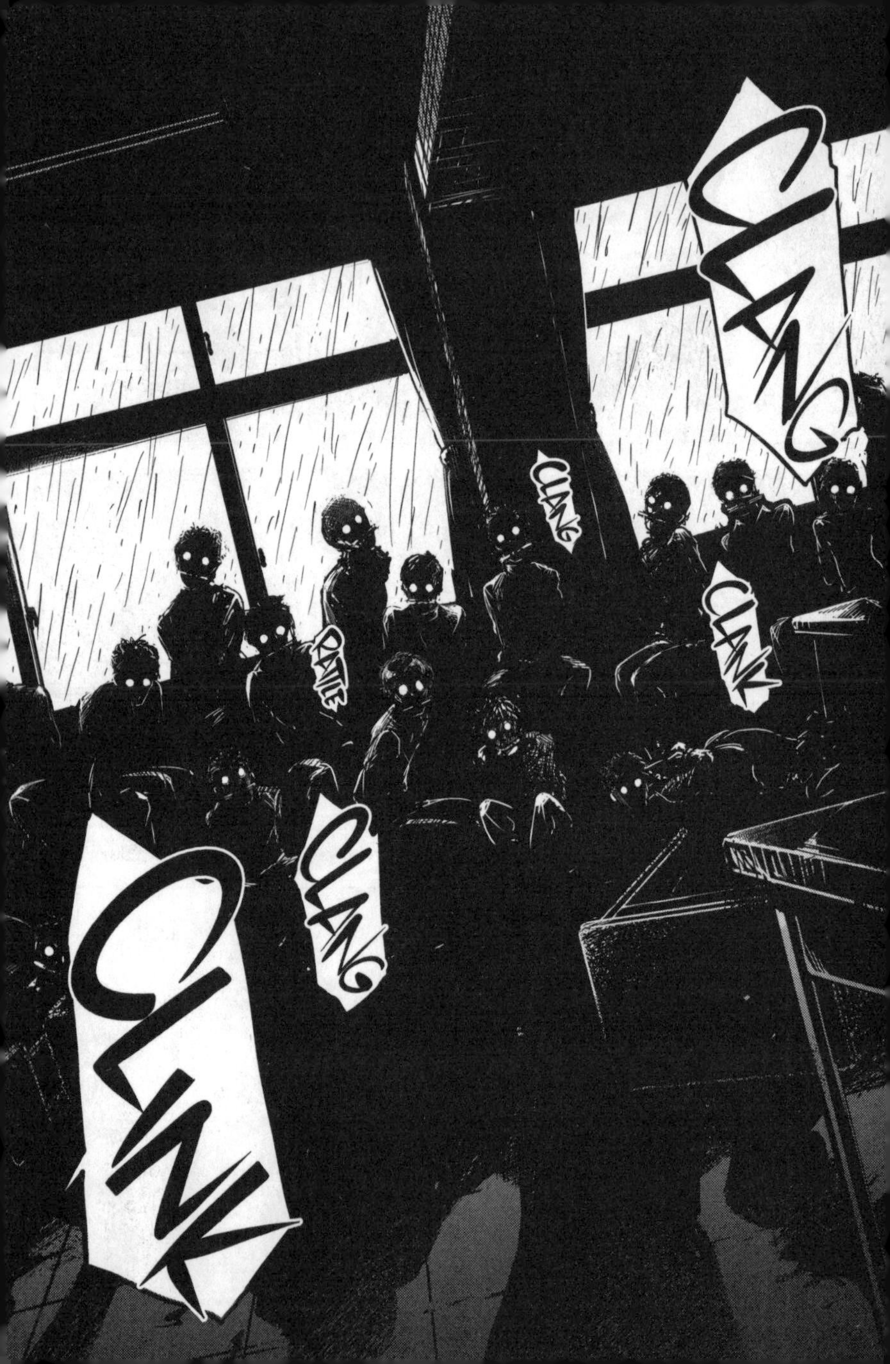
CLANG
CLANG
CLANK
RATTLE
CLANG
CLANK

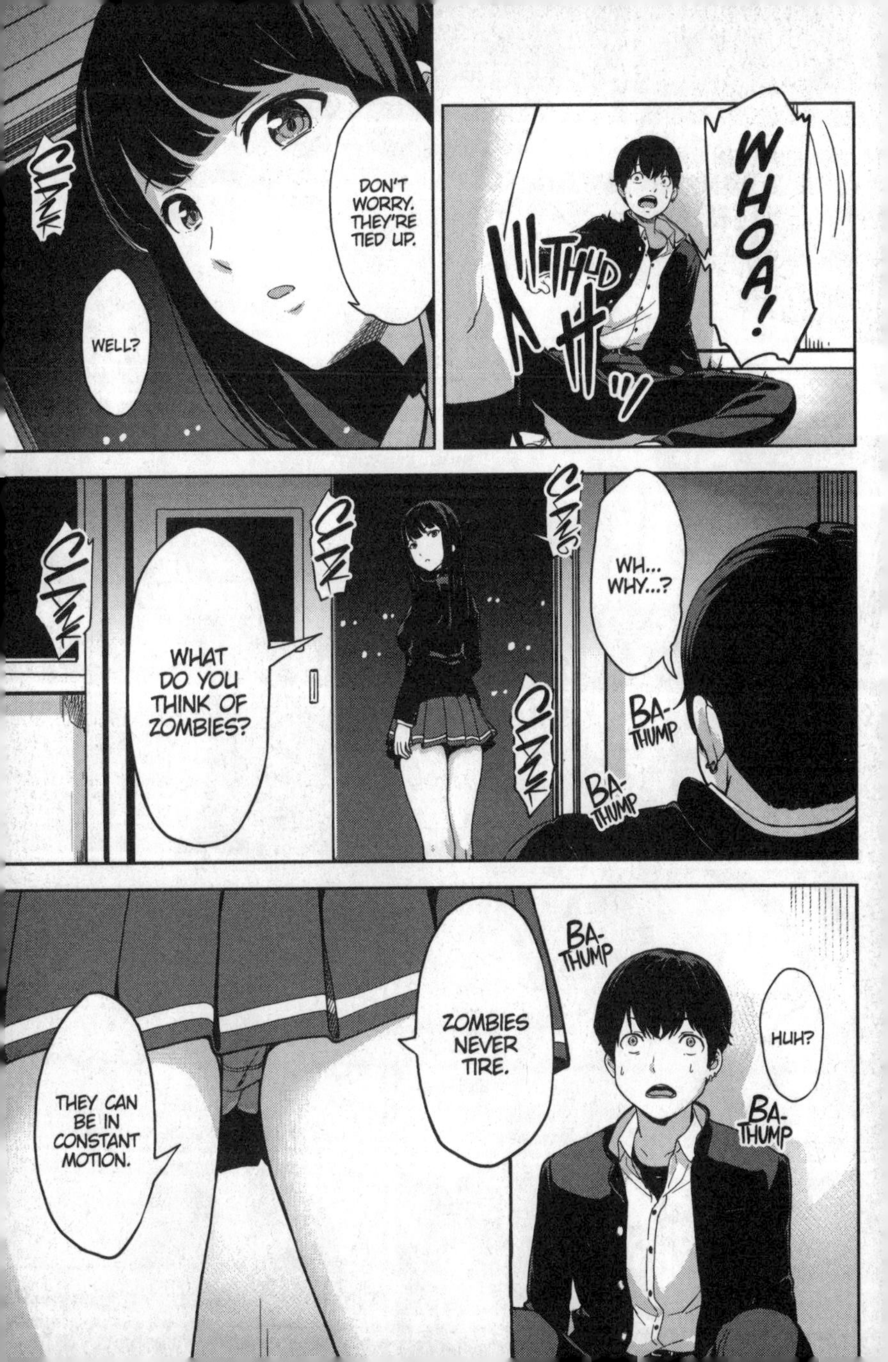
WHOA!
THUD
DON'T WORRY. THEY'RE TIED UP.
CLANK
WELL?
CLANG
WH... WHY...?
BA-THUMP
BA-THUMP
CLANK
CLANK
WHAT DO YOU THINK OF ZOMBIES?
CLANK
BA-THUMP
HUH?
BA-THUMP
ZOMBIES NEVER TIRE.
THEY CAN BE IN CONSTANT MOTION.

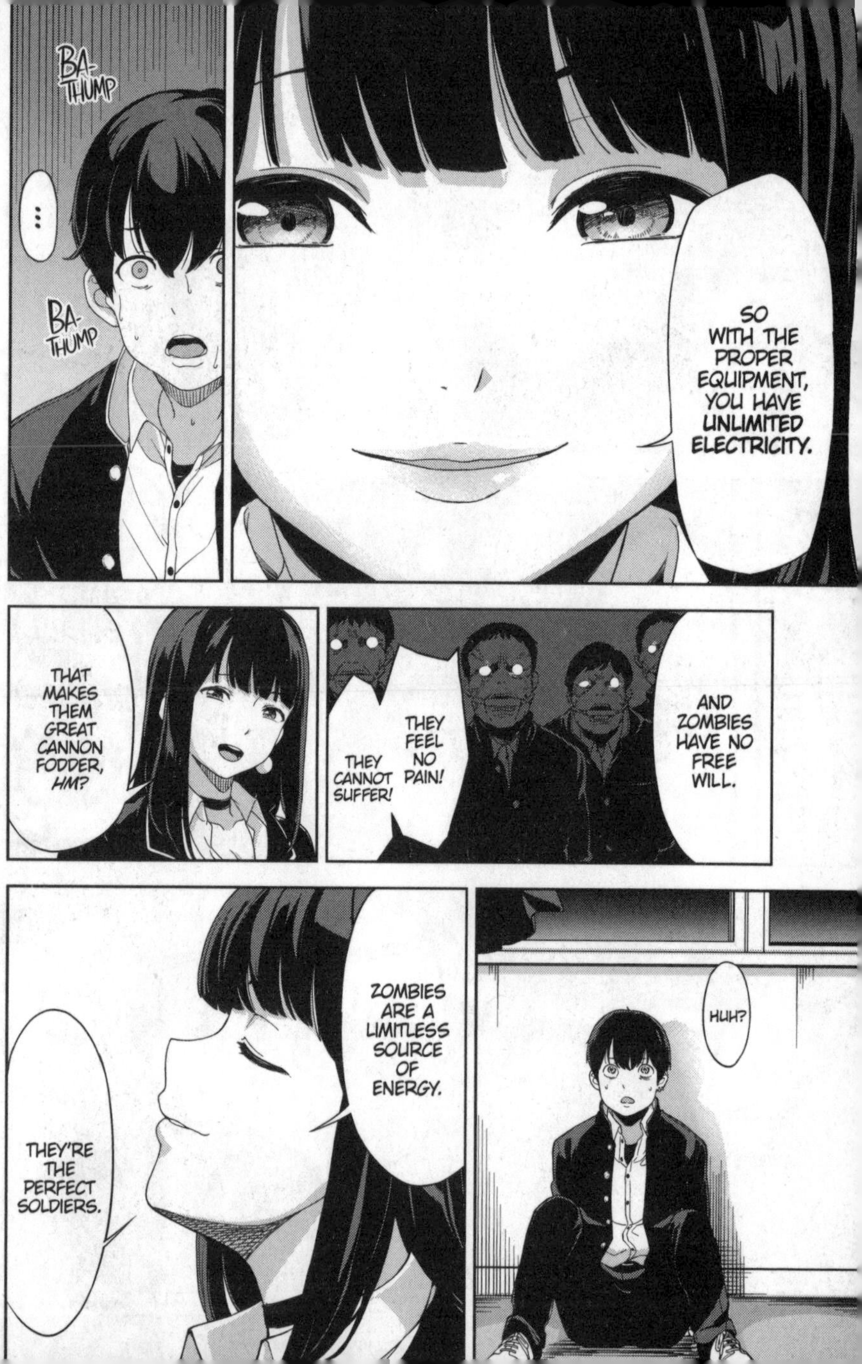
SO WITH THE PROPER EQUIPMENT, YOU HAVE UNLIMITED ELECTRICITY.
BA-THUMP
...
BA-THUMP
AND ZOMBIES HAVE NO FREE WILL.
THEY FEEL NO PAIN!
THEY CANNOT SUFFER!
THAT MAKES THEM GREAT CANNON FODDER, *HM?*
HUH?
ZOMBIES ARE A LIMITLESS SOURCE OF ENERGY.
THEY'RE THE PERFECT SOLDIERS.

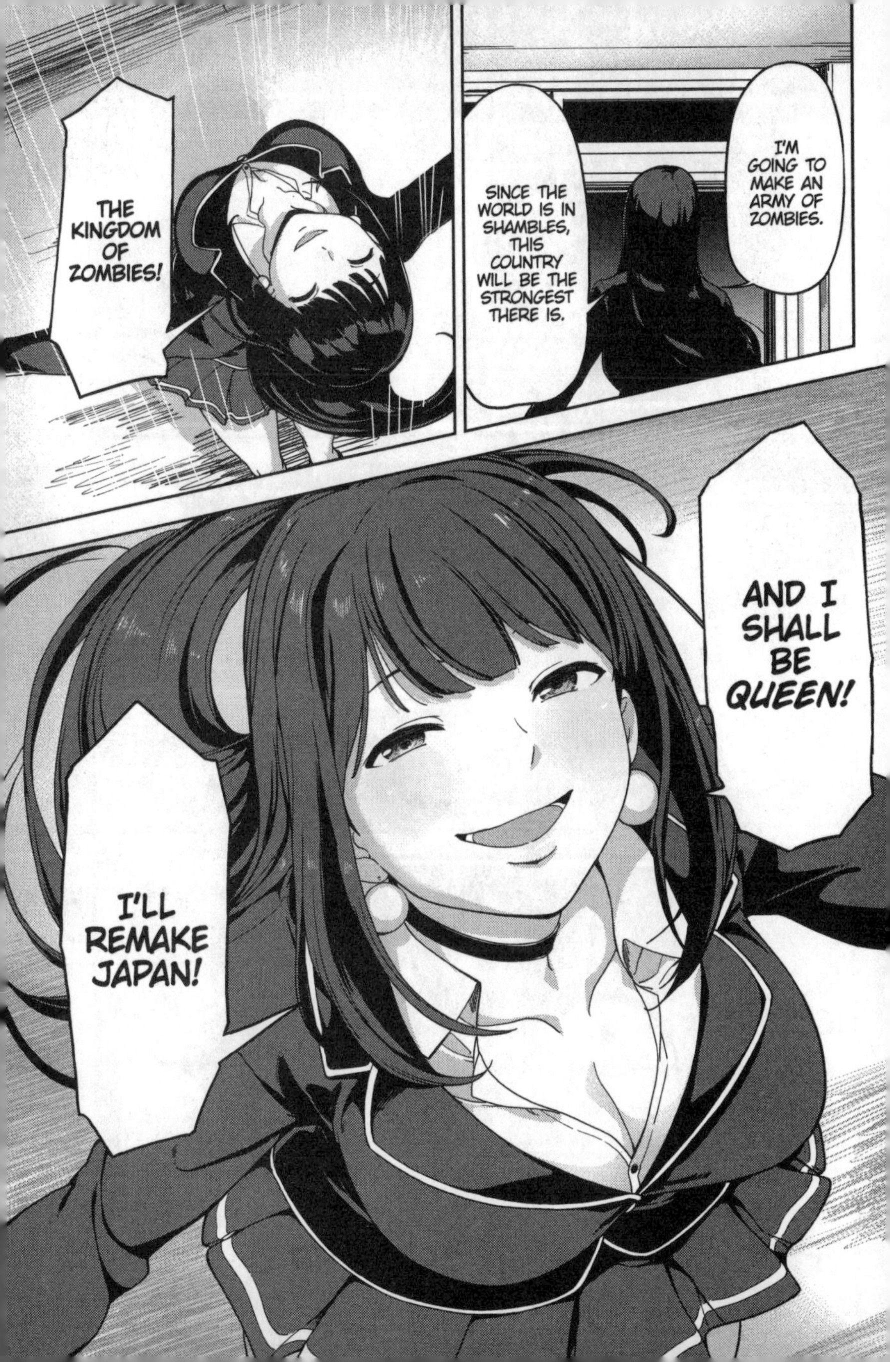
I'M GOING TO MAKE AN ARMY OF ZOMBIES.
SINCE THE WORLD IS IN SHAMBLES, THIS COUNTRY WILL BE THE STRONGEST THERE IS.
THE KINGDOM OF ZOMBIES!
AND I SHALL BE QUEEN!
I'LL REMAKE JAPAN!

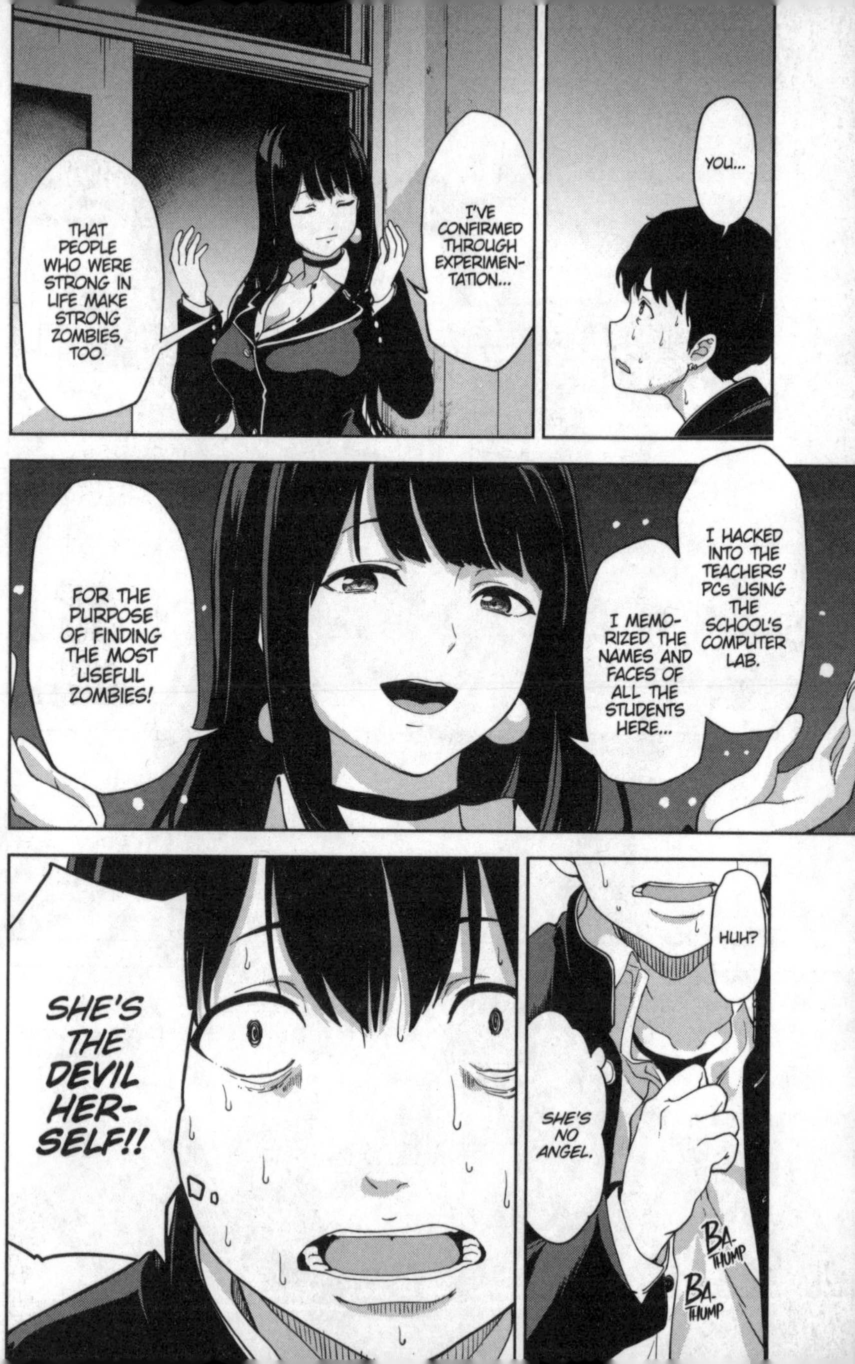
YOU...
I'VE CONFIRMED THROUGH EXPERIMENTATION...
THAT PEOPLE WHO WERE STRONG IN LIFE MAKE STRONG ZOMBIES, TOO.
I HACKED INTO THE TEACHERS' PCs USING THE SCHOOL'S COMPUTER LAB.
I MEMORIZED THE NAMES AND FACES OF ALL THE STUDENTS HERE...
FOR THE PURPOSE OF FINDING THE MOST USEFUL ZOMBIES!
HUH?
SHE'S NO ANGEL.
BA-THUMP
BA-THUMP
SHE'S THE DEVIL HERSELF!!

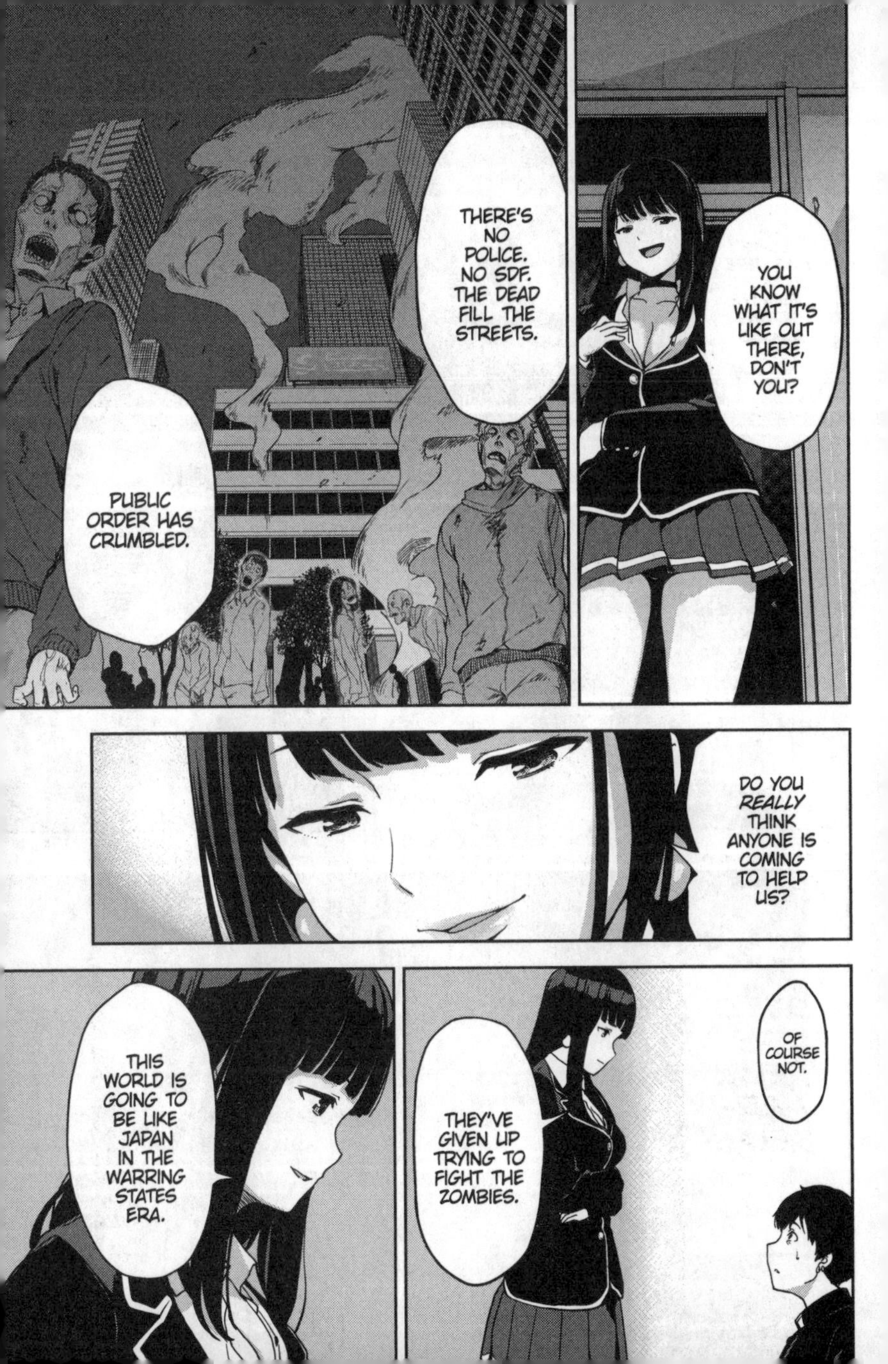
YOU KNOW WHAT IT'S LIKE OUT THERE, DON'T YOU?
THERE'S NO POLICE. NO SDF. THE DEAD FILL THE STREETS.
PUBLIC ORDER HAS CRUMBLED.
DO YOU *REALLY* THINK ANYONE IS COMING TO HELP US?
OF COURSE NOT.
THEY'VE GIVEN UP TRYING TO FIGHT THE ZOMBIES.
THIS WORLD IS GOING TO BE LIKE JAPAN IN THE WARRING STATES ERA.

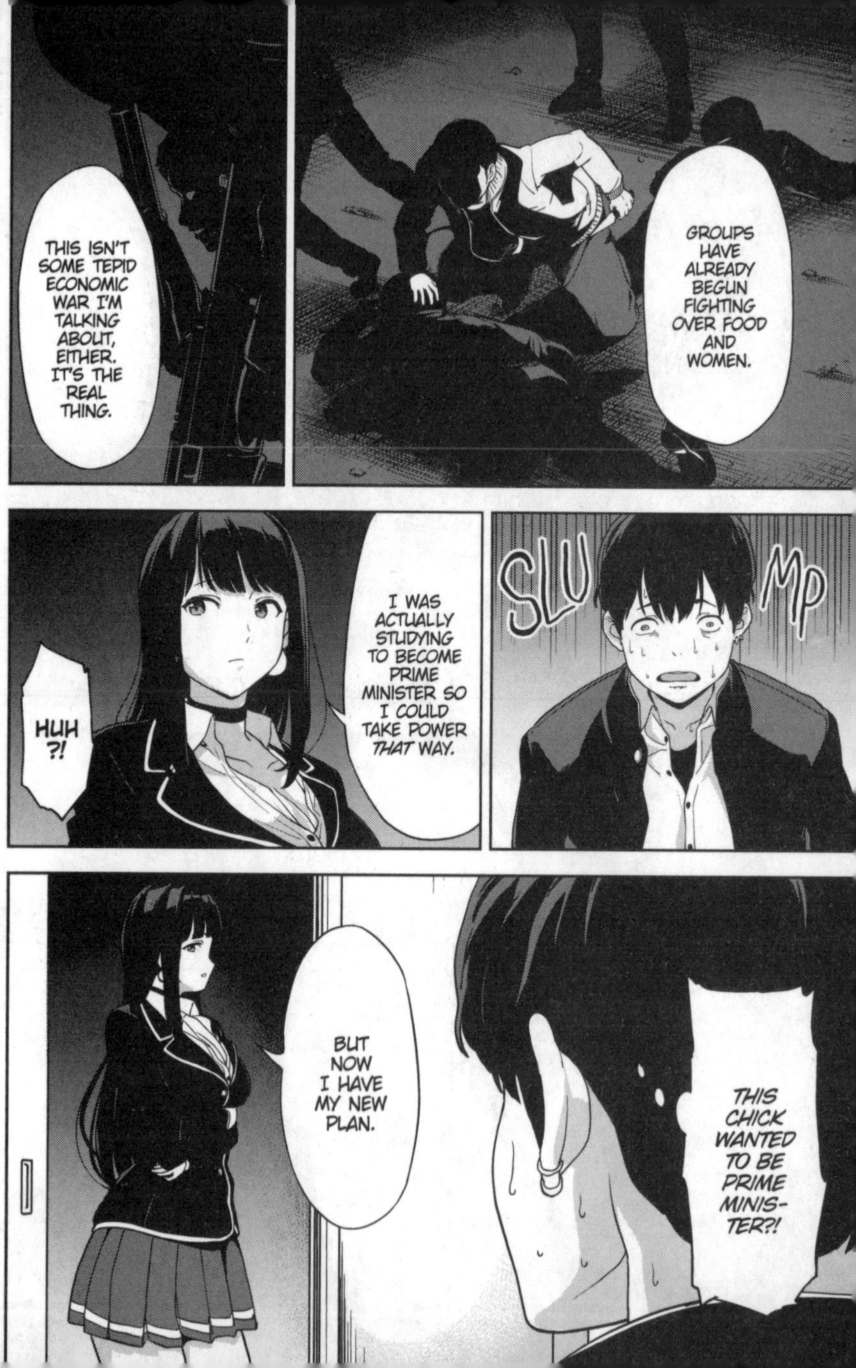
GROUPS HAVE ALREADY BEGUN FIGHTING OVER FOOD AND WOMEN.
THIS ISN'T SOME TEPID ECONOMIC WAR I'M TALKING ABOUT, EITHER. IT'S THE REAL THING.
SLUMP
I WAS ACTUALLY STUDYING TO BECOME PRIME MINISTER SO I COULD TAKE POWER *THAT* WAY.
HUH?!
BUT NOW I HAVE MY NEW PLAN.
THIS CHICK WANTED TO BE PRIME MINIS-TER?!

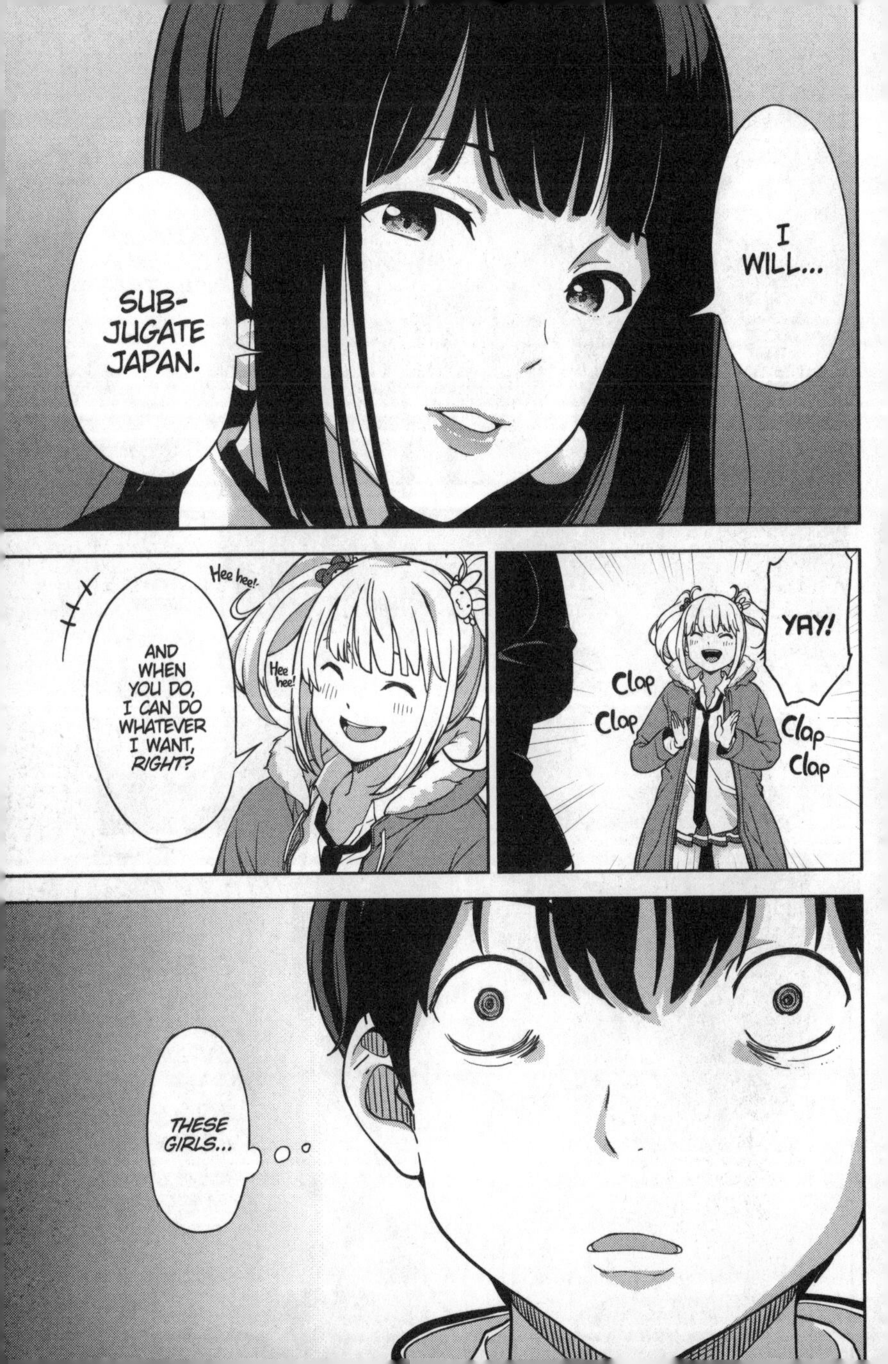
I WILL...
SUB-JUGATE JAPAN.
YAY!
Clap
Clap
Clap
Clap
Hee hee!
Hee hee!
AND WHEN YOU DO, I CAN DO WHATEVER I WANT, *RIGHT?*
THESE GIRLS...

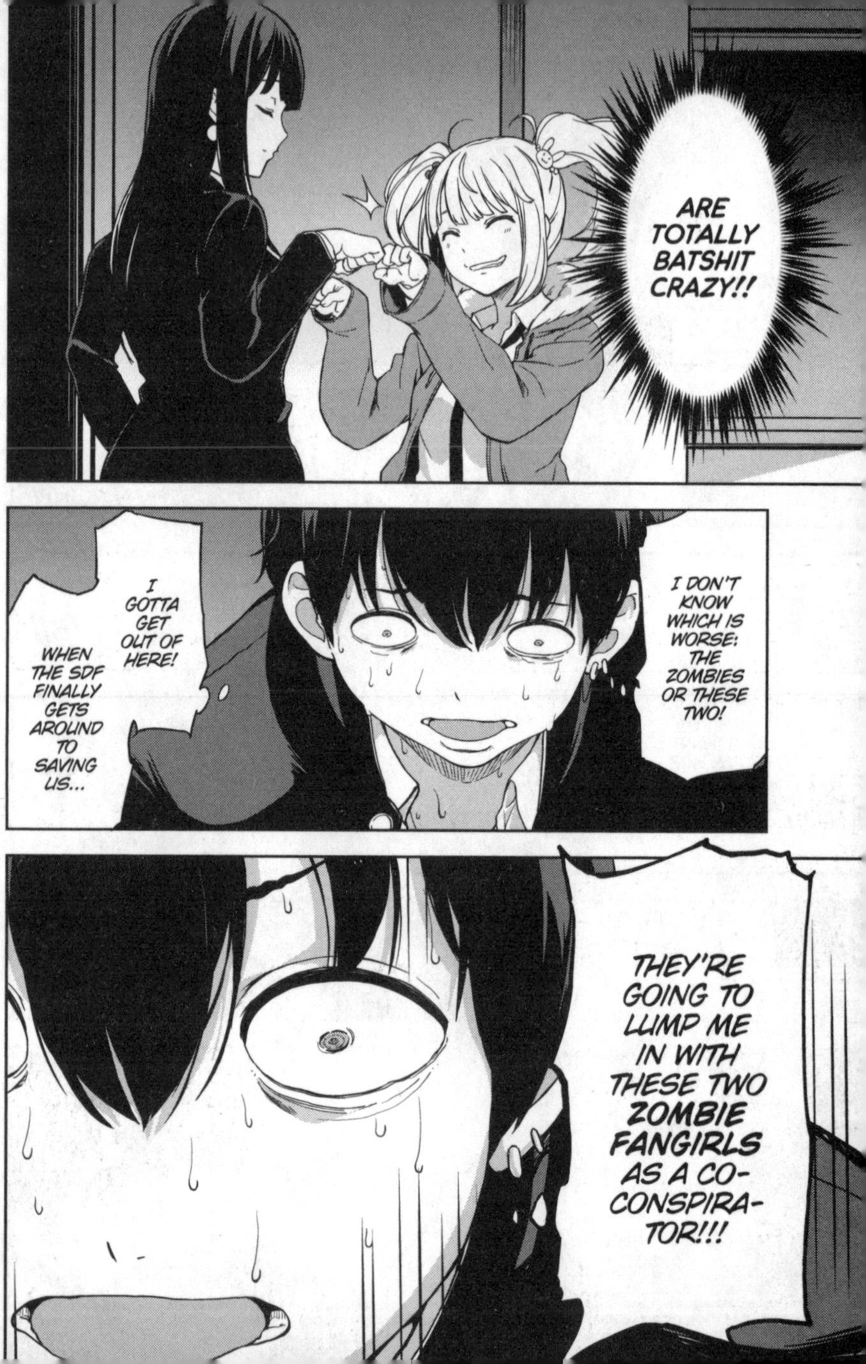
ARE TOTALLY BATSHIT CRAZY!!
I DON'T KNOW WHICH IS WORSE: THE ZOMBIES OR THESE TWO!
I GOTTA GET OUT OF HERE!
WHEN THE SDF FINALLY GETS AROUND TO SAVING US...
THEY'RE GOING TO LUMP ME IN WITH THESE TWO ZOMBIE FANGIRLS AS A CO-CONSPIRATOR!!!

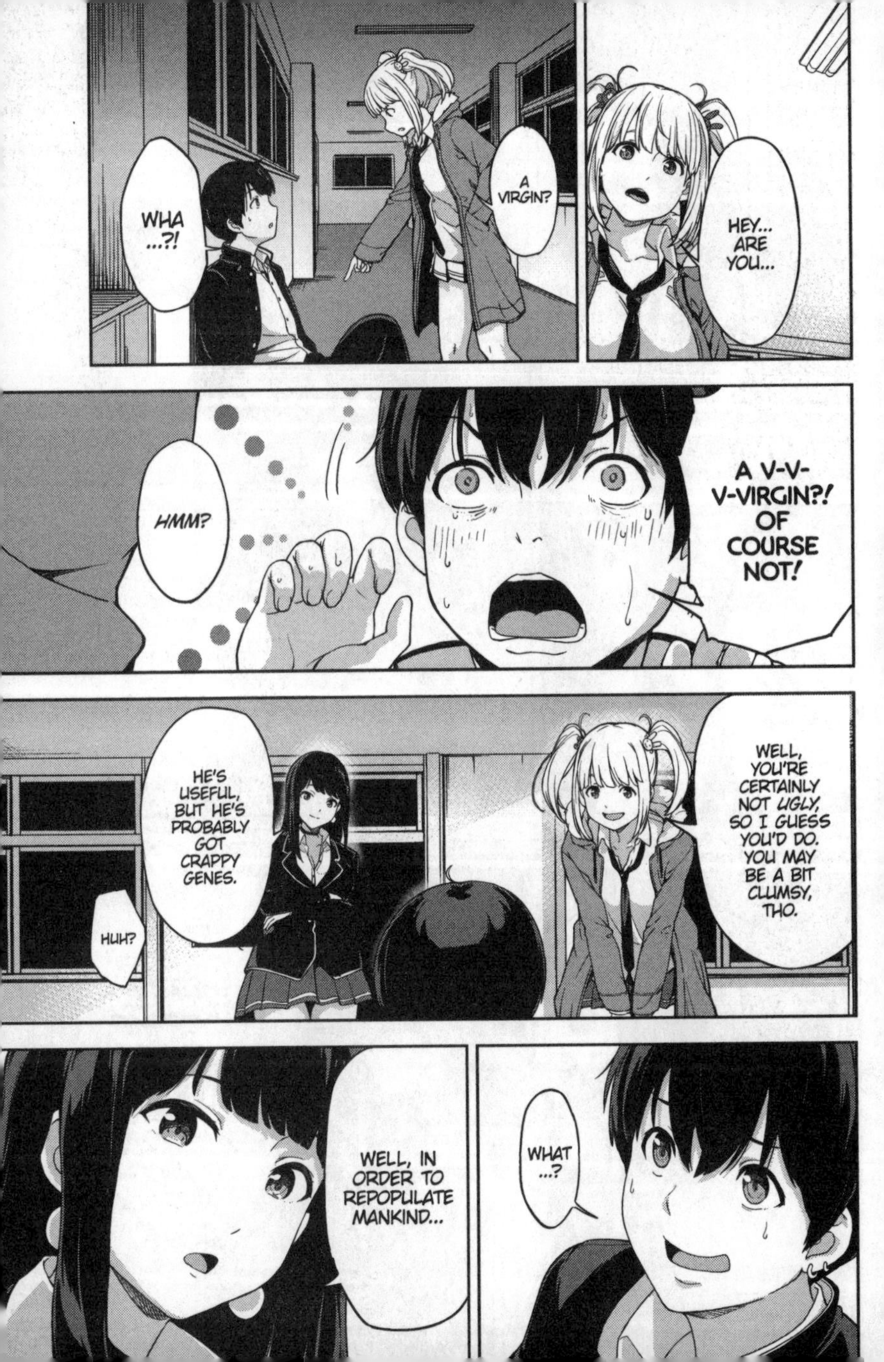
HEY... ARE YOU...
A VIRGIN?
WHA ...?!
A V-V-V-VIRGIN?! OF COURSE NOT!
HMM?
WELL, YOU'RE CERTAINLY NOT *UGLY*, SO I GUESS YOU'D DO. YOU MAY BE A BIT CLUMSY, THO.
HE'S USEFUL, BUT HE'S PROBABLY GOT CRAPPY GENES.
HUH?
WHAT ...?
WELL, IN ORDER TO REPOPULATE MANKIND...

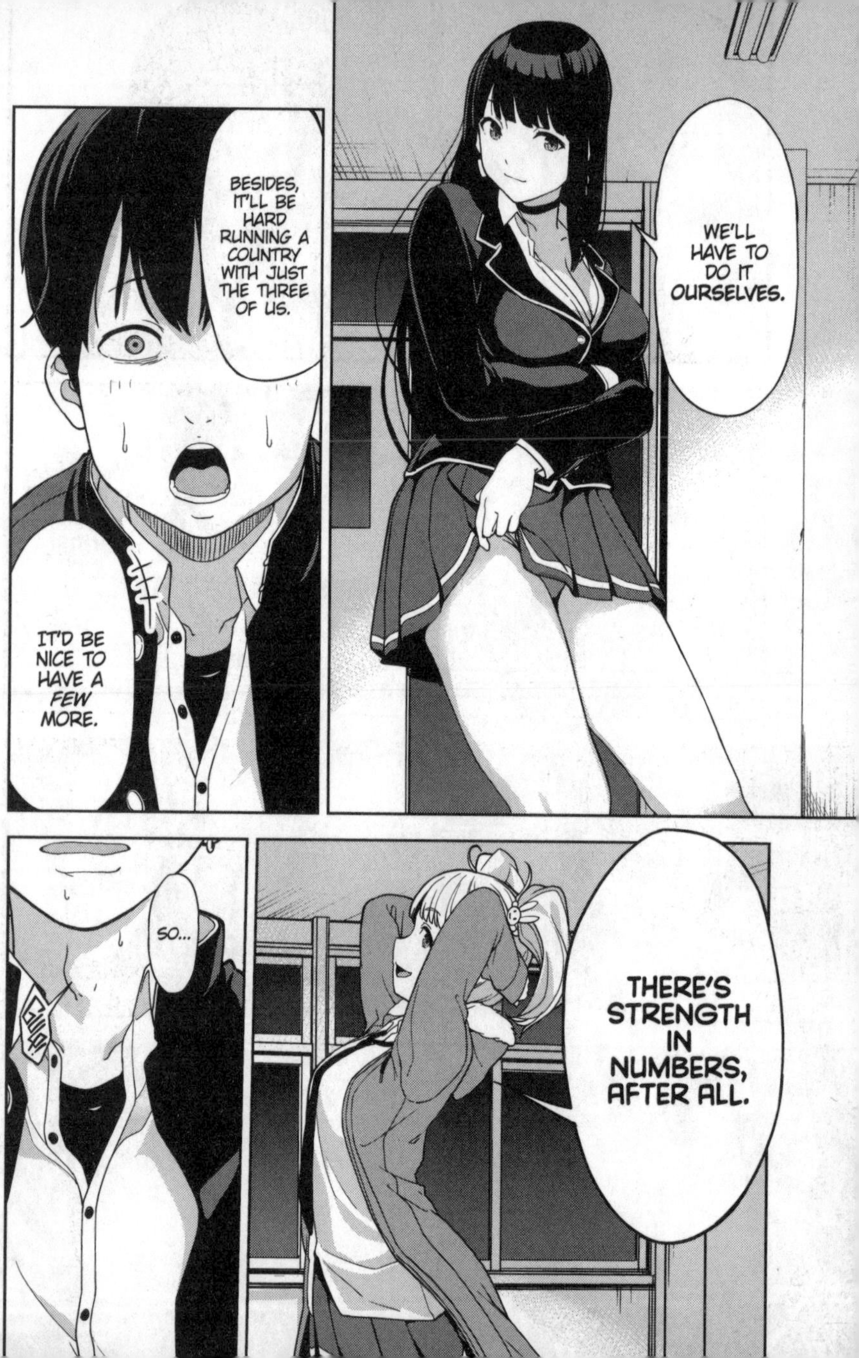
WE'LL HAVE TO DO IT OURSELVES.
BESIDES, IT'LL BE HARD RUNNING A COUNTRY WITH JUST THE THREE OF US.
IT'D BE NICE TO HAVE A *FEW* MORE.
THERE'S STRENGTH IN NUMBERS, AFTER ALL.
SO...

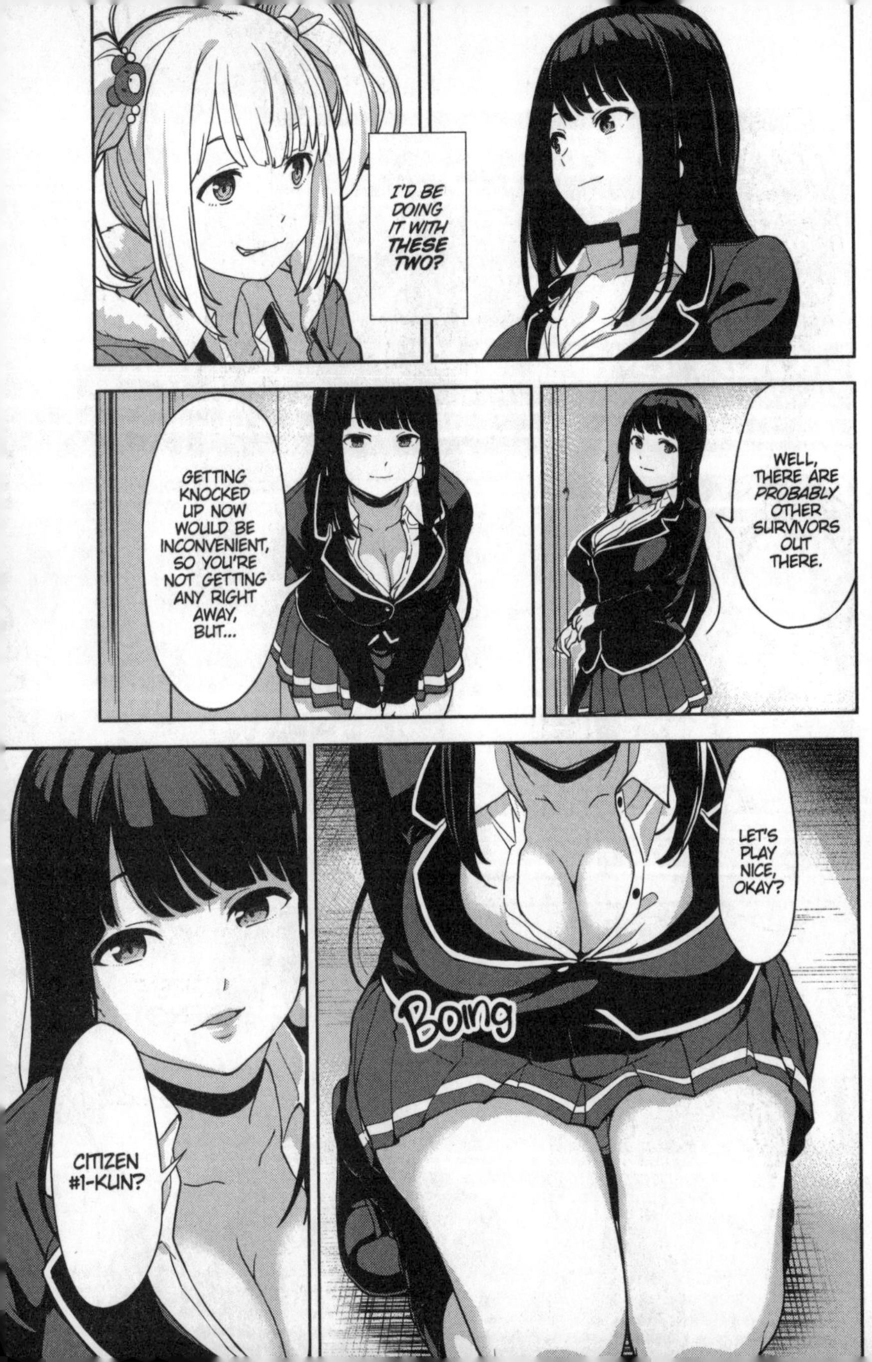
I'D BE DOING IT WITH THESE TWO?
WELL, THERE ARE PROBABLY OTHER SURVIVORS OUT THERE.
GETTING KNOCKED UP NOW WOULD BE INCONVENIENT, SO YOU'RE NOT GETTING ANY RIGHT AWAY, BUT...
LET'S PLAY NICE, OKAY?
Boing
CITIZEN #1-KUN?

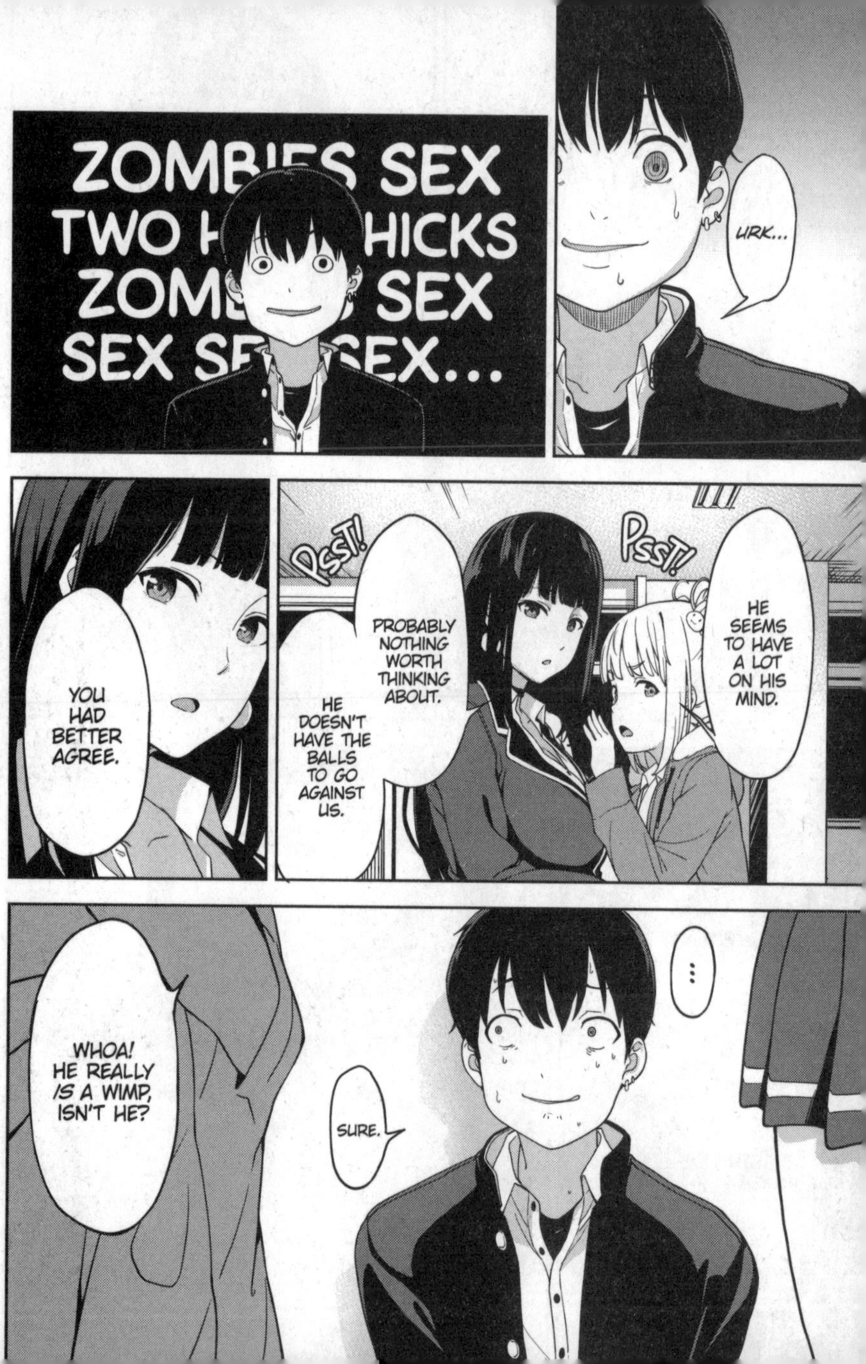
URK...
ZOMB ES SEX
TWO H HICKS
ZOMB SEX
SEX SE SEX...
PSST!
HE SEEMS TO HAVE A LOT ON HIS MIND.
PSST!
PROBABLY NOTHING WORTH THINKING ABOUT.
HE DOESN'T HAVE THE BALLS TO GO AGAINST US.
YOU HAD BETTER AGREE.
...
SURE.
WHOA! HE REALLY IS A WIMP, ISN'T HE?

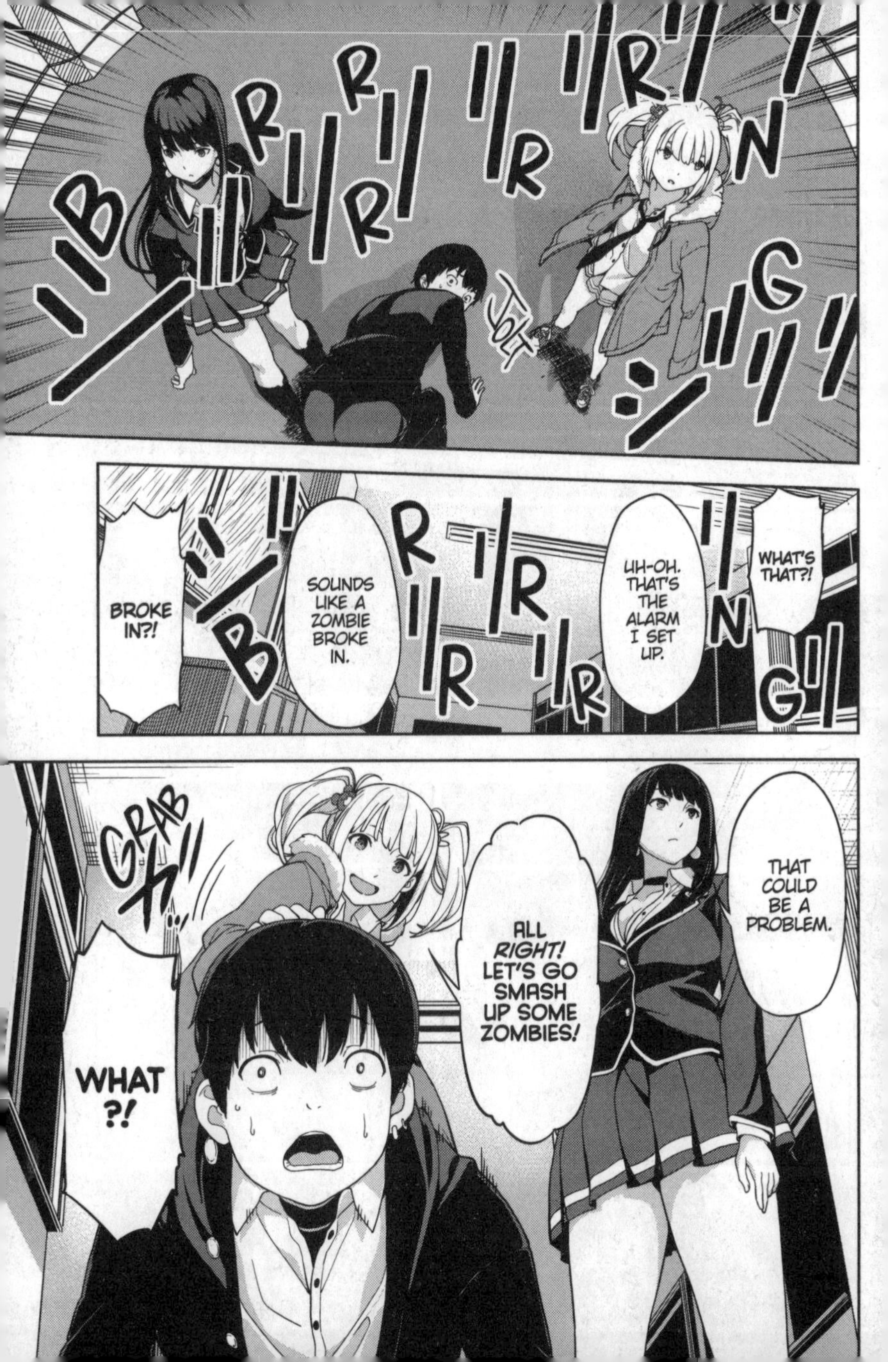
JOLT
WHAT'S THAT?!
UH-OH. THAT'S THE ALARM I SET UP.
SOUNDS LIKE A ZOMBIE BROKE IN.
BROKE IN?!
THAT COULD BE A PROBLEM.
ALL *RIGHT!* LET'S GO SMASH UP SOME ZOMBIES!
GRAB
WHAT?!

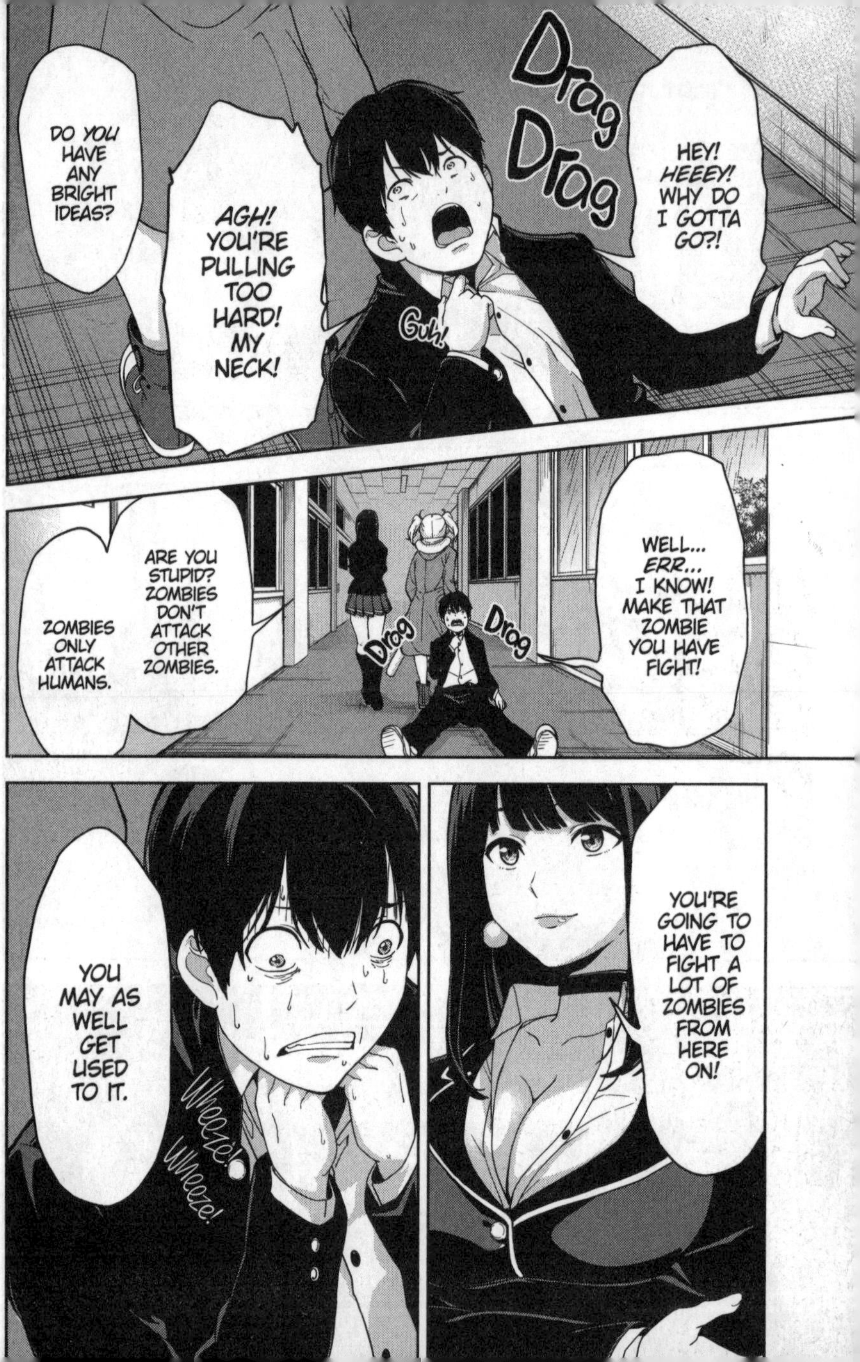
HEY! HEEEY! WHY DO I GOTTA GO?!
Drag Drag
AGH! YOU'RE PULLING TOO HARD! MY NECK!
Guh!
DO YOU HAVE ANY BRIGHT IDEAS?
WELL... ERR... I KNOW! MAKE THAT ZOMBIE YOU HAVE FIGHT!
Drag Drag
ARE YOU STUPID? ZOMBIES DON'T ATTACK OTHER ZOMBIES.
ZOMBIES ONLY ATTACK HUMANS.
YOU'RE GOING TO HAVE TO FIGHT A LOT OF ZOMBIES FROM HERE ON!
YOU MAY AS WELL GET USED TO IT.
Wheeze! Wheeze!

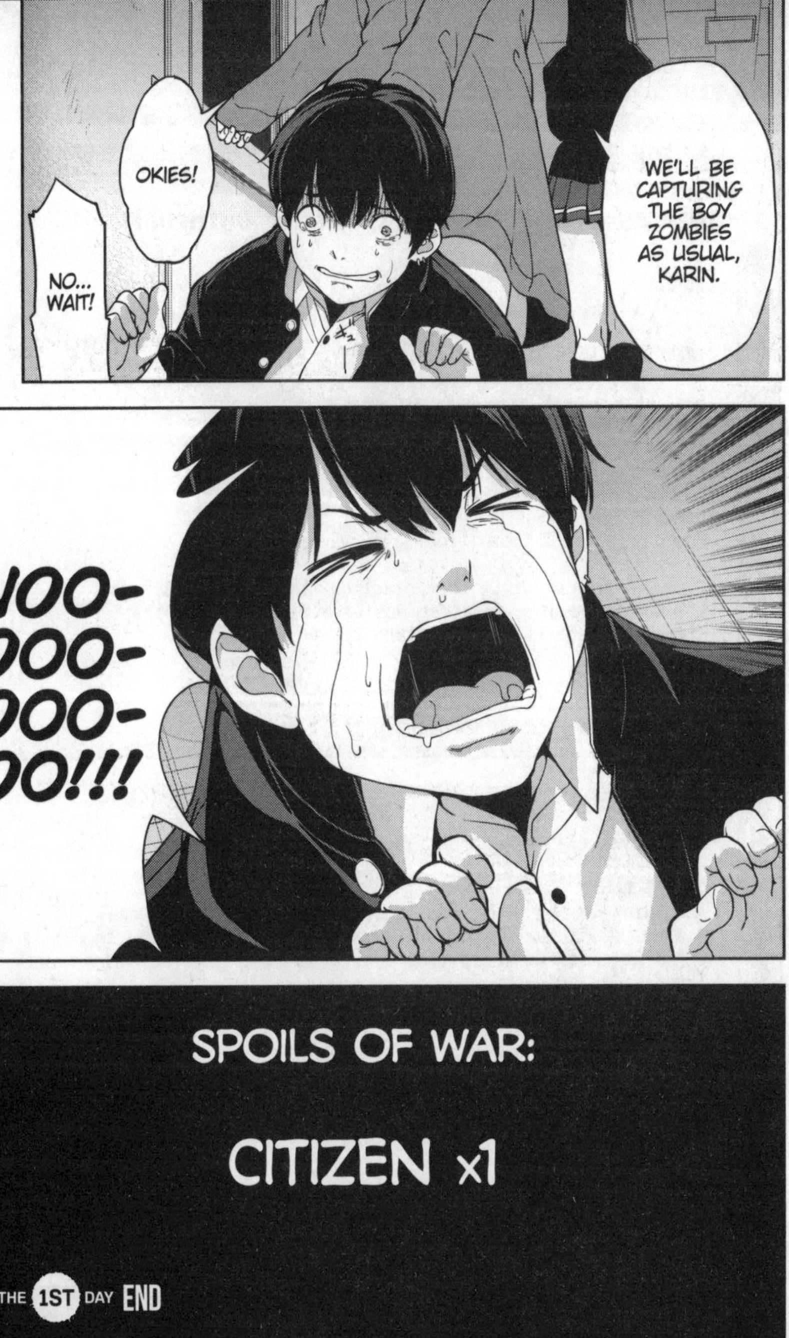
WE'LL BE CAPTURING THE BOY ZOMBIES AS USUAL, KARIN.
OKIES!
NO... WAIT!
NOO-OOO-OOO-OO!!!
SPOILS OF WAR:
CITIZEN x1
THE 1ST DAY END

Miki's Log - Two Weeks After Outbreak

10/1
Zombies appeared around the world roughly simultaneously.

Teamed up with Nagiri Karin.
Took back the computer lab.
Set up our base of operations there.

10/2
Began clearing the schoolground
(Karin is especially good at this).
Schoolground almost clear.
Zombies left to chase fleeing survivors.

I have confirmed that the infection spread quickest in
low-populated areas and regions with military organizations.
I never thought they could take on the military...

Addendum, 10/4
One soldier was probably bitten and he became a super-zombie.
The infection spread throughout the group.
Areas close to military bases are likely very dangerous.
Beware of the SDF.

10/3
The source of the outbreak is being hotly debated on the internet.

2018/5/12
According to the news, ten patients in South Africa were
diagnosed with an unknown disease. Doctors from around the
world were sent to help find a cure.
The details are unknown.

5/22
According to the newspapers, those 10 patients died.
There is a possibility the virus spread when those doctors
returned to their home countries.
The disease could have spread in the airports. Maybe there's
a time lag from the initial stages to the incubation period?

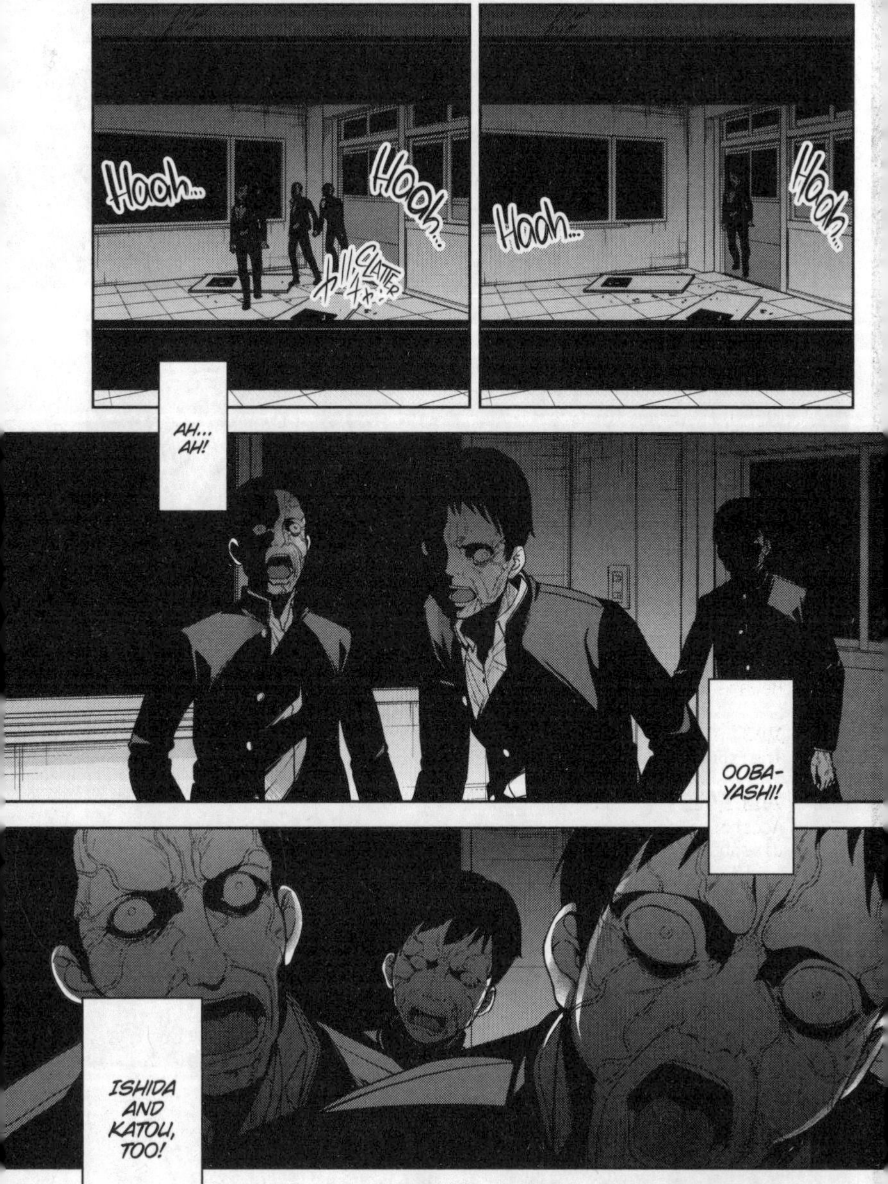

Haah...
Haah...
Haah...
Haah...
CLATTER
AH... AH!
OOBA-YASHI!
ISHIDA AND KATOU, TOO!

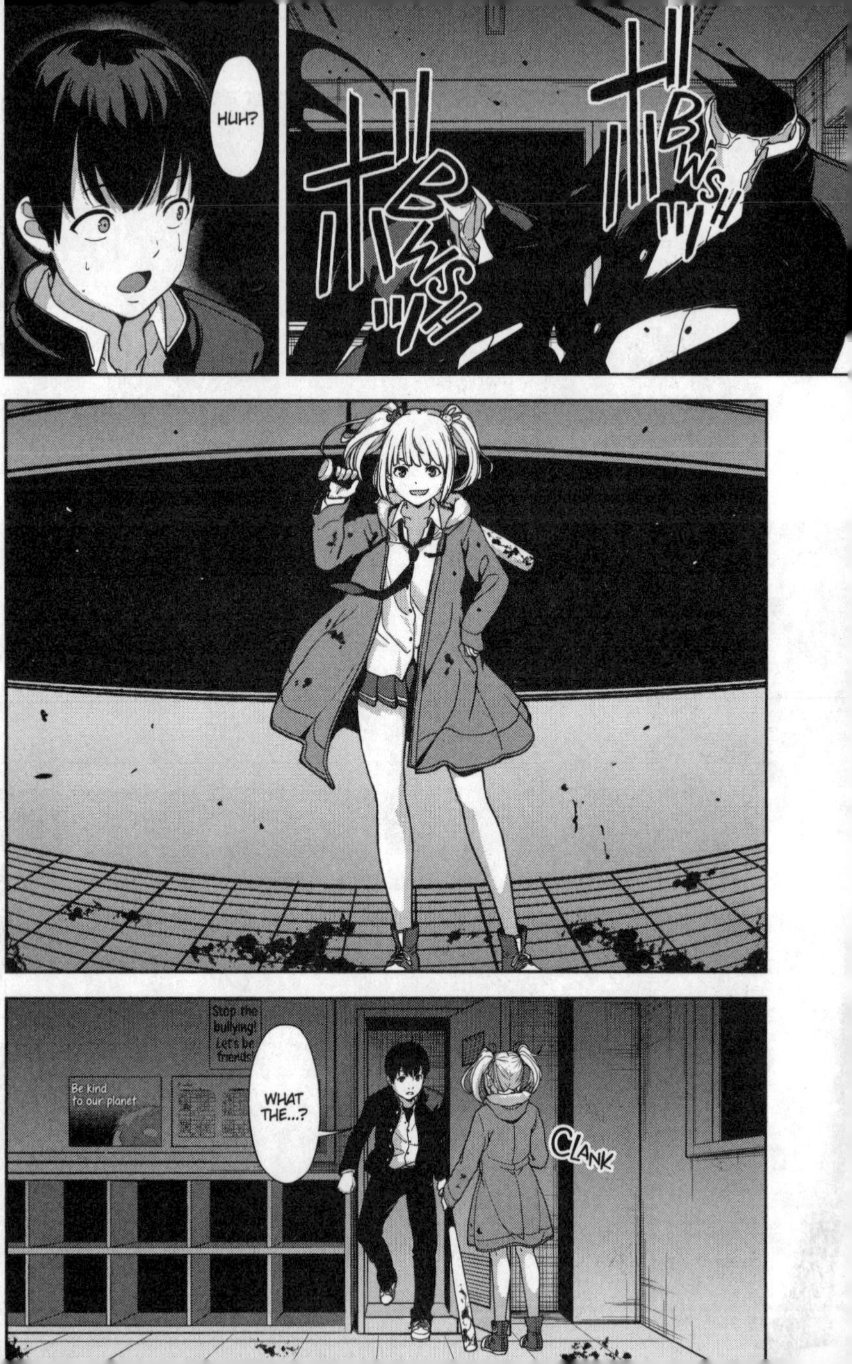
BWSH
BWSH
HUH?
Stop the bullying! Let's be friends!
CLANK
WHAT THE...?
Be kind to our planet

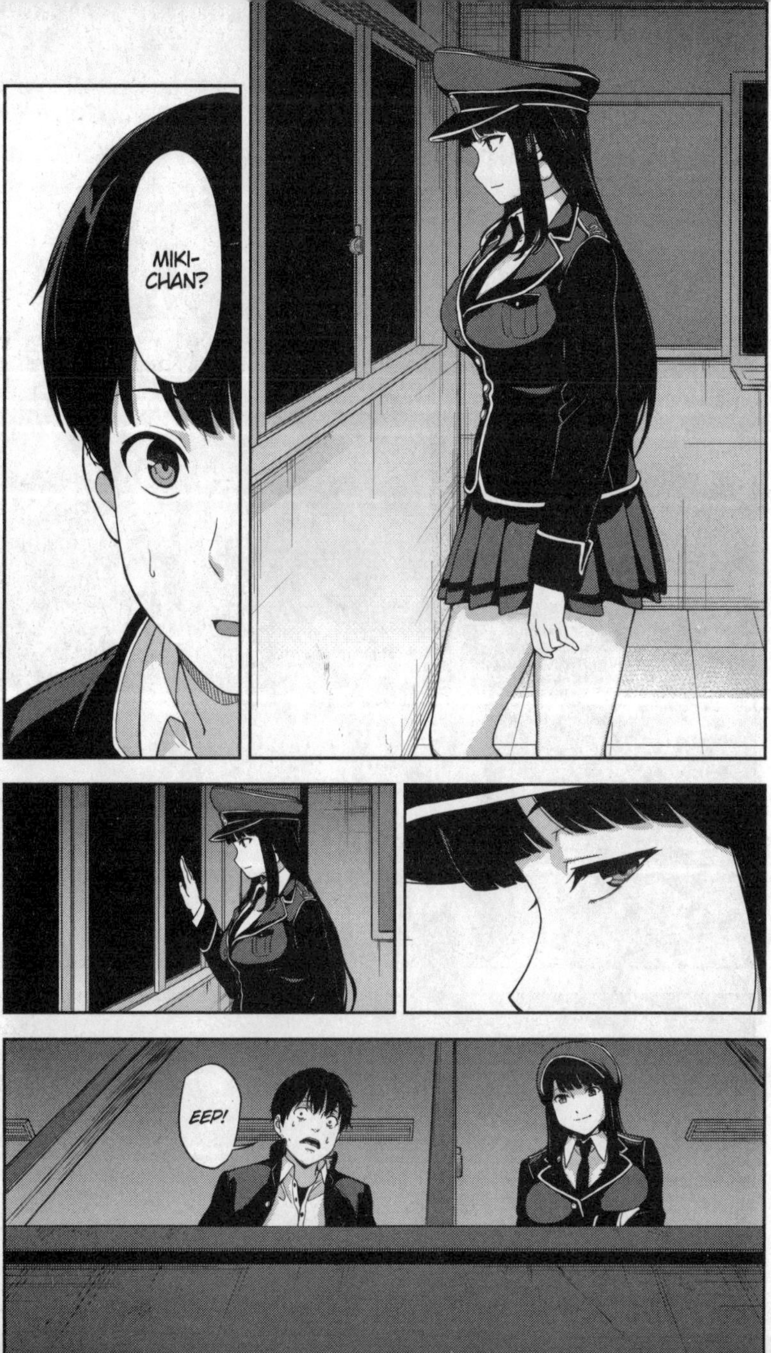
MIKI-CHAN?
EEP!

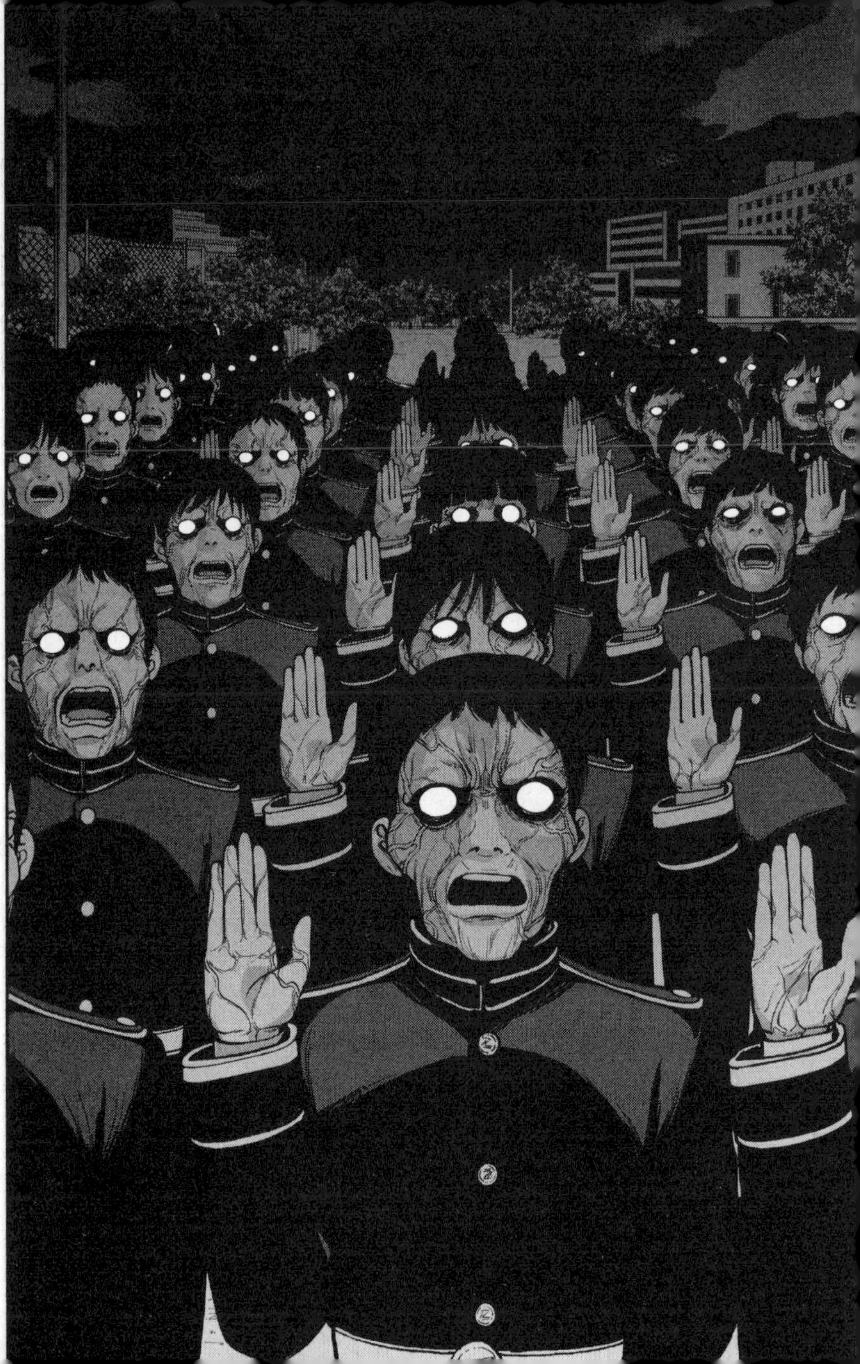

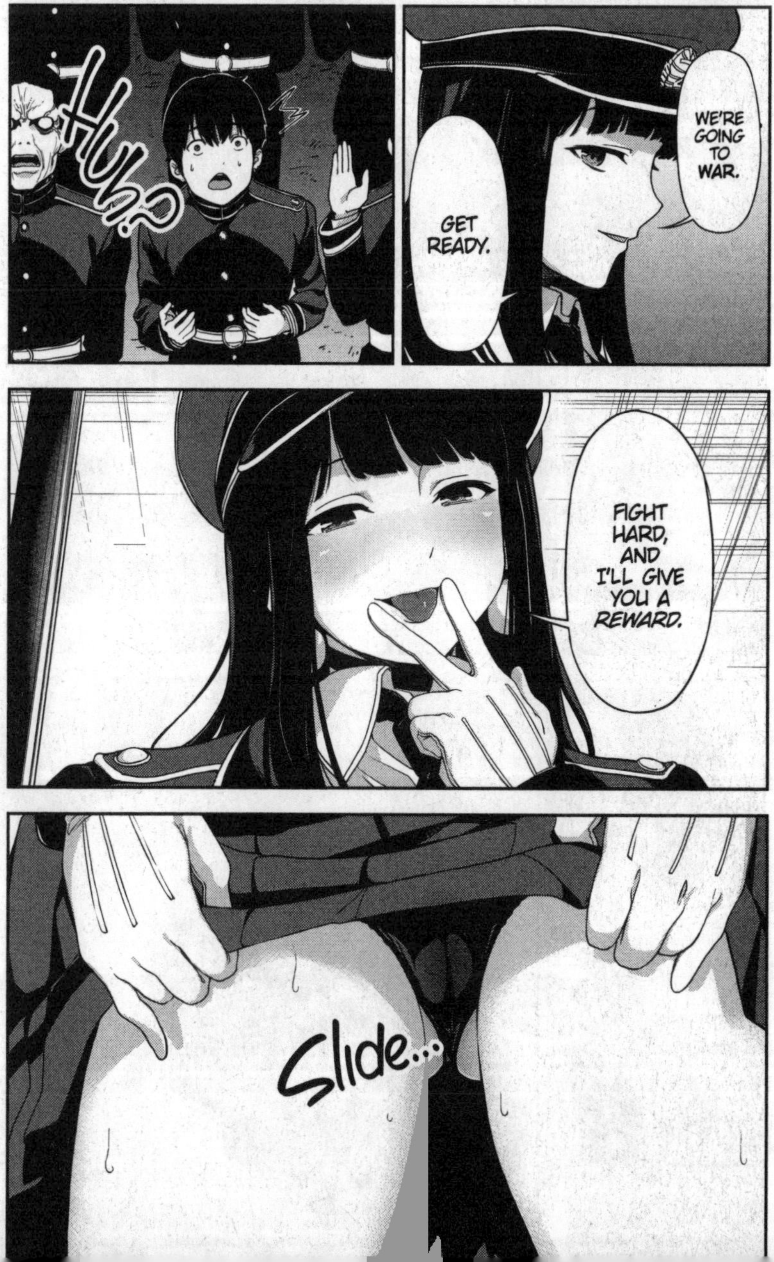
WE'RE GOING TO WAR.
GET READY.
HUH?
FIGHT HARD, AND I'LL GIVE YOU A REWARD.
Slide...

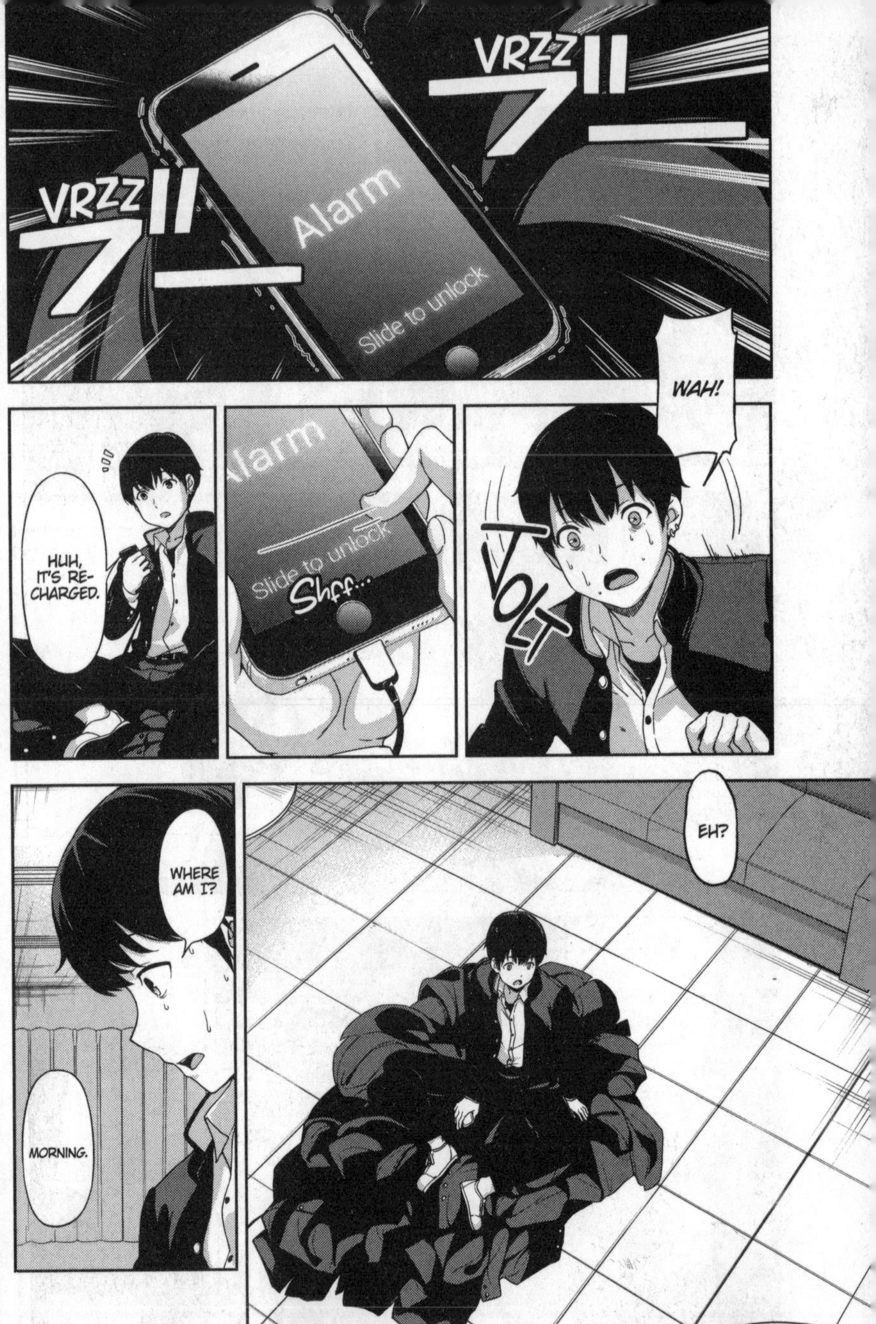
VRZZ
ブー
VRZZ
ブー
Alarm
Slide to unlock
WAH!
VOLT
Alarm
Slide to unlock
Shff...
HUH, IT'S RE-CHARGED.
EH?
WHERE AM I?
MORNING.

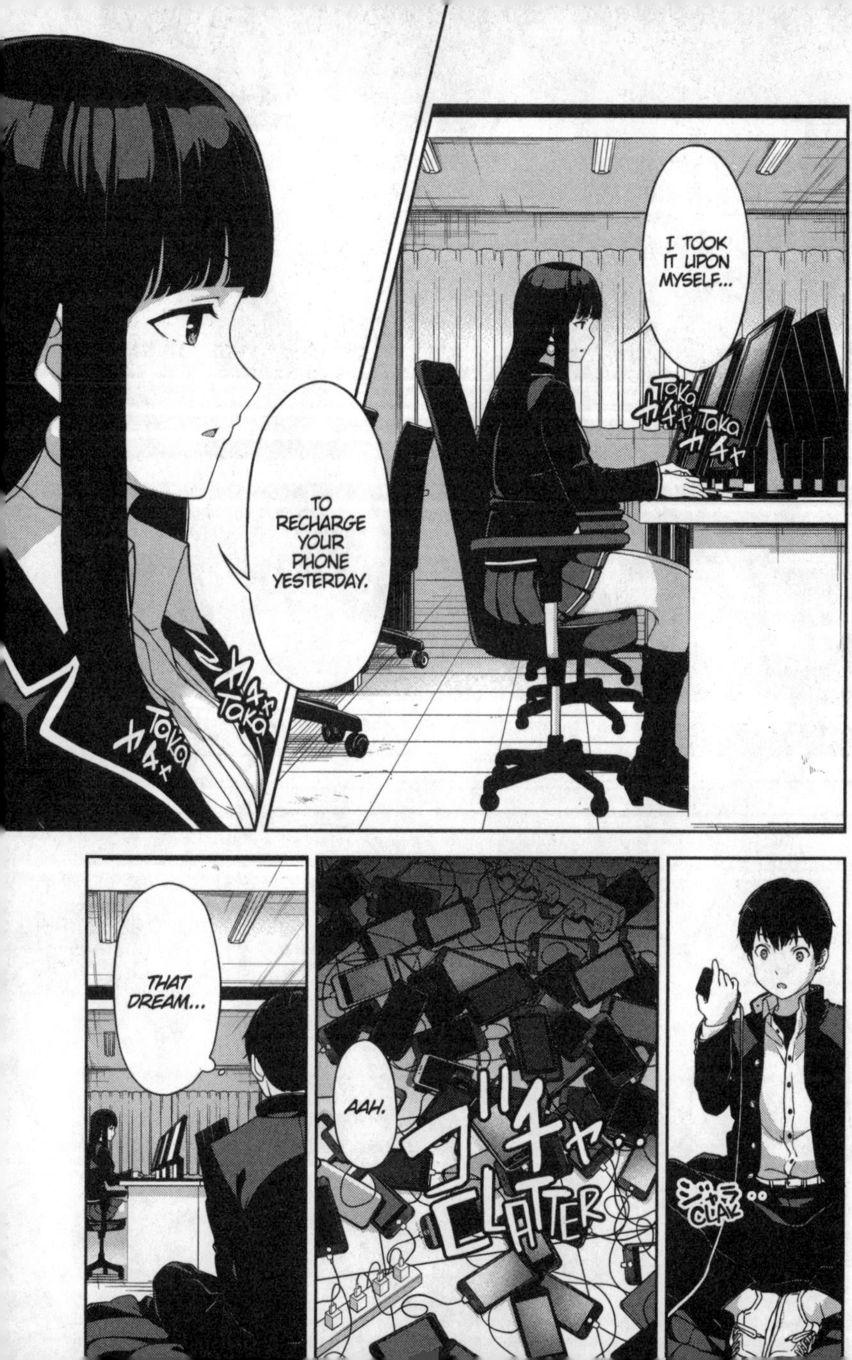
I TOOK IT UPON MYSELF...
Taka Taka
Taka Taka
TO RECHARGE YOUR PHONE YESTERDAY.
Taka Taka
Taka Taka
CLAK
AAH.
CLATTER
THAT DREAM...

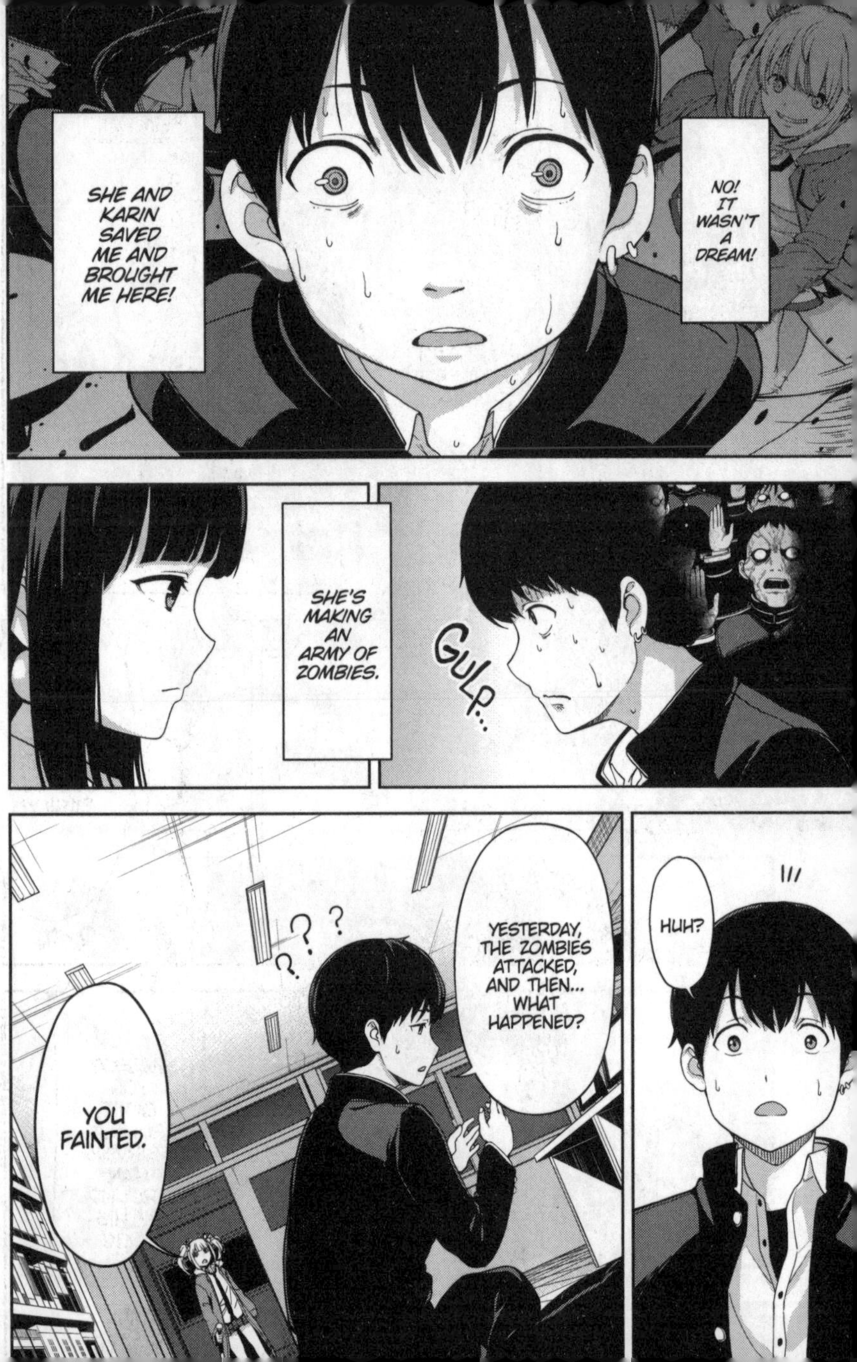
NO! IT WASN'T A DREAM!
SHE AND KARIN SAVED ME AND BROUGHT ME HERE!
GULP...
SHE'S MAKING AN ARMY OF ZOMBIES.
HUH?
YESTERDAY, THE ZOMBIES ATTACKED, AND THEN... WHAT HAPPENED?
YOU FAINTED.

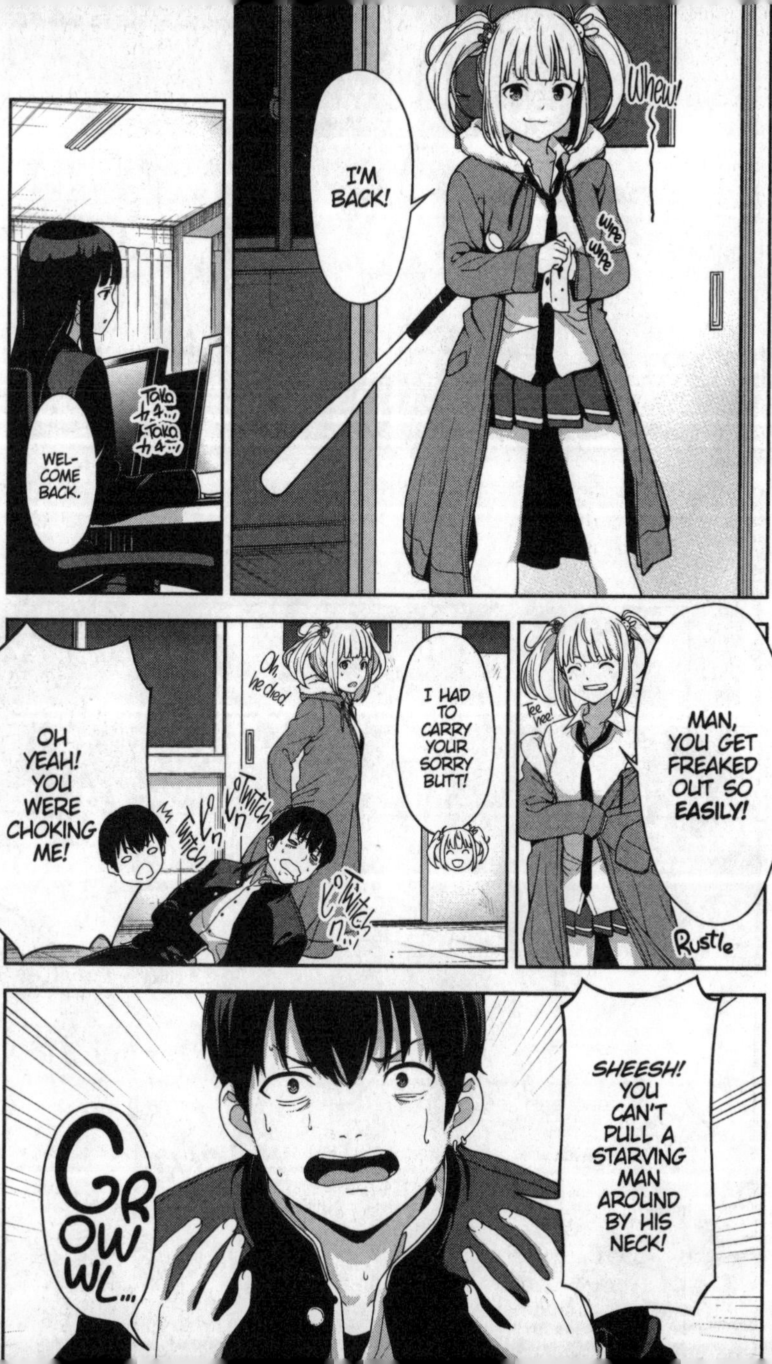
Whew!
I'M BACK!
wipe wipe
Taka
Taka
WEL-COME BACK.
MAN, YOU GET FREAKED OUT SO EASILY!
Tee hee!
Rustle
I HAD TO CARRY YOUR SORRY BUTT!
Oh, he died.
Twitch
Twitch
Twitch
OH YEAH! YOU WERE CHOKING ME!
SHEESH! YOU CAN'T PULL A STARVING MAN AROUND BY HIS NECK!
GROWL...

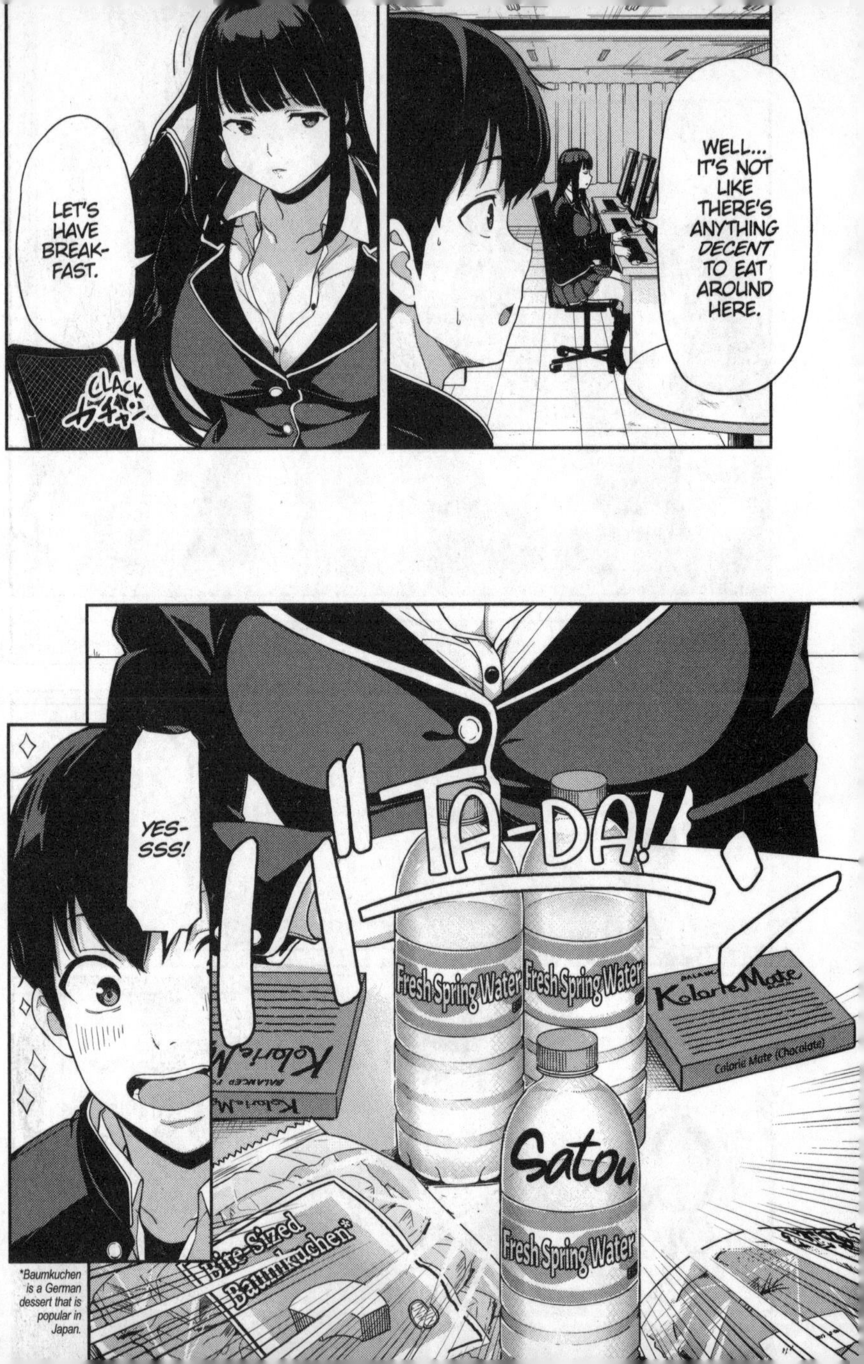
WELL... IT'S NOT LIKE THERE'S ANYTHING *DECENT* TO EAT AROUND HERE.
LET'S HAVE BREAK-FAST.
CLACK
TA-DA!
YES-SSS!
Fresh Spring Water
Fresh Spring Water
Kolorie Mate
Calorie Mate (Chocolate)
Satou
Fresh Spring Water
Bite-Sized Baumkuchen*

*Baumkuchen is a German dessert that is popular in Japan.

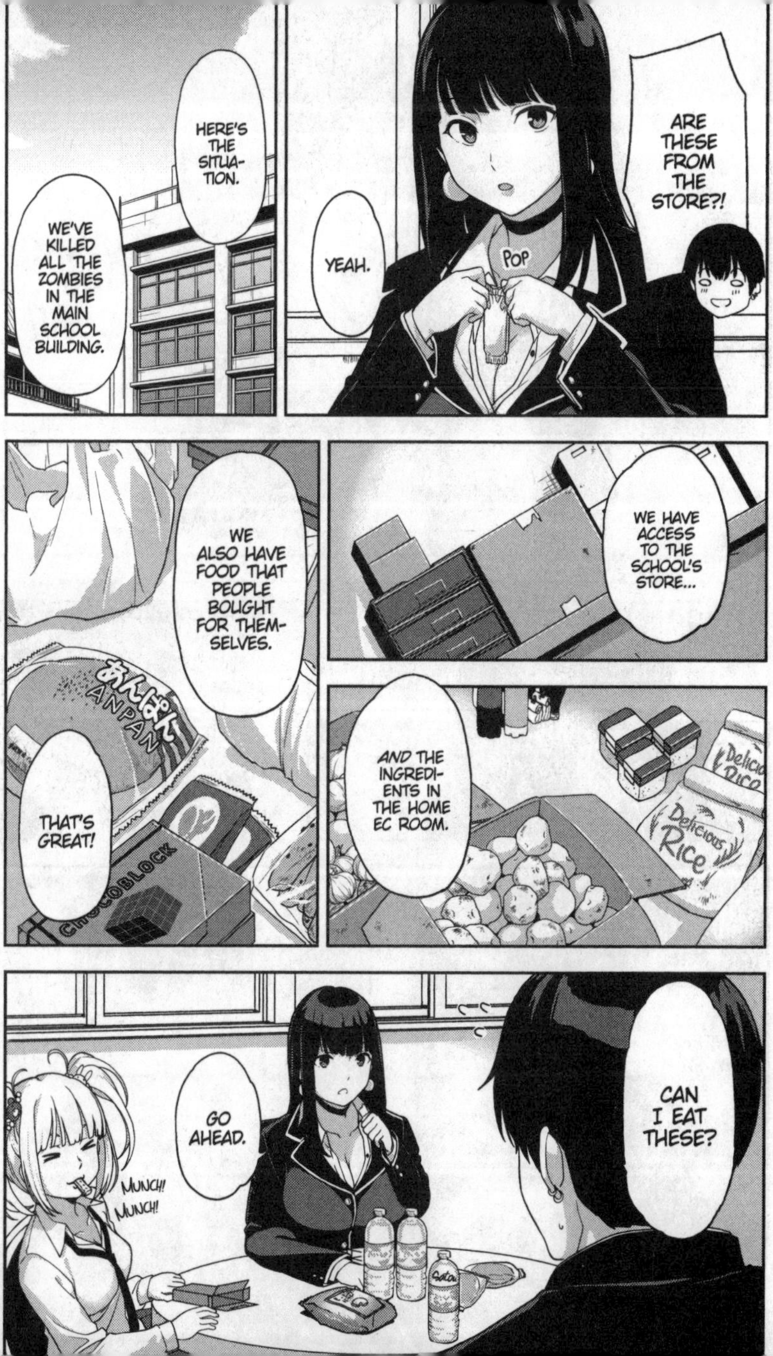
ARE THESE FROM THE STORE?!
POP
YEAH.
HERE'S THE SITUA-TION.
WE'VE KILLED ALL THE ZOMBIES IN THE MAIN SCHOOL BUILDING.
WE HAVE ACCESS TO THE SCHOOL'S STORE...
Delicious Rice
Delicious Rice
AND THE INGREDI-ENTS IN THE HOME EC ROOM.
WE ALSO HAVE FOOD THAT PEOPLE BOUGHT FOR THEM-SELVES.
あんぱん ANPAN
THAT'S GREAT!
CHOCOBLOCK
CAN I EAT THESE?
GO AHEAD.
MUNCH!! MUNCH!

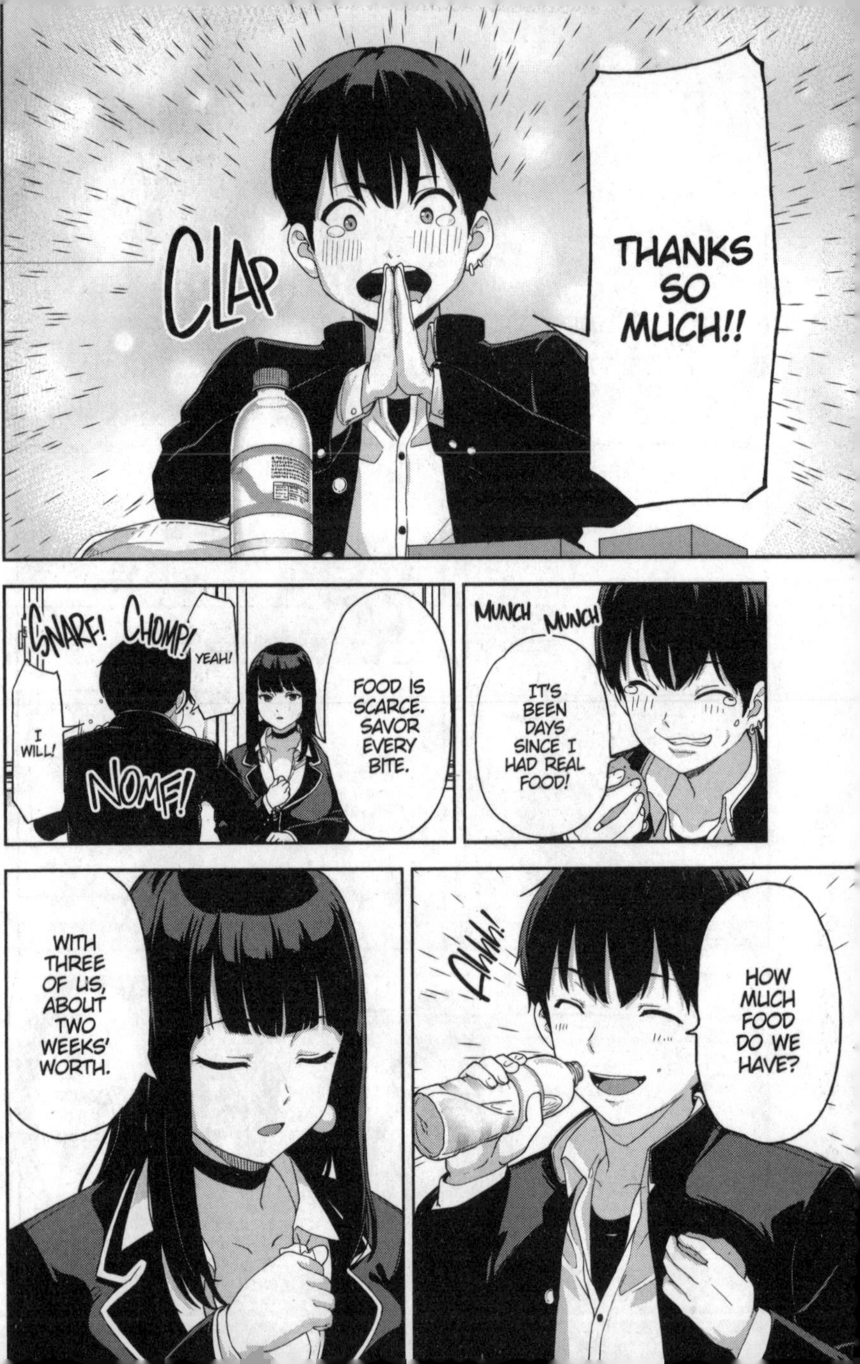
THANKS SO MUCH!!
CLAP
MUNCH
MUNCH
IT'S BEEN DAYS SINCE I HAD REAL FOOD!
FOOD IS SCARCE. SAVOR EVERY BITE.
YEAH!
CHOMP!
SNARF!
I WILL!
NOMF!
HOW MUCH FOOD DO WE HAVE?
Ahhh!
WITH THREE OF US, ABOUT TWO WEEKS' WORTH.

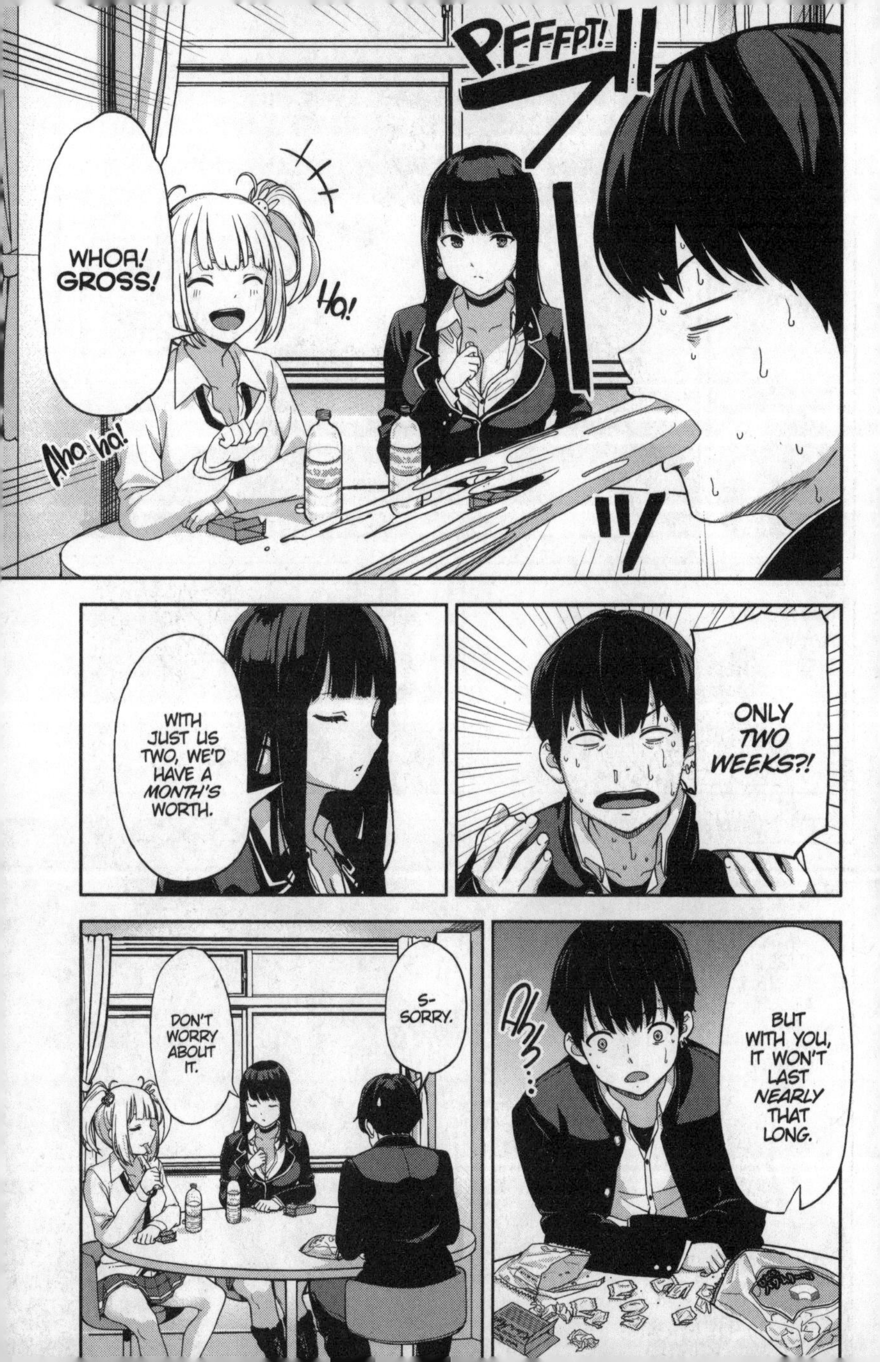
PFFFPT!
Ha!
WHOA! GROSS!
Aha ha!
ONLY TWO WEEKS?!
WITH JUST US TWO, WE'D HAVE A MONTH'S WORTH.
BUT WITH YOU, IT WON'T LAST NEARLY THAT LONG.
Ah...
S-SORRY.
DON'T WORRY ABOUT IT.

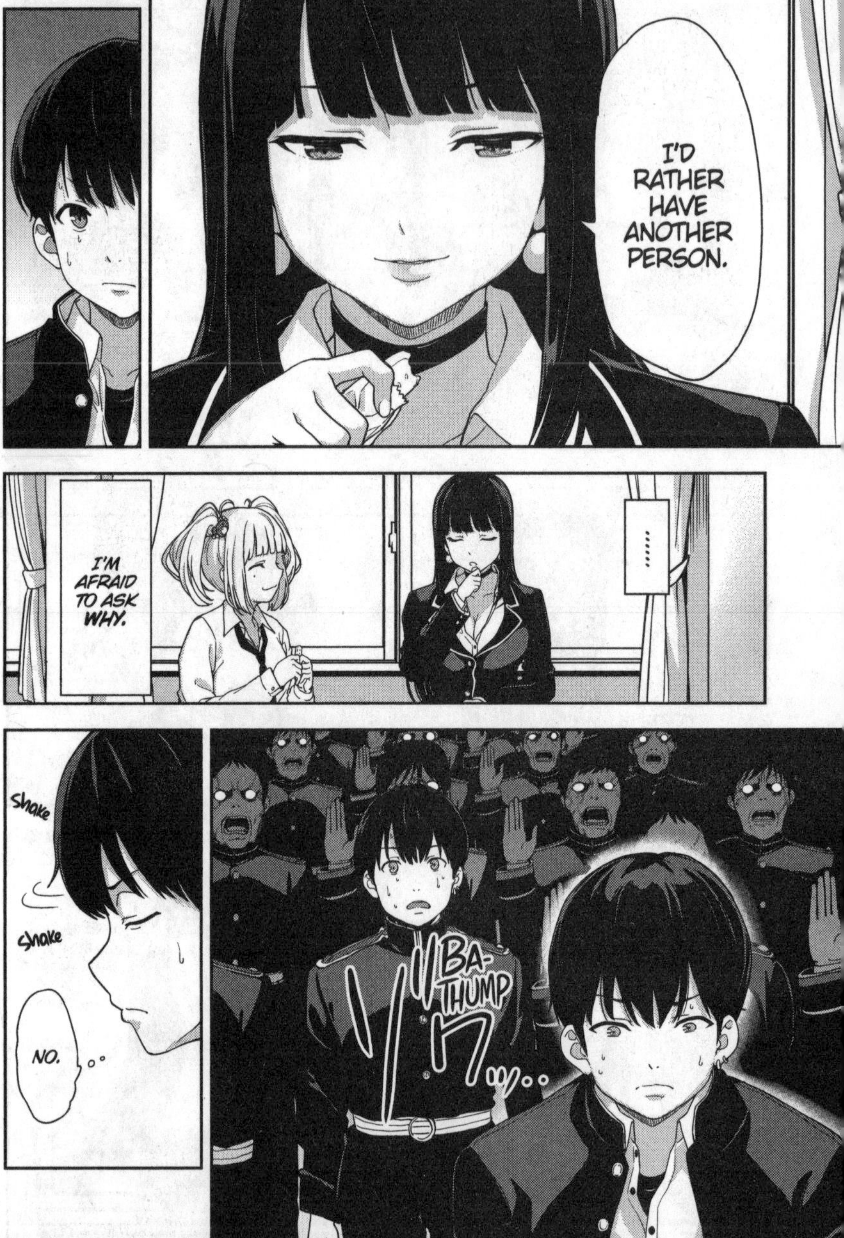
I'D RATHER HAVE ANOTHER PERSON.
......
I'M AFRAID TO ASK WHY.
BA-THUMP
Shake
Shake
NO.

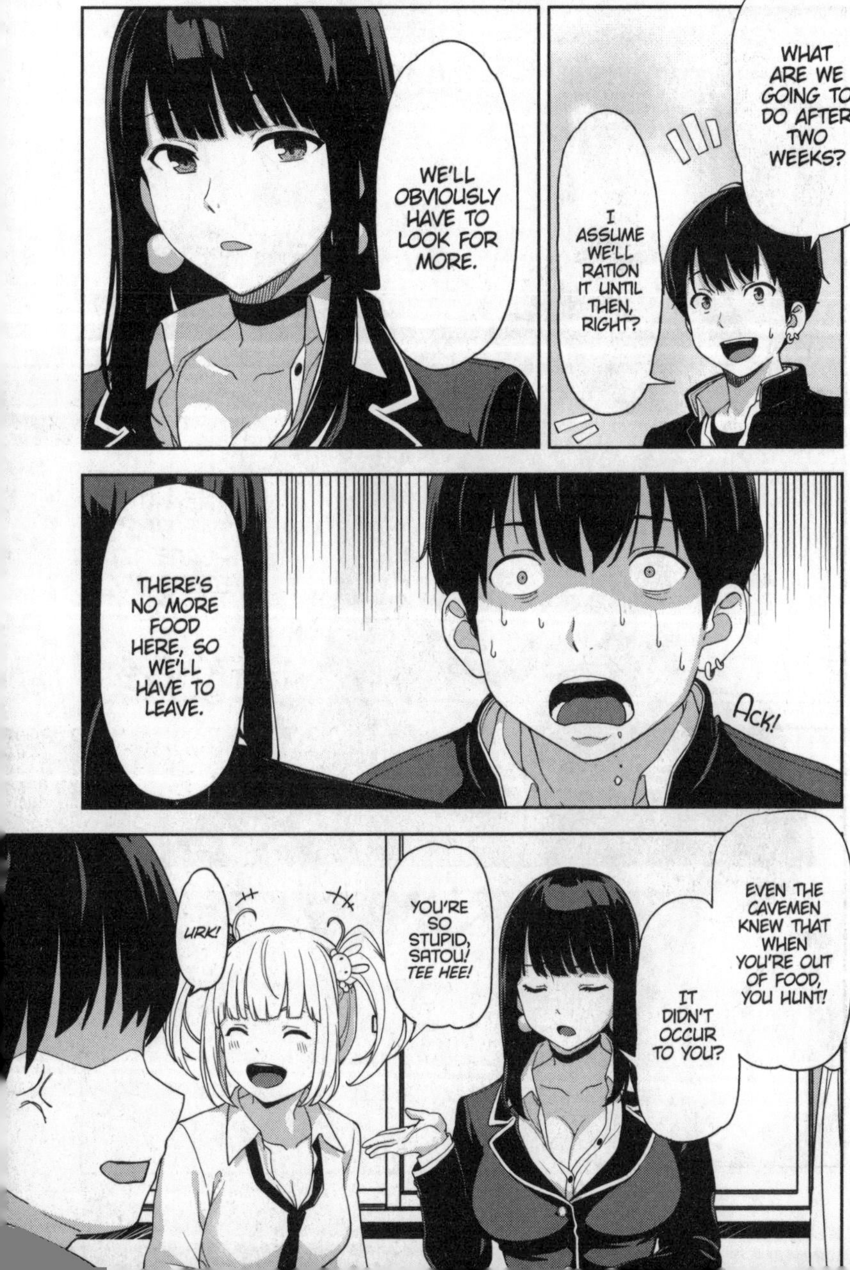

WHAT ARE WE GOING TO DO AFTER TWO WEEKS?
I ASSUME WE'LL RATION IT UNTIL THEN, RIGHT?
WE'LL OBVIOUSLY HAVE TO LOOK FOR MORE.
THERE'S NO MORE FOOD HERE, SO WE'LL HAVE TO LEAVE.
ACK!
EVEN THE CAVEMEN KNEW THAT WHEN YOU'RE OUT OF FOOD, YOU HUNT!
IT DIDN'T OCCUR TO YOU?
YOU'RE SO STUPID, SATOU! *TEE HEE!*
URK!

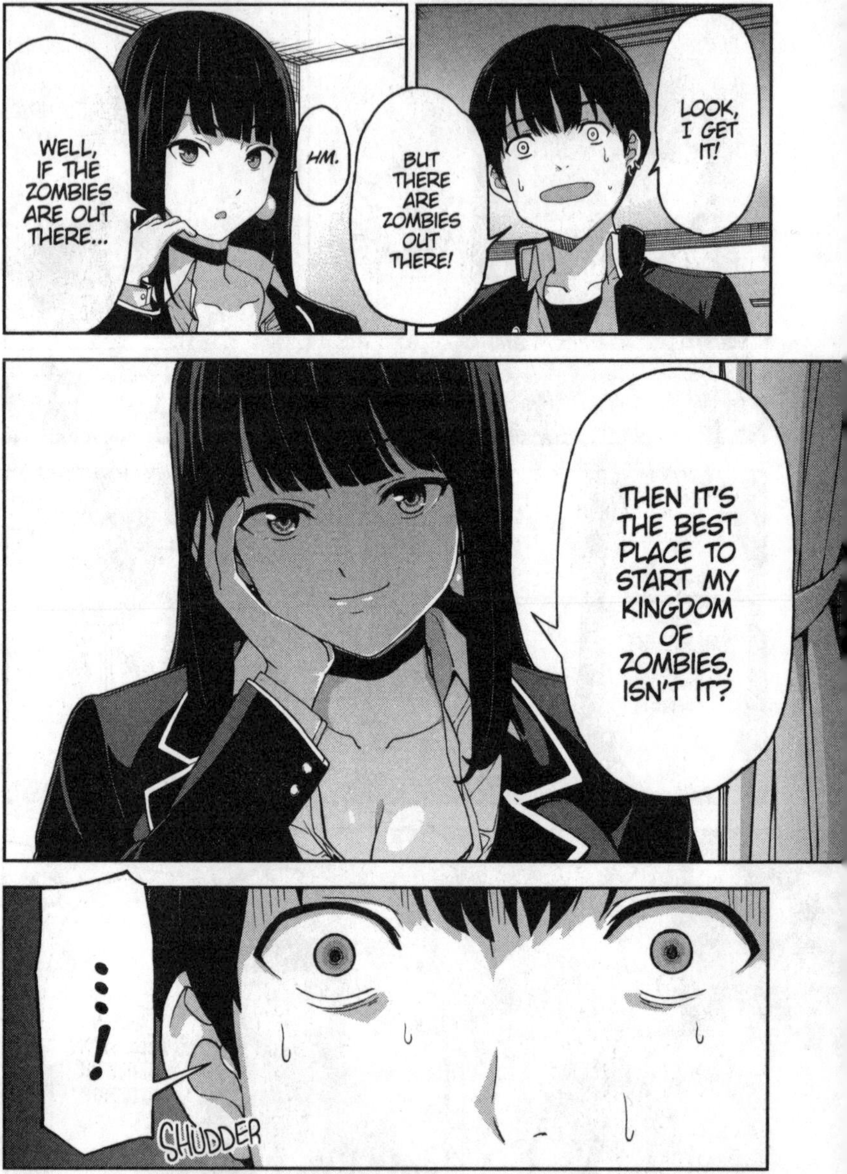
LOOK, I GET IT!
BUT THERE ARE ZOMBIES OUT THERE!
HM.
WELL, IF THE ZOMBIES ARE OUT THERE...
THEN IT'S THE BEST PLACE TO START MY KINGDOM OF ZOMBIES, ISN'T IT?
...!
SHUDDER

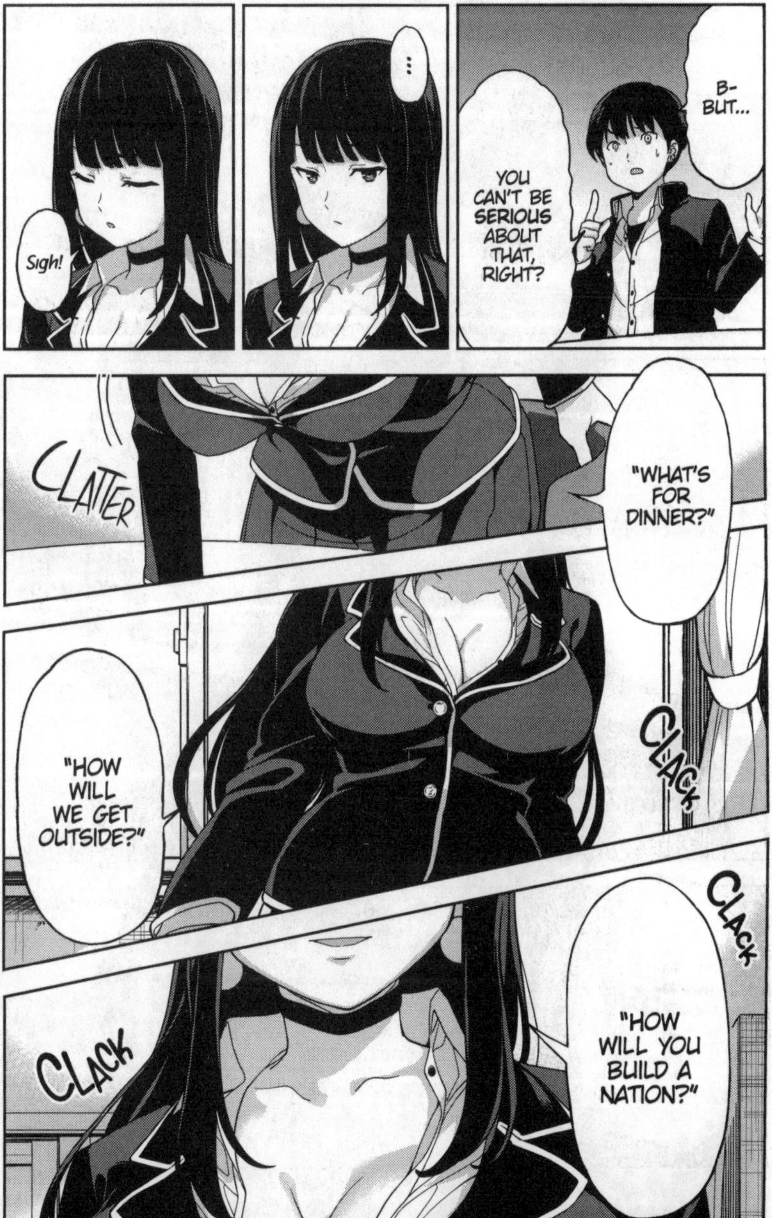
B-BUT...
YOU CAN'T BE SERIOUS ABOUT THAT, RIGHT?
...
Sigh!
"WHAT'S FOR DINNER?"
CLATTER
CLACK
"HOW WILL WE GET OUTSIDE?"
CLACK
"HOW WILL YOU BUILD A NATION?"
CLACK

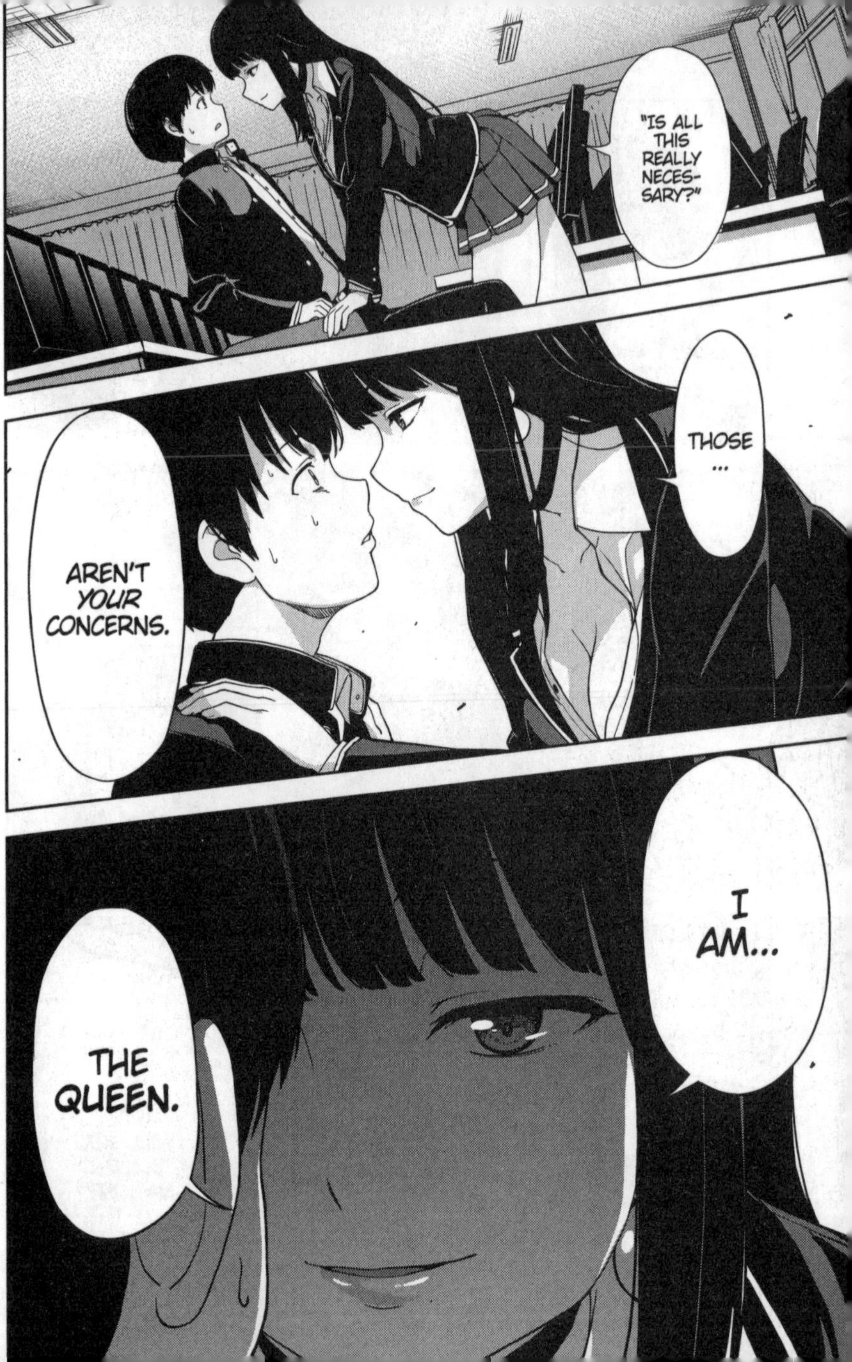
"IS ALL THIS REALLY NECES-SARY?"
THOSE ...
AREN'T YOUR CONCERNS.
I AM...
THE QUEEN.

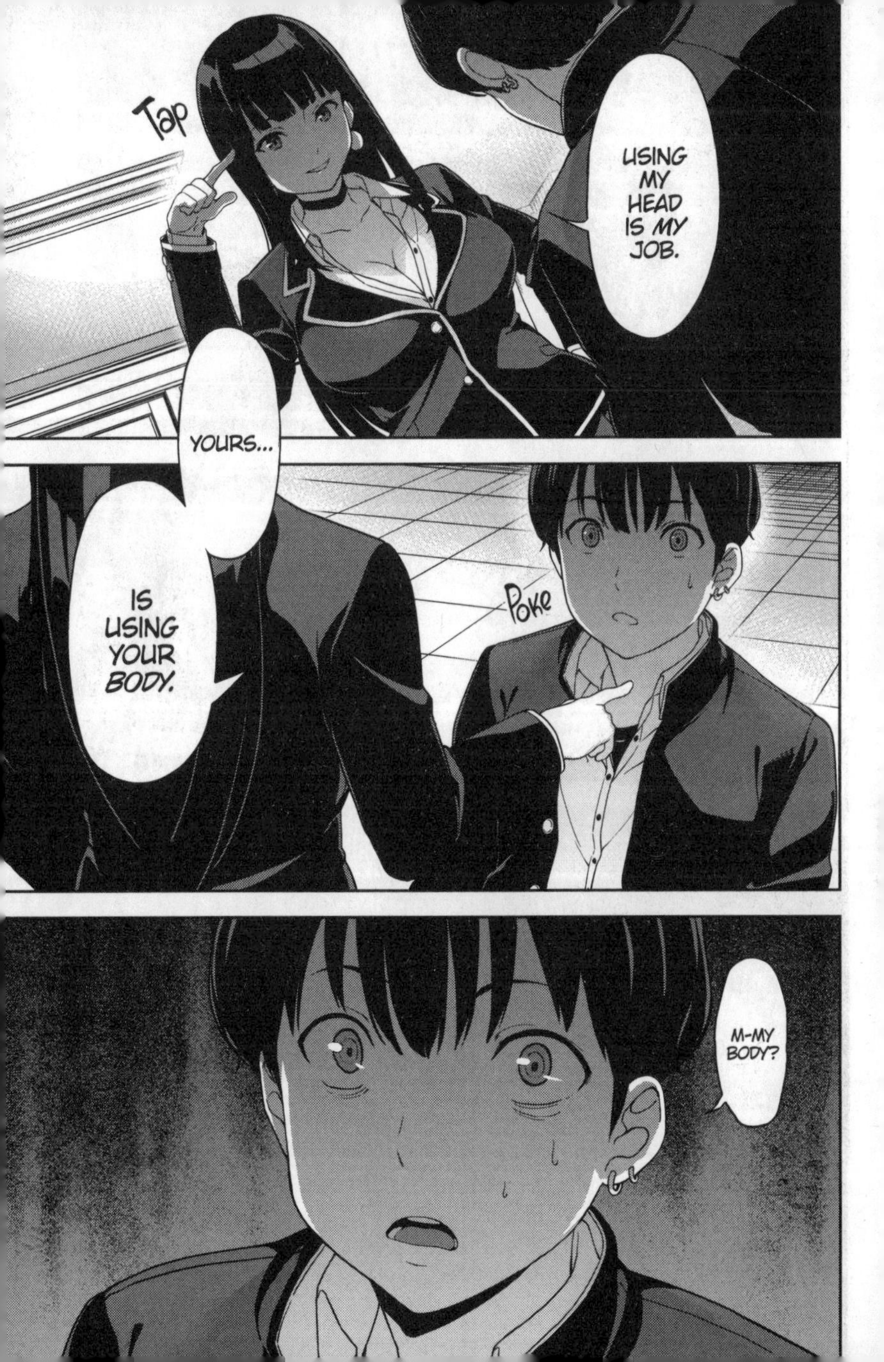
USING MY HEAD IS MY JOB.
Tap
YOURS...
IS USING YOUR BODY.
Poke
M-MY BODY?

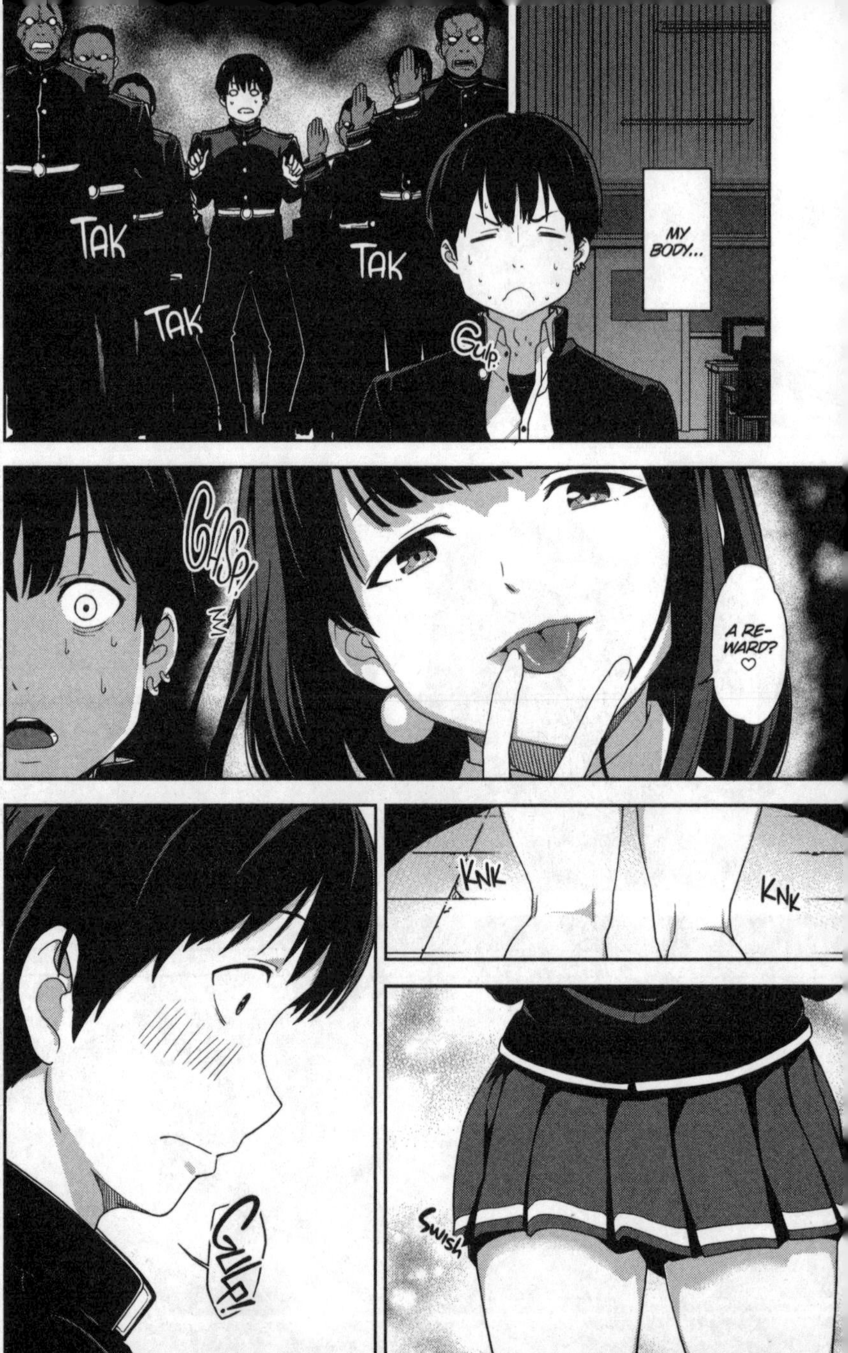

MY BODY...
Gulp.
TAK
TAK
TAK
A RE-WARD? ♡
GASP!
KNK
KNK
Swish
GULP!

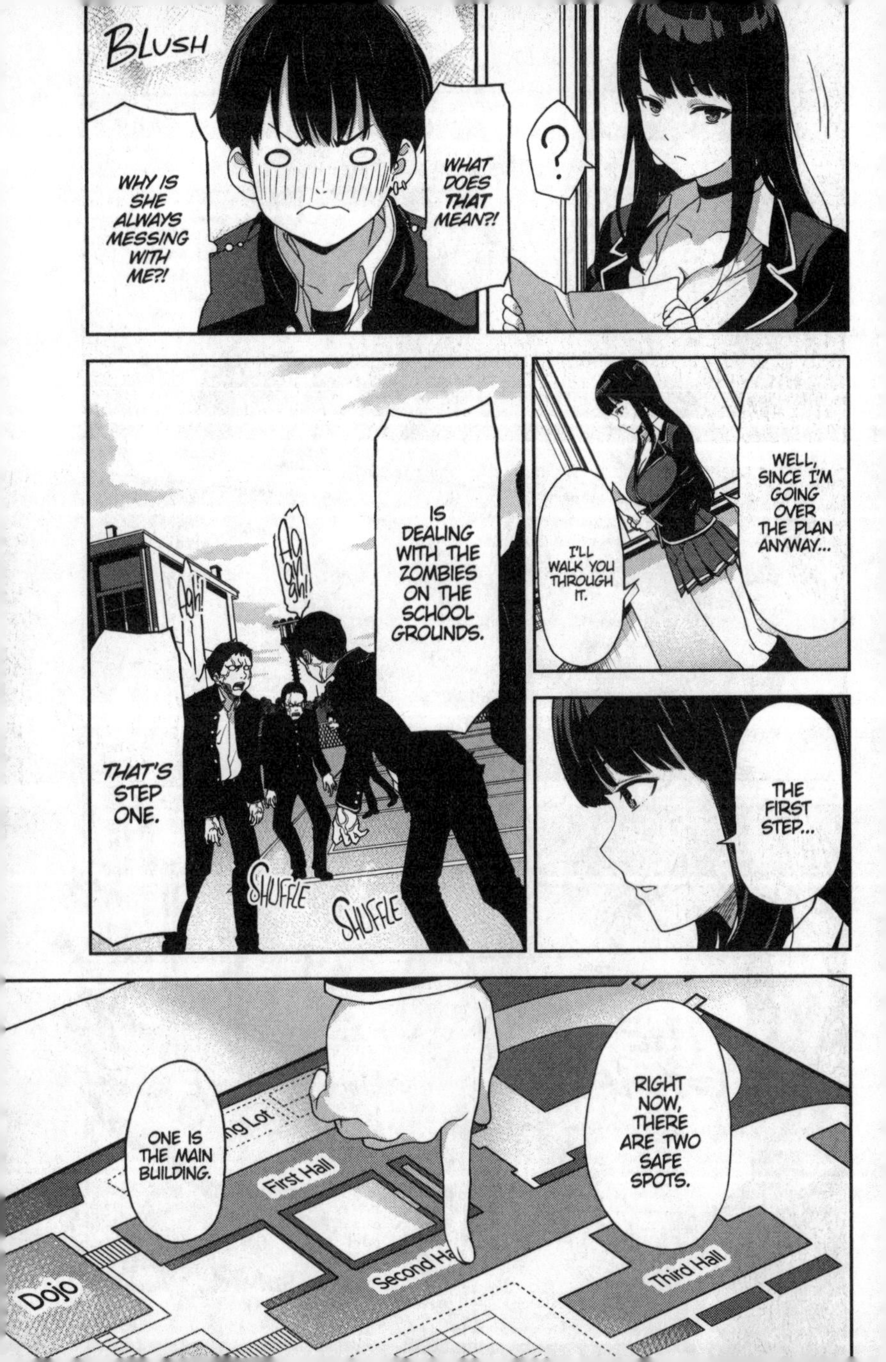
?
WHAT DOES THAT MEAN?!
WHY IS SHE ALWAYS MESSING WITH ME?!
BLUSH
WELL, SINCE I'M GOING OVER THE PLAN ANYWAY...
I'LL WALK YOU THROUGH IT.
THE FIRST STEP...
IS DEALING WITH THE ZOMBIES ON THE SCHOOL GROUNDS.
Haargh!
Agh!
THAT'S STEP ONE.
SHUFFLE
SHUFFLE
RIGHT NOW, THERE ARE TWO SAFE SPOTS.
ONE IS THE MAIN BUILDING.
ng Lot
First Hall
Second Ha
Third Hall
Dojo

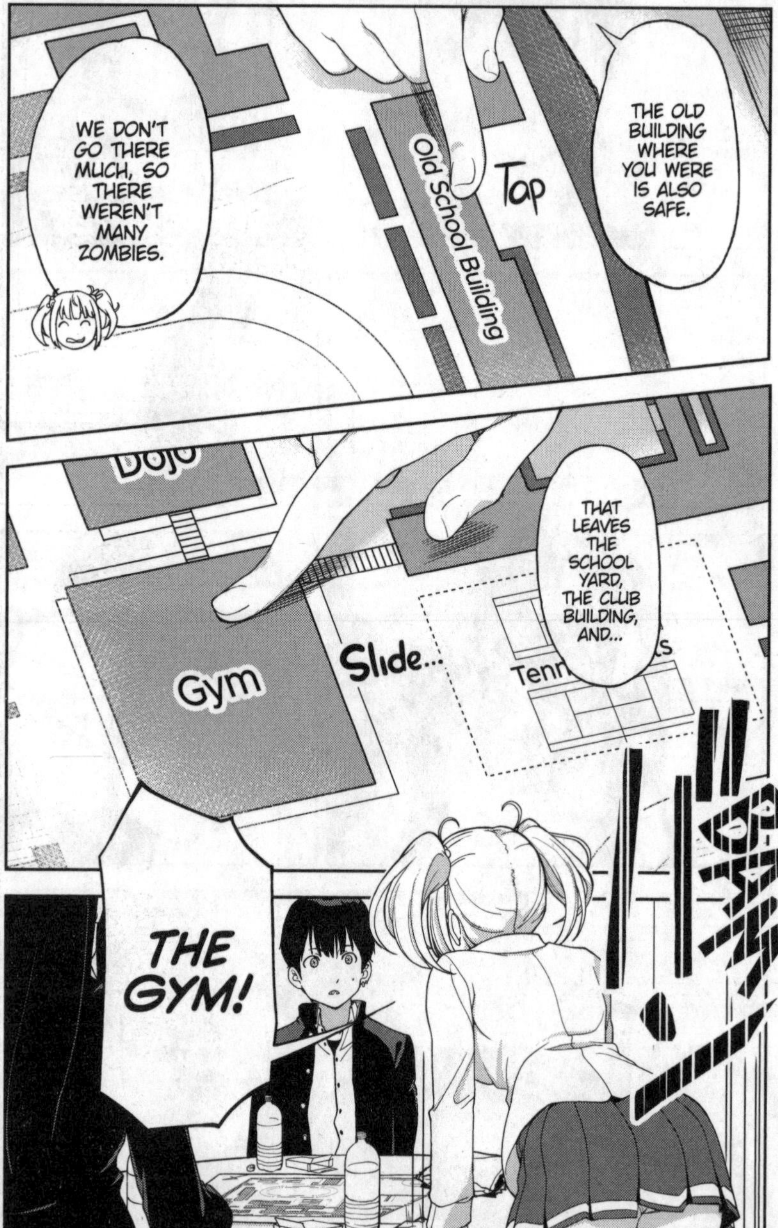
THE OLD BUILDING WHERE YOU WERE IS ALSO SAFE.
Tap
Old School Building
WE DON'T GO THERE MUCH, SO THERE WEREN'T MANY ZOMBIES.
THAT LEAVES THE SCHOOL YARD, THE CLUB BUILDING, AND...
Dojo
Slide...
Gym
BAM!!
THE GYM!

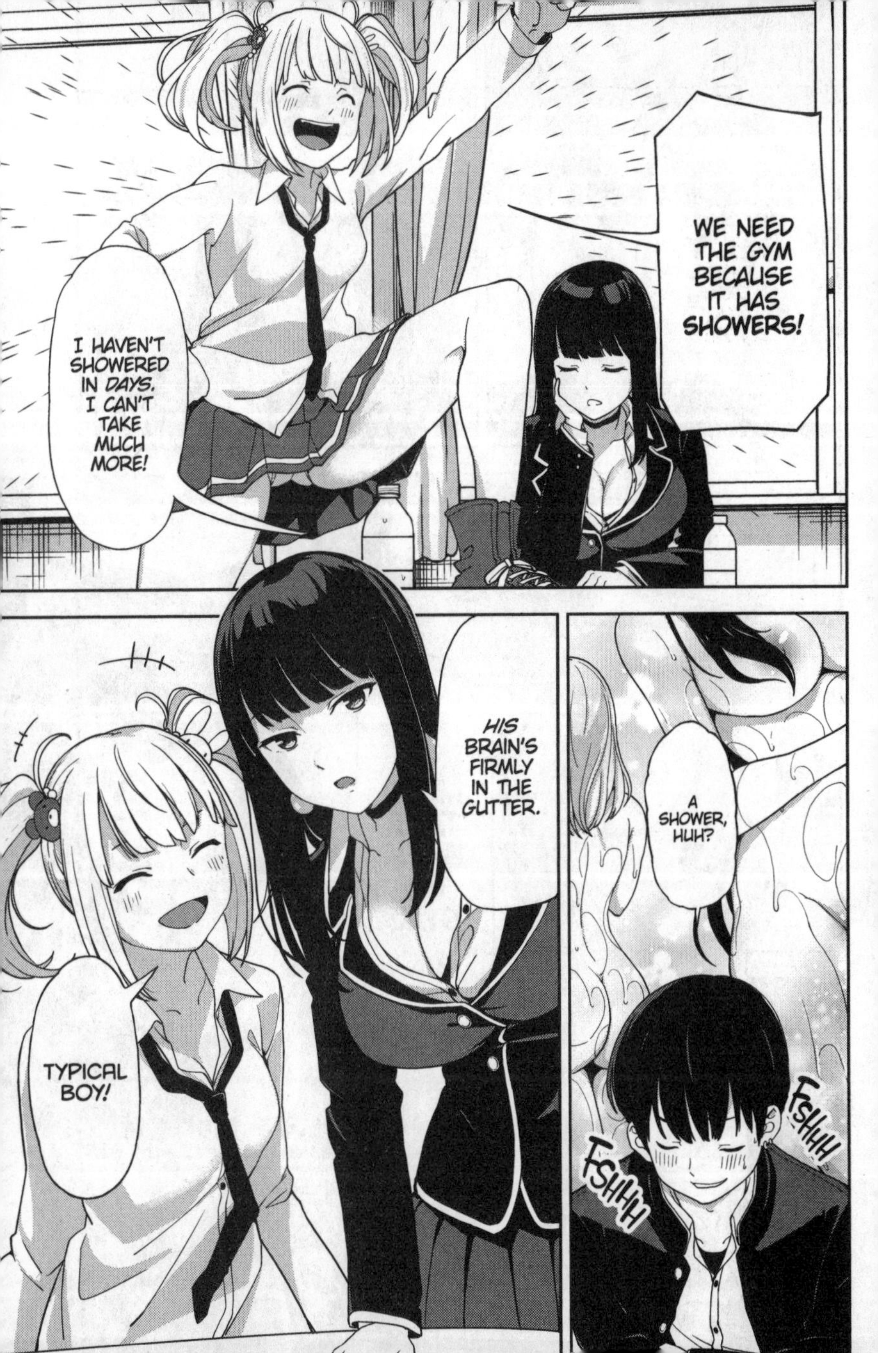
WE NEED THE GYM BECAUSE IT HAS SHOWERS!
I HAVEN'T SHOWERED IN *DAYS*. I CAN'T TAKE MUCH MORE!
A SHOWER, HUH?
FSHHH
FSHHH
HIS BRAIN'S FIRMLY IN THE GUTTER.
TYPICAL BOY!

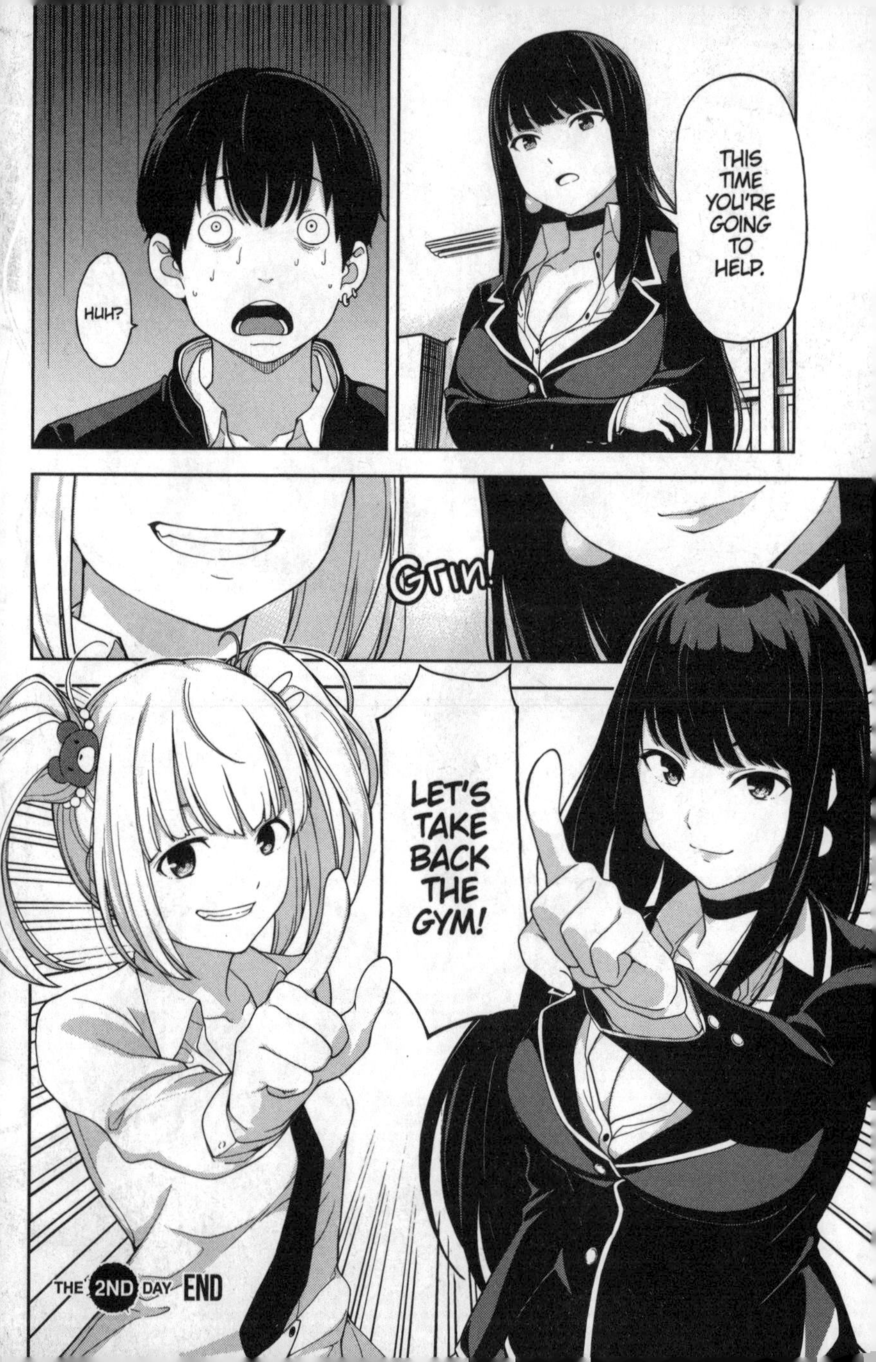
THIS TIME YOU'RE GOING TO HELP.
HUH?
Grin!
LET'S TAKE BACK THE GYM!
THE 2ND DAY END

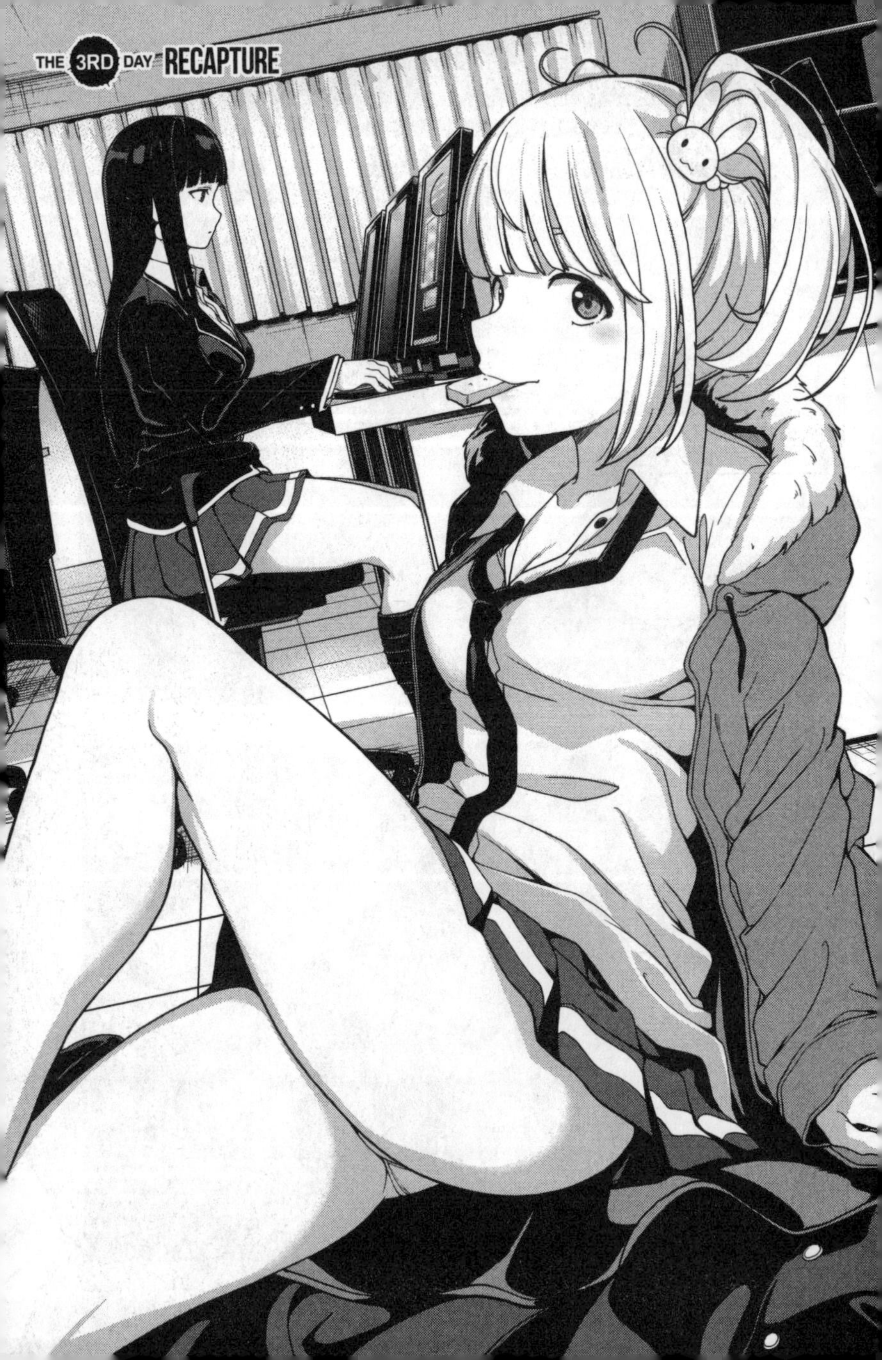
THE 3RD DAY RECAPTURE

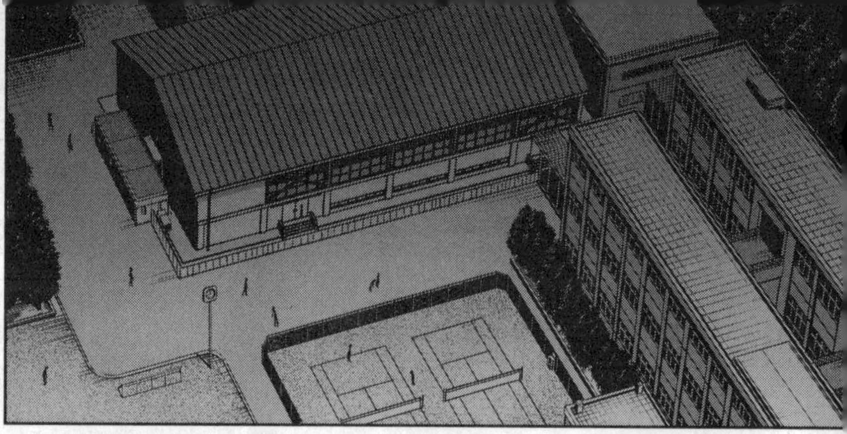
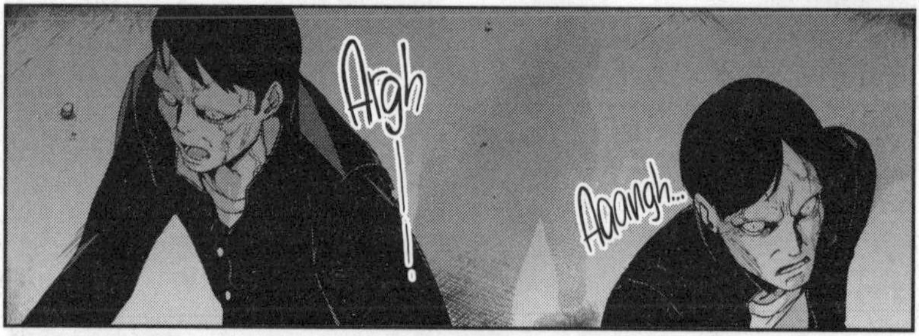
Aaargh...
Argh!!
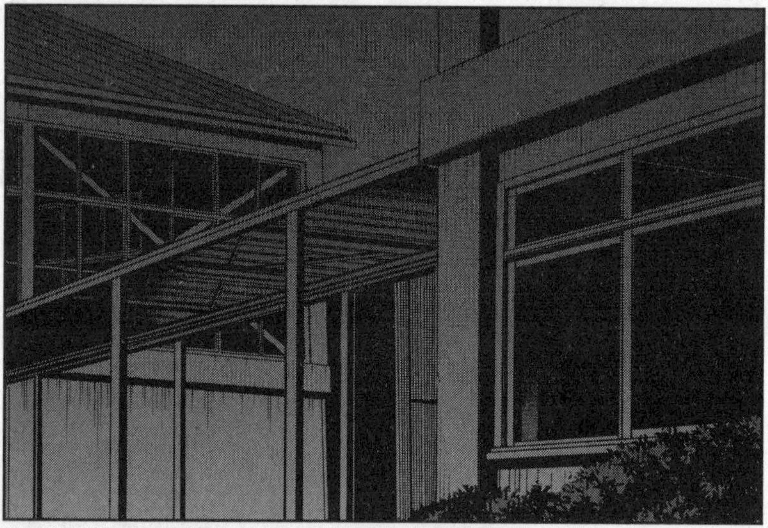

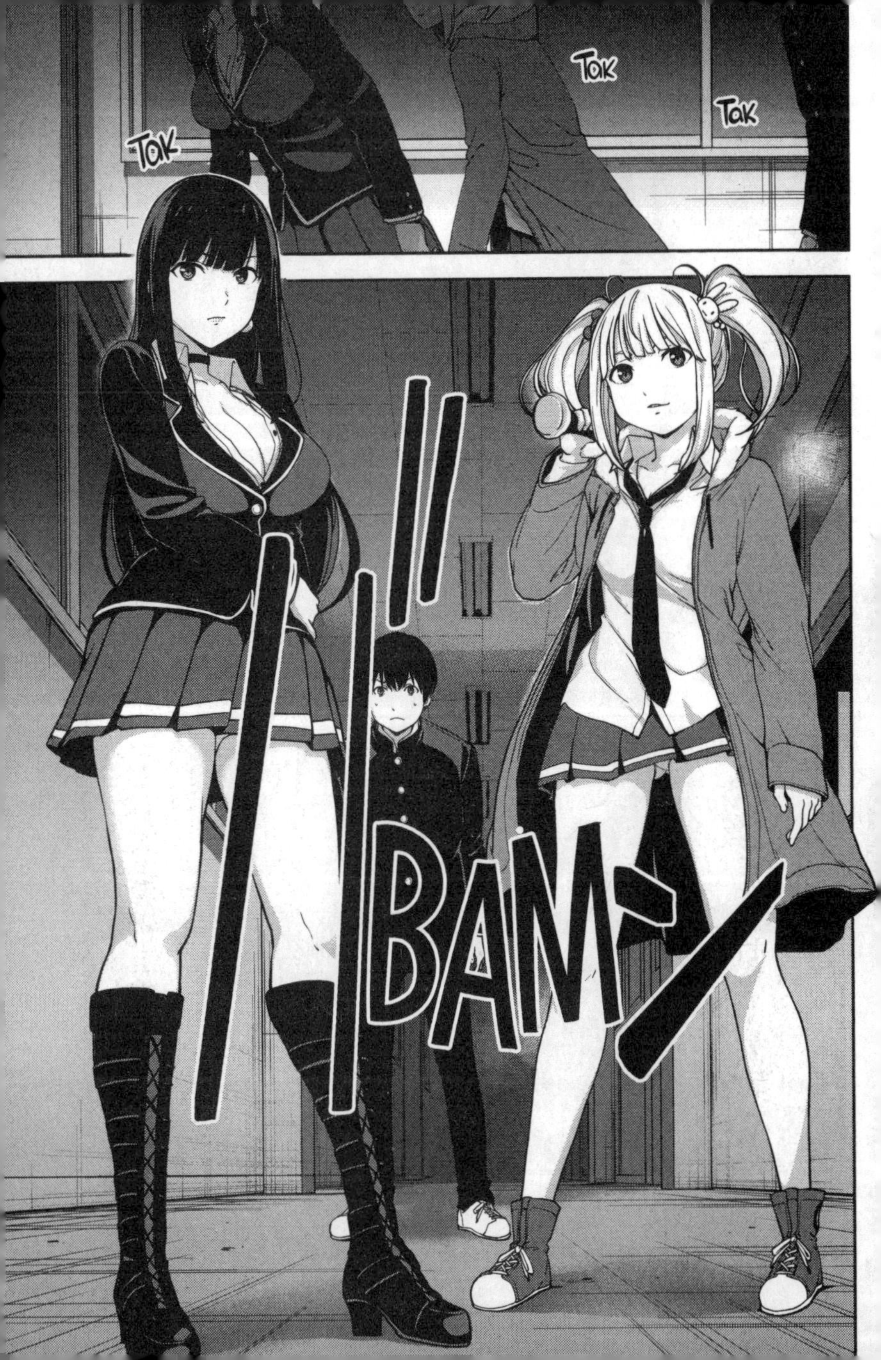
TAK
TOK
TOK
BAM

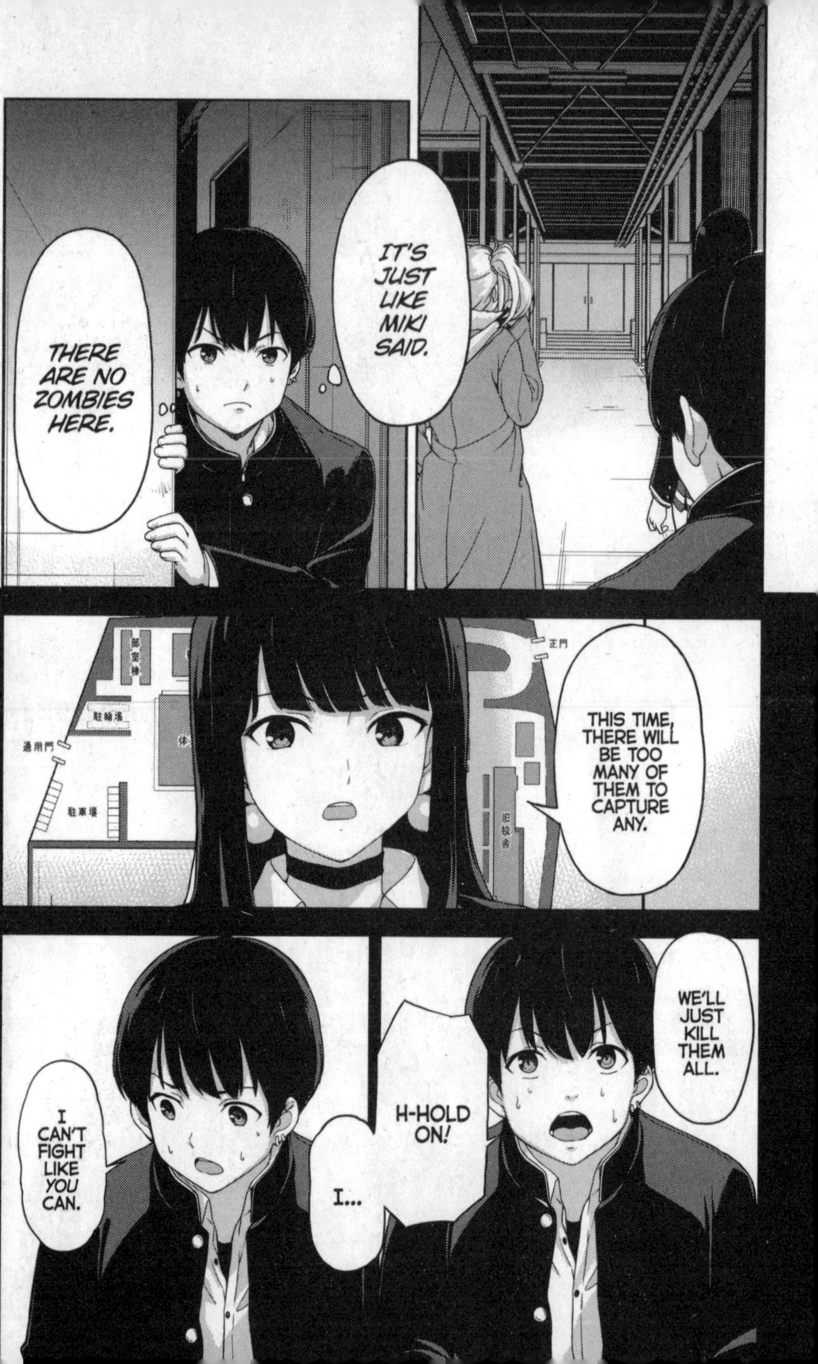
IT'S JUST LIKE MIKI SAID.
THERE ARE NO ZOMBIES HERE.
正門
部室棟
駐輪場
通用門
駐車場
旧校舎
THIS TIME, THERE WILL BE TOO MANY OF THEM TO CAPTURE ANY.
WE'LL JUST KILL THEM ALL.
H-HOLD ON!
I...
I CAN'T FIGHT LIKE YOU CAN.

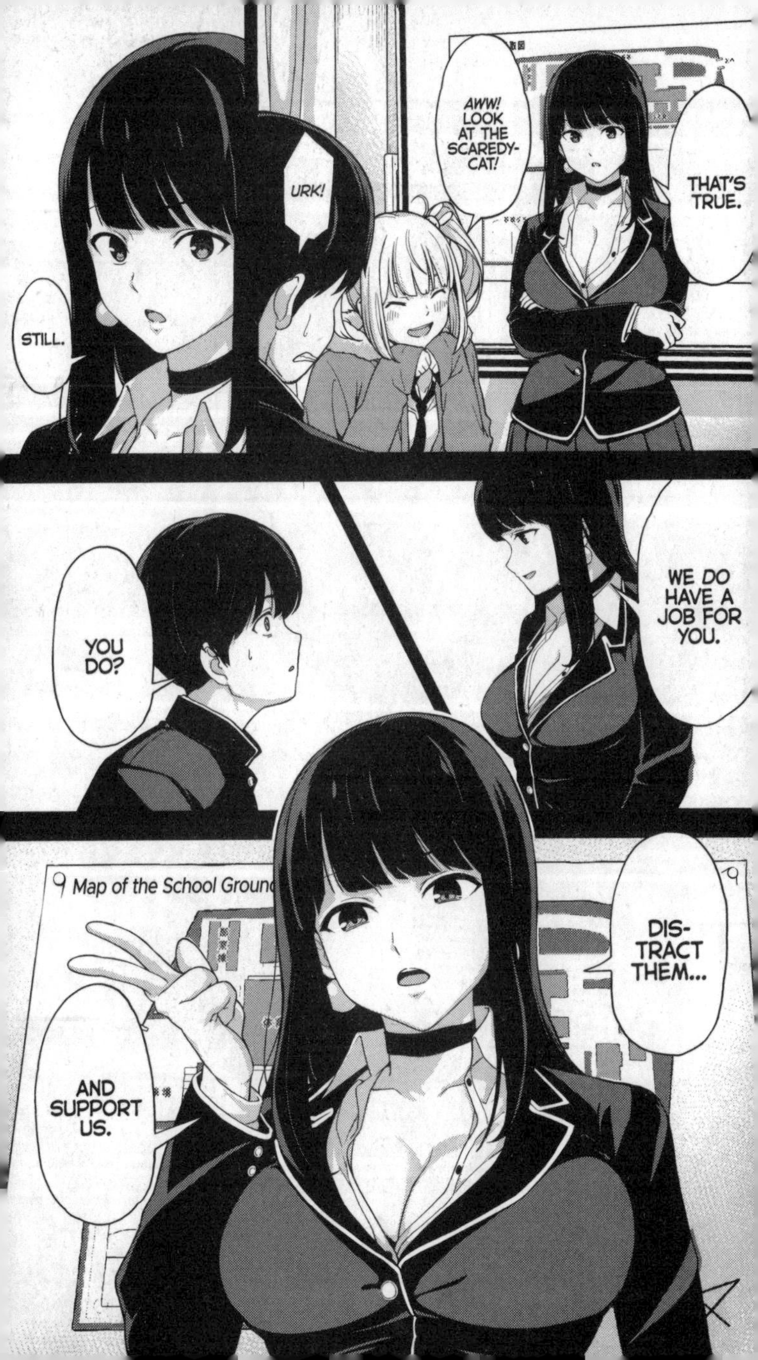
THAT'S TRUE.
AWW! LOOK AT THE SCAREDY-CAT!
URK!
STILL.
WE *DO* HAVE A JOB FOR YOU.
YOU DO?
DIS-TRACT THEM...
Map of the School Ground
AND SUPPORT US.

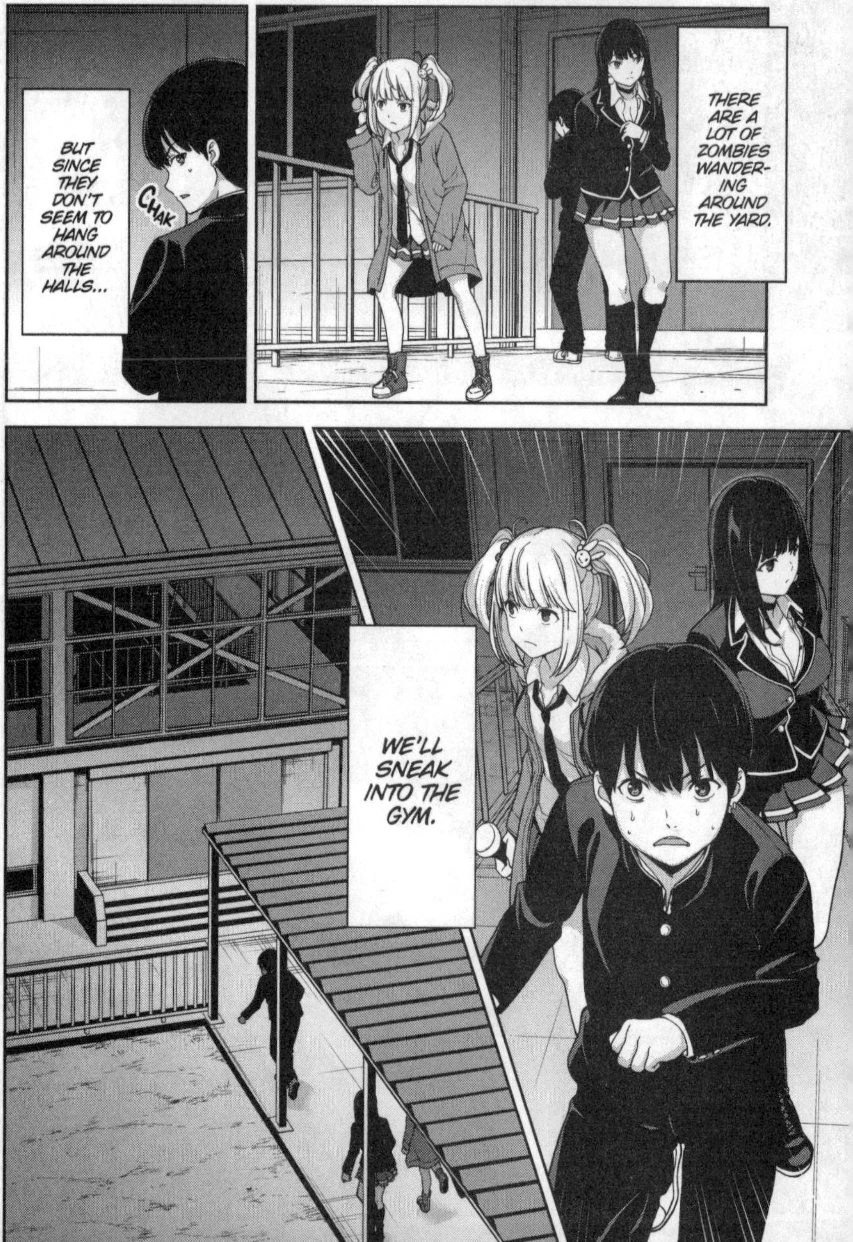
THERE ARE A LOT OF ZOMBIES WANDER-ING AROUND THE YARD.
BUT SINCE THEY DON'T SEEM TO HANG AROUND THE HALLS...
CHAK
WE'LL SNEAK INTO THE GYM.

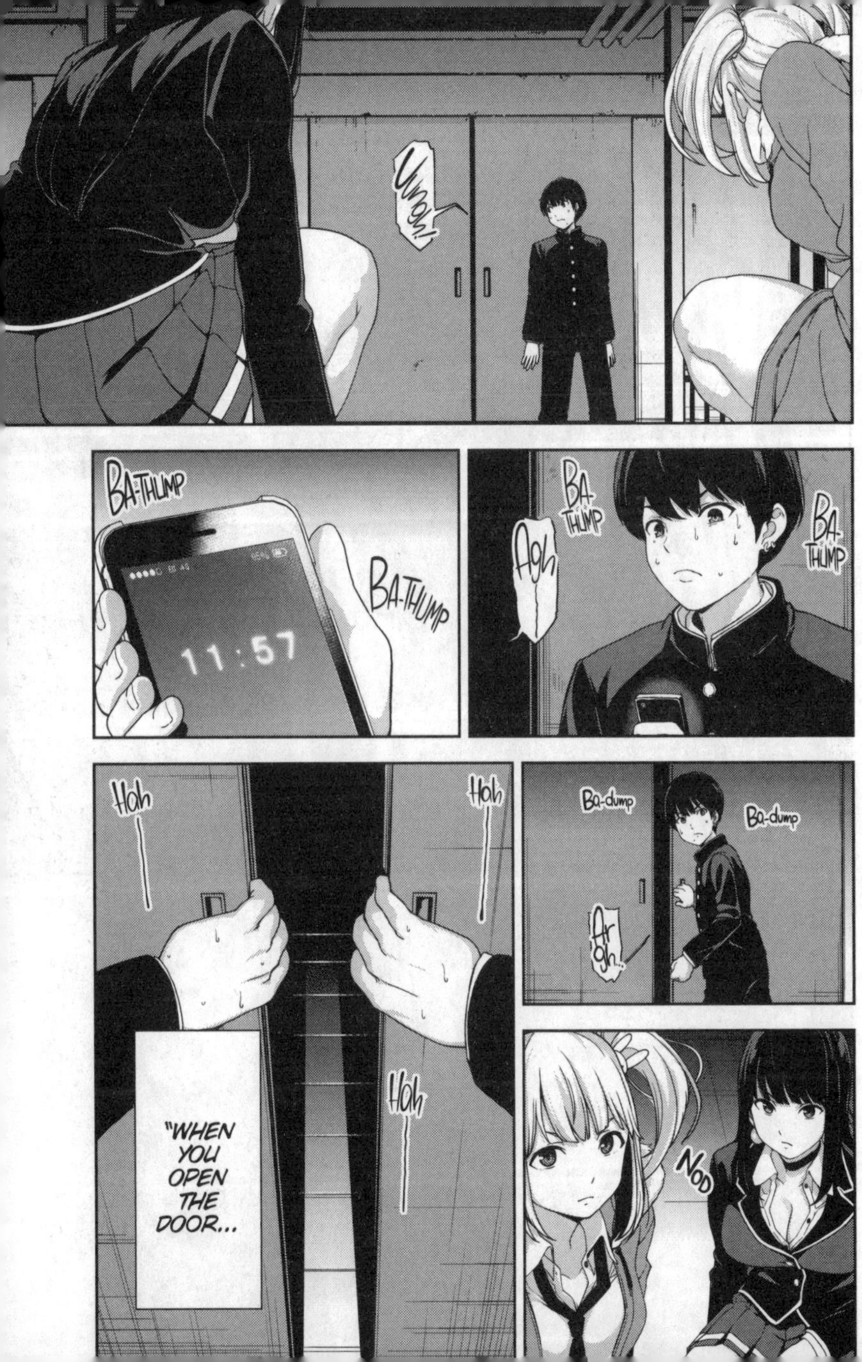
Umgh!
BA-THUMP
BA-THUMP
Agh
BA-THUMP
11:57
BA-THUMP
Ba-dump
Ba-dump
Argh...
Nod
Hah
Hah
Hah
"WHEN YOU OPEN THE DOOR...

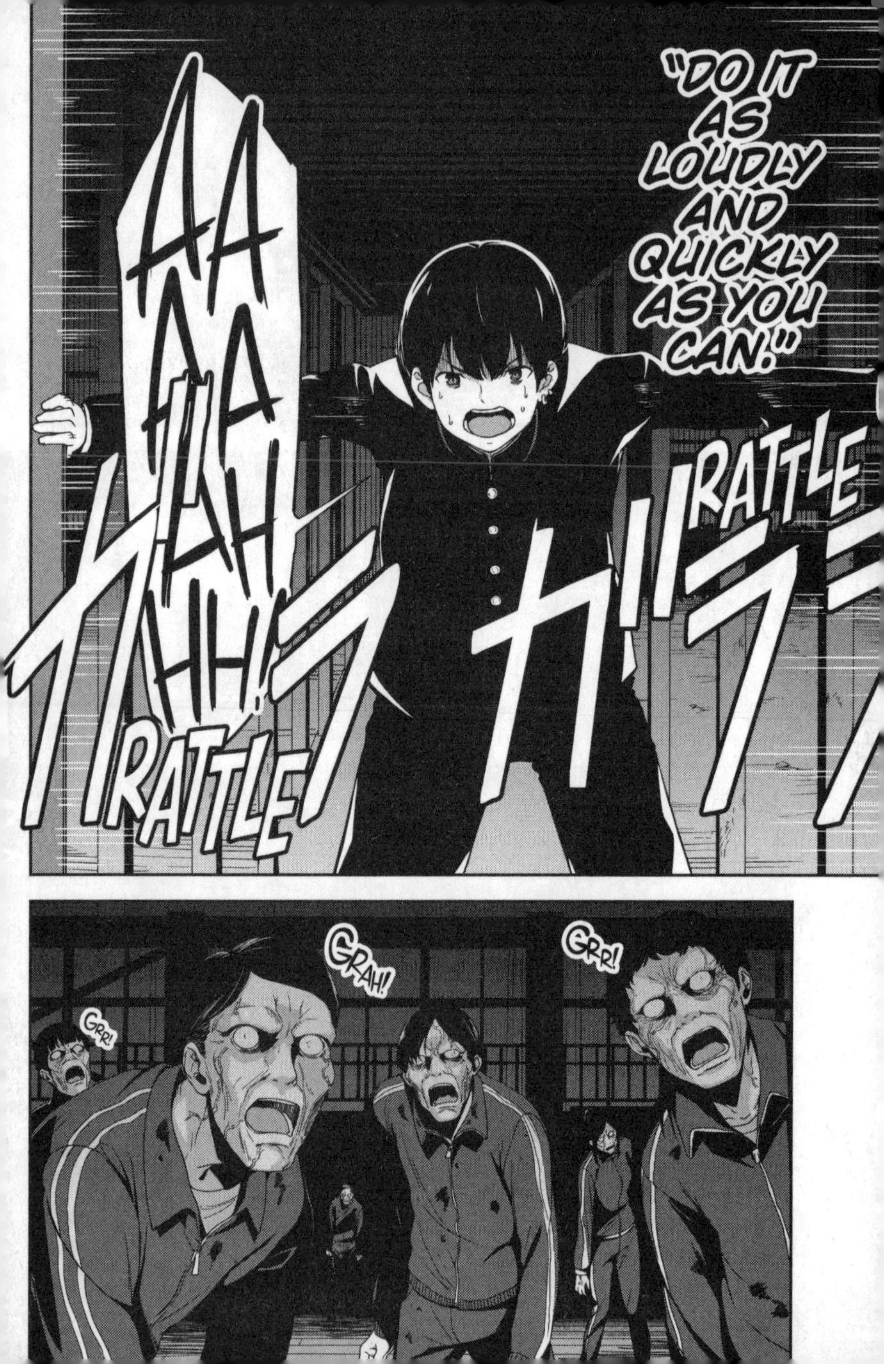

"DO IT AS LOUDLY AND QUICKLY AS YOU CAN."
RATTLE
AAAAAAHH!
RATTLE
GRR!
GRAH!
GRR!

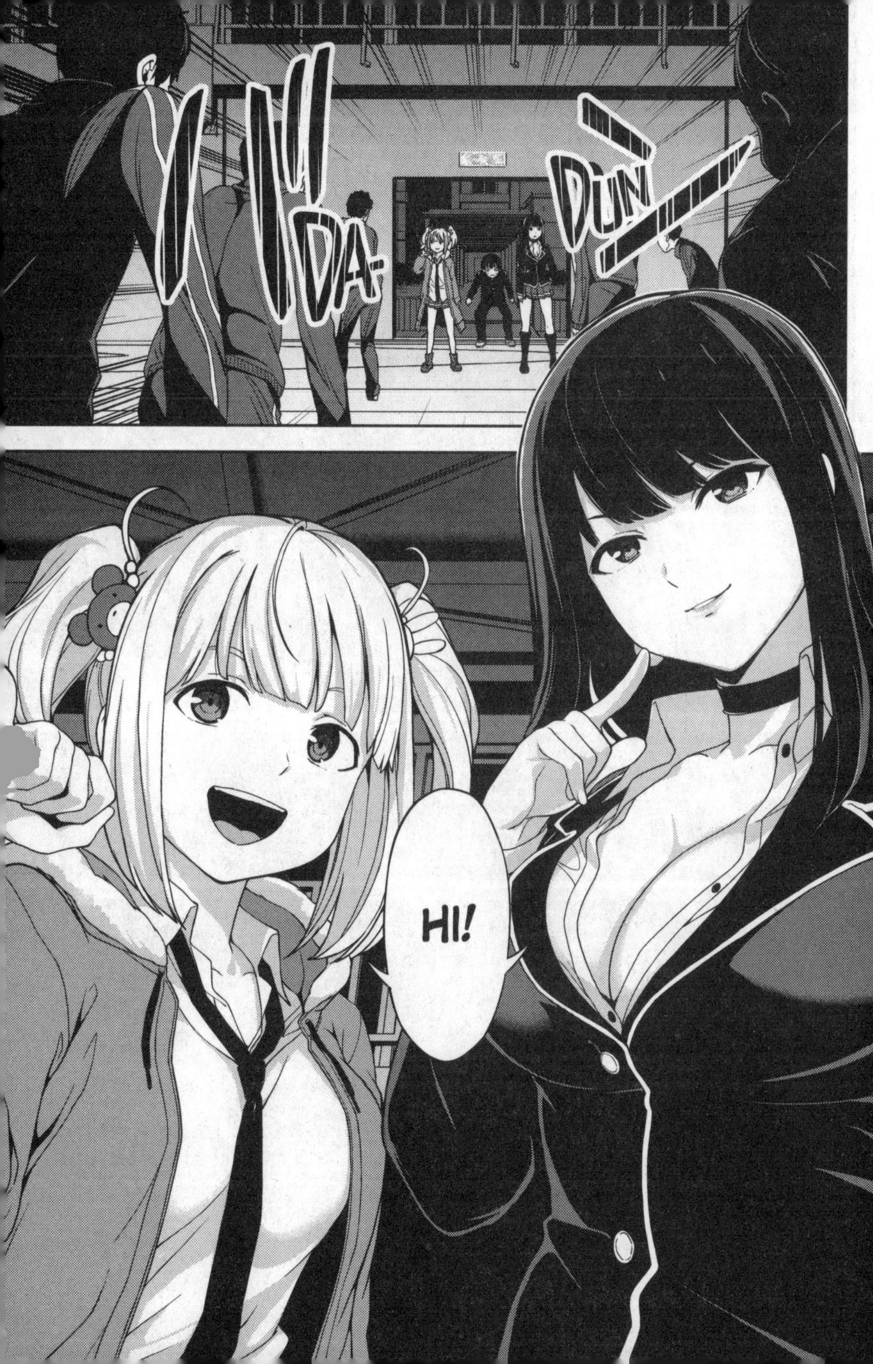
DA-
DUN
HI!

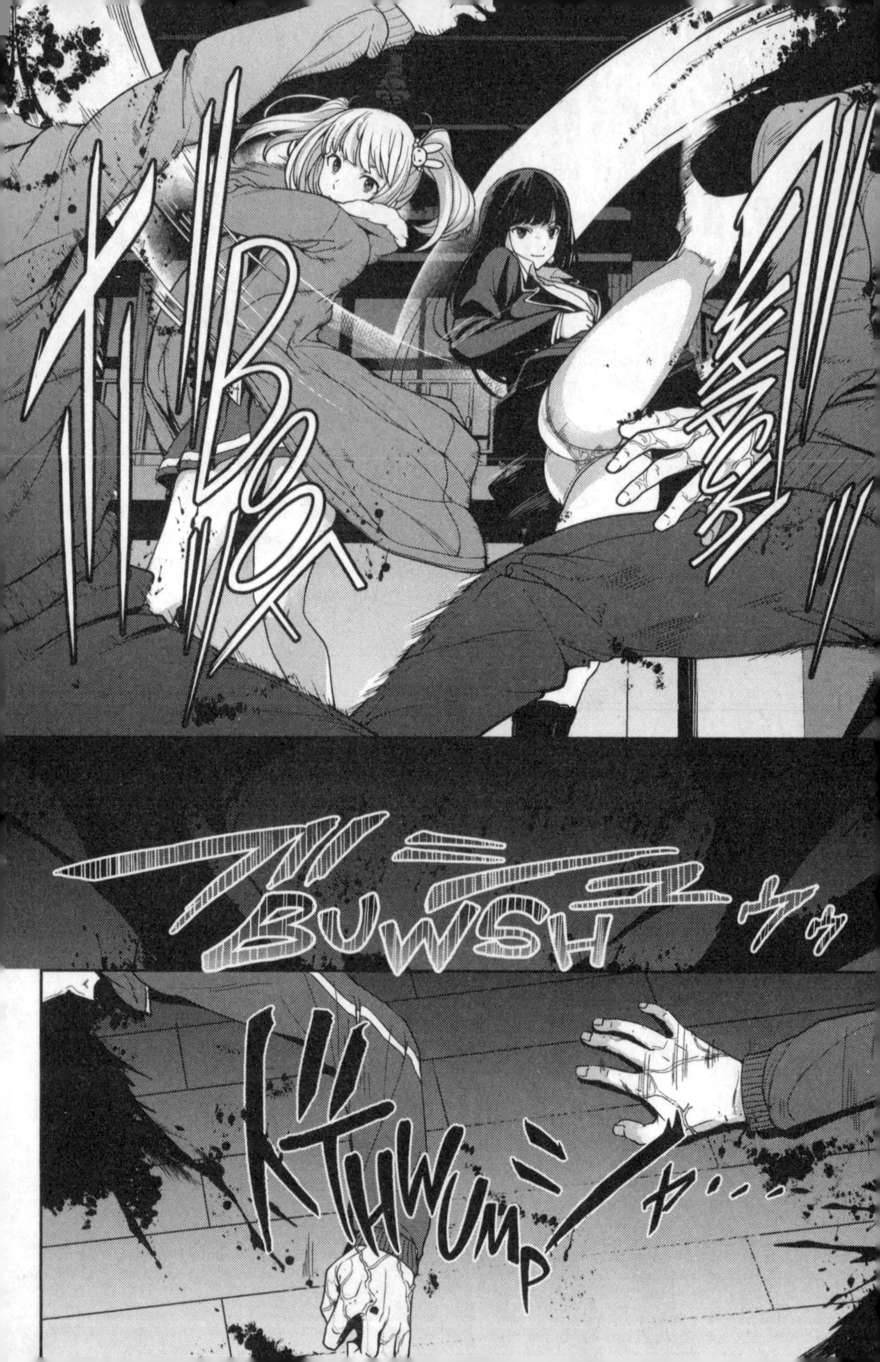
WHACK!!
BDOOF
BUWSH
KTHWUMP

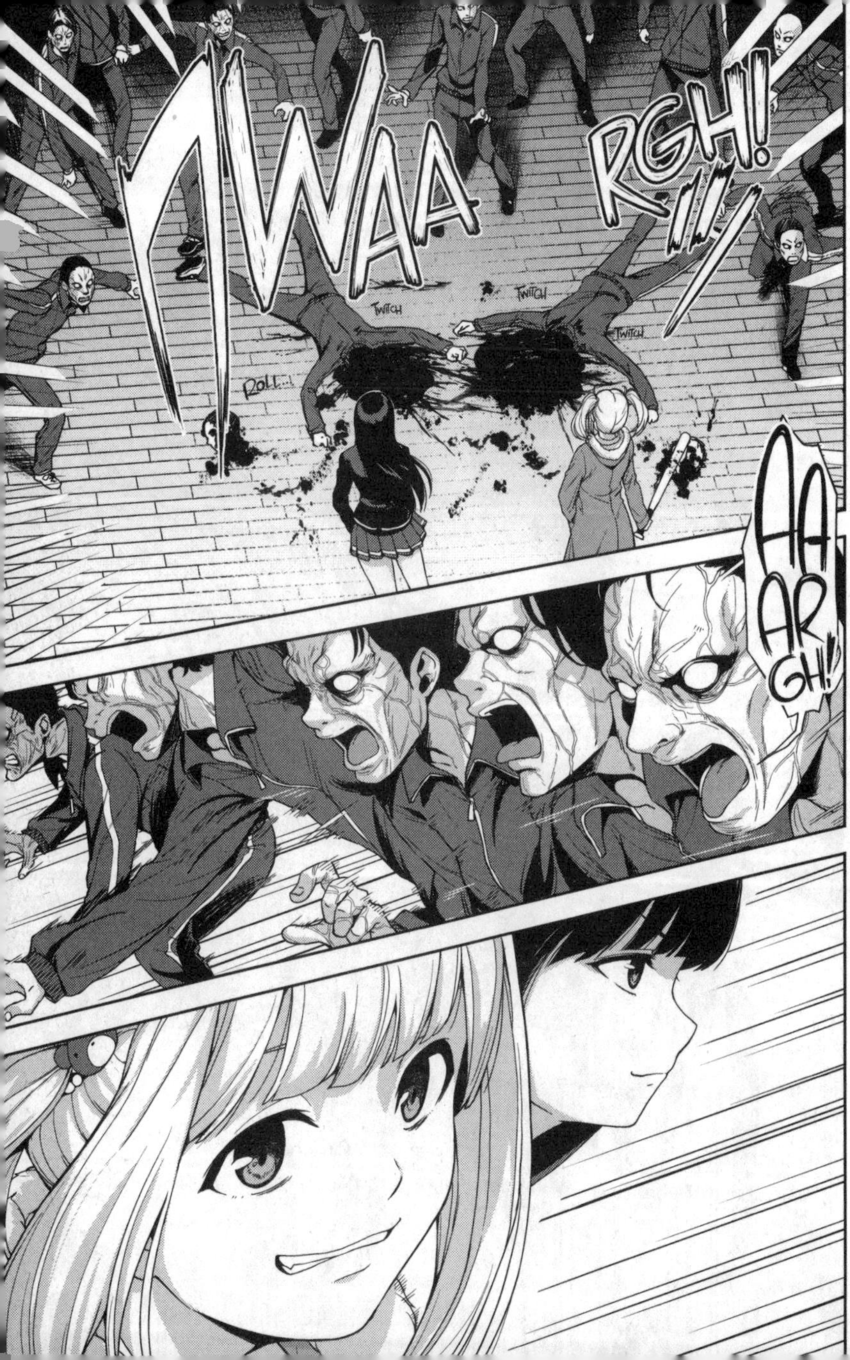

WAAARGH!!
TWITCH
TWITCH
TWITCH
ROLL...
AAARGH!!

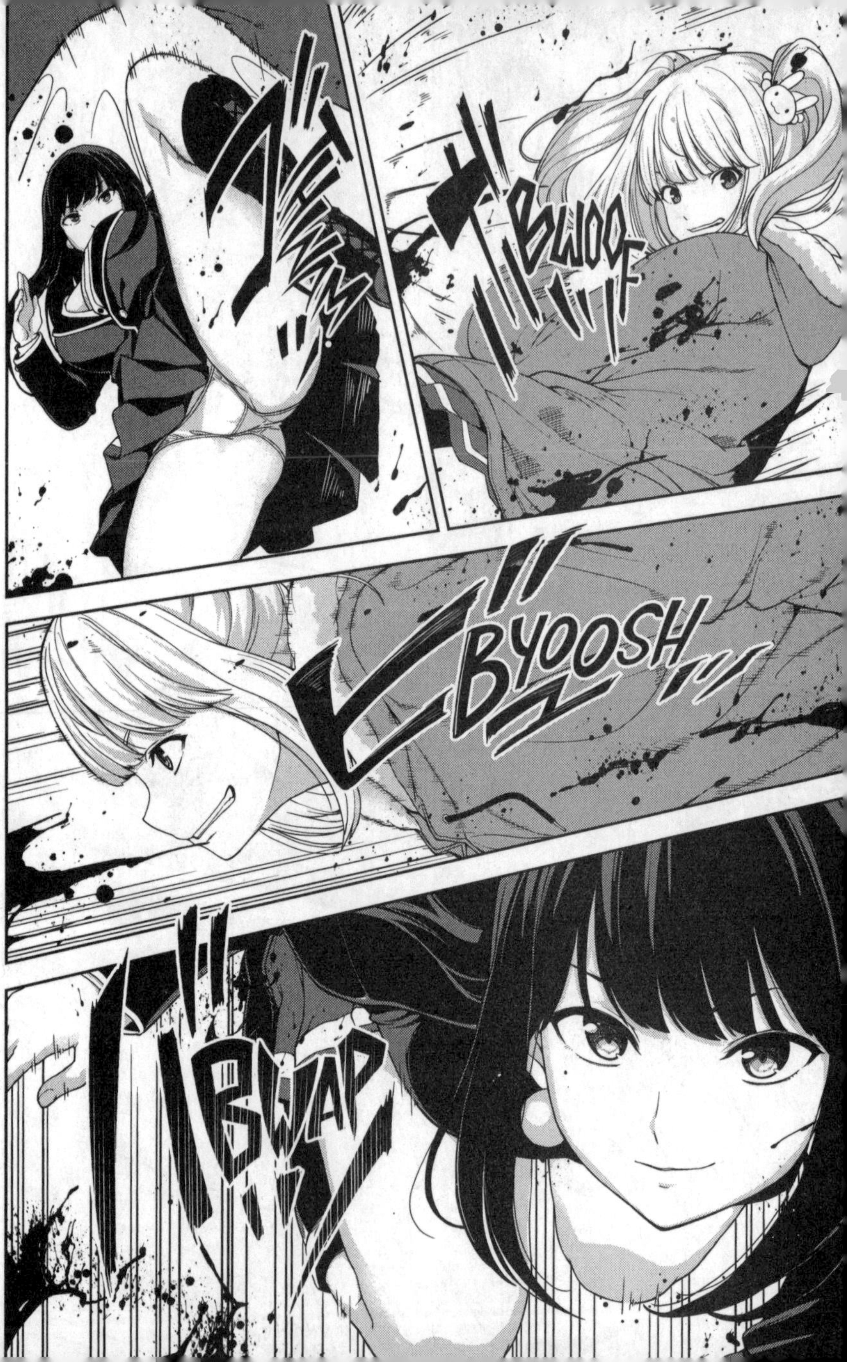
BWOOF
WHAM!
BYOOSH
BWAP

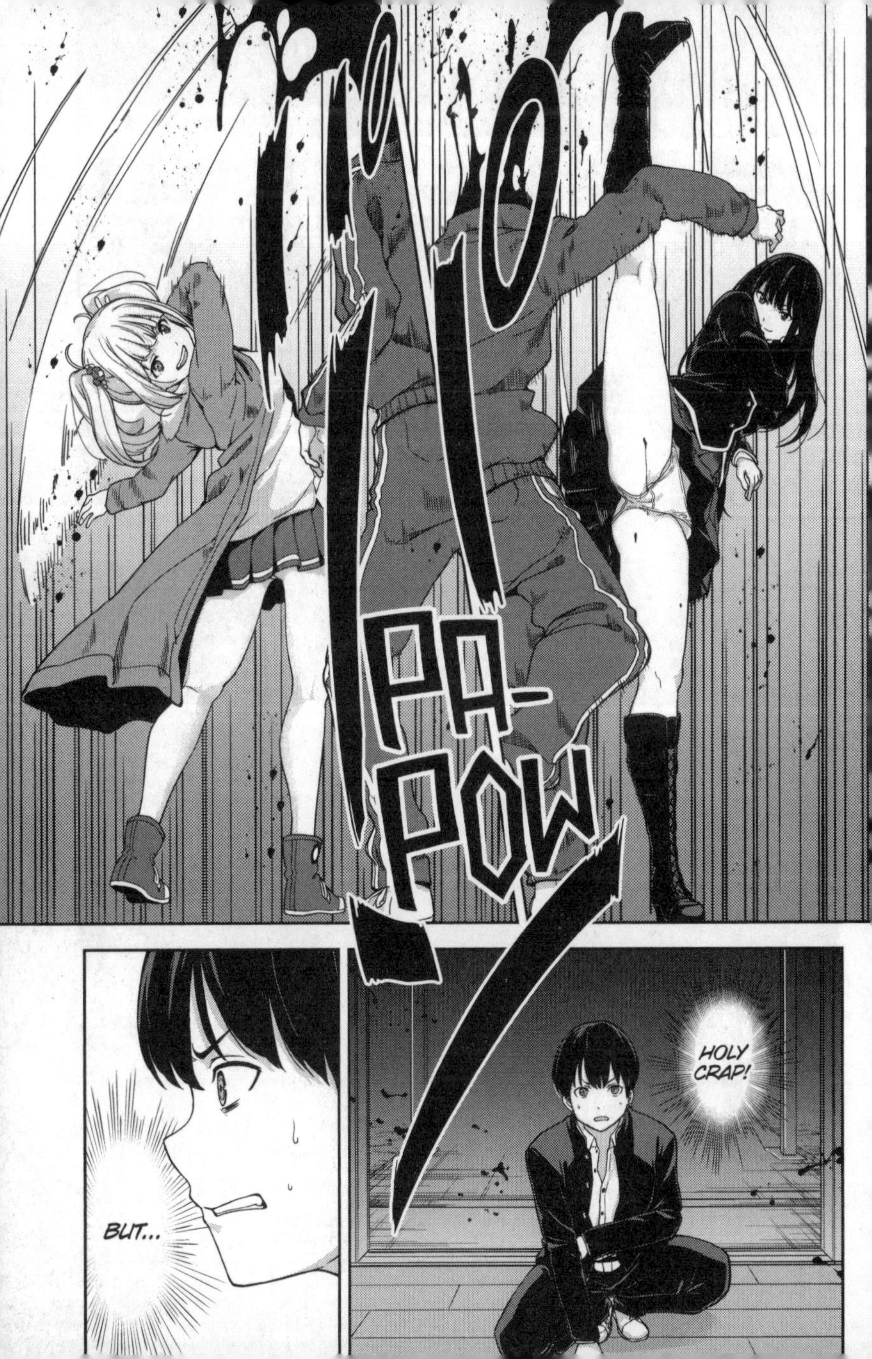
PA-POW
HOLY CRAP!
BUT...

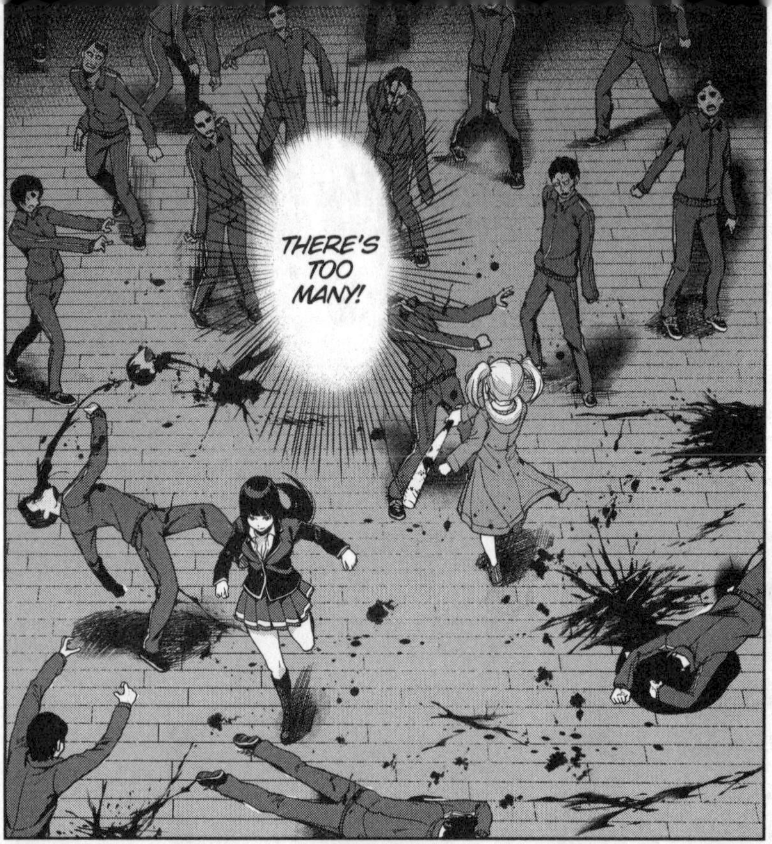
THERE'S TOO MANY!

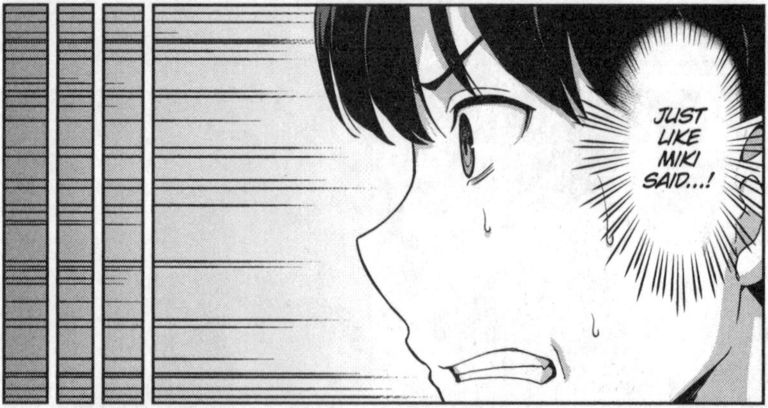
JUST LIKE MIKI SAID...!

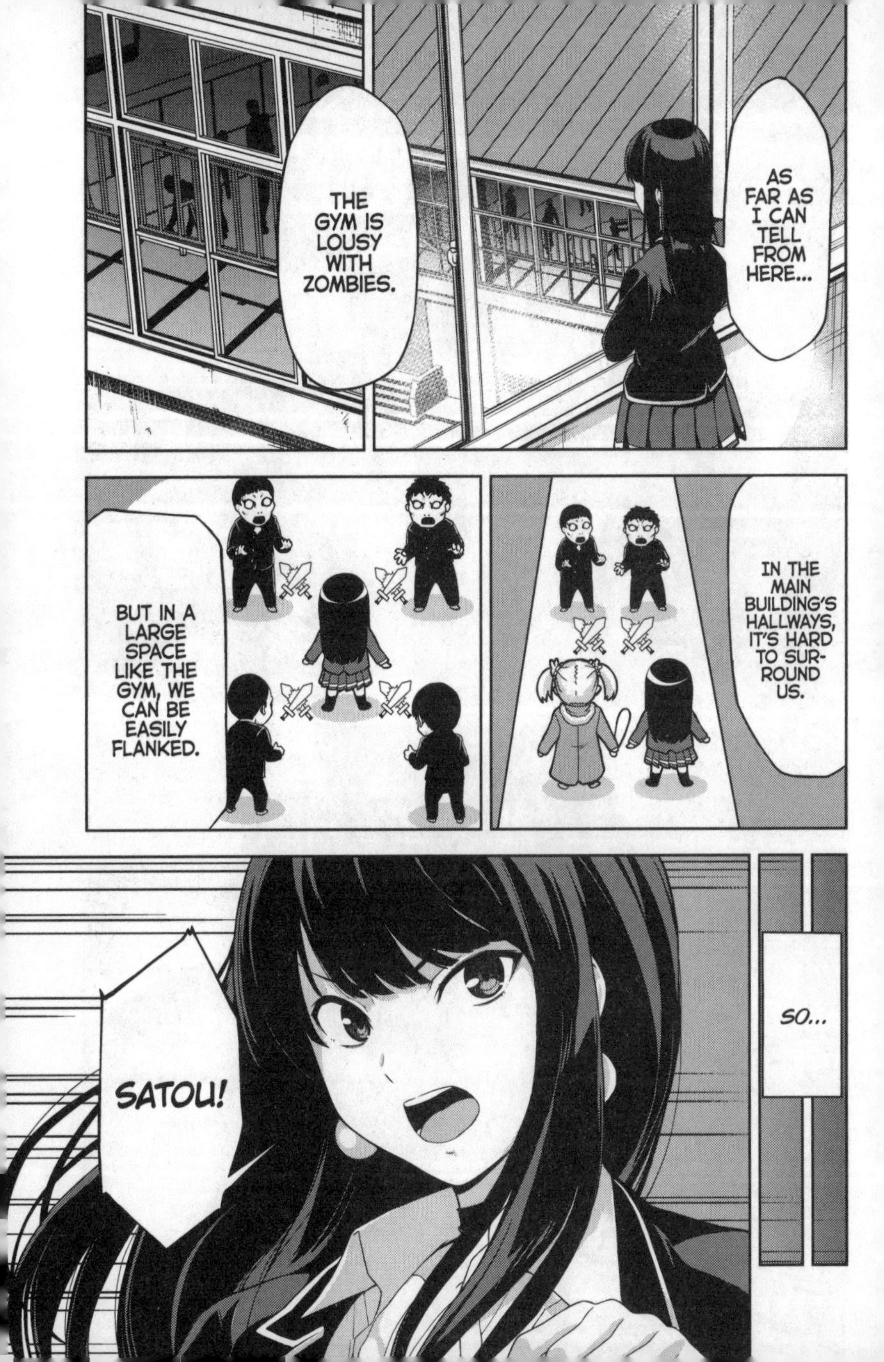
AS FAR AS I CAN TELL FROM HERE...
THE GYM IS LOUSY WITH ZOMBIES.
IN THE MAIN BUILDING'S HALLWAYS, IT'S HARD TO SUR-ROUND US.
BUT IN A LARGE SPACE LIKE THE GYM, WE CAN BE EASILY FLANKED.
SO...
SATOU!

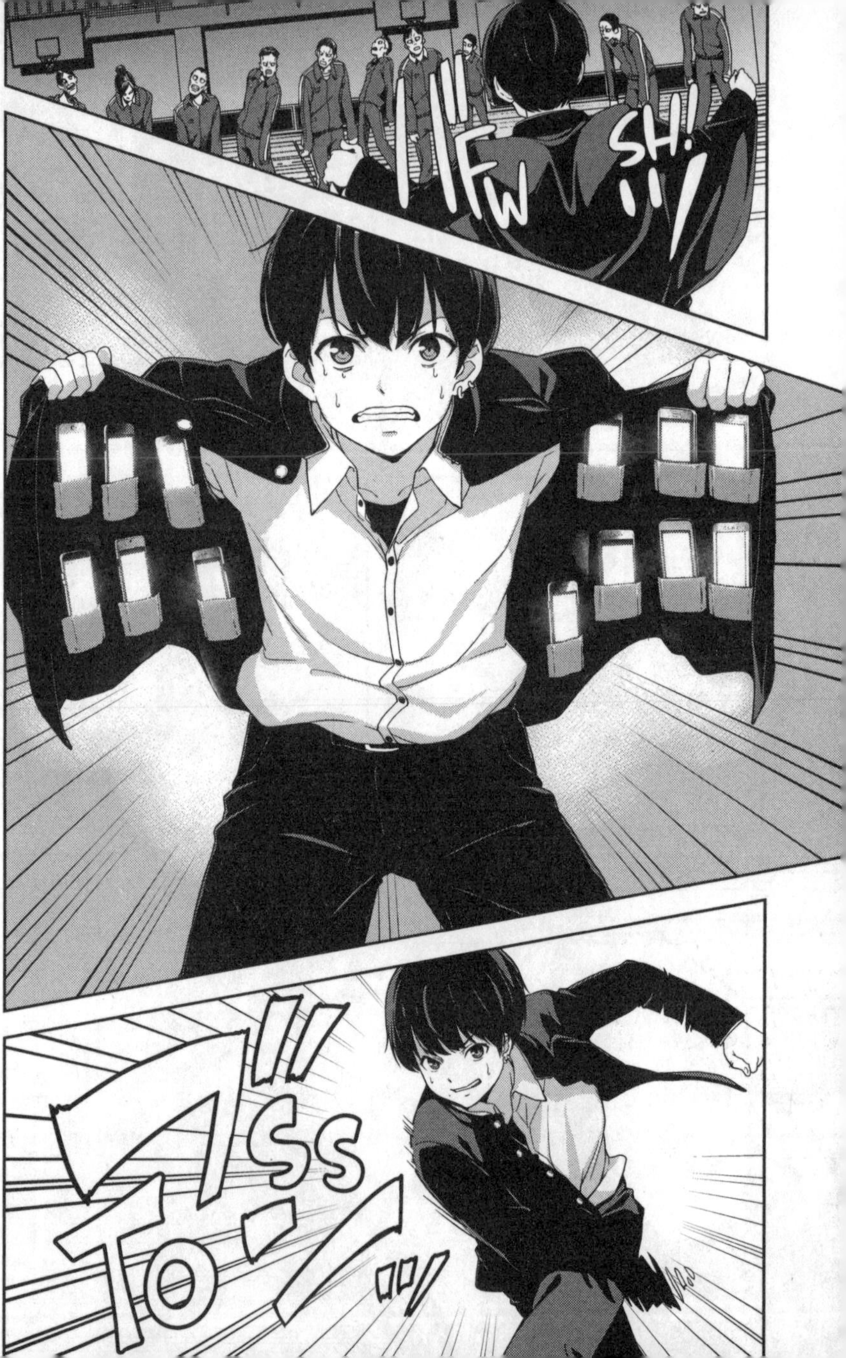
FwSH!
TOSS

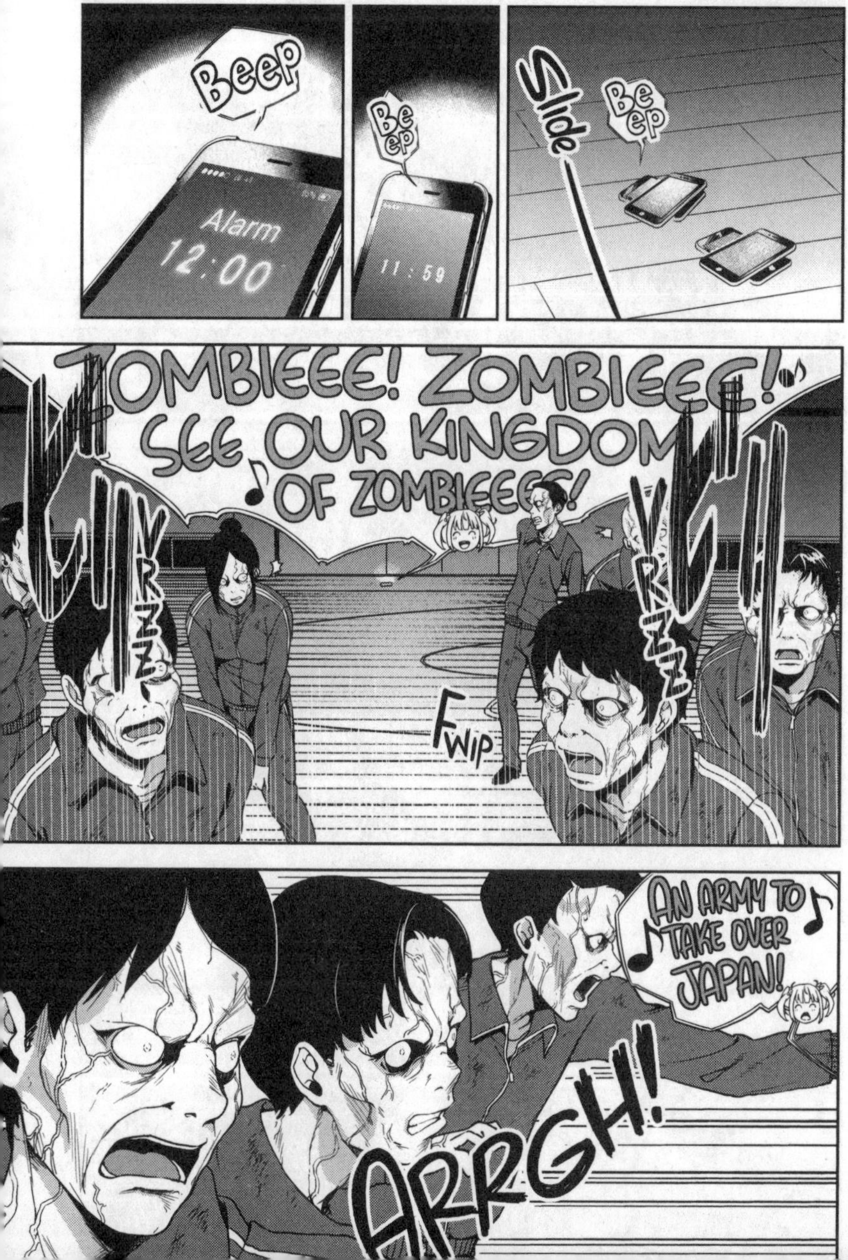
Slide
Beep
Beep
11:59
Beep
Alarm
12:00
ZOMBIEEE! ZOMBIEEE! SEE OUR KINGDOM OF ZOMBIEEES!
FWIP
AN ARMY TO TAKE OVER JAPAN!
ARRGH!

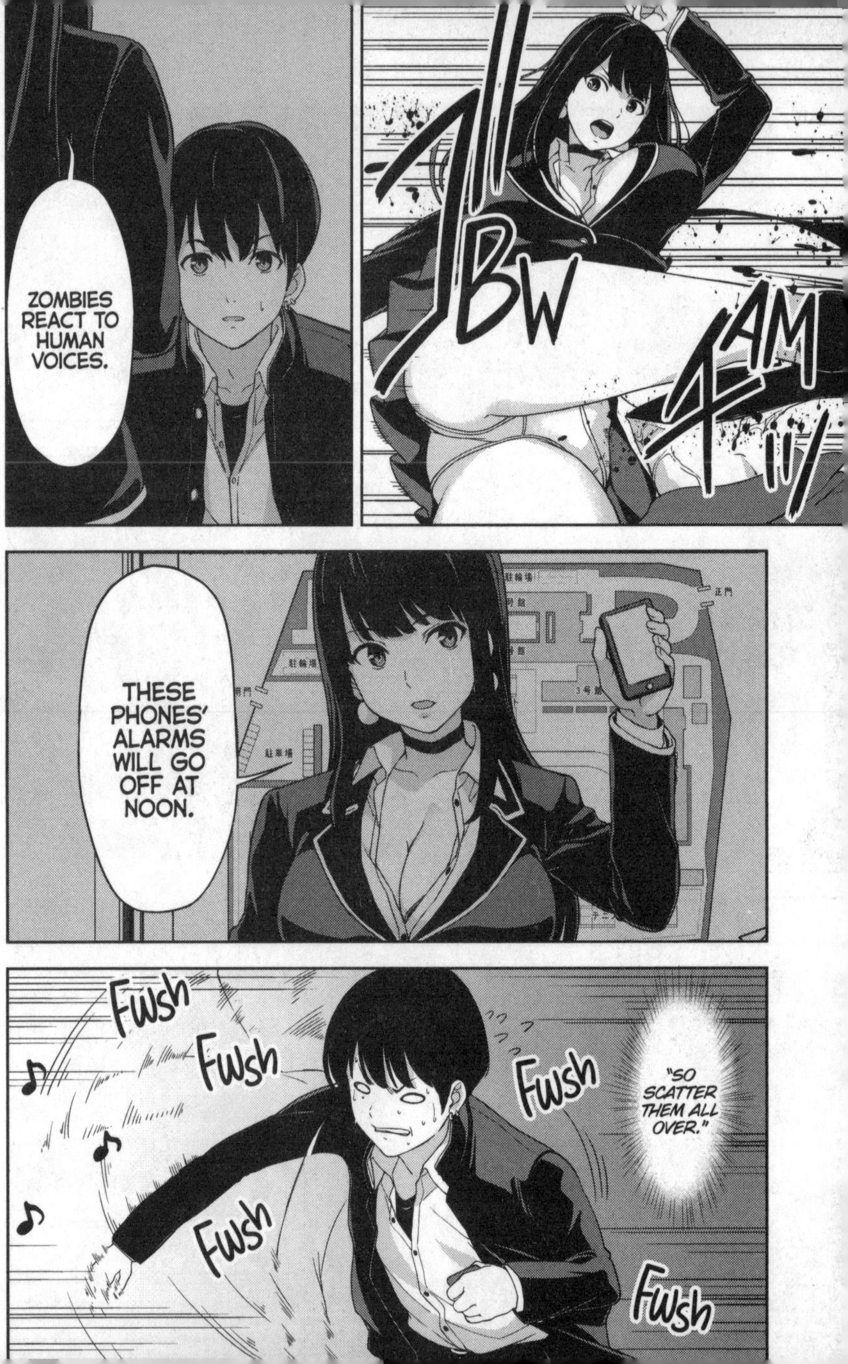
BWAM!!
ZOMBIES REACT TO HUMAN VOICES.
THESE PHONES' ALARMS WILL GO OFF AT NOON.
"SO SCATTER THEM ALL OVER."
Fwsh
Fwsh
Fwsh
Fwsh
Fwsh

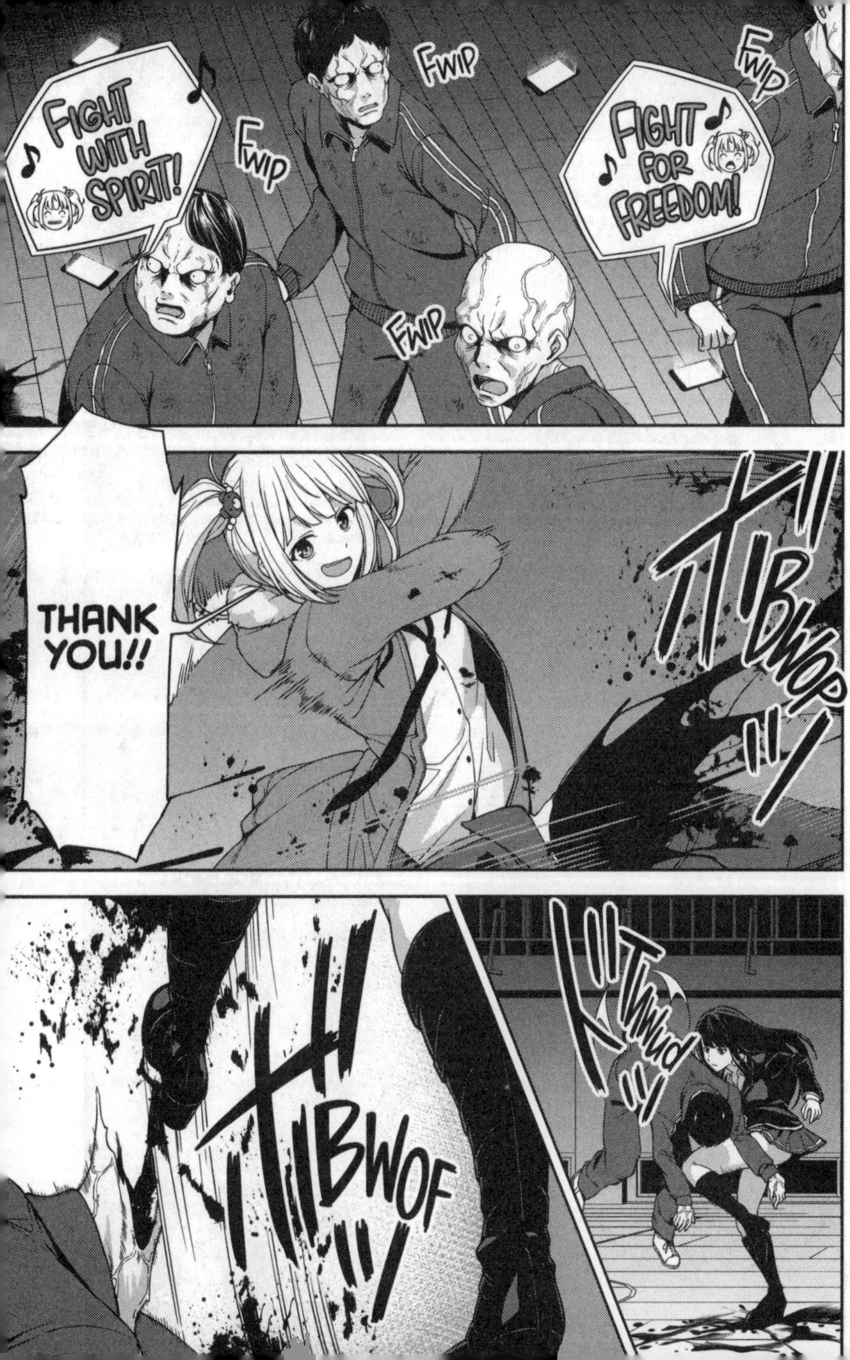

Fwip
FIGHT FOR FREEDOM!
Fwip
Fwip
FIGHT WITH SPIRIT!
Fwip
BWOP
THANK YOU!!
Thwud
BWOF

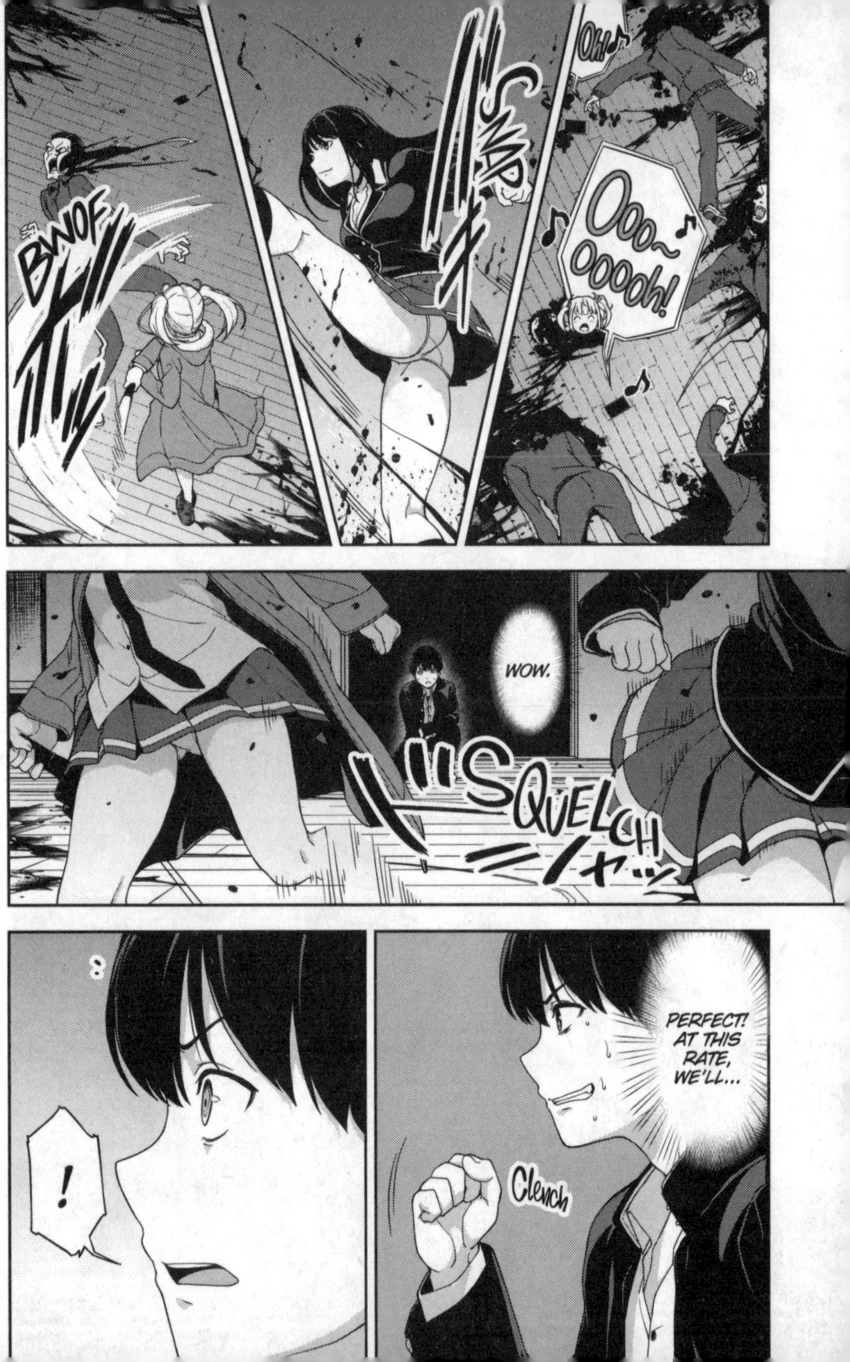
OH!♪
Ooo~ooooh!
SMAP
BWOF
WOW.
SQUELCH
PERFECT! AT THIS RATE, WE'LL...
Clench
!

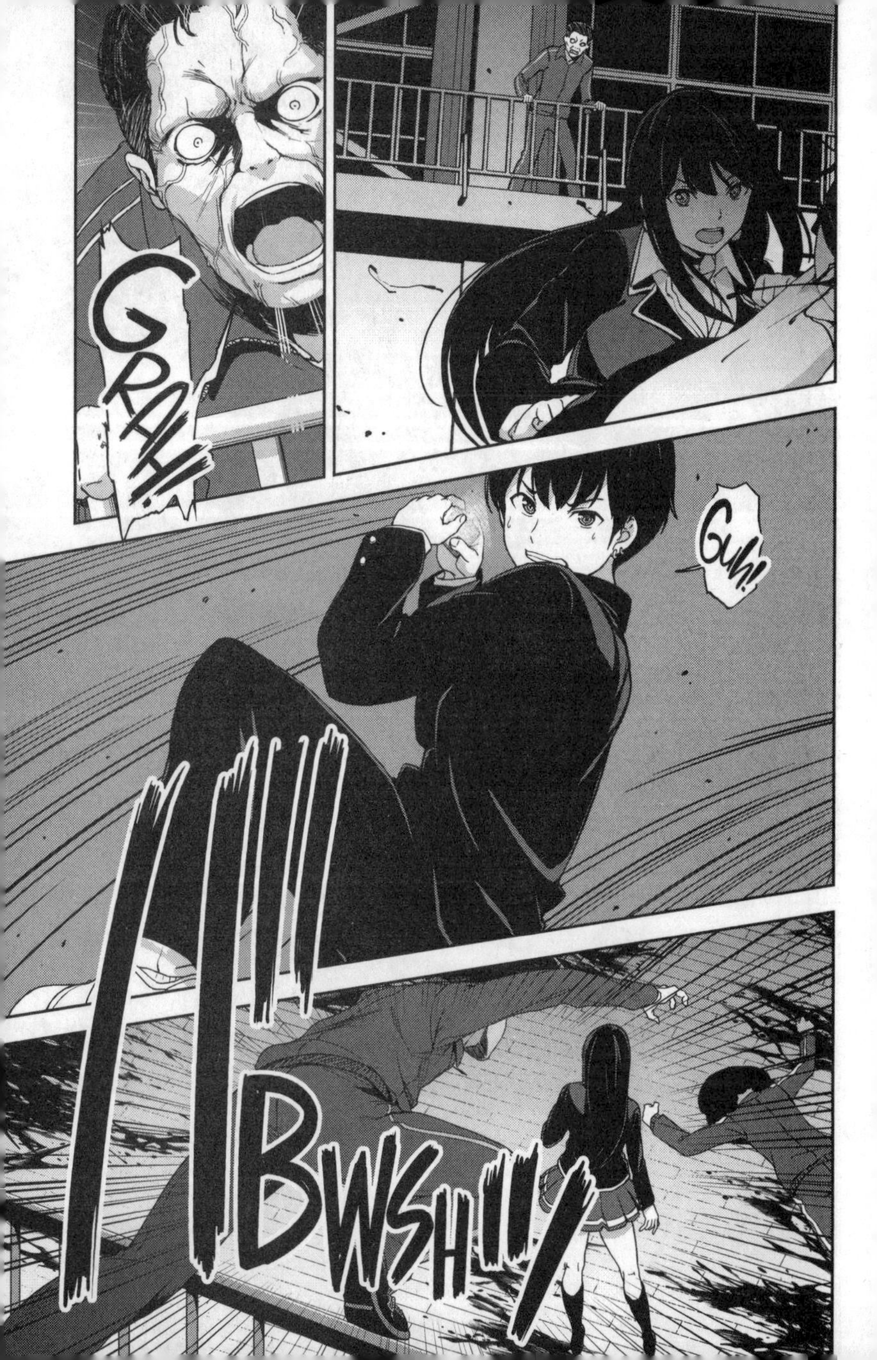
GRAH!!
GUH!
BWSH!!

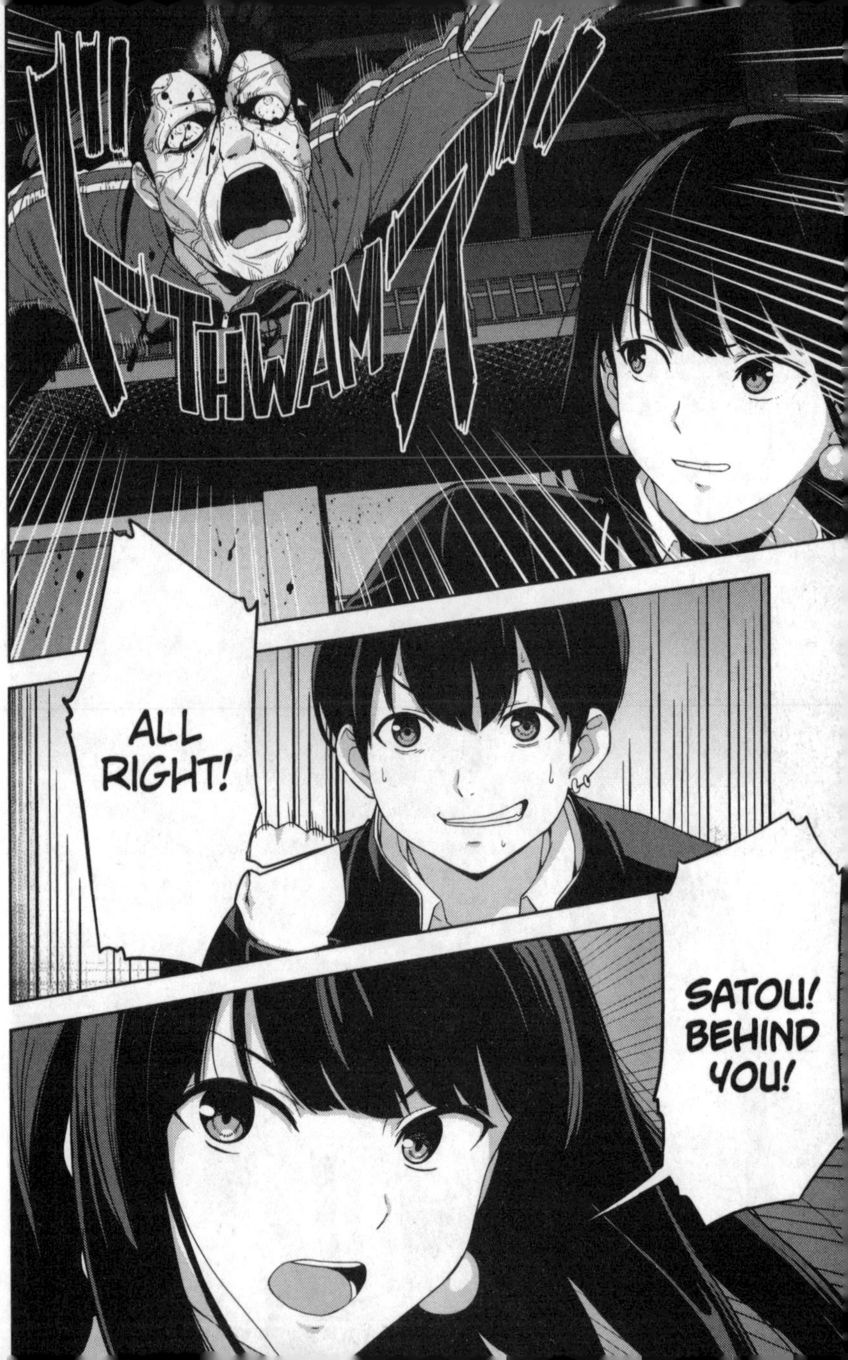
THWAM
ALL RIGHT!
SATOU! BEHIND YOU!

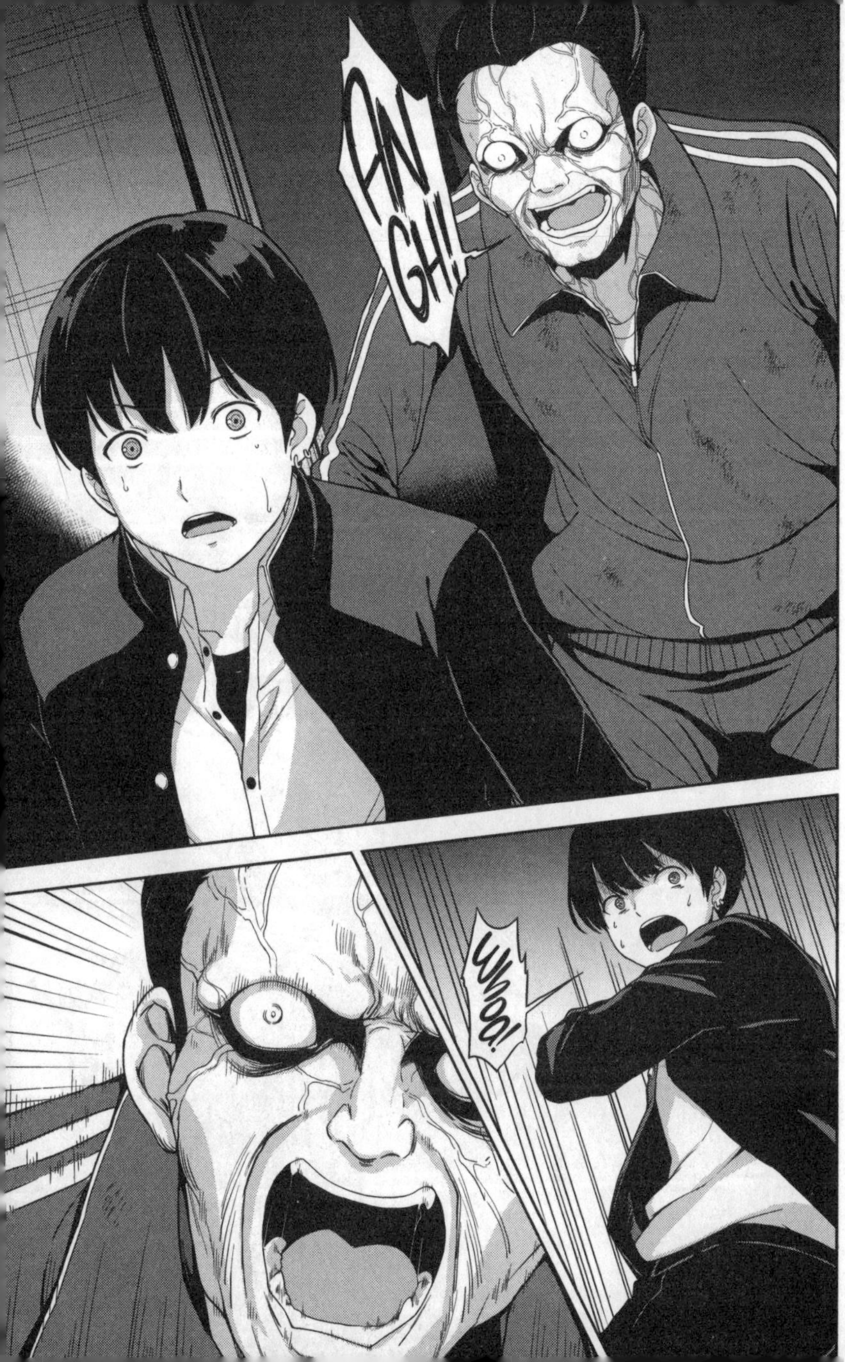

AAN GH!!
Whoa!

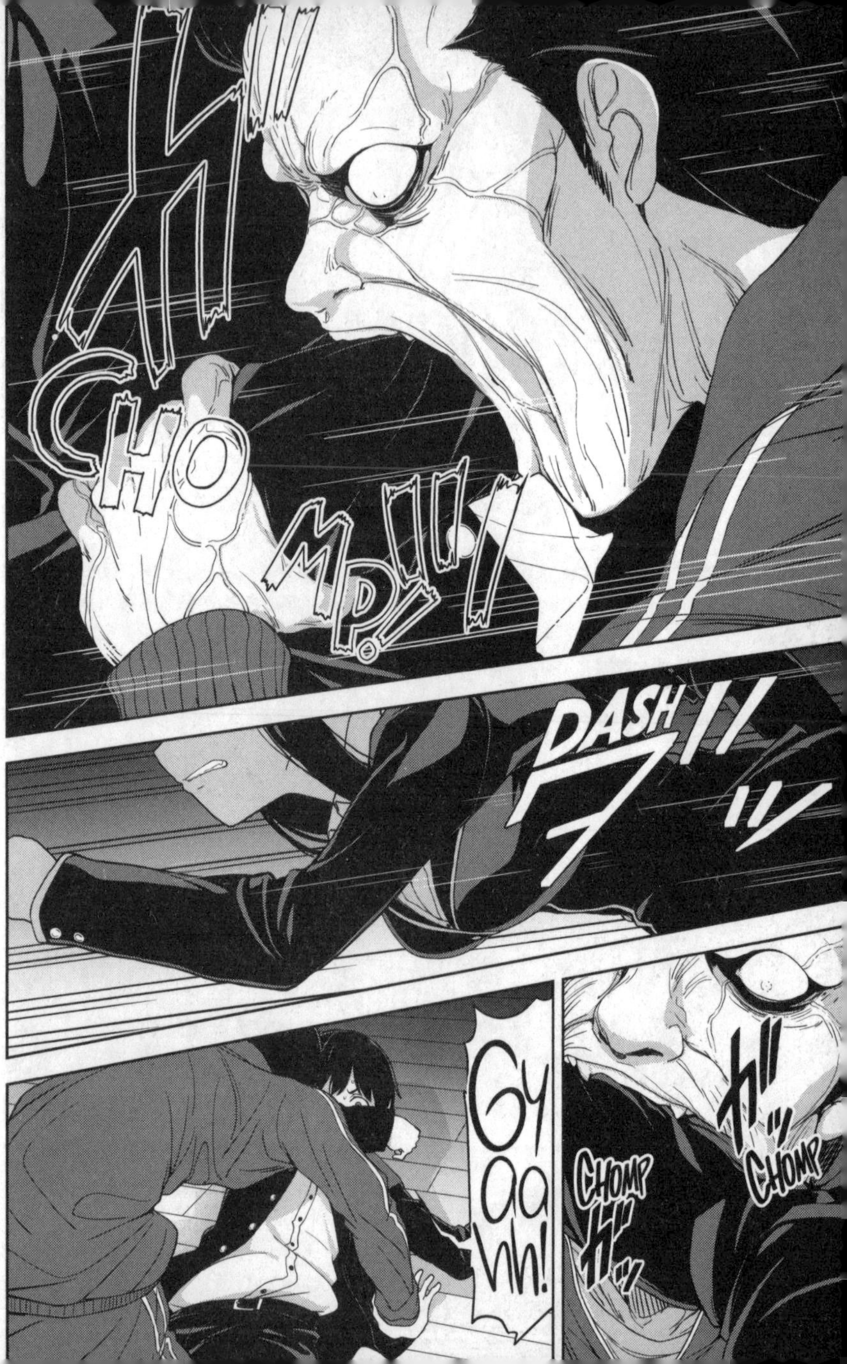
CHOMP!!!!!
DASH
ダッ
ガッ
CHOMP
CHOMP
ガッ
Gyaahh!

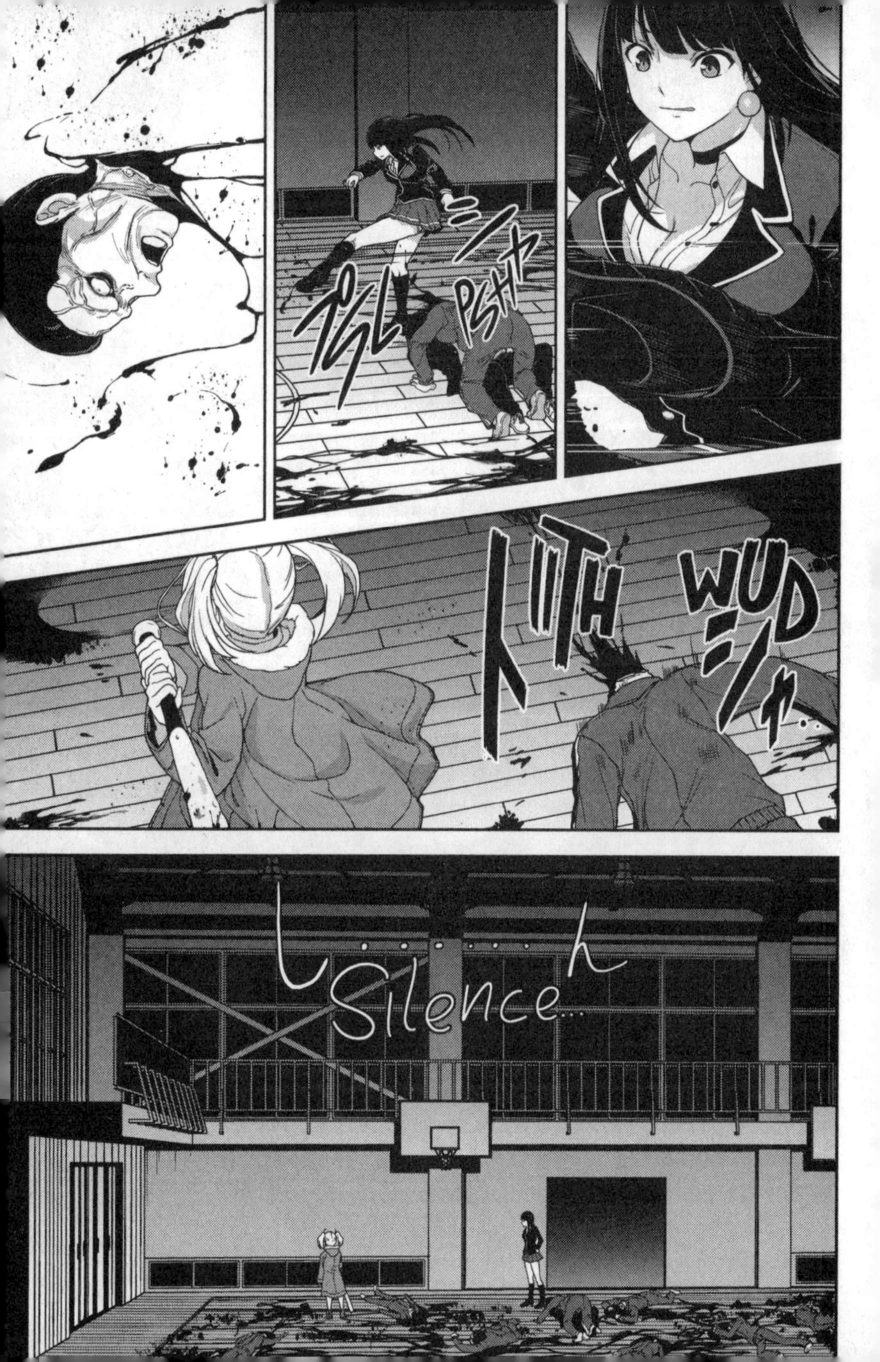
PSHA
WUD
Silence...

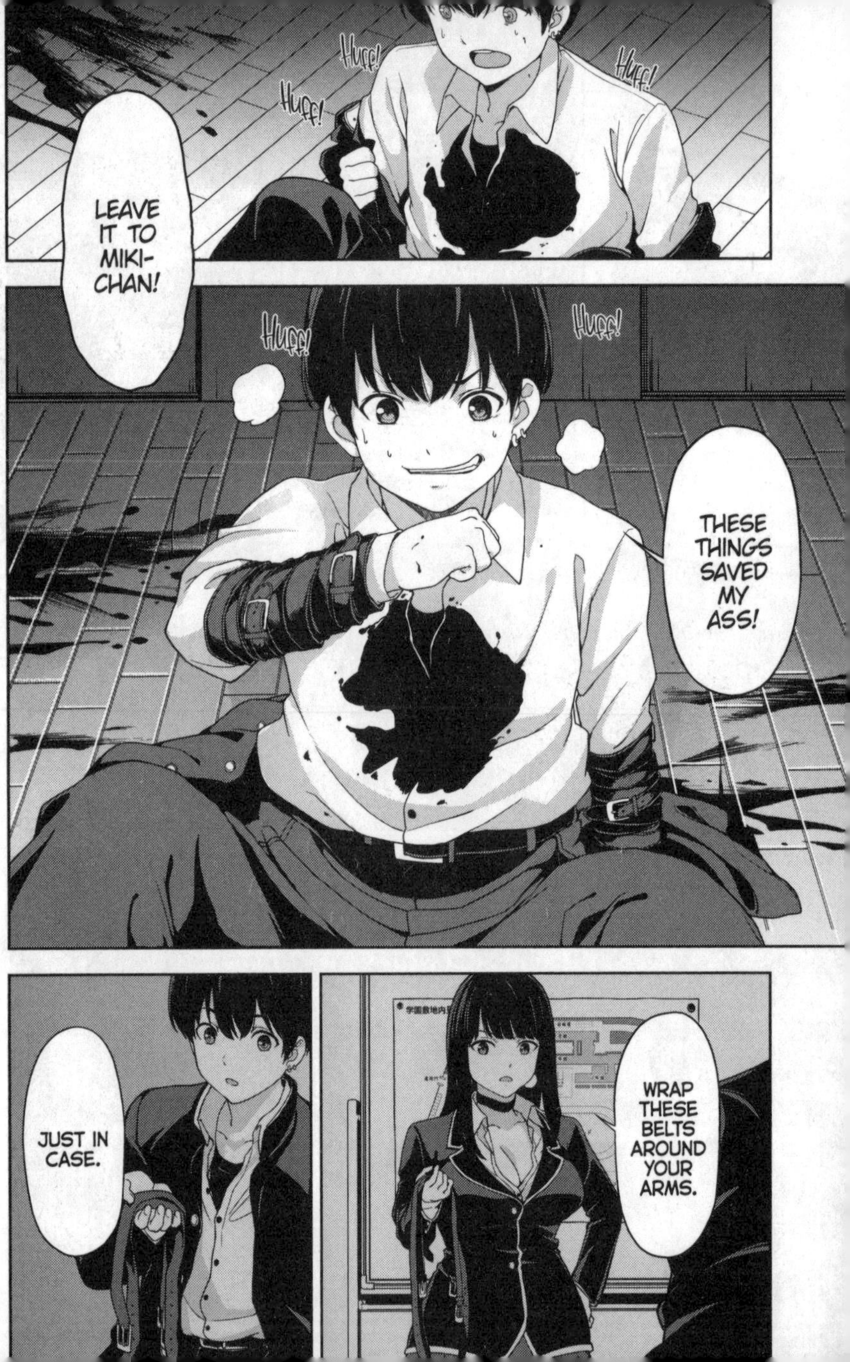
Huff!
Huff!
Huff!
LEAVE IT TO MIKI-CHAN!
Huff!
Huff!
THESE THINGS SAVED MY ASS!
WRAP THESE BELTS AROUND YOUR ARMS.
JUST IN CASE.

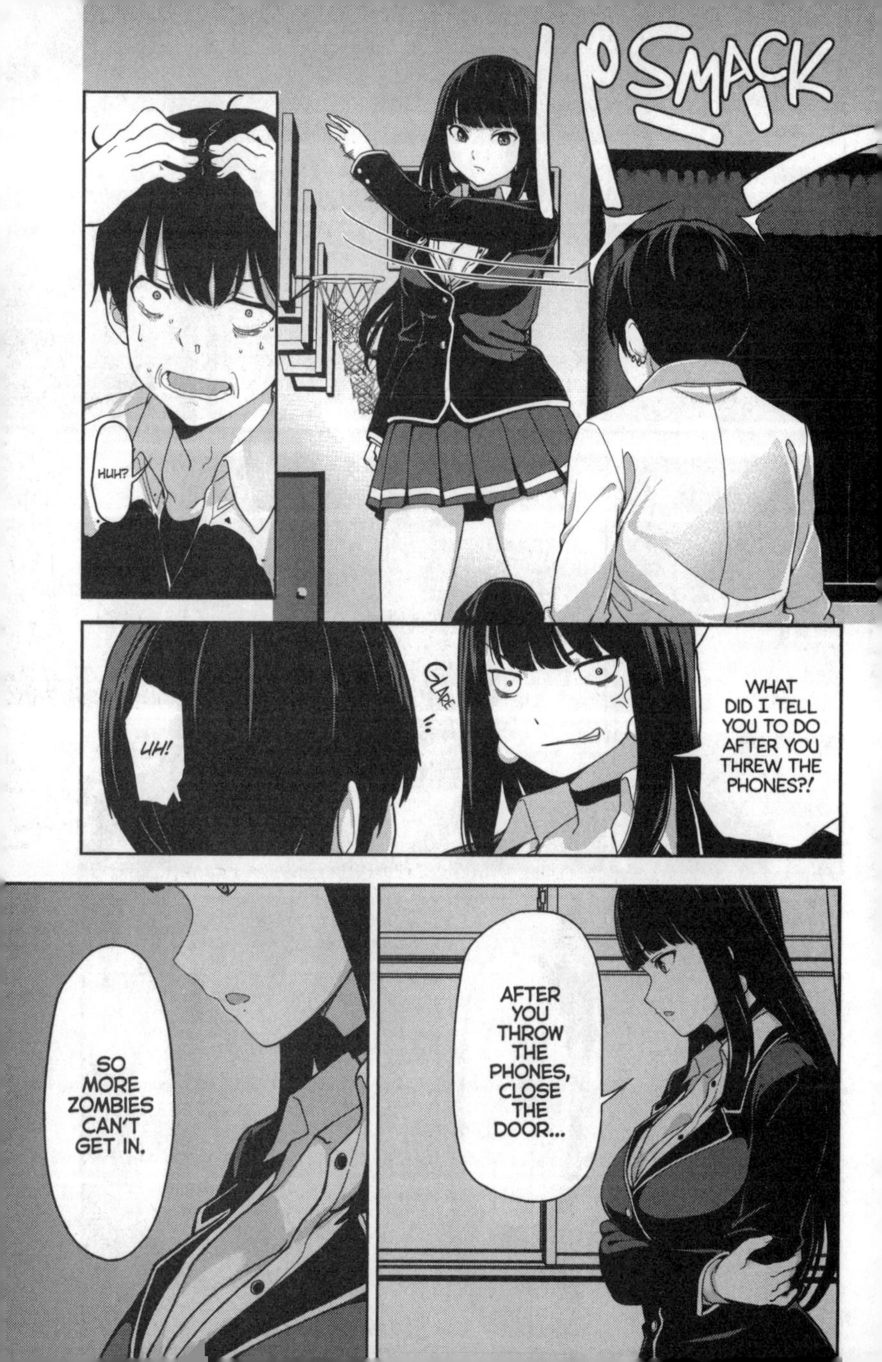
SMACK
HUH?
WHAT DID I TELL YOU TO DO AFTER YOU THREW THE PHONES?!
GLARE
UH!
AFTER YOU THROW THE PHONES, CLOSE THE DOOR...
SO MORE ZOMBIES CAN'T GET IN.

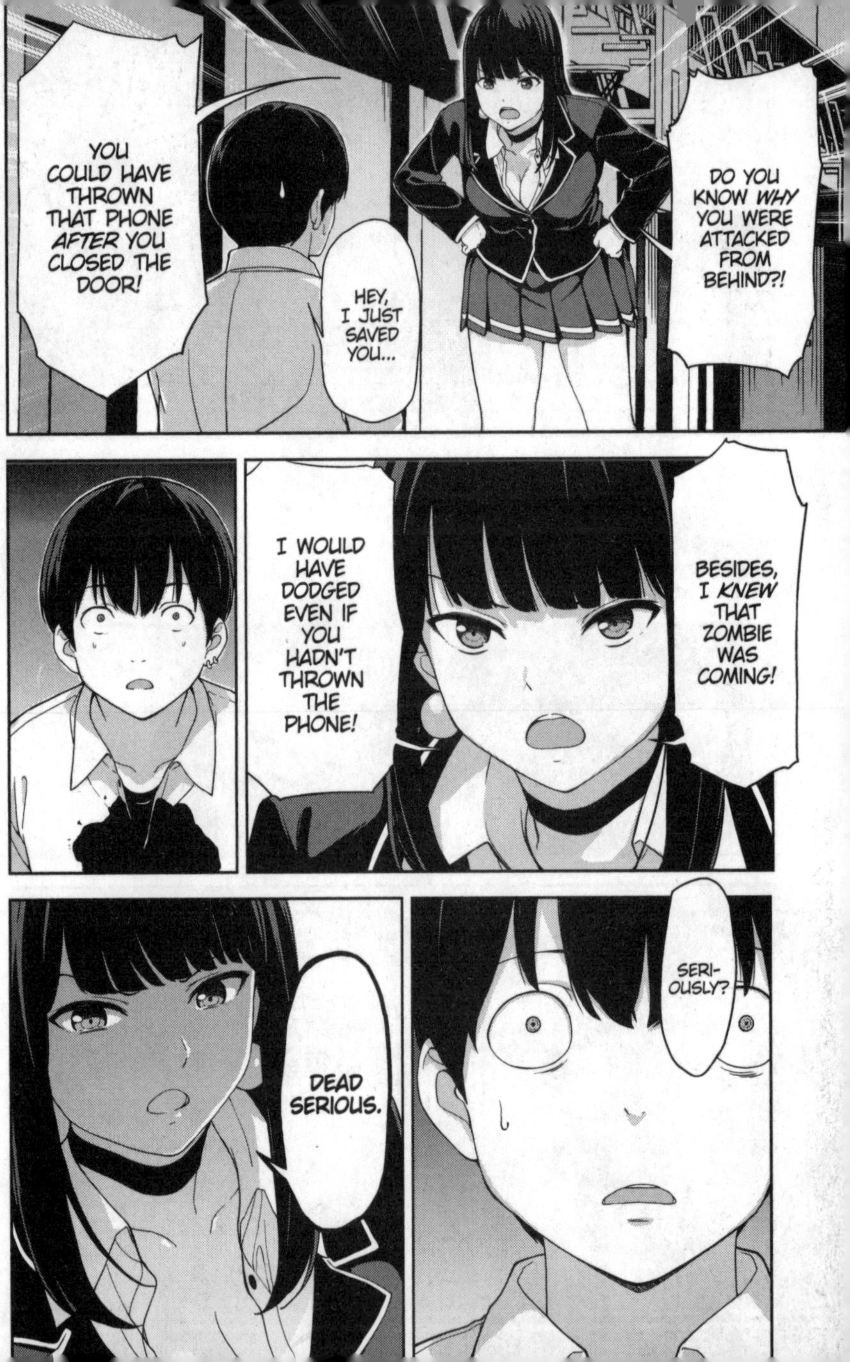
DO YOU KNOW *WHY* YOU WERE ATTACKED FROM BEHIND?!
HEY, I JUST SAVED YOU...
YOU COULD HAVE THROWN THAT PHONE *AFTER* YOU CLOSED THE DOOR!
BESIDES, I *KNEW* THAT ZOMBIE WAS COMING!
I WOULD HAVE DODGED EVEN IF YOU HADN'T THROWN THE PHONE!
SERI-OUSLY?
DEAD SERIOUS.

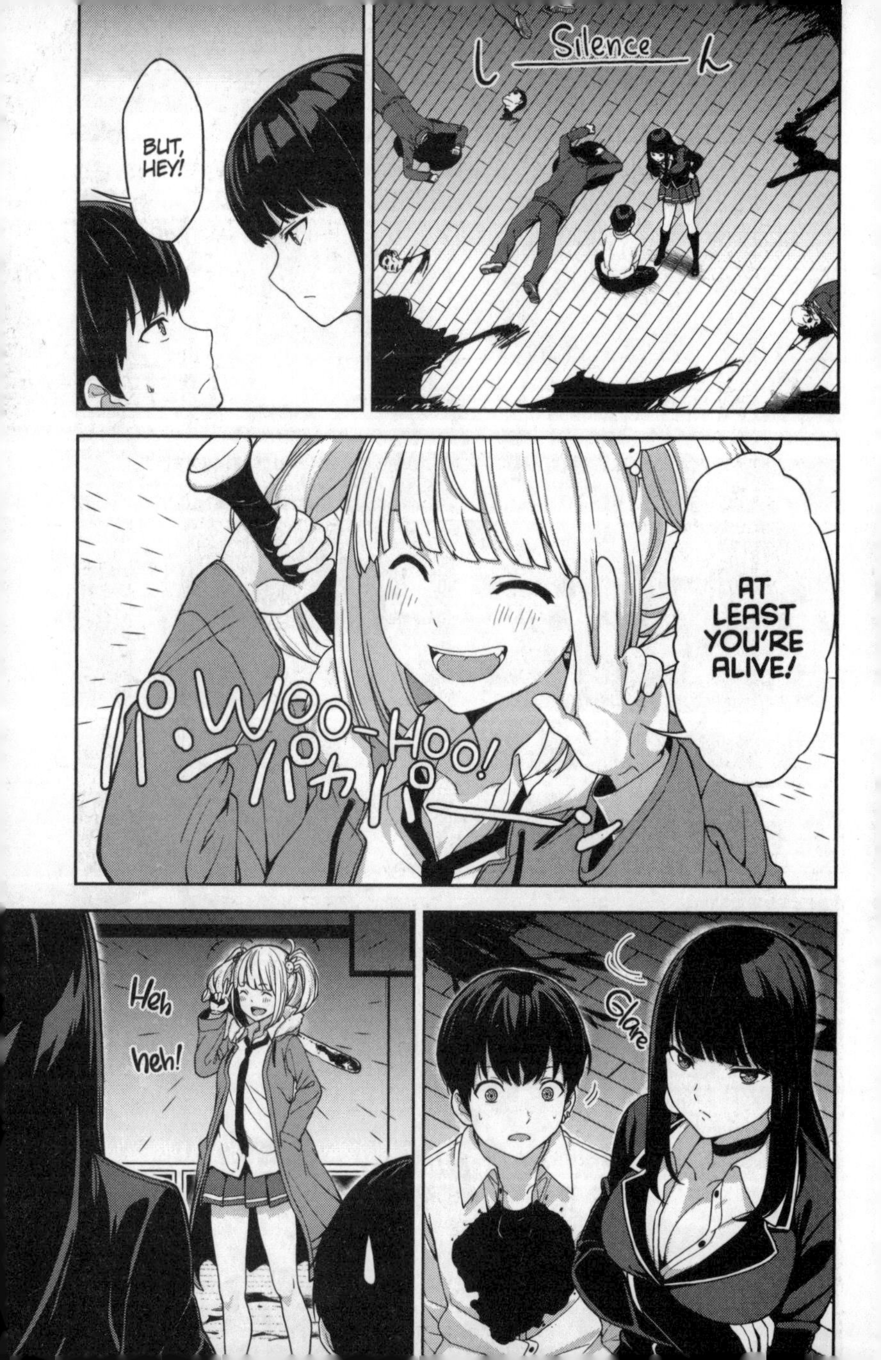
Silence
BUT, HEY!
AT LEAST YOU'RE ALIVE!
WOO-HOO!
Glare
Heh heh!

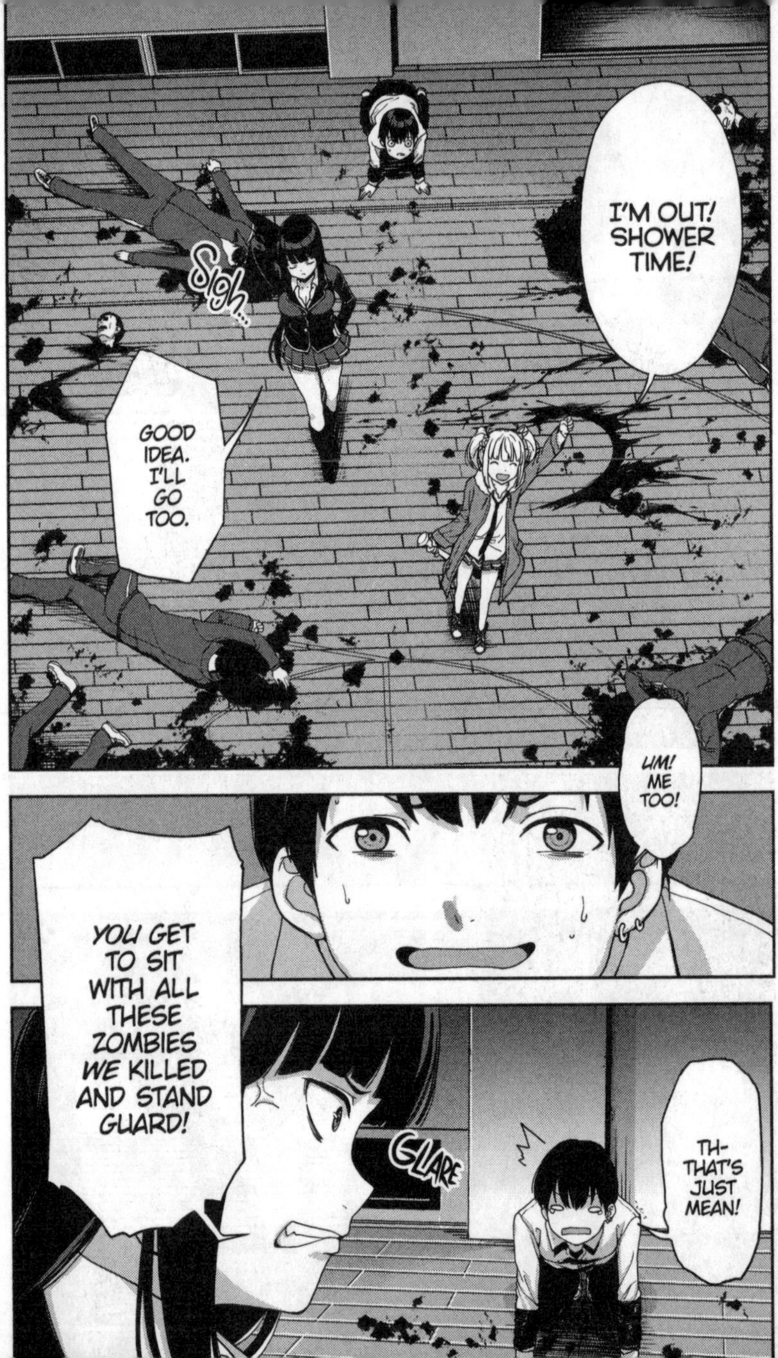
I'M OUT! SHOWER TIME!
Sigh...
GOOD IDEA. I'LL GO TOO.
UM! ME TOO!
YOU GET TO SIT WITH ALL THESE ZOMBIES WE KILLED AND STAND GUARD!
GLARE
TH-THAT'S JUST MEAN!

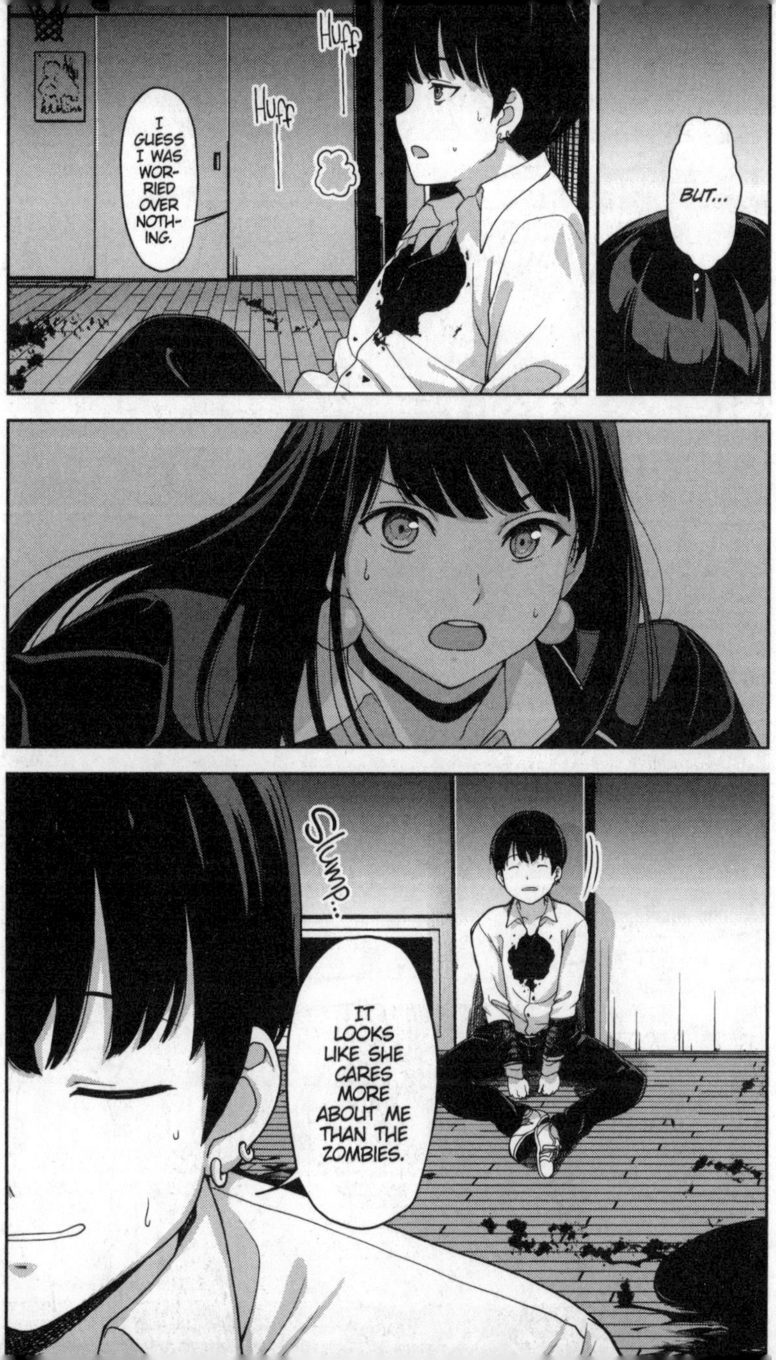
BUT...
Huff
Huff
I GUESS I WAS WORRIED OVER NOTHING.
Slump...
IT LOOKS LIKE SHE CARES MORE ABOUT ME THAN THE ZOMBIES.

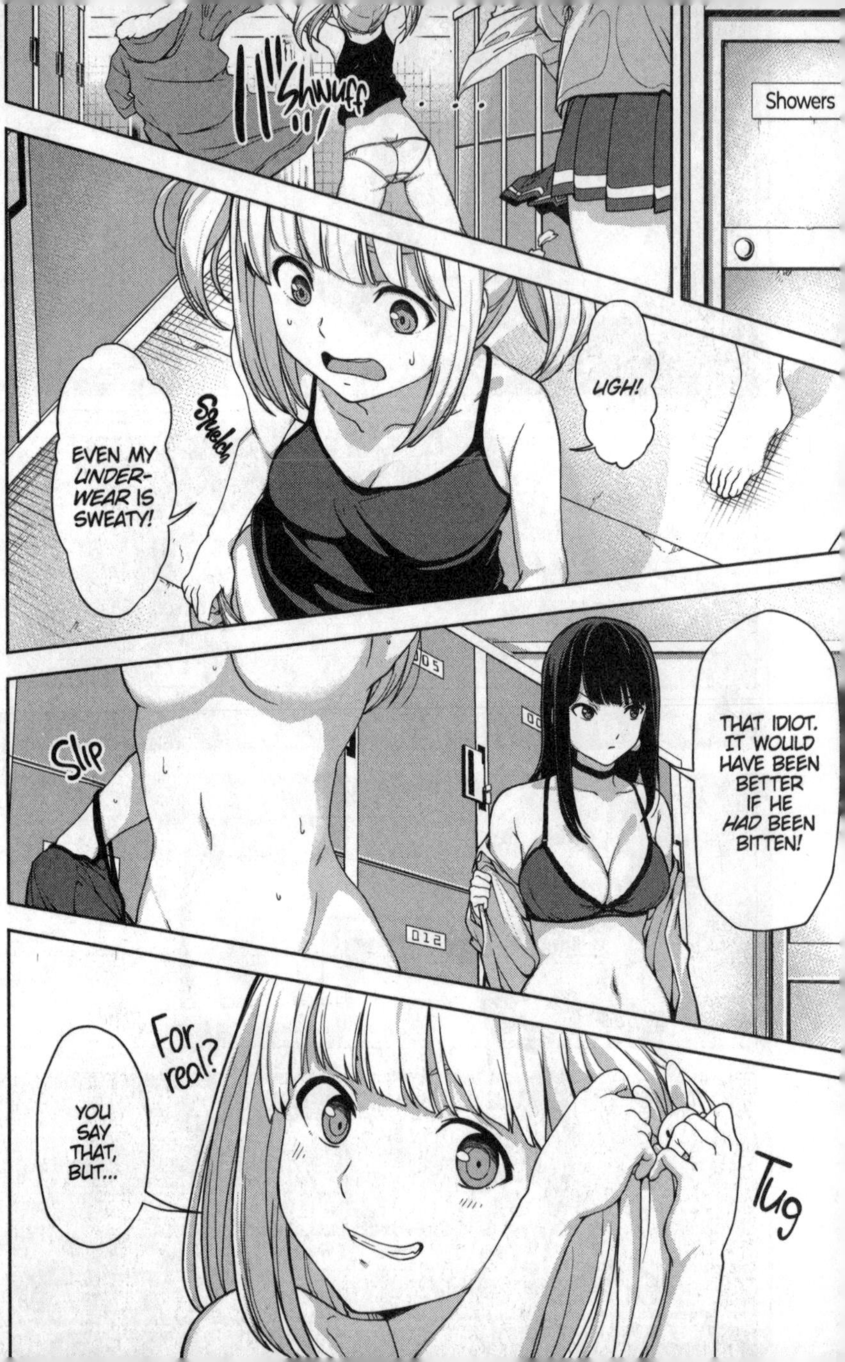
Showers
Shwuff
UGH!
Squelch
EVEN MY UNDER-WEAR IS SWEATY!
THAT IDIOT. IT WOULD HAVE BEEN BETTER IF HE *HAD* BEEN BITTEN!
Slip
Tug
For real?
YOU SAY THAT, BUT...

NYO HA HA!

YOU SHIT A *BRICK* WHEN YOU SAW HE WAS IN TROUBLE!

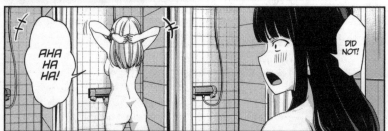

AHA HA HA!

DID NOT!

ぽっ—Sob—ん

Aha ha ha! I did not!

AT LEAST *THEY'RE* HAVING FUN.

SPOILS OF WAR:

GYMNASIUM SHOWER ROOM

THE 3RD DAY END

10/4
Cleared the main school building.
Discovered there is a huge difference in the strength
between individual zombies.
There is a possibility that they can use weapons.

10/5
Found Satou Masaru.
As a former member of a sports club, he may have useful skills.
He seems easily manipulated.

10/7
Took back the gym.
Satou has a good arm, but he's a loser. Nervous disposition.

10/9
While we were cleaning up, I did some experiments.
Fire: ✓

10/10
A news blog in NY failed to refresh.
Information from the United States has been cut off.

10/12
An aid group in Osaka has stopped giving updates.

10/14
We have finished clearing out the school.
Tomorrow we will light a signal fire.

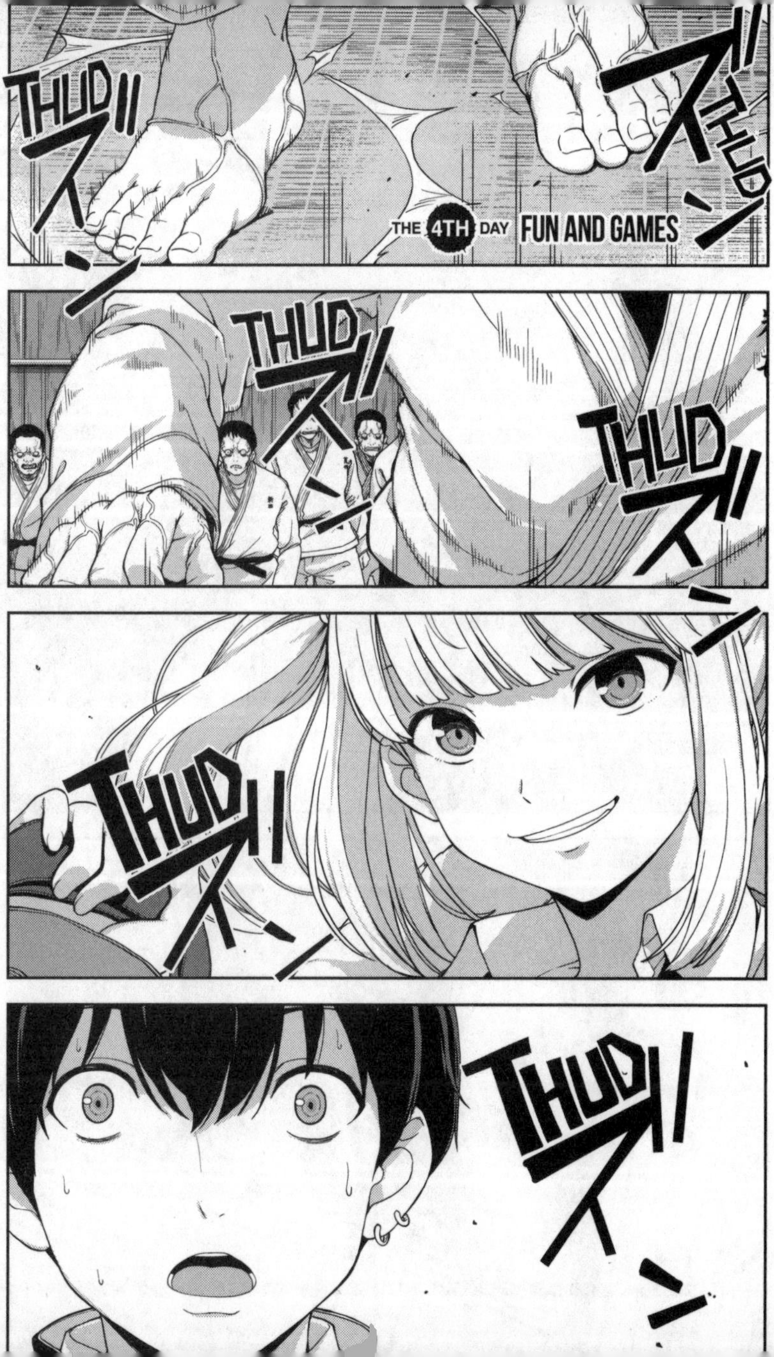
THUD
THUD
THE 4TH DAY FUN AND GAMES
THUD
THUD
THUD
THUD

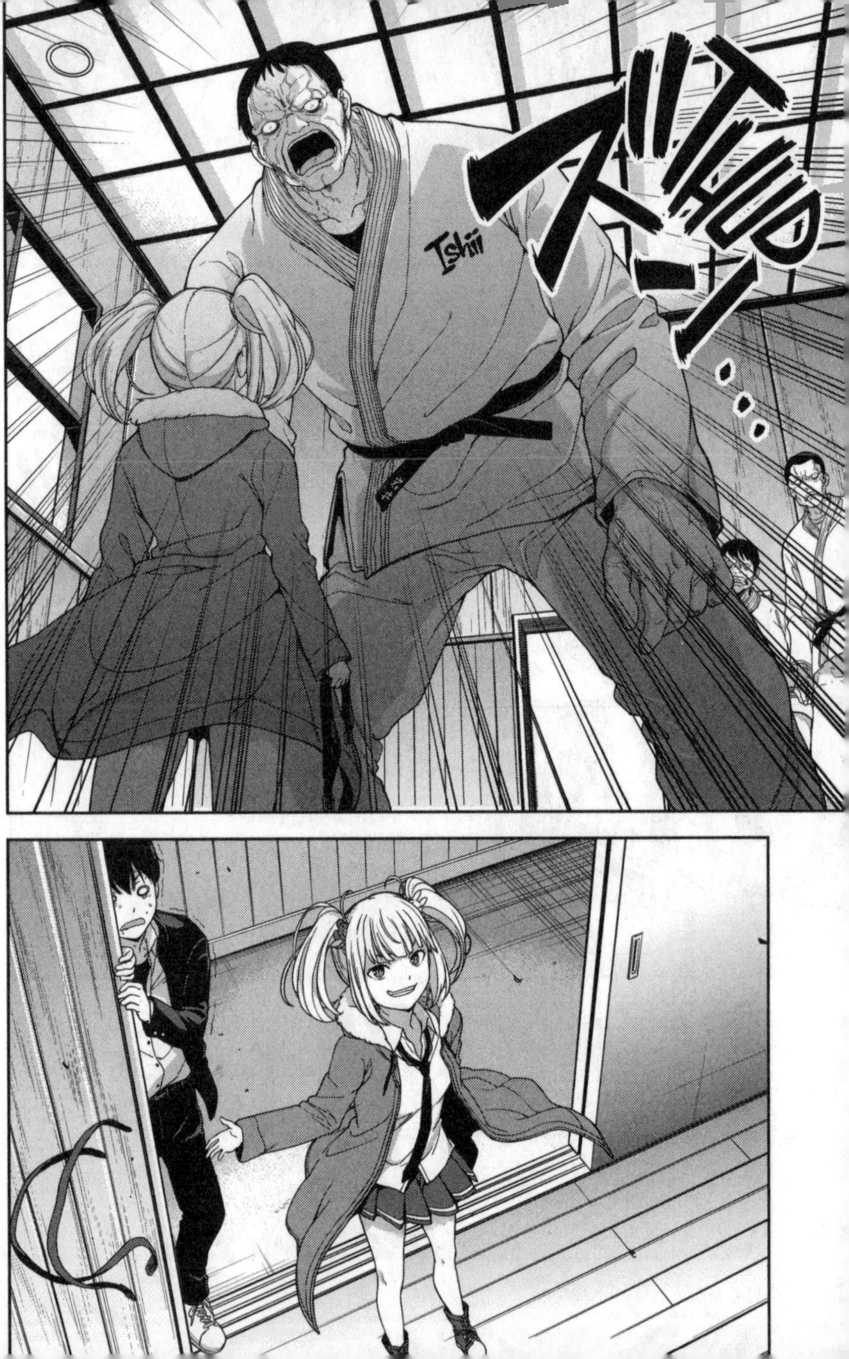
THUD
Ishii

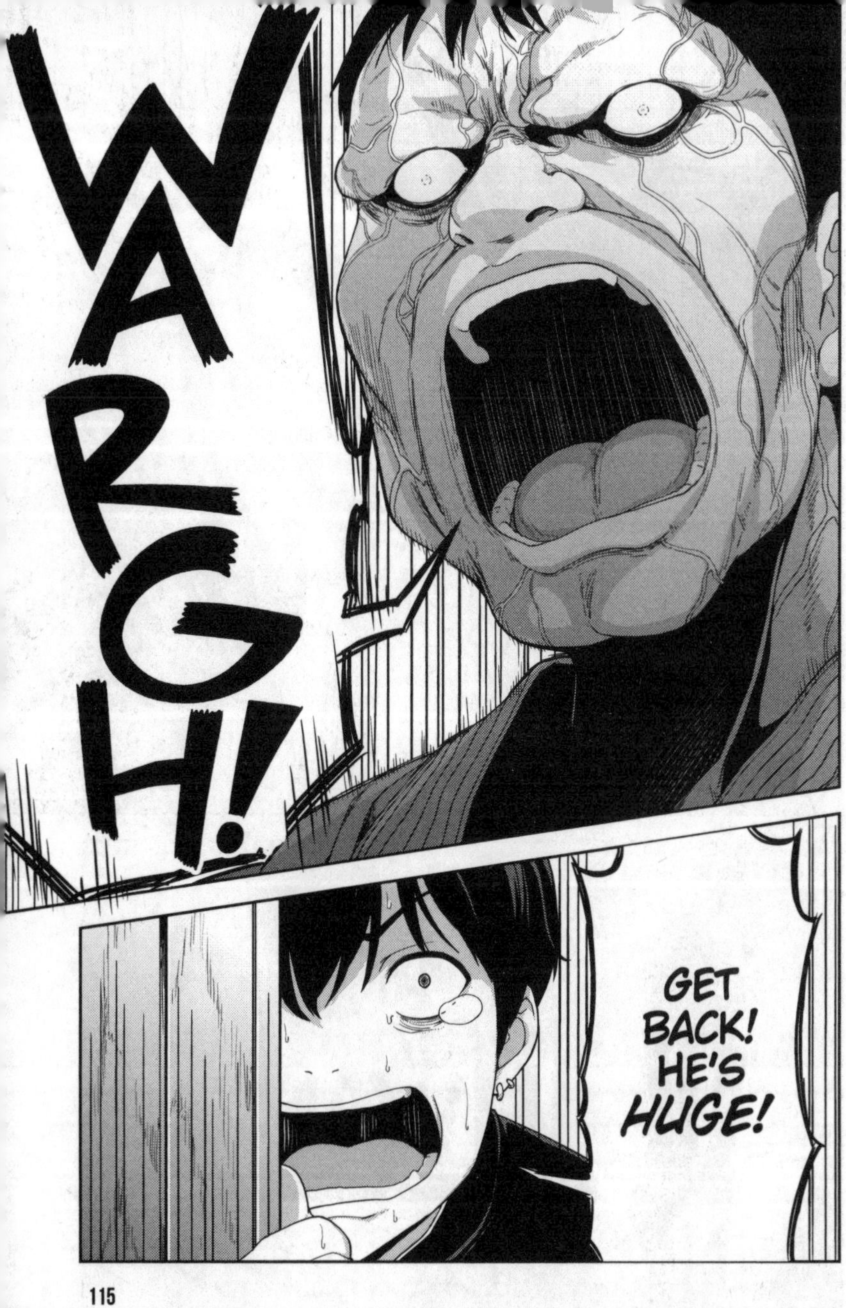
WARGH!
GET BACK! HE'S HUGE!

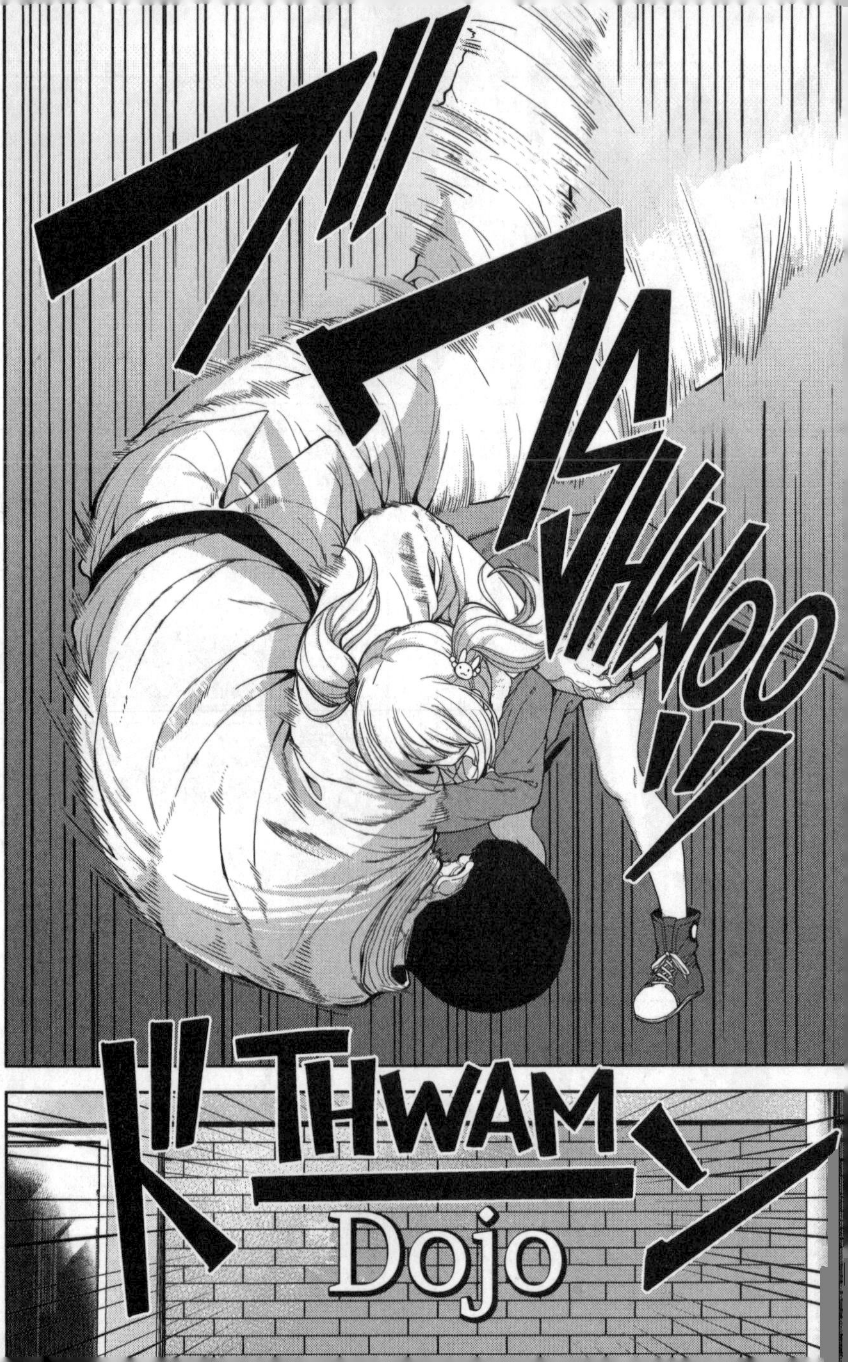
SHWOO!!!
THWAM
Dojo

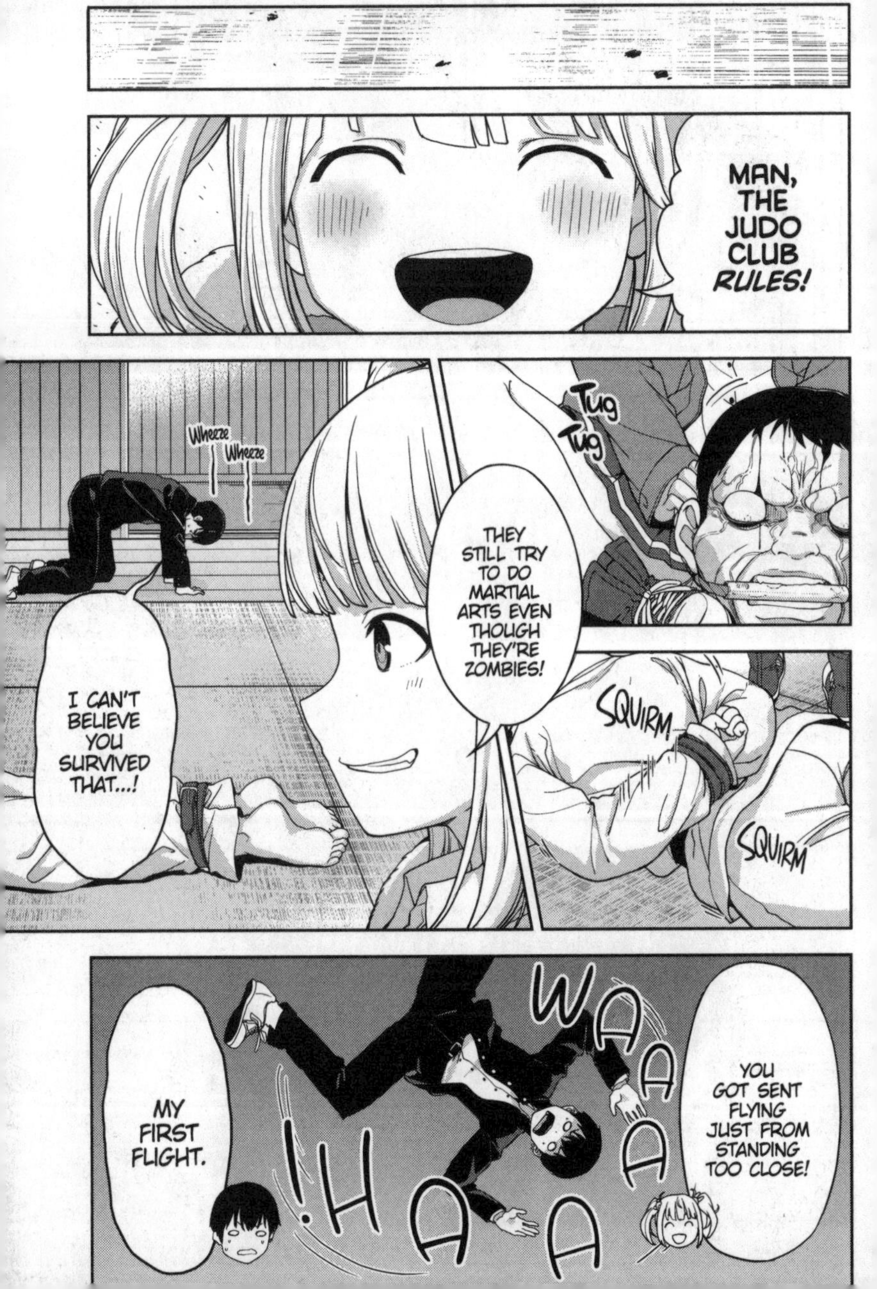
MAN, THE JUDO CLUB RULES!
Tug Tug
SQUIRM
SQUIRM
THEY STILL TRY TO DO MARTIAL ARTS EVEN THOUGH THEY'RE ZOMBIES!
Wheeze Wheeze
I CAN'T BELIEVE YOU SURVIVED THAT...!
YOU GOT SENT FLYING JUST FROM STANDING TOO CLOSE!
WAAAAAAAH!
MY FIRST FLIGHT.

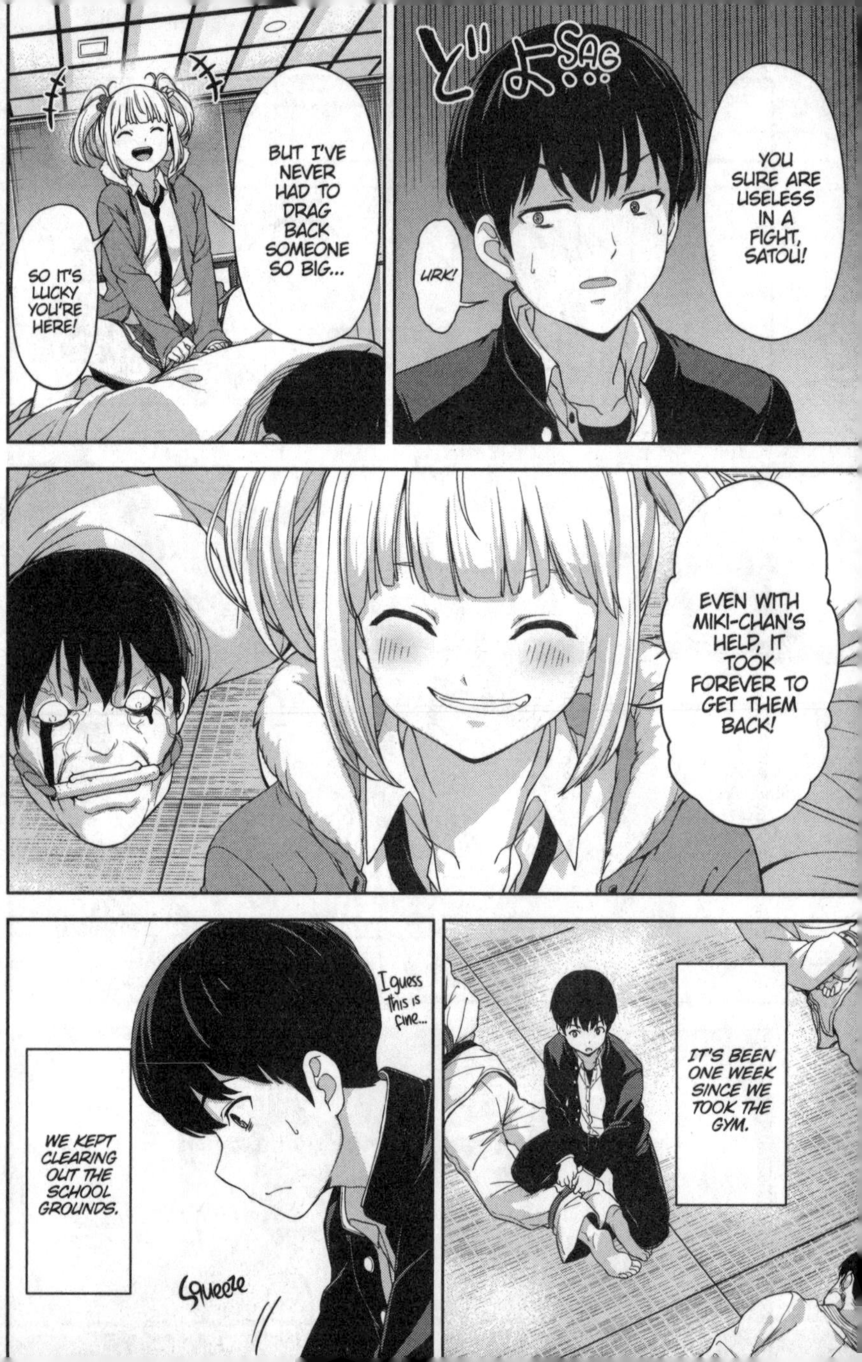
どよ SAG
YOU SURE ARE USELESS IN A FIGHT, SATOU!
URK!
BUT I'VE NEVER HAD TO DRAG BACK SOMEONE SO BIG...
SO IT'S LUCKY YOU'RE HERE!
EVEN WITH MIKI-CHAN'S HELP, IT TOOK FOREVER TO GET THEM BACK!
IT'S BEEN ONE WEEK SINCE WE TOOK THE GYM.
I guess this is fine...
WE KEPT CLEARING OUT THE SCHOOL GROUNDS.
Squeeze

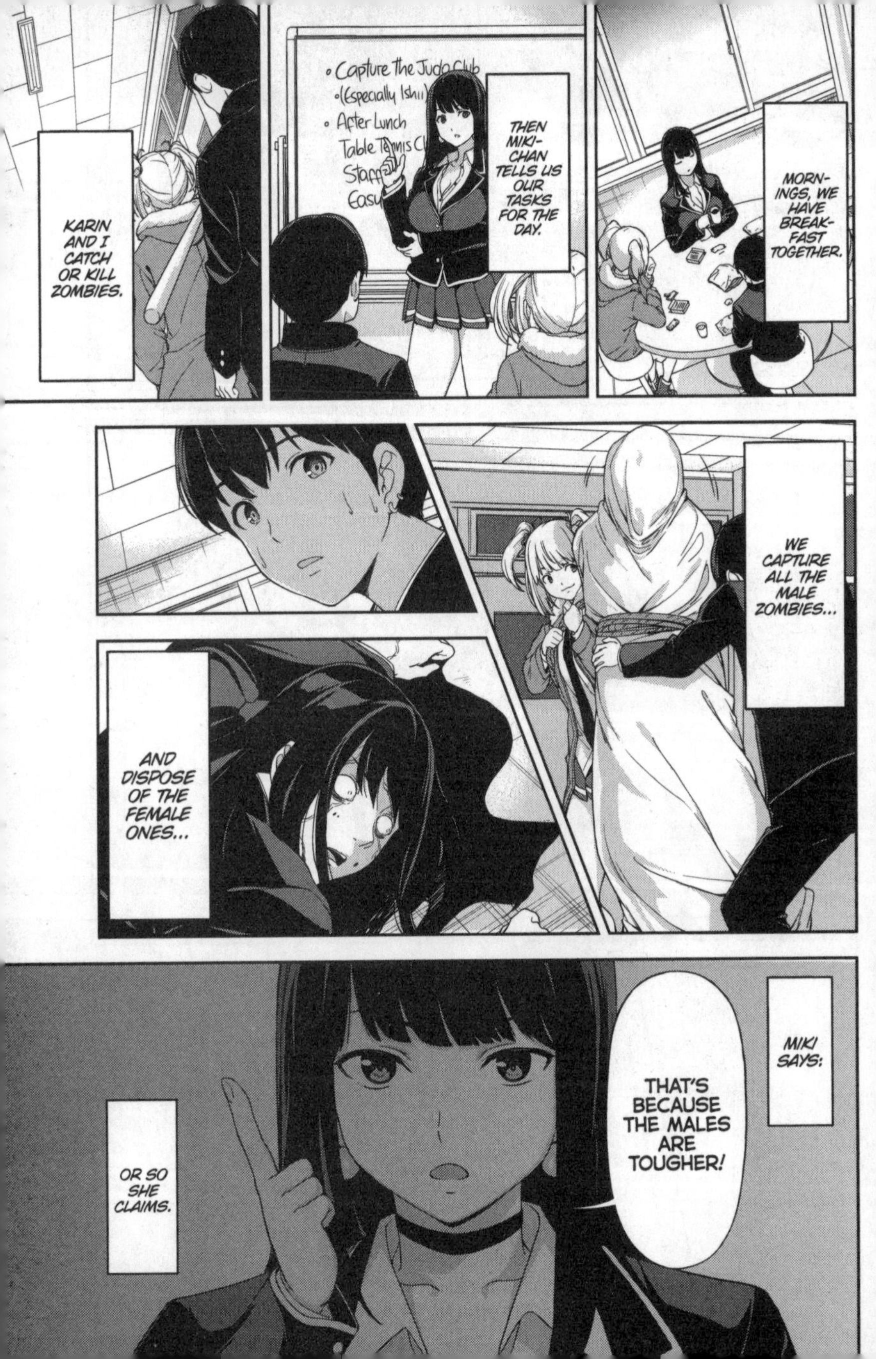
MORNINGS, WE HAVE BREAKFAST TOGETHER.
THEN MIKI-CHAN TELLS US OUR TASKS FOR THE DAY.
Capture the Judo Club
(Especially Ishii)
After Lunch
KARIN AND I CATCH OR KILL ZOMBIES.
WE CAPTURE ALL THE MALE ZOMBIES...
AND DISPOSE OF THE FEMALE ONES...
MIKI SAYS:
THAT'S BECAUSE THE MALES ARE TOUGHER!
OR SO SHE CLAIMS.

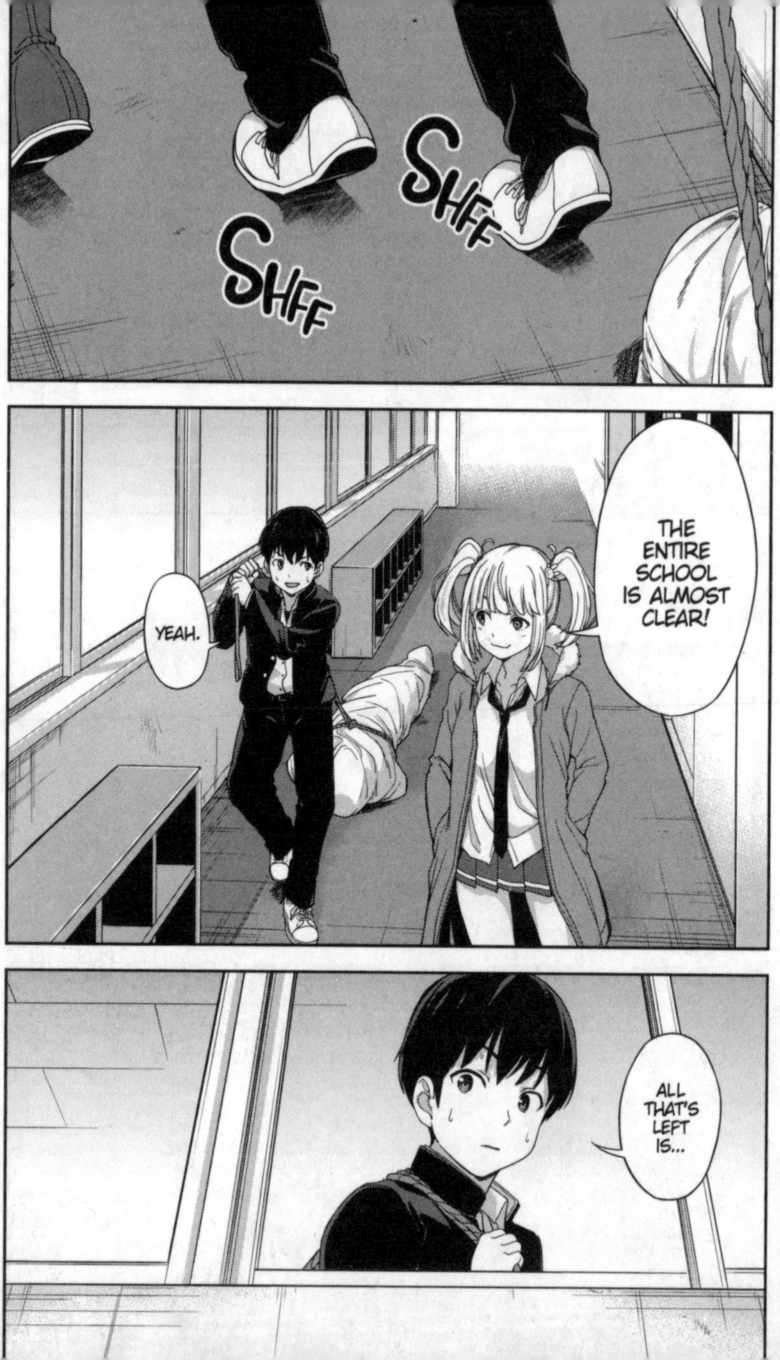
SHFF
SHFF
THE ENTIRE SCHOOL IS ALMOST CLEAR!
YEAH.
ALL THAT'S LEFT IS...

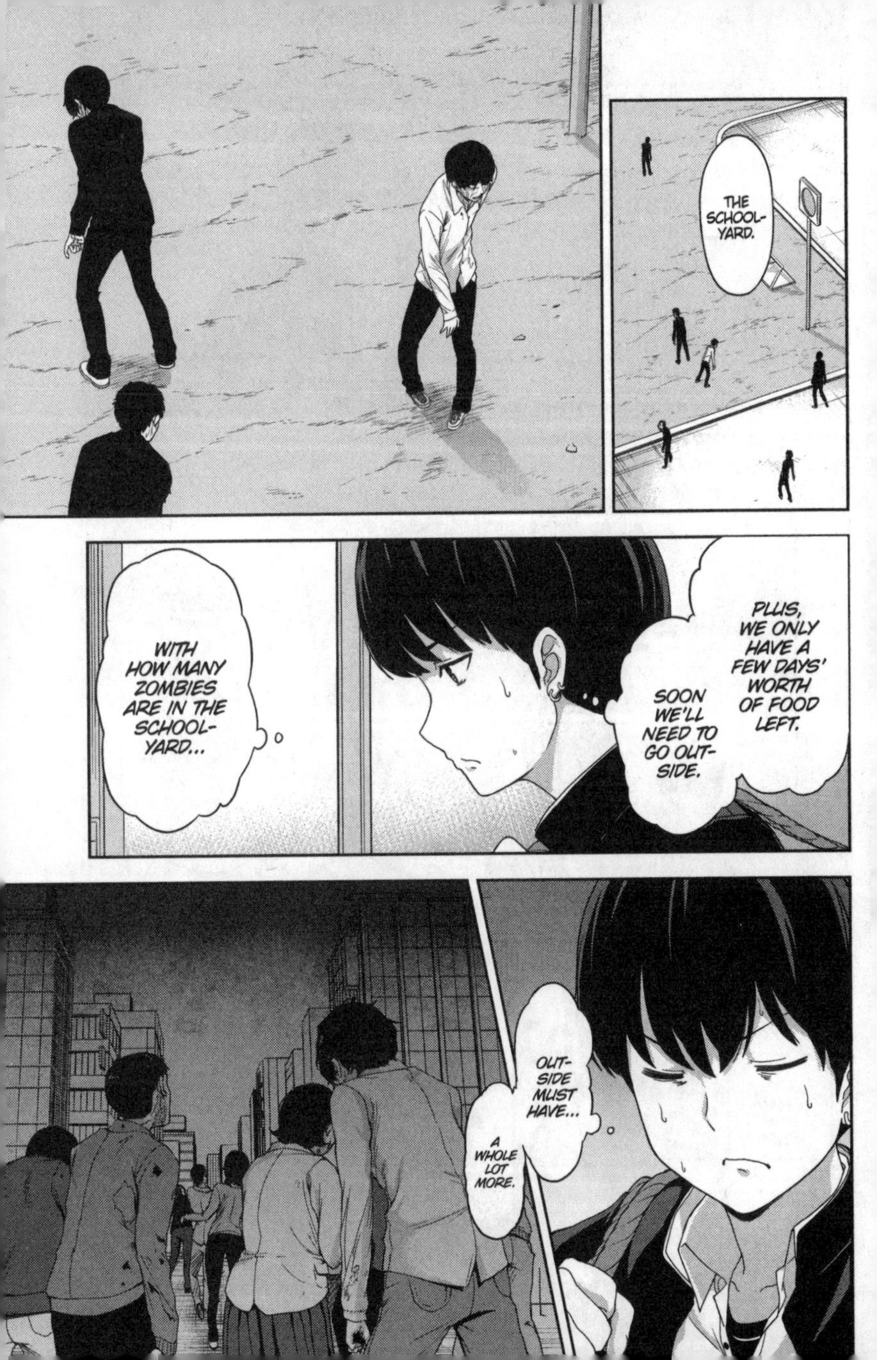
THE SCHOOLYARD.
PLUS, WE ONLY HAVE A FEW DAYS' WORTH OF FOOD LEFT.
SOON WE'LL NEED TO GO OUTSIDE.
WITH HOW MANY ZOMBIES ARE IN THE SCHOOLYARD...
OUTSIDE MUST HAVE...
A WHOLE LOT MORE.

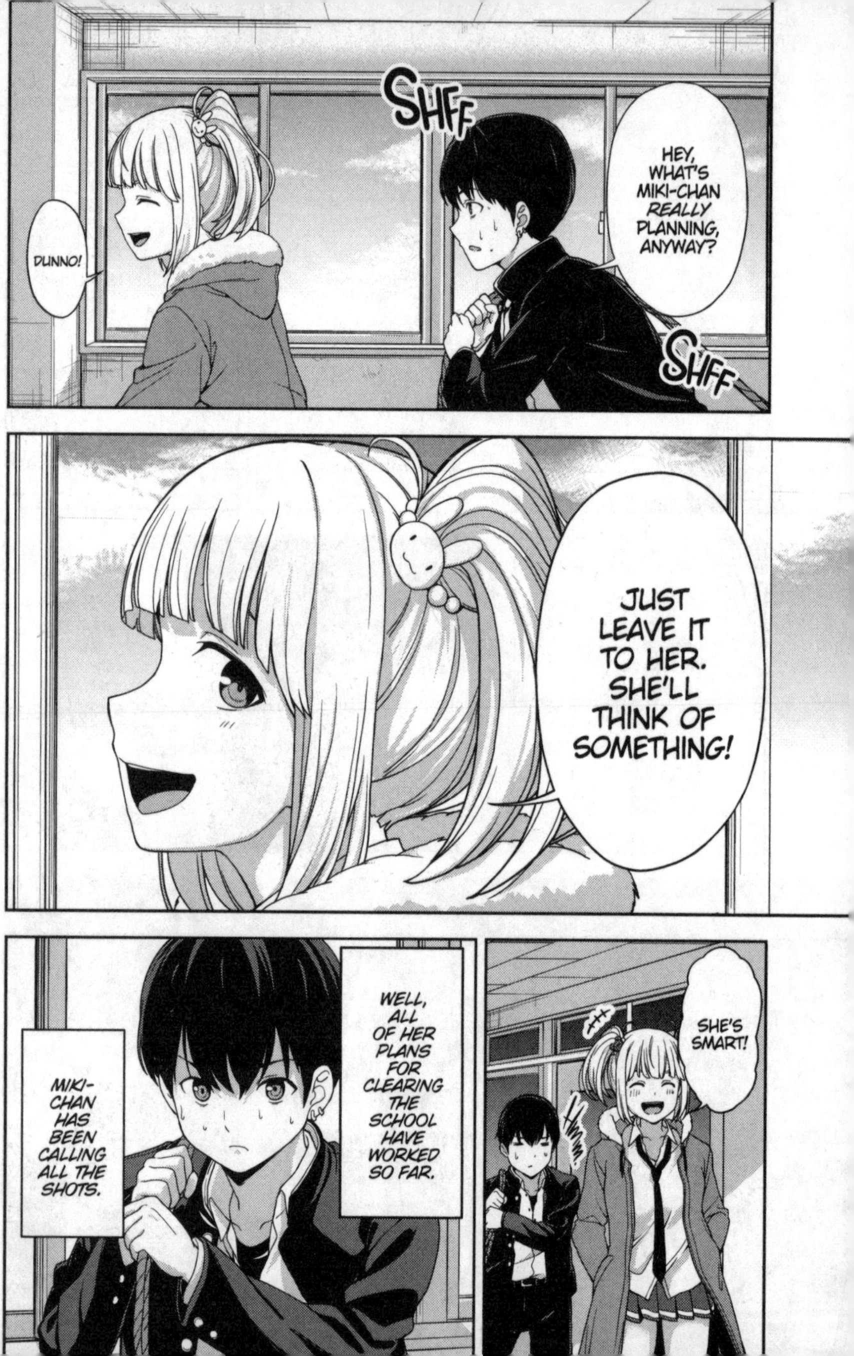

SHFF
HEY, WHAT'S MIKI-CHAN *REALLY* PLANNING, ANYWAY?
SHFF
DUNNO!
JUST LEAVE IT TO HER. SHE'LL THINK OF SOMETHING!
SHE'S SMART!
WELL, ALL OF HER PLANS FOR CLEARING THE SCHOOL HAVE WORKED SO FAR.
MIKI-CHAN HAS BEEN CALLING ALL THE SHOTS.

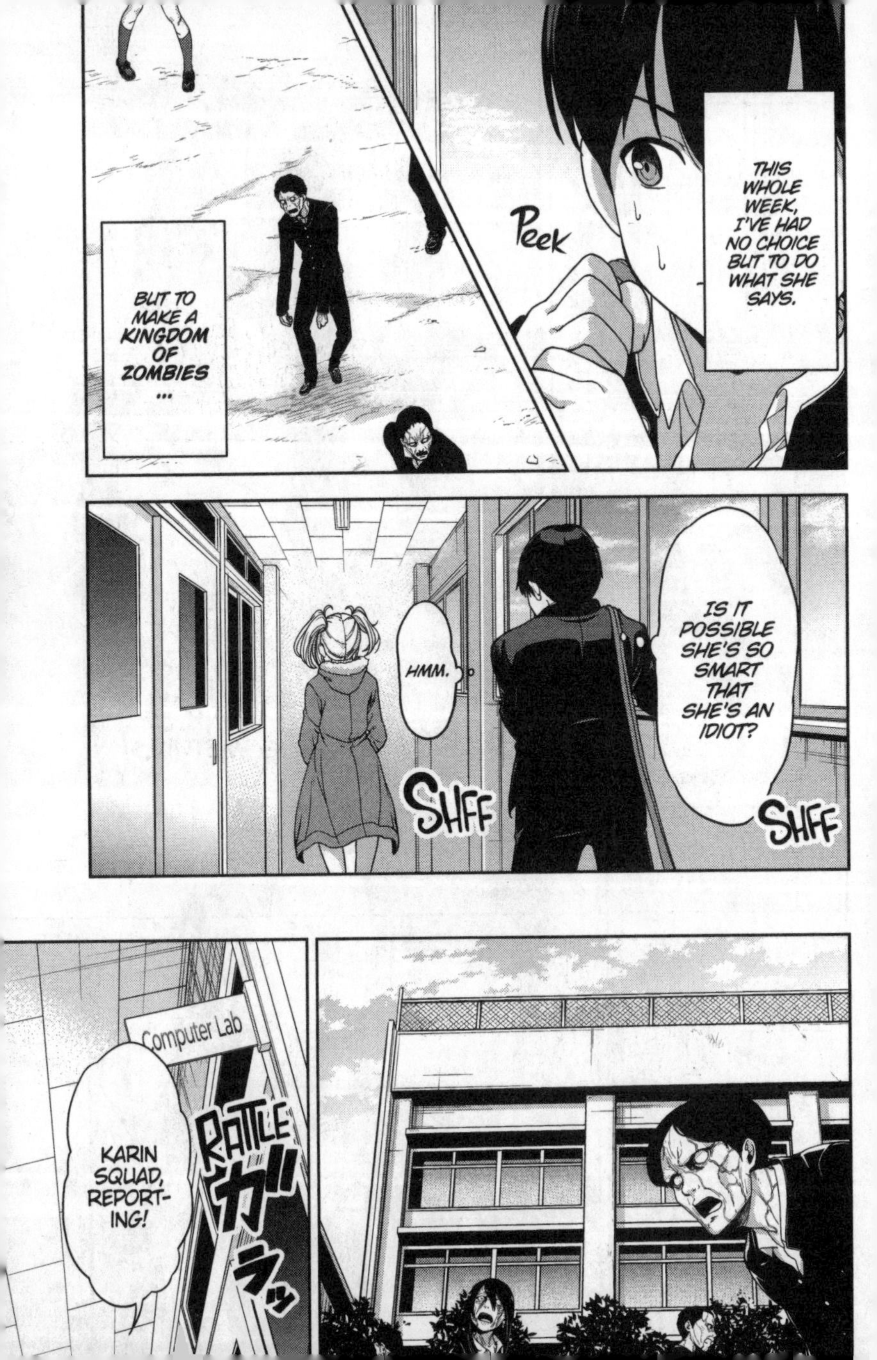
THIS WHOLE WEEK, I'VE HAD NO CHOICE BUT TO DO WHAT SHE SAYS.
Peek
BUT TO MAKE A KINGDOM OF ZOMBIES ...
IS IT POSSIBLE SHE'S SO SMART THAT SHE'S AN IDIOT?
HMM.
SHFF
SHFF
Computer Lab
RATTLE
ガラッ
KARIN SQUAD, REPORTING!

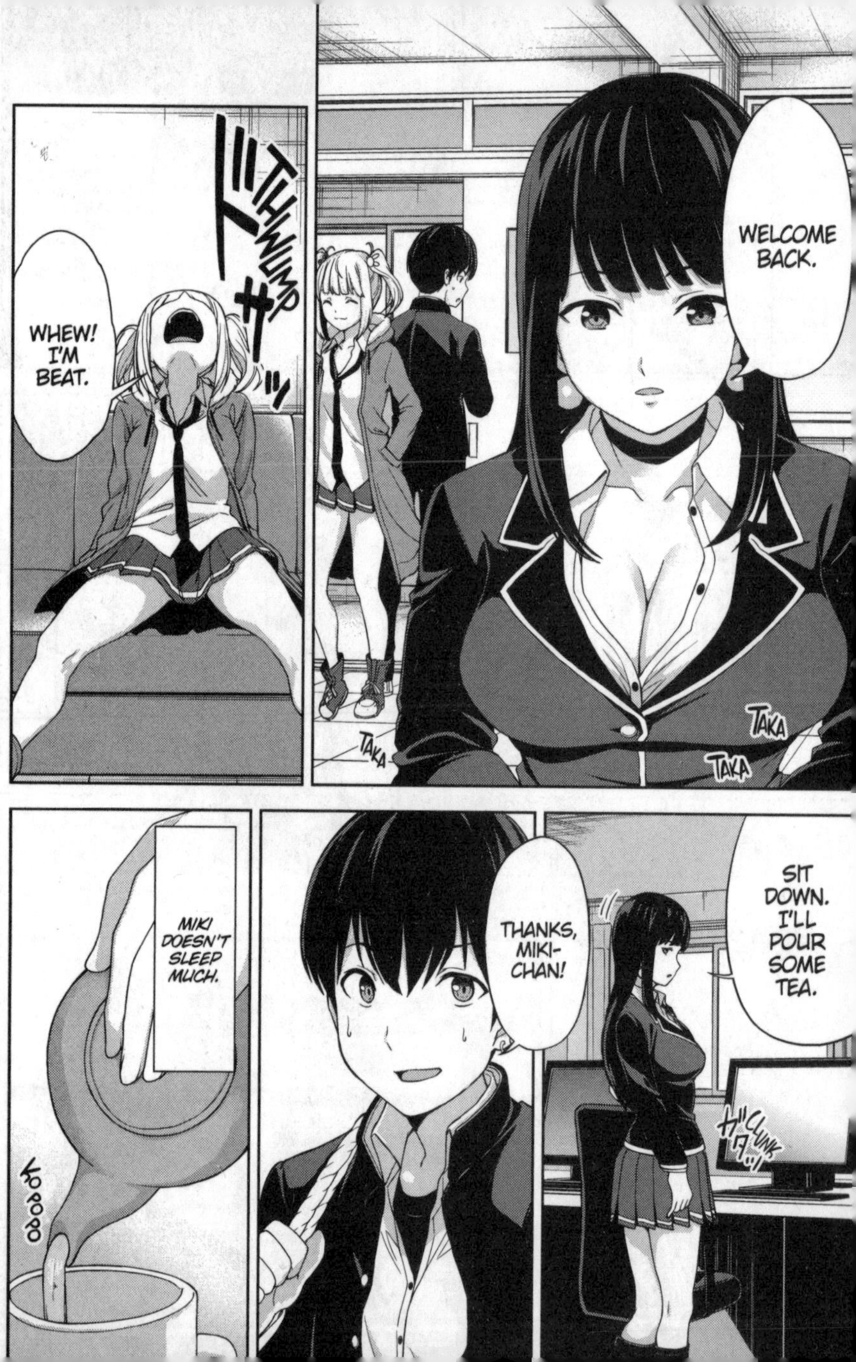
WELCOME BACK.
TAKA
TAKA
TAKA
THWUMP
WHEW! I'M BEAT.
SIT DOWN. I'LL POUR SOME TEA.
CLUNK
THANKS, MIKI-CHAN!
MIKI DOESN'T SLEEP MUCH.
KOPOPO

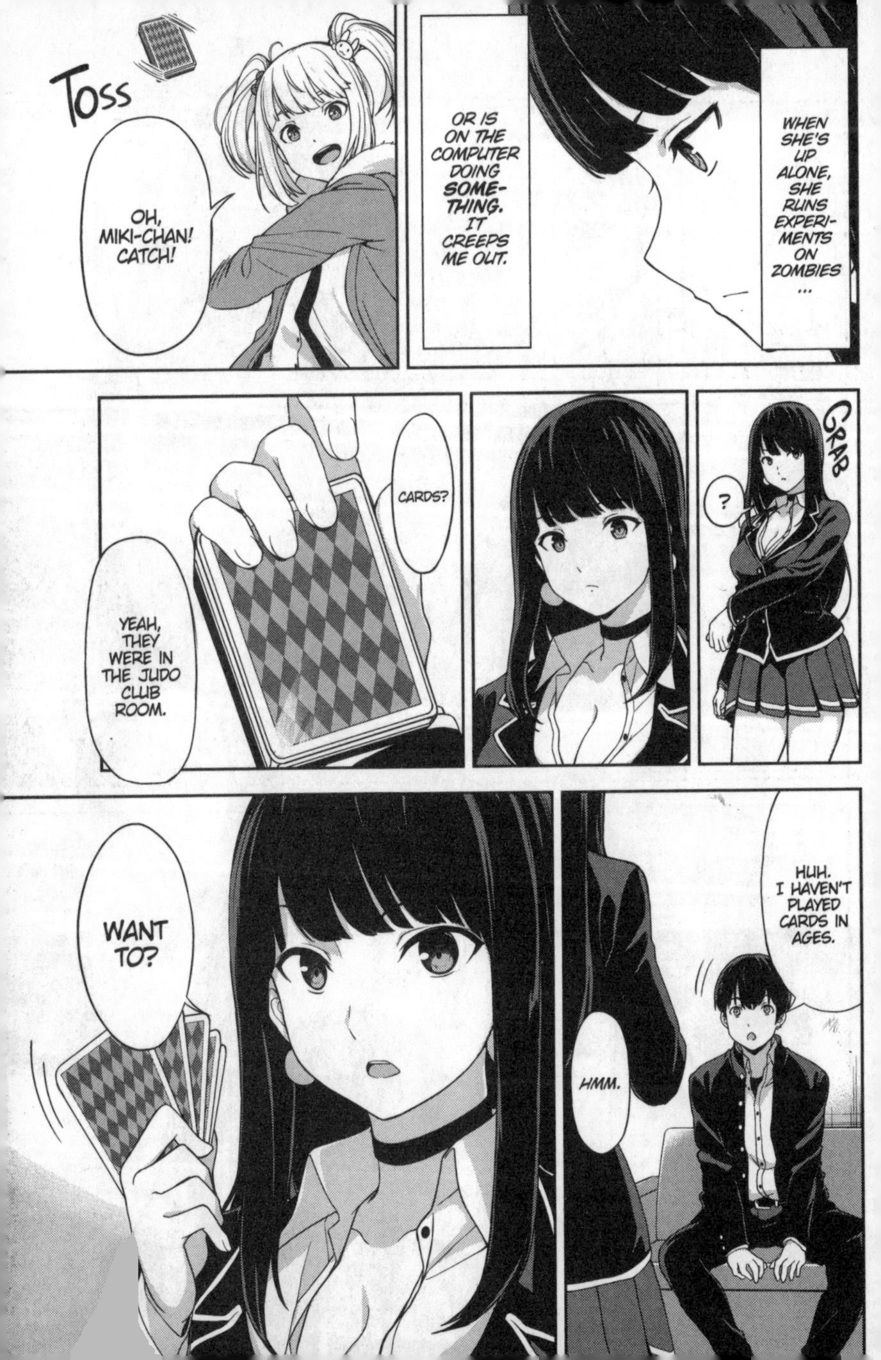
WHEN SHE'S UP ALONE, SHE RUNS EXPERIMENTS ON ZOMBIES ...
OR IS ON THE COMPUTER DOING SOMETHING. IT CREEPS ME OUT.
TOSS
OH, MIKI-CHAN! CATCH!
GRAB
?
CARDS?
YEAH, THEY WERE IN THE JUDO CLUB ROOM.
HUH. I HAVEN'T PLAYED CARDS IN AGES.
HMM.
WANT TO?

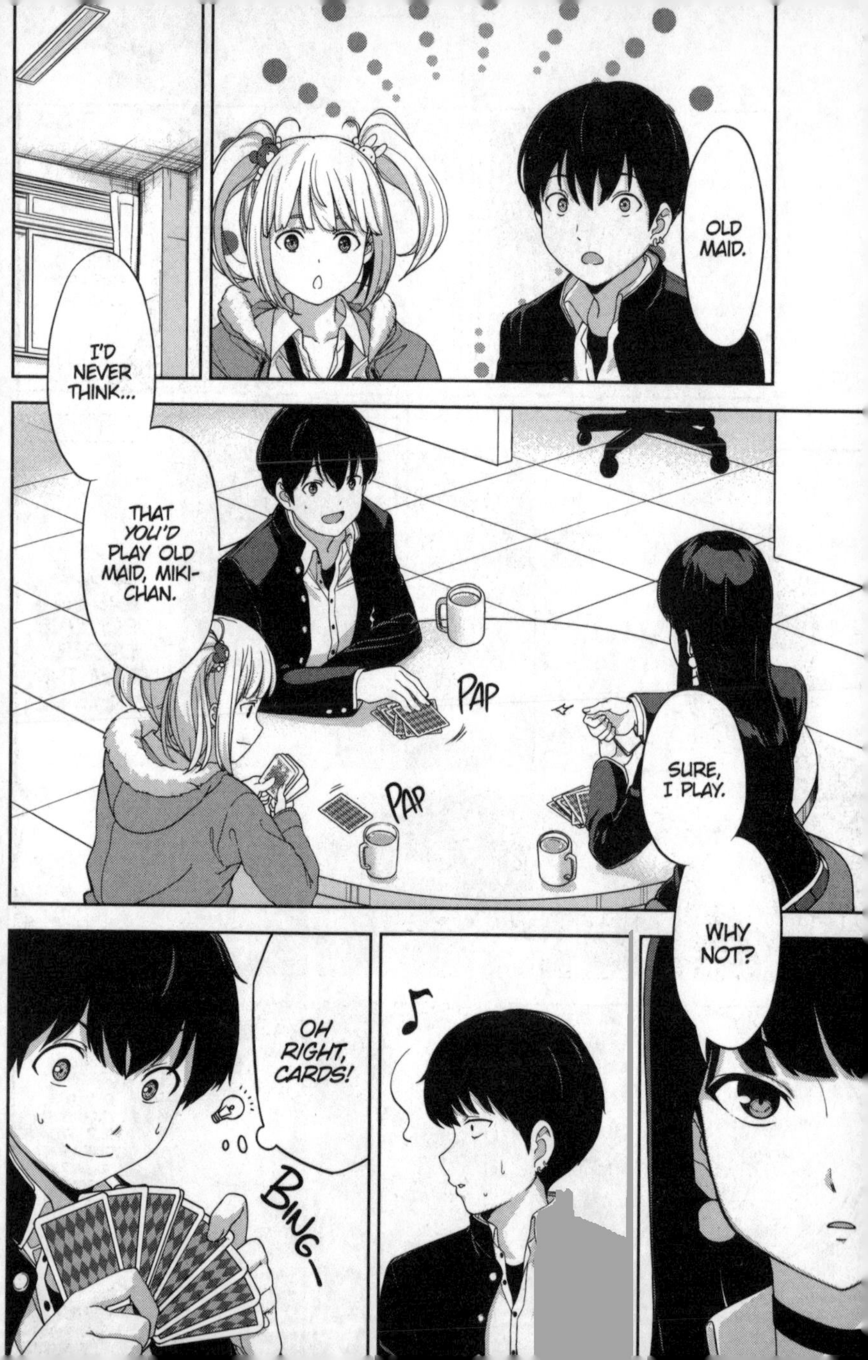
OLD MAID.
I'D NEVER THINK...
THAT YOU'D PLAY OLD MAID, MIKI-CHAN.
SURE, I PLAY.
PAP
PAP
WHY NOT?
OH RIGHT, CARDS!
BING

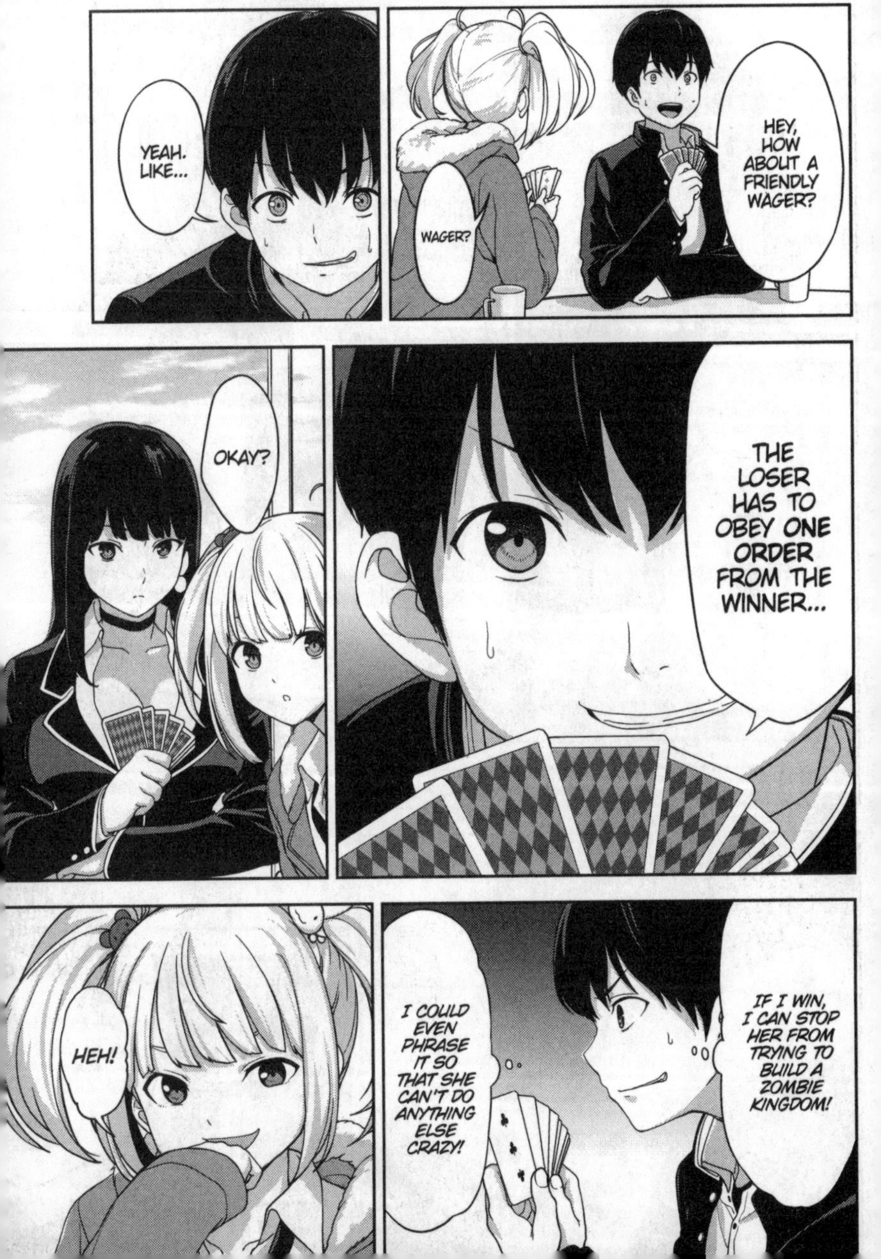
HEY, HOW ABOUT A FRIENDLY WAGER?
WAGER?
YEAH. LIKE...
THE LOSER HAS TO OBEY ONE ORDER FROM THE WINNER...
OKAY?
IF I WIN, I CAN STOP HER FROM TRYING TO BUILD A ZOMBIE KINGDOM!
I COULD EVEN PHRASE IT SO THAT SHE CAN'T DO ANYTHING ELSE CRAZY!
HEH!

GAH!!

THAT'S NOT WHAT I MEANT!

I DON'T MIND.

Ohhh my!

WHAT A PERV!

WHAT?! HUH?!

LET'S GET STARTED. I'M FIRST.

YOU DON'T?!

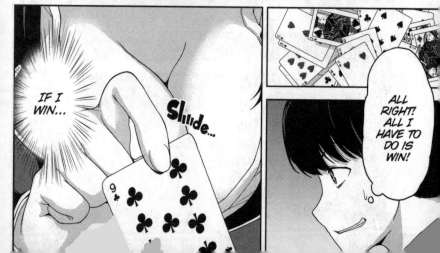

IF I WIN...

Sliide...

ALL RIGHT! ALL I HAVE TO DO IS WIN!

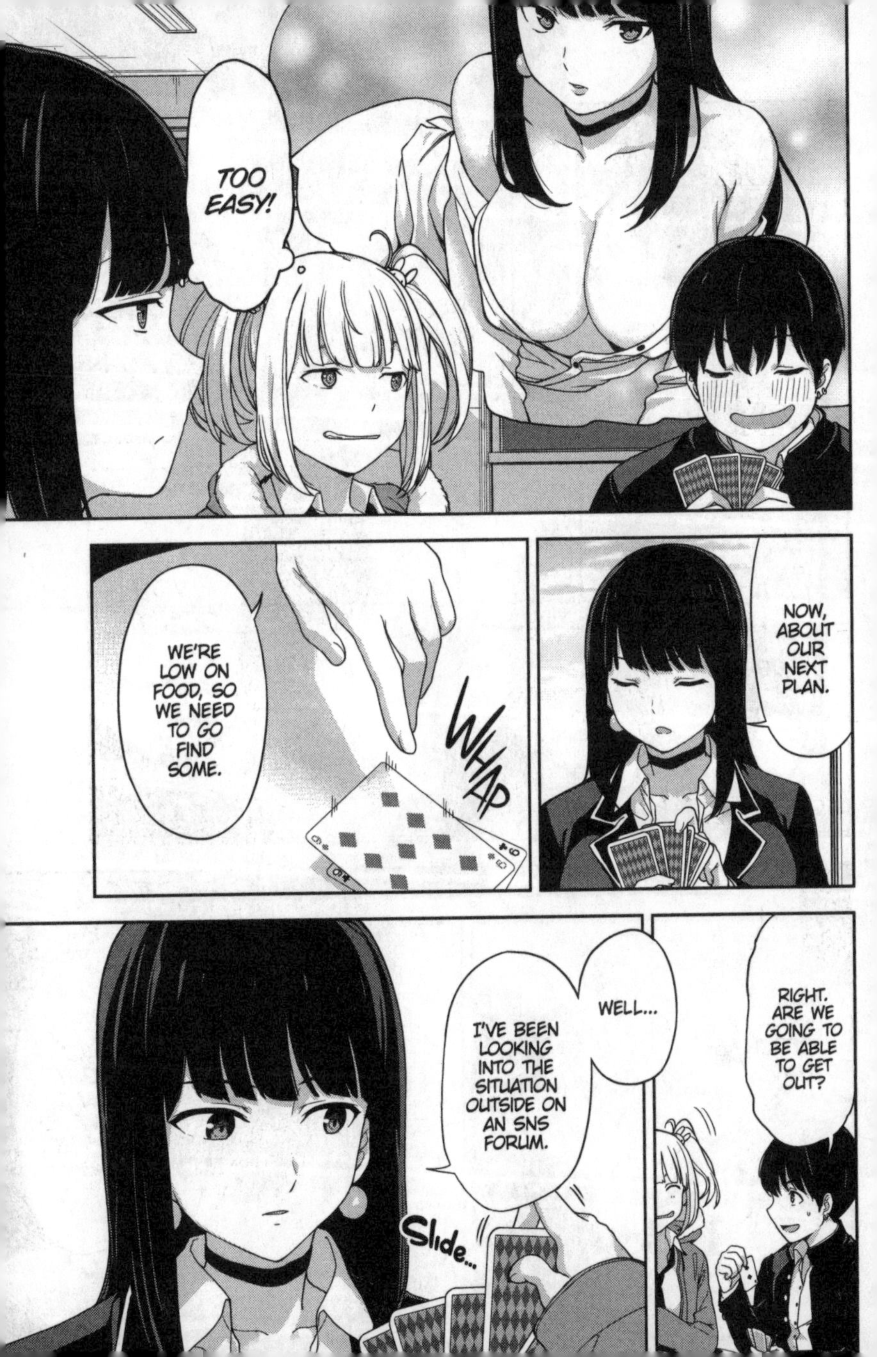

TOO EASY!
NOW, ABOUT OUR NEXT PLAN.
WE'RE LOW ON FOOD, SO WE NEED TO GO FIND SOME.
WHAP
RIGHT. ARE WE GOING TO BE ABLE TO GET OUT?
WELL...
I'VE BEEN LOOKING INTO THE SITUATION OUTSIDE ON AN SNS FORUM.
Slide...

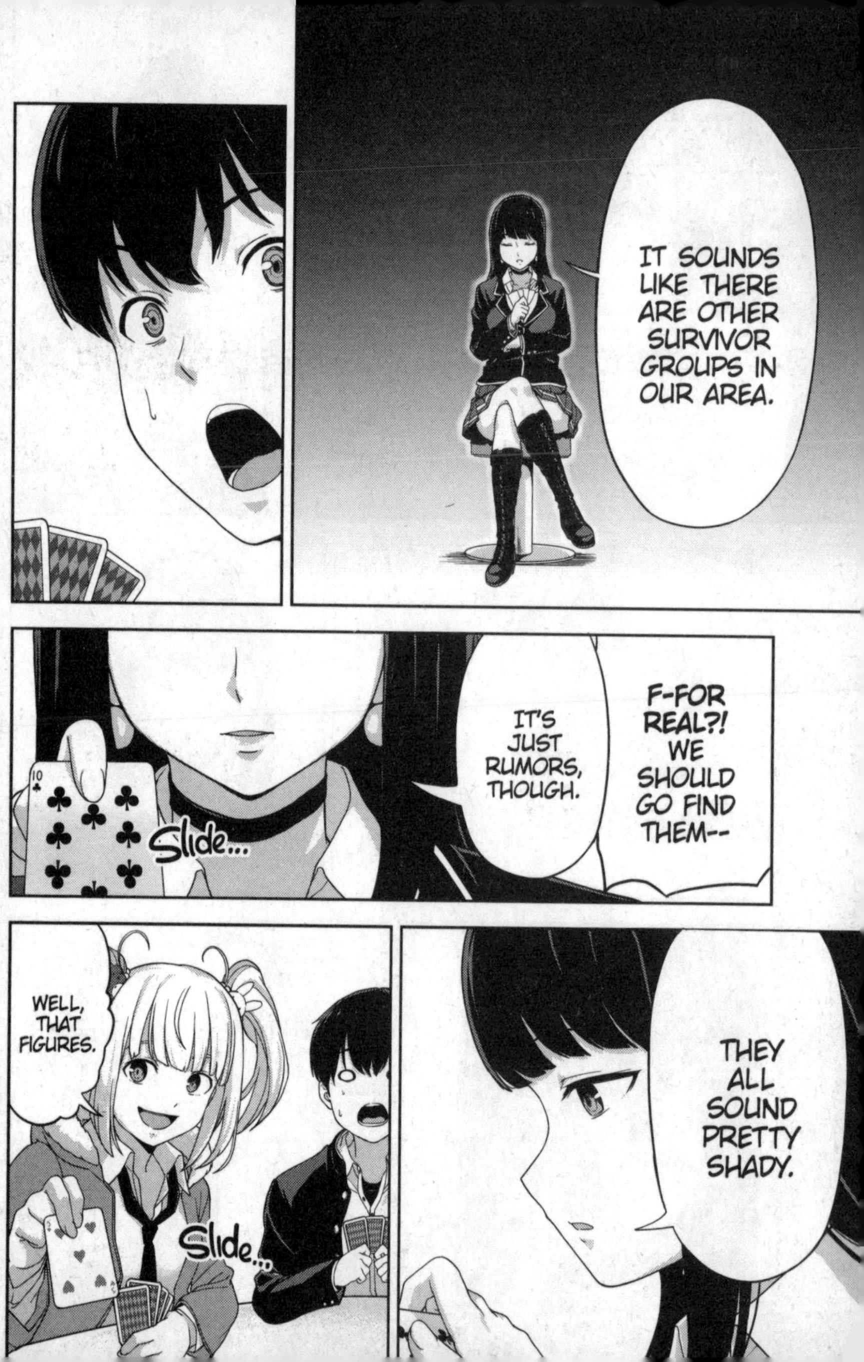
IT SOUNDS LIKE THERE ARE OTHER SURVIVOR GROUPS IN OUR AREA.
F-FOR REAL?! WE SHOULD GO FIND THEM--
IT'S JUST RUMORS, THOUGH.
Slide...
THEY ALL SOUND PRETTY SHADY.
WELL, THAT FIGURES.
Slide...

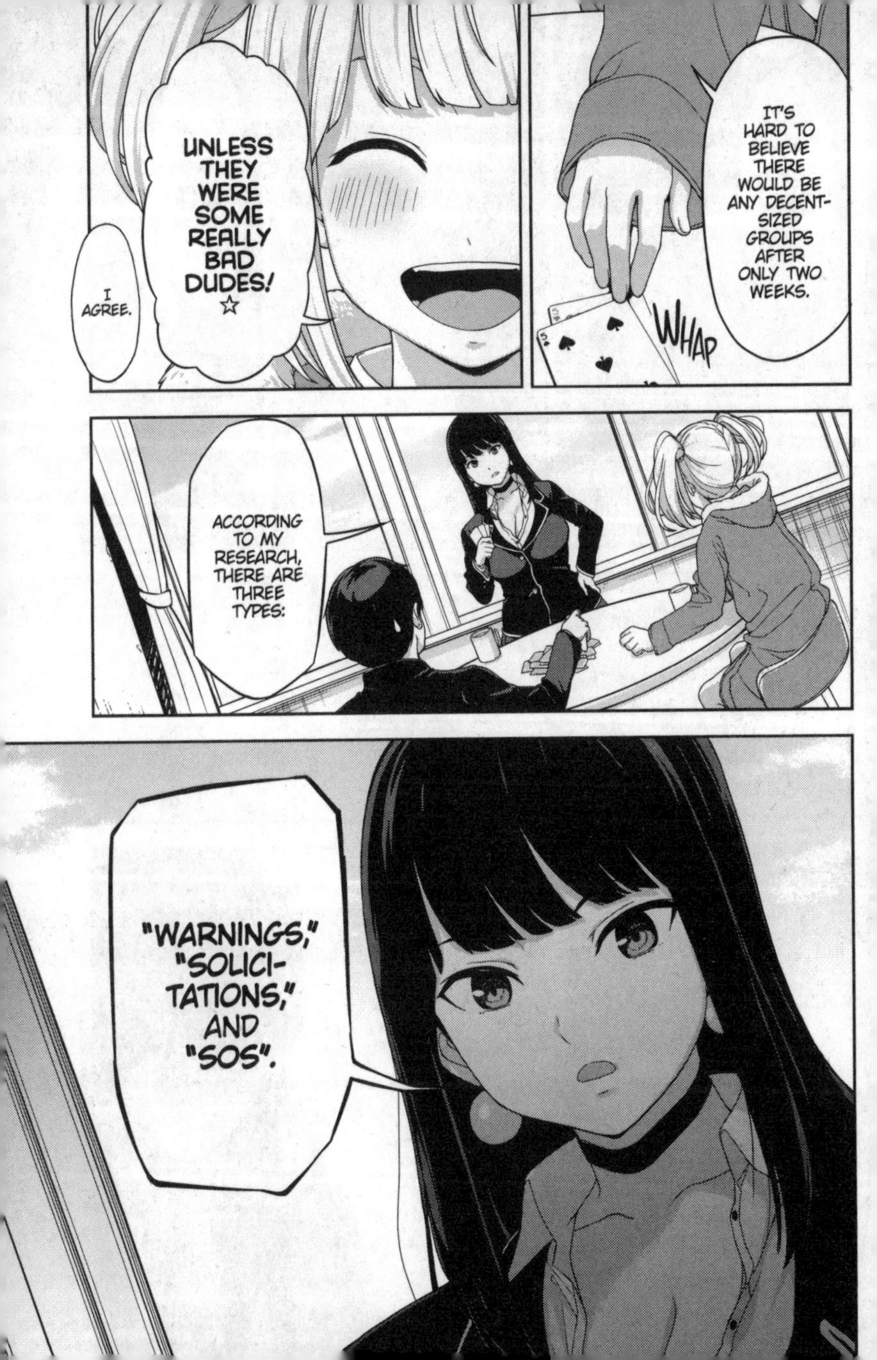
IT'S HARD TO BELIEVE THERE WOULD BE ANY DECENT-SIZED GROUPS AFTER ONLY TWO WEEKS.
WHAP
UNLESS THEY WERE SOME REALLY BAD DUDES! ☆
I AGREE.
ACCORDING TO MY RESEARCH, THERE ARE THREE TYPES:
"WARNINGS," "SOLICITATIONS," AND "SOS".

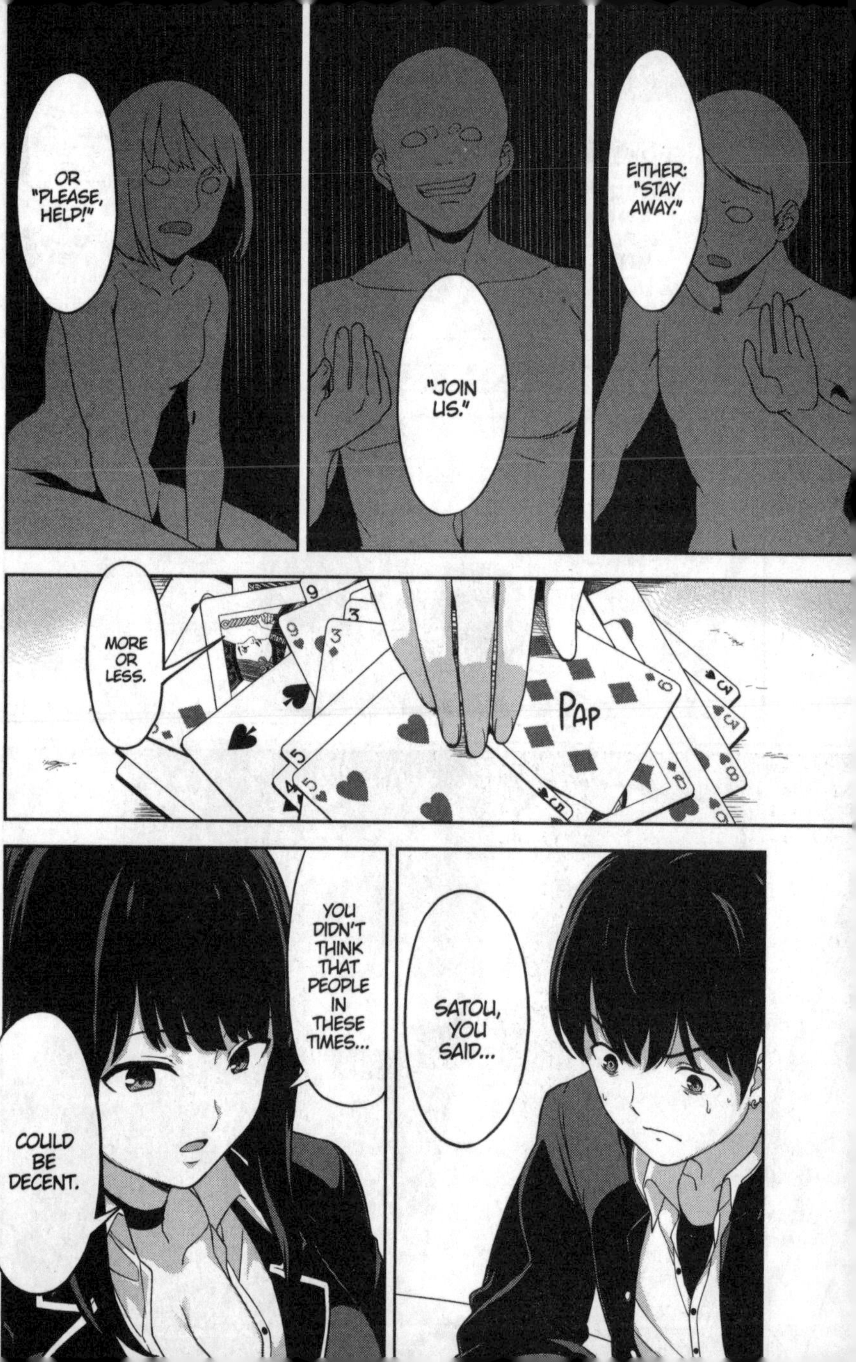
EITHER: "STAY AWAY."
"JOIN US."
OR "PLEASE, HELP!"
MORE OR LESS.
PAP
SATOU, YOU SAID...
YOU DIDN'T THINK THAT PEOPLE IN THESE TIMES...
COULD BE DECENT.

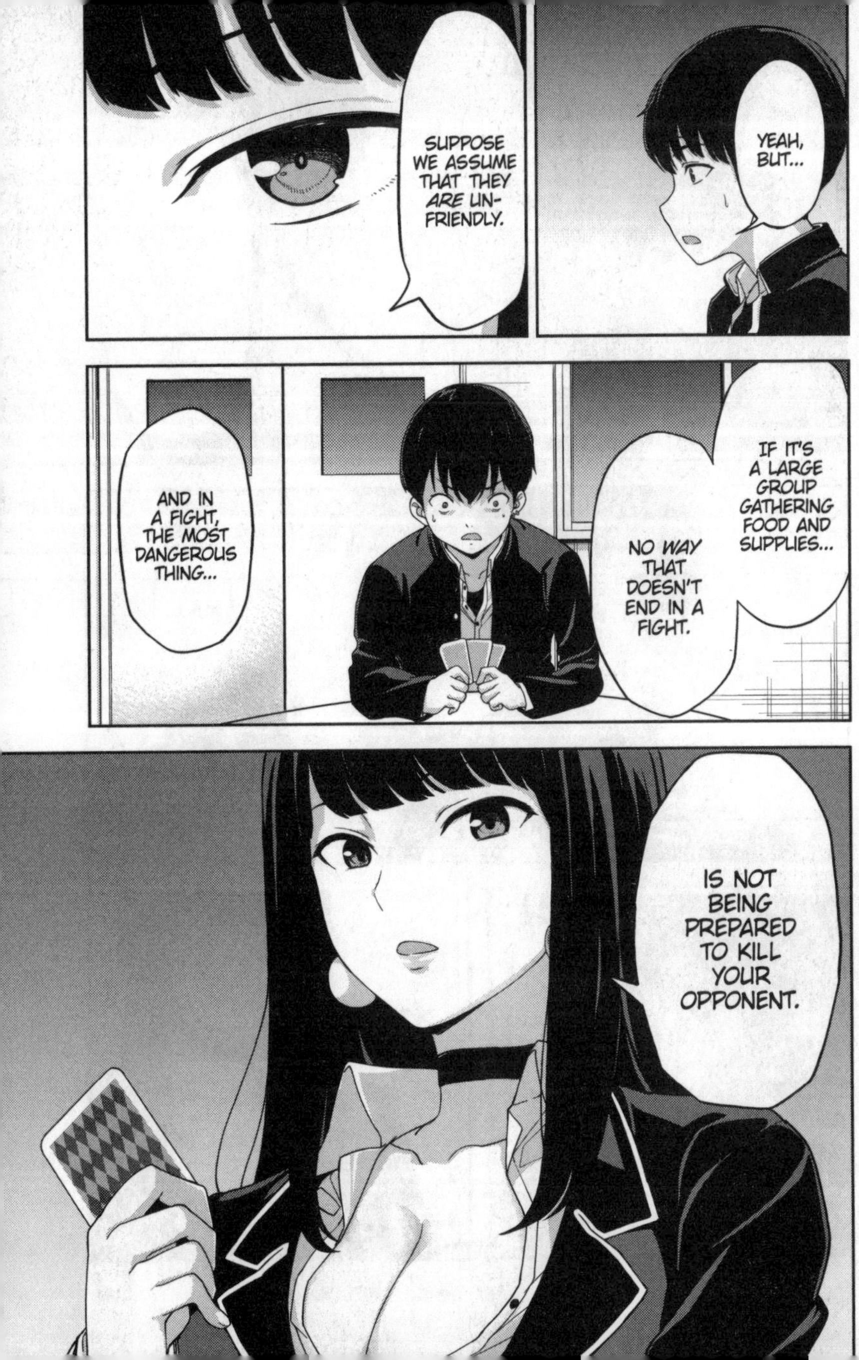
YEAH, BUT...
SUPPOSE WE ASSUME THAT THEY *ARE* UN-FRIENDLY.
IF IT'S A LARGE GROUP GATHERING FOOD AND SUPPLIES...
NO *WAY* THAT DOESN'T END IN A FIGHT.
AND IN A FIGHT, THE MOST DANGEROUS THING...
IS NOT BEING PREPARED TO KILL YOUR OPPONENT.

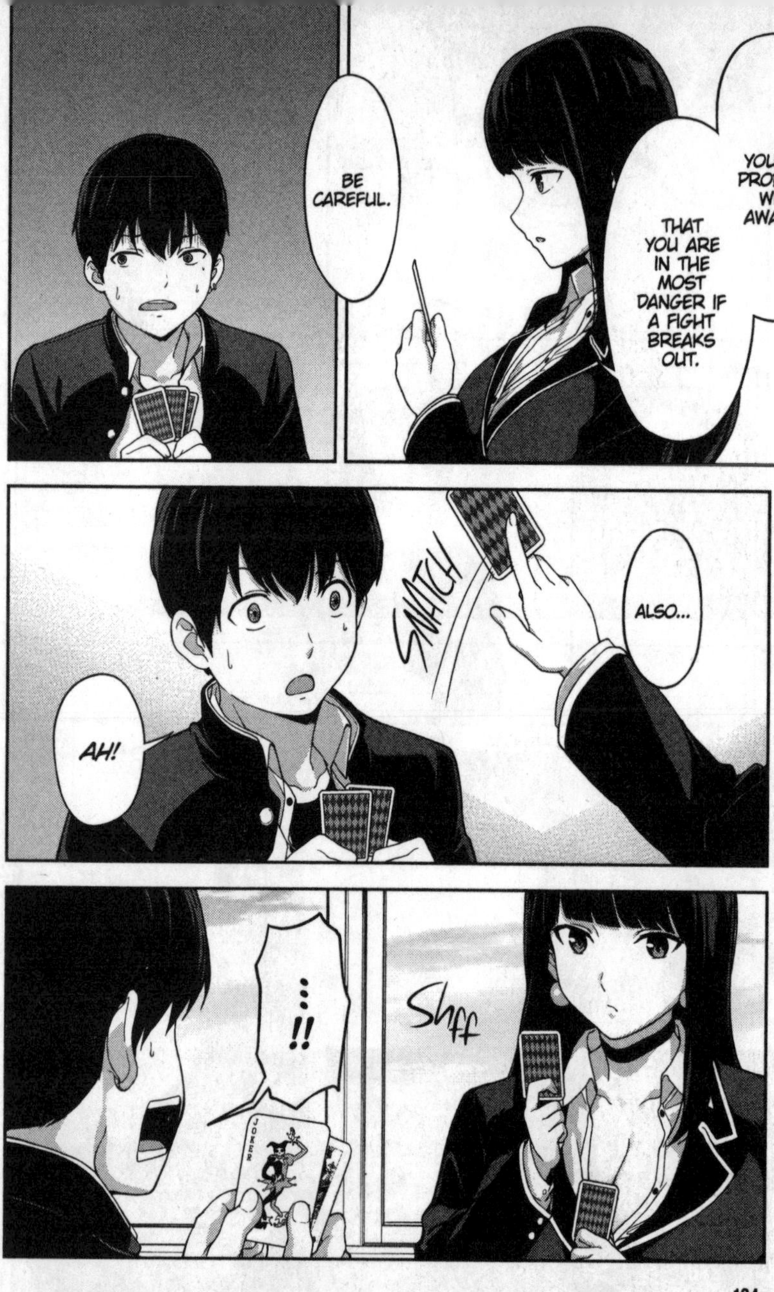
YOU ARE PROBABLY WELL AWARE...
THAT YOU ARE IN THE MOST DANGER IF A FIGHT BREAKS OUT.
BE CAREFUL.
ALSO...
SNATCH
AH!
Shff
...!!
JOKER

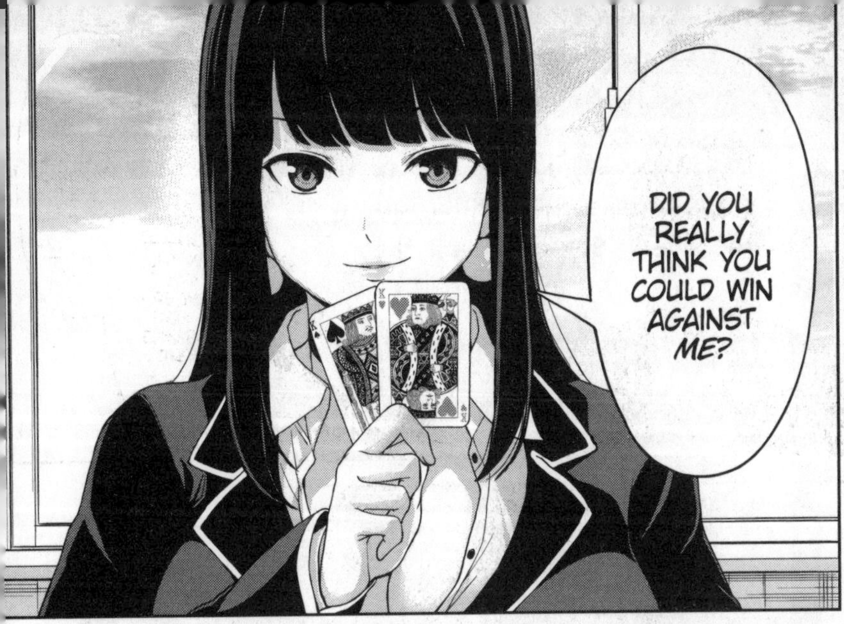
DID YOU REALLY THINK YOU COULD WIN AGAINST ME?

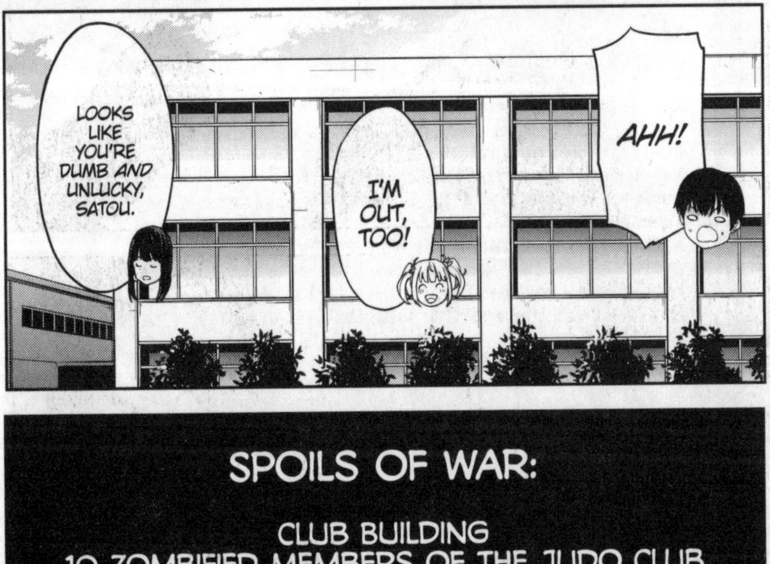
AHH!
I'M OUT, TOO!
LOOKS LIKE YOU'RE DUMB AND UNLUCKY, SATOU.

SPOILS OF WAR:

CLUB BUILDING
10 ZOMBIFIED MEMBERS OF THE JUDO CLUB
INFO ON ENEMY GROUPS?

THE 4TH DAY END

A Note Regarding Infrastructure
Recorder: Sekigahara Miki

10/1↵
10/4↵
Electricity, gas, and water infrastructure
has been cut off in places.

It is unknown when or if more areas
will be cut off.

The school has power and running water,
but I'm worried the water is contaminated.
For now, it would be best to continue
drinking bottled water for as long as we can.
I am currently thinking of how to deal
with electricity and radio.

10/9↵
Regarding electricity and radio:
It is possible that people who work within
the facilities are still alive, but it is
equally likely that the facilities are running
on their own automated processes.
Worst case scenario, the zombified former
employees there could be working the systems
themselves...
When I think of the experiments I've
performed on the zombies I've been able
to capture, performing specific tasks
isn't out of the realm of possibility.

There may be a possibility to seize control
of these sooner rather than later.

THE 5TH DAY SIGNAL FIRE

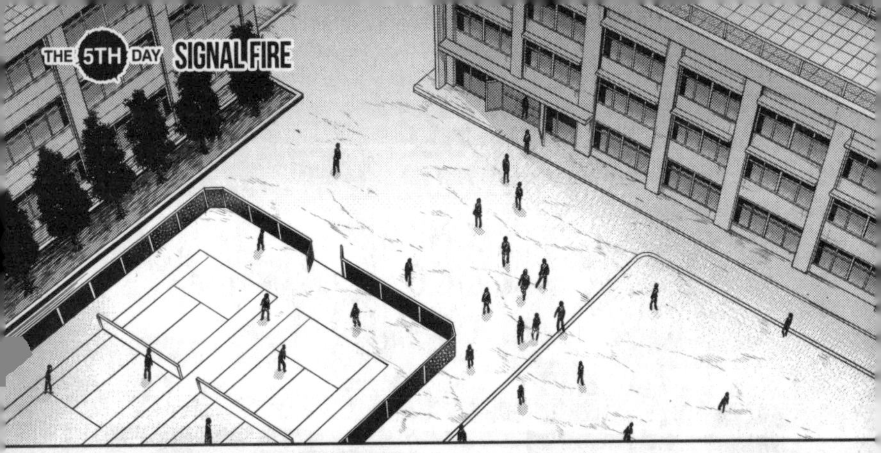

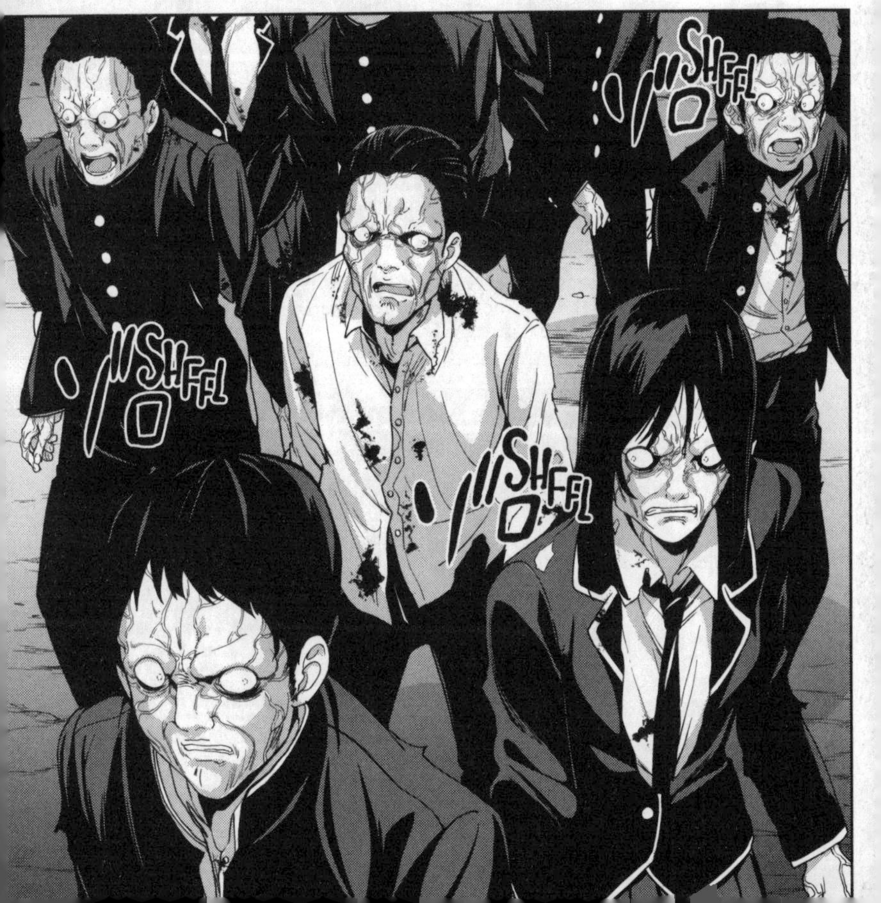
SHFFL
SHFFL
SHFFL

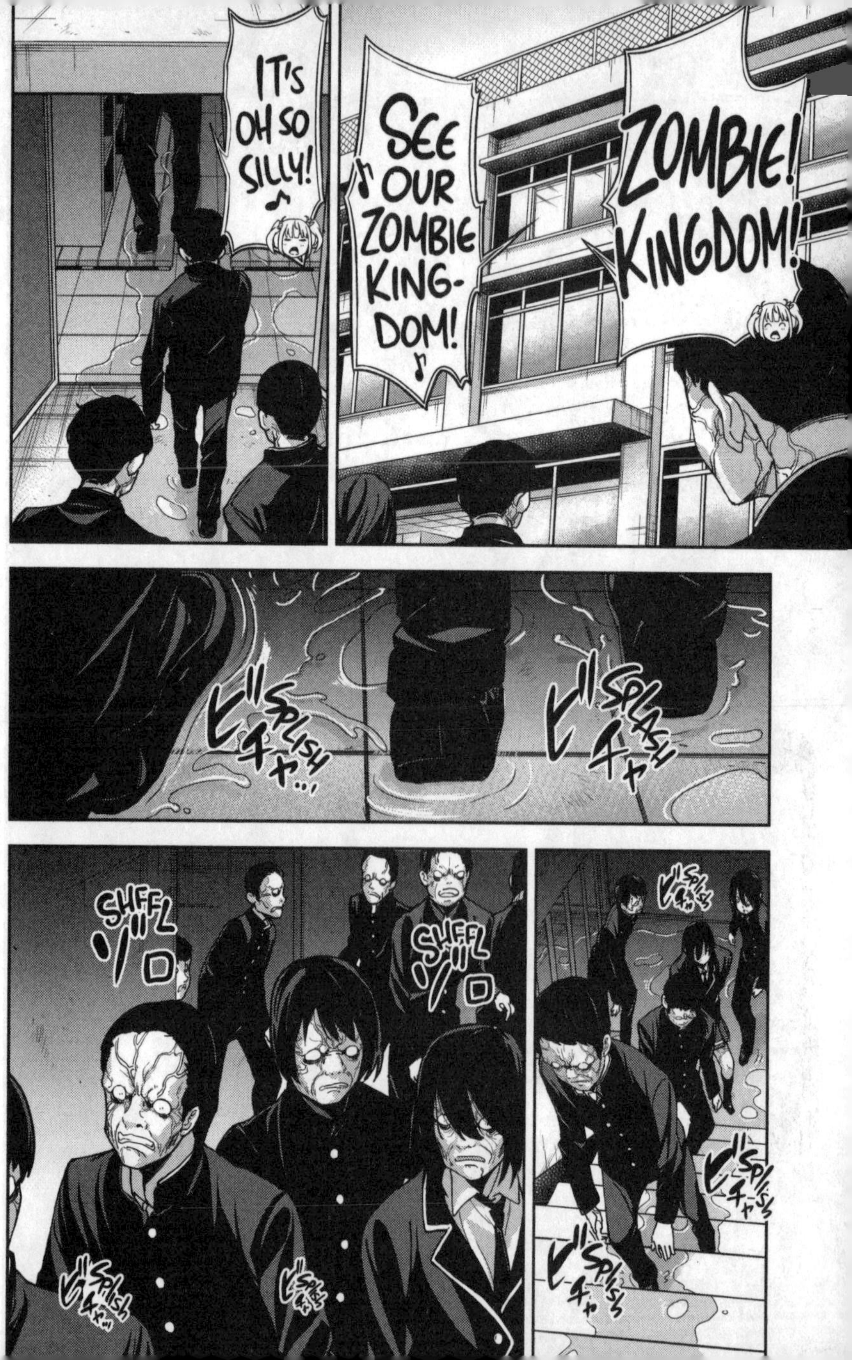
ZOMBIE! KINGDOM!
SEE OUR ZOMBIE KING-DOM!
IT'S OH SO SILLY!
SPLASH
SPLISH
SPLISH
SPLISH
SPLISH
SHFFL
SHFFL
SPLISH
SPLISH

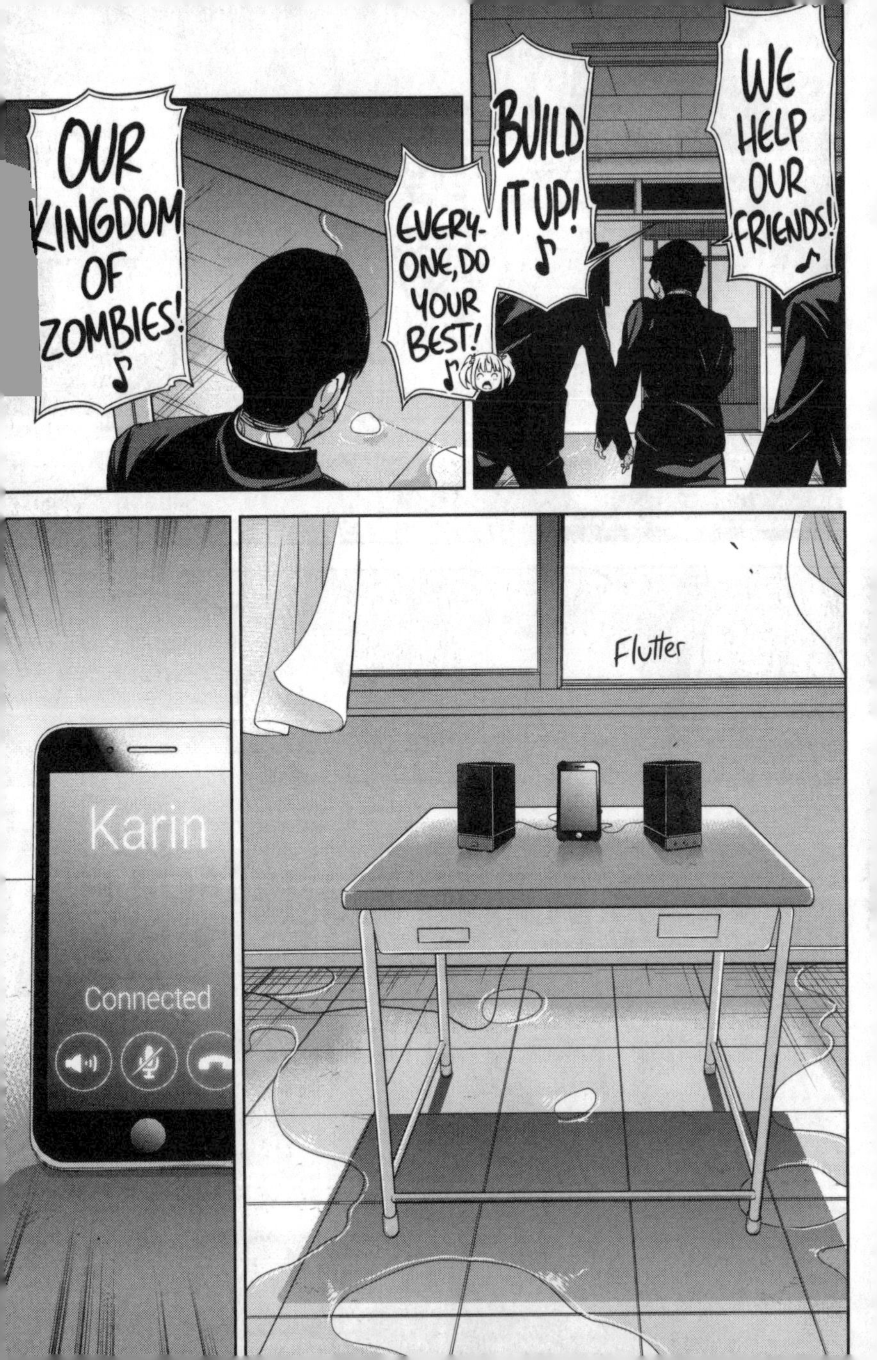
WE HELP OUR FRIENDS! ♪
BUILD IT UP! ♪
EVERY-ONE, DO YOUR BEST! ♪
OUR KINGDOM OF ZOMBIES! ♪
Flutter
Karin
Connected

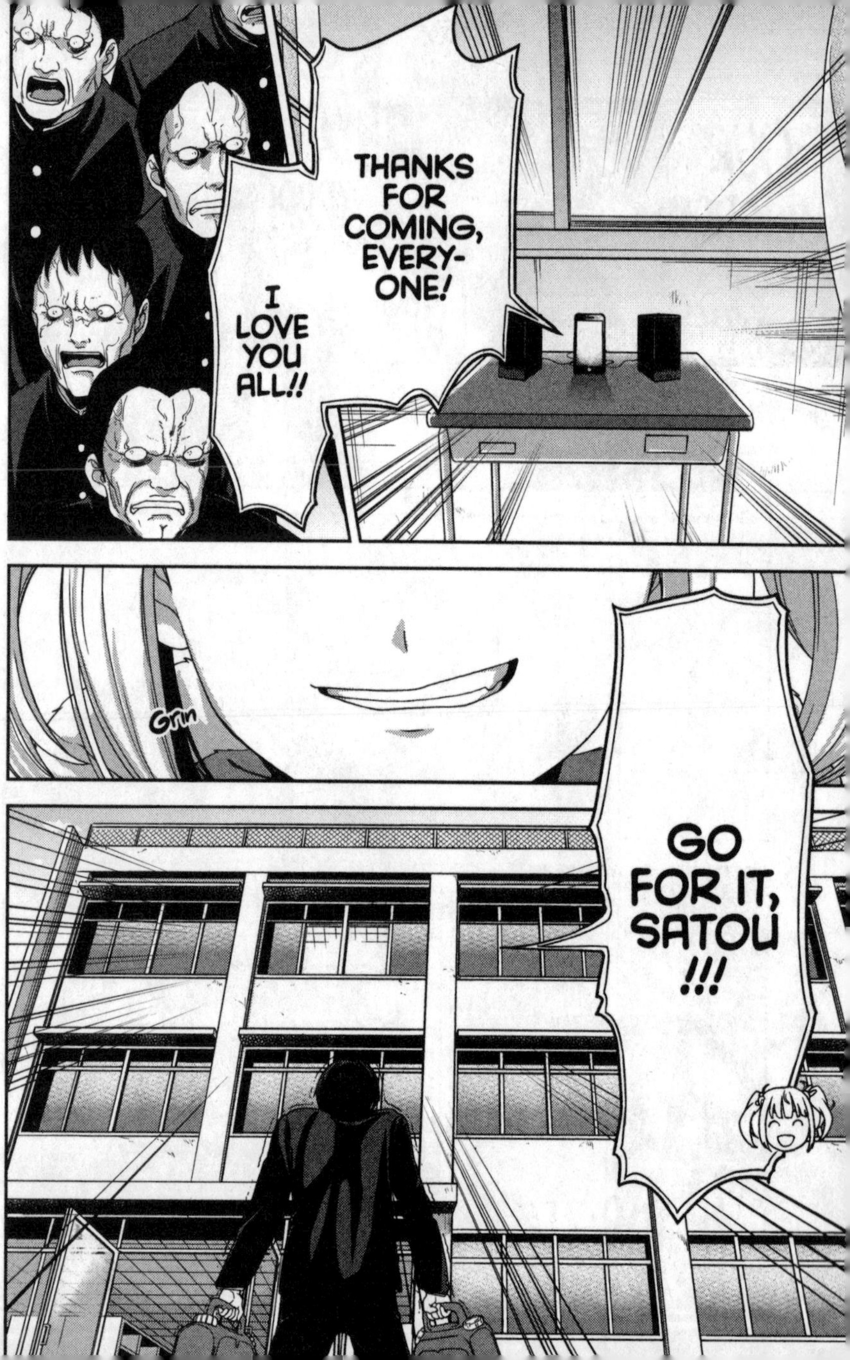
THANKS FOR COMING, EVERY-ONE!
I LOVE YOU ALL!!
Grin
GO FOR IT, SATOU!!!

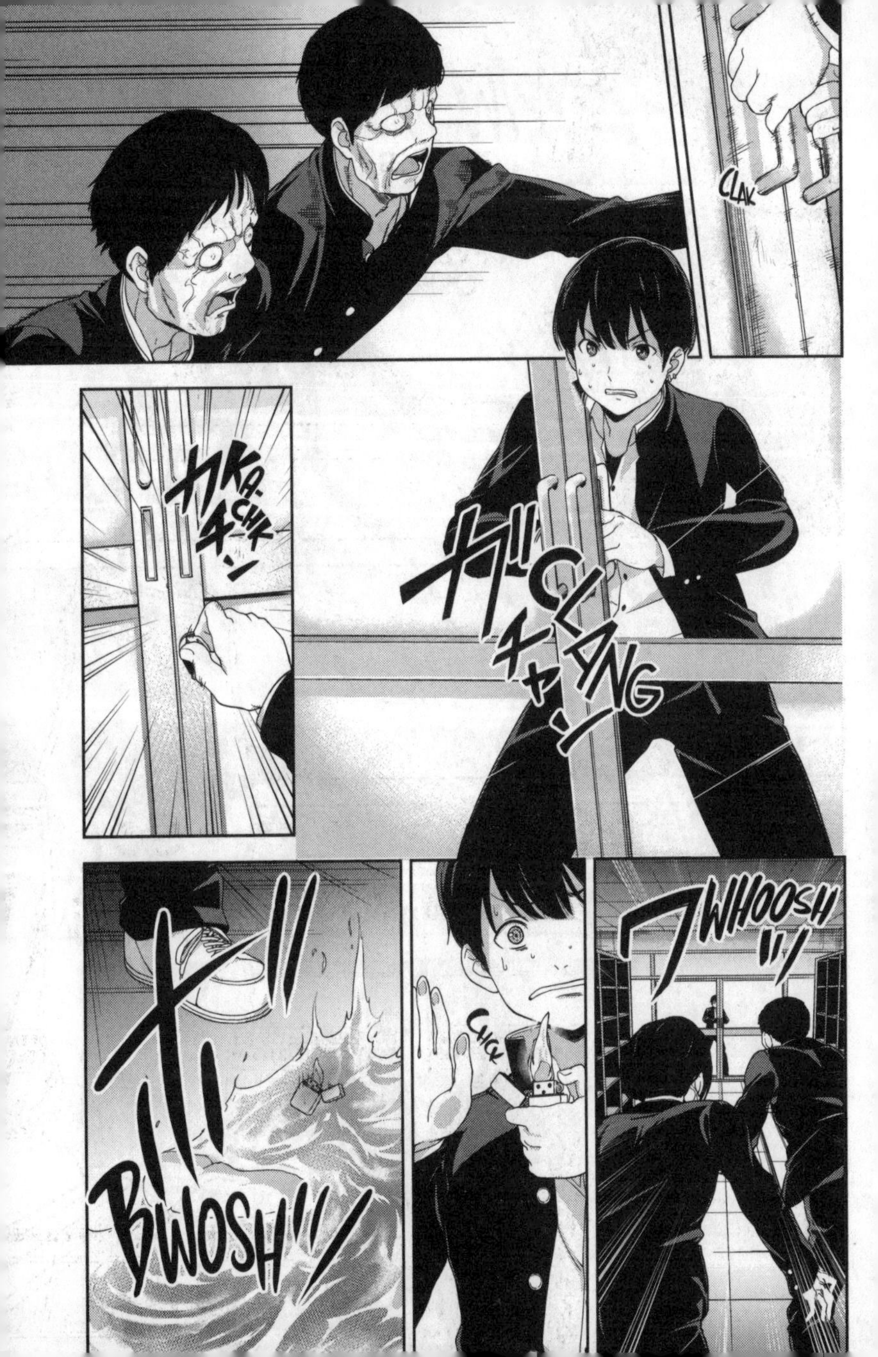

CLAK
CLANG
KA-CHK
WHOOSH
CHCK
BWOSH!!

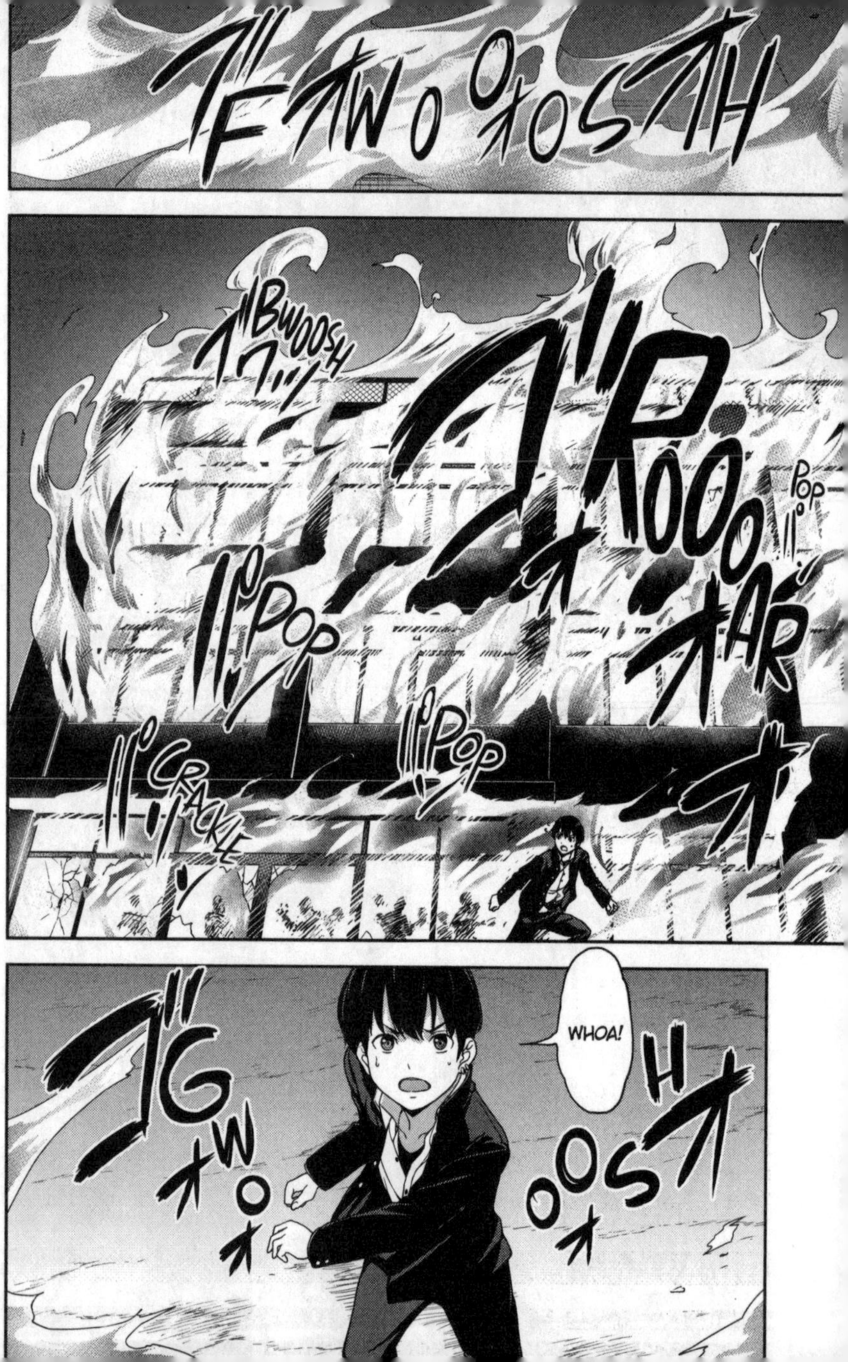
FWOOOSH
ROOOAR
POP
BWOOSH
POP
POP
CRACKLE
WHOA!
GWOOOSH

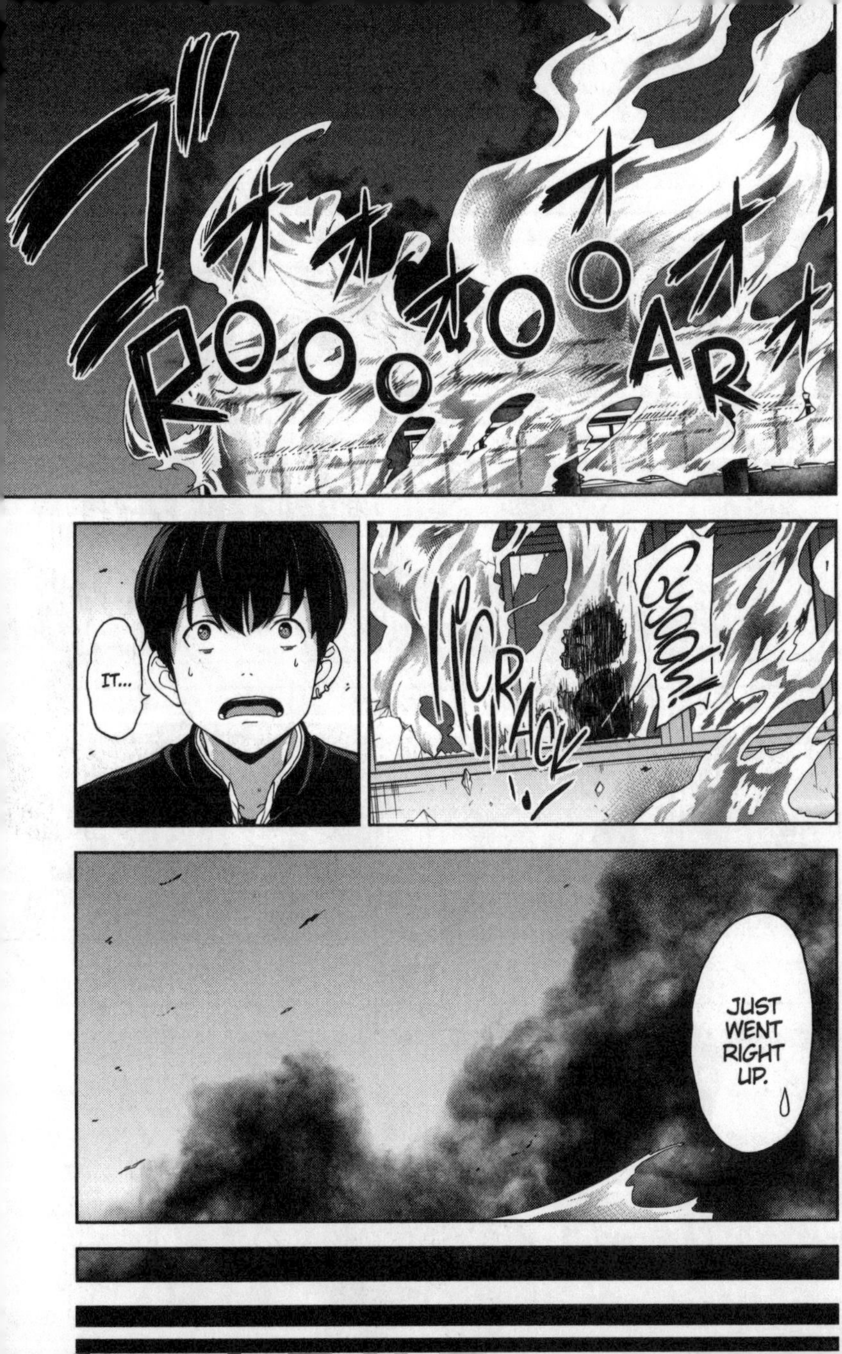
ROOOOOOAR
CRACK
GYOOH!
IT...
JUST WENT RIGHT UP.

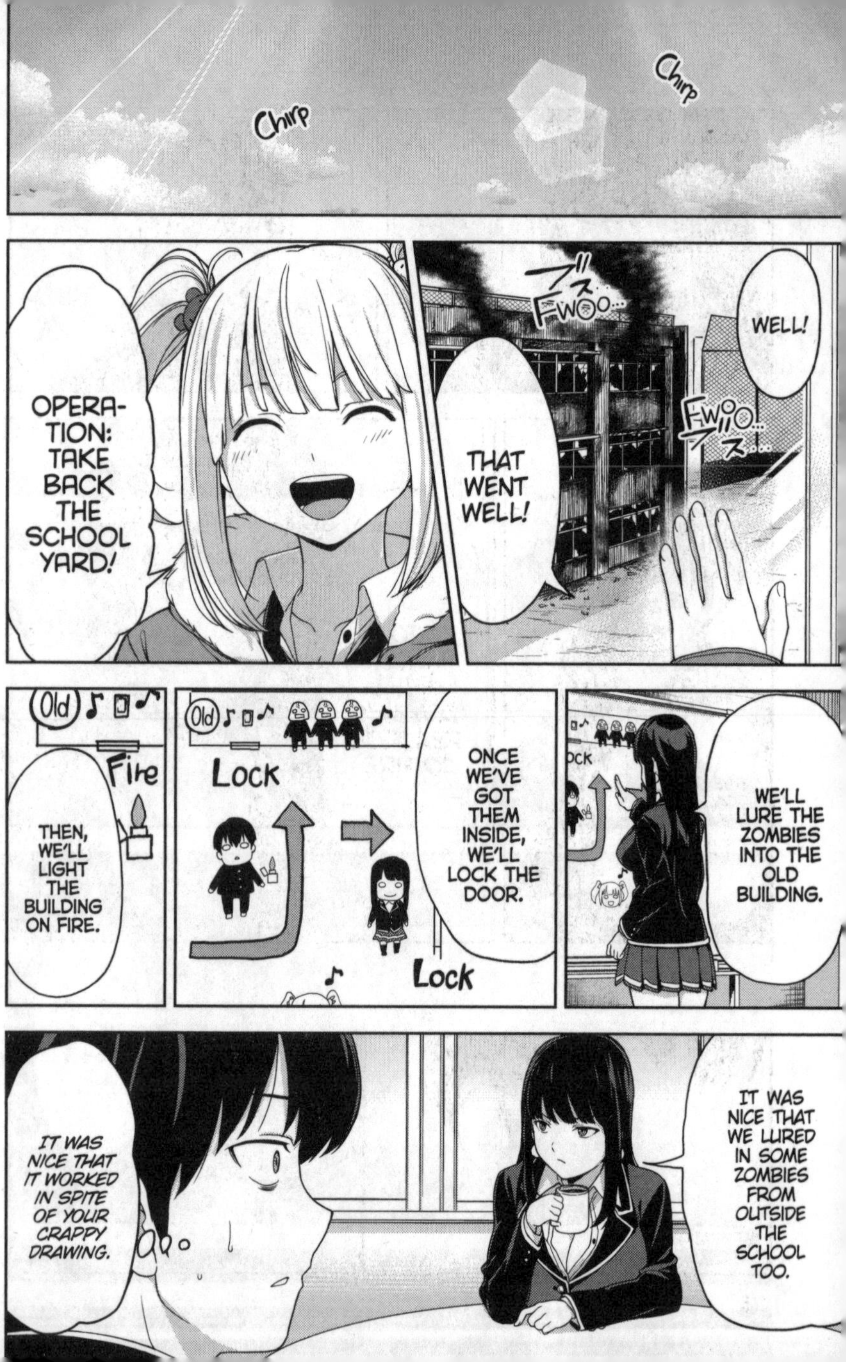
Chirp
Chirp
ブス
FWOO...
WELL!
THAT WENT WELL!
FWOO...
ブス...
OPERATION: TAKE BACK THE SCHOOL YARD!
WE'LL LURE THE ZOMBIES INTO THE OLD BUILDING.
ONCE WE'VE GOT THEM INSIDE, WE'LL LOCK THE DOOR.
Old
Lock
Lock
Old
Fire
THEN, WE'LL LIGHT THE BUILDING ON FIRE.
IT WAS NICE THAT WE LURED IN SOME ZOMBIES FROM OUTSIDE THE SCHOOL TOO.
IT WAS NICE THAT IT WORKED IN SPITE OF YOUR CRAPPY DRAWING.

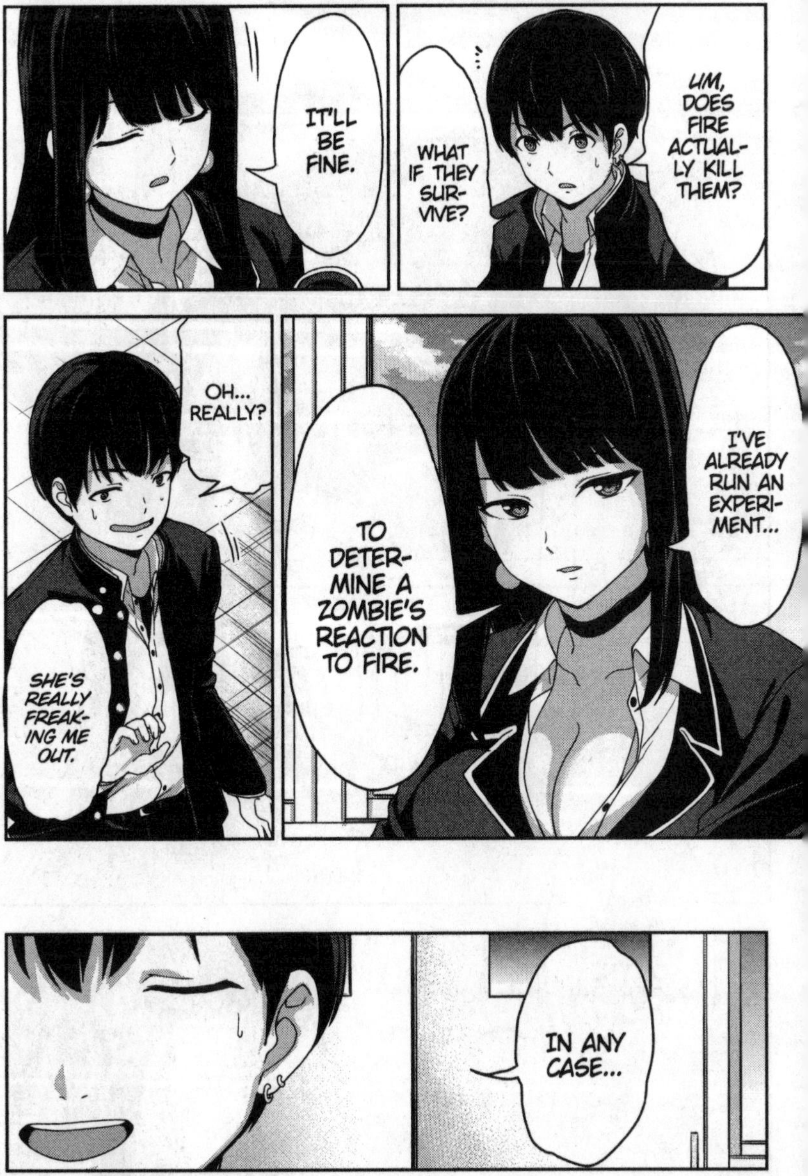
UM, DOES FIRE ACTUALLY KILL THEM?
WHAT IF THEY SURVIVE?
IT'LL BE FINE.
I'VE ALREADY RUN AN EXPERIMENT...
TO DETERMINE A ZOMBIE'S REACTION TO FIRE.
OH... REALLY?
SHE'S REALLY FREAKING ME OUT.
IN ANY CASE...

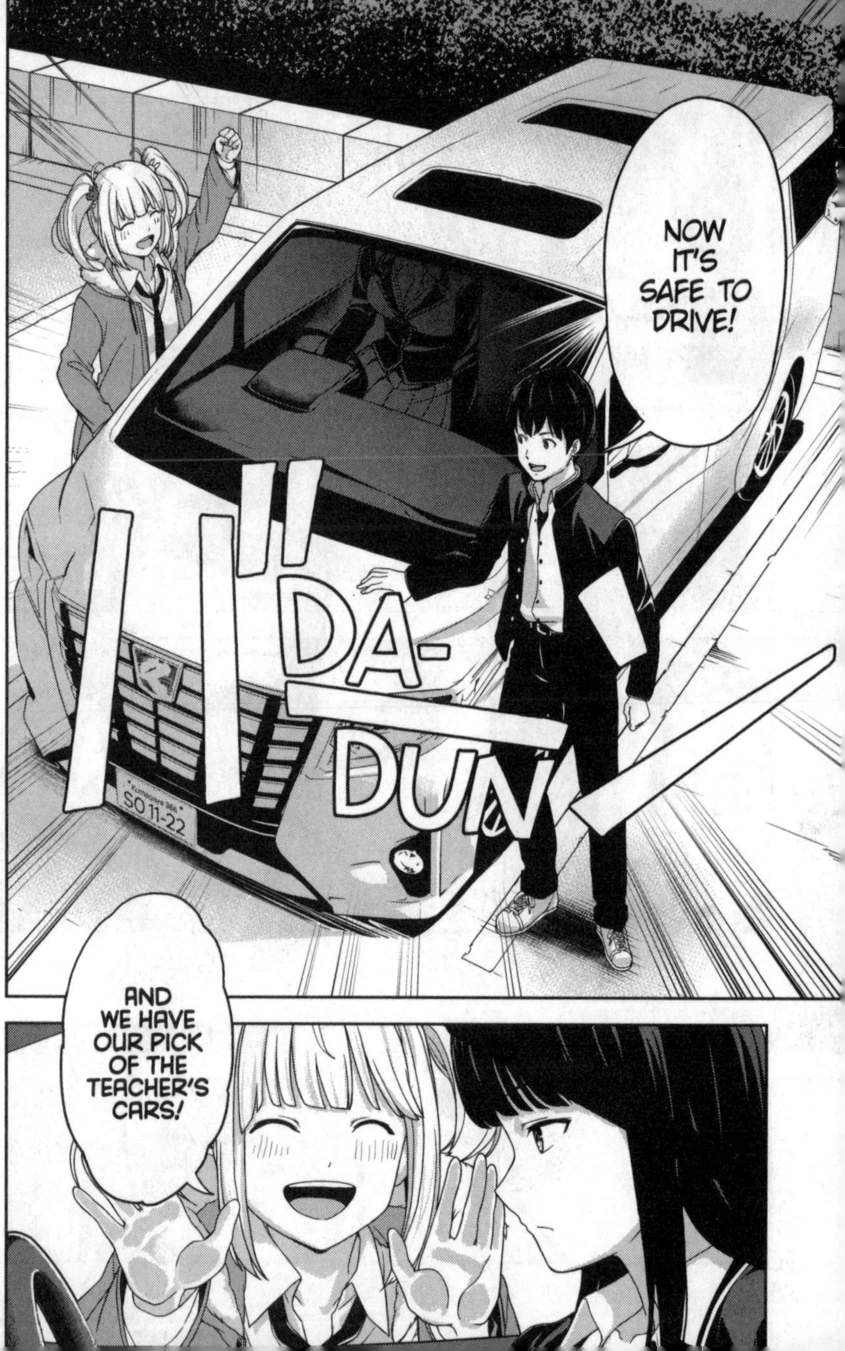
NOW IT'S SAFE TO DRIVE!
DA-DUN
SO 11-22
AND WE HAVE OUR PICK OF THE TEACHER'S CARS!

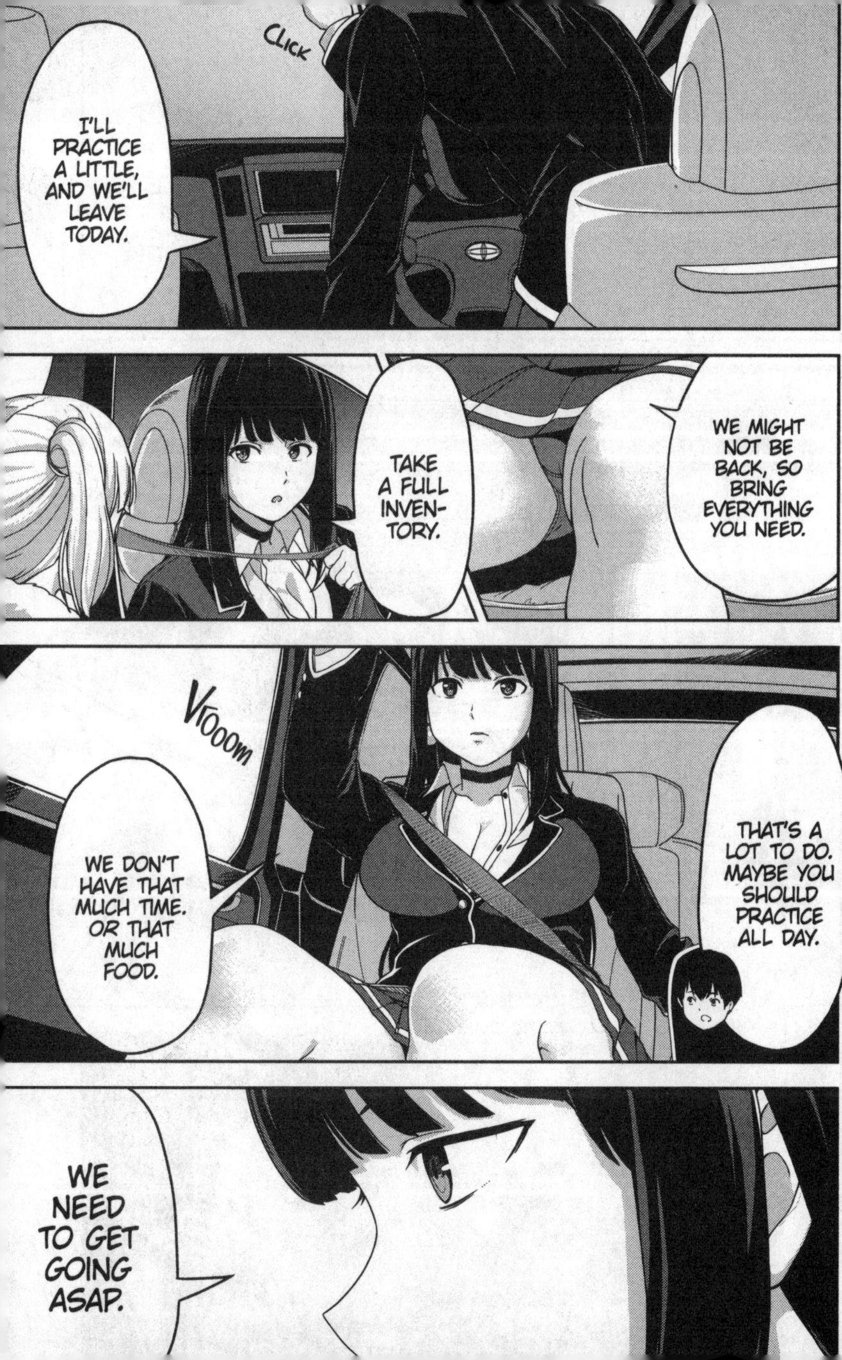
CLICK
I'LL PRACTICE A LITTLE, AND WE'LL LEAVE TODAY.
WE MIGHT NOT BE BACK, SO BRING EVERYTHING YOU NEED.
TAKE A FULL INVEN-TORY.
THAT'S A LOT TO DO. MAYBE YOU SHOULD PRACTICE ALL DAY.
Vrooom
WE DON'T HAVE THAT MUCH TIME. OR THAT MUCH FOOD.
WE NEED TO GET GOING ASAP.

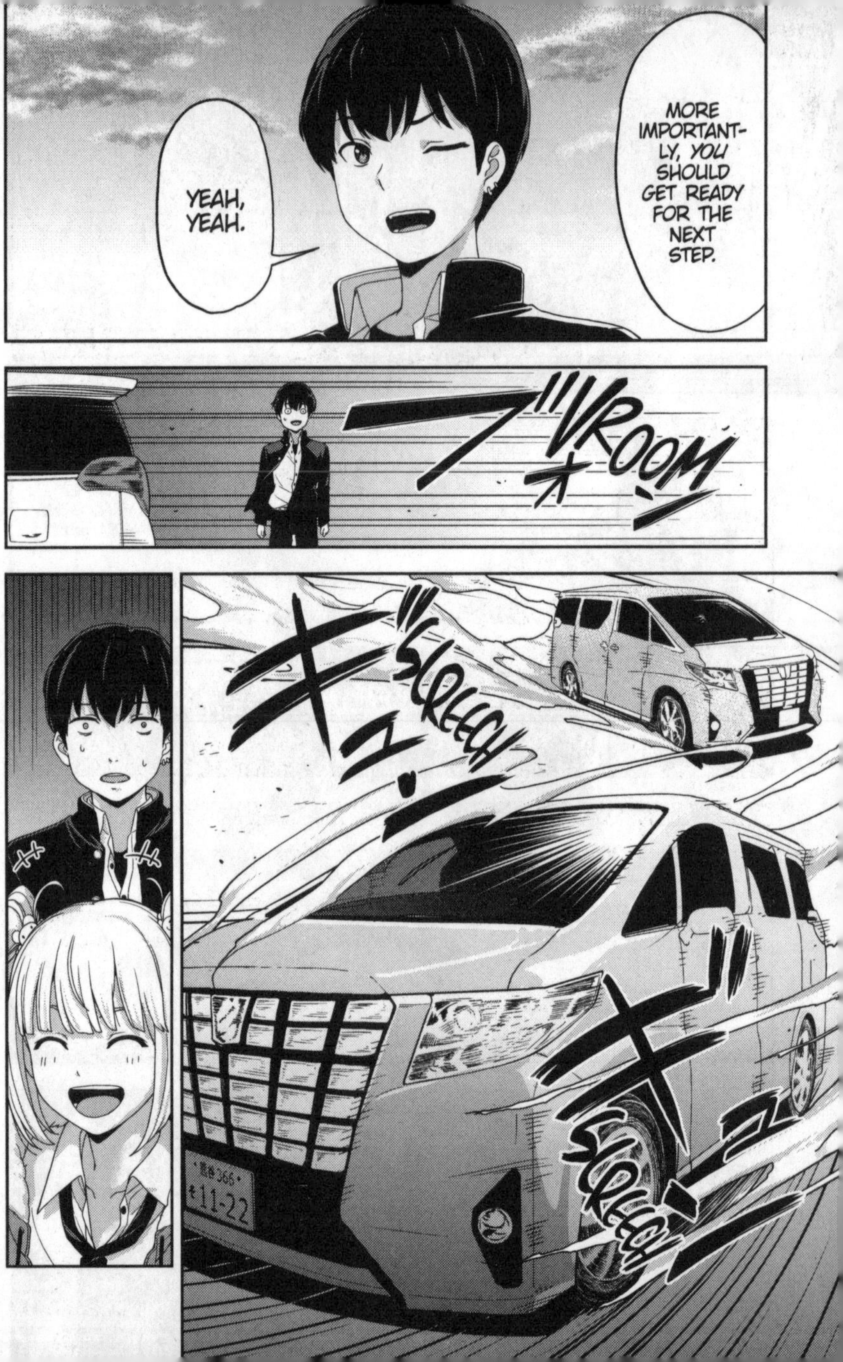
MORE IMPORTANT-LY, YOU SHOULD GET READY FOR THE NEXT STEP.
YEAH, YEAH.
VROOM
SCREECH
SCREECH

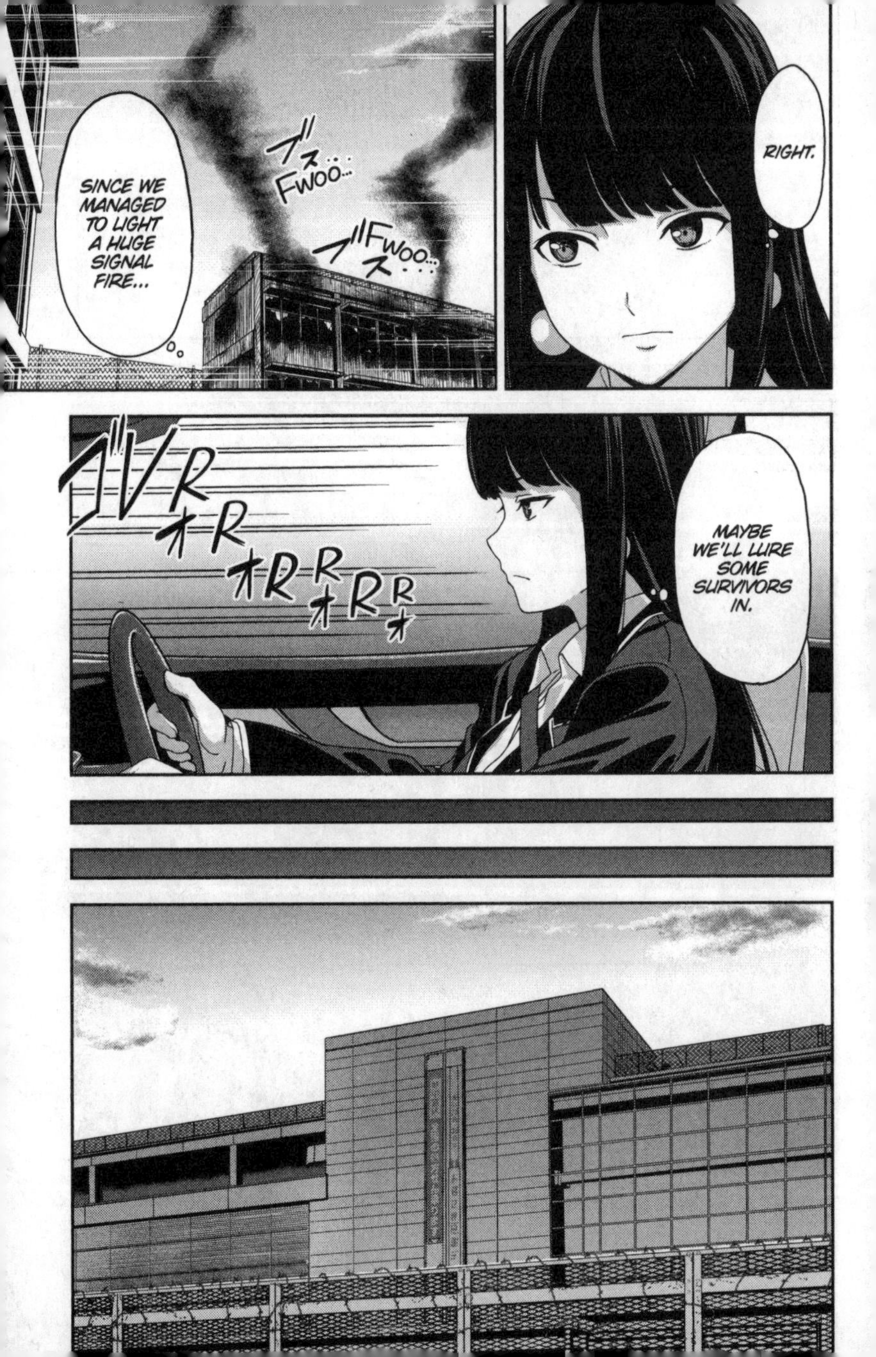
RIGHT.
Fwoo...
Fwoo...
SINCE WE MANAGED TO LIGHT A HUGE SIGNAL FIRE...
MAYBE WE'LL LURE SOME SURVIVORS IN.
RRRRRR

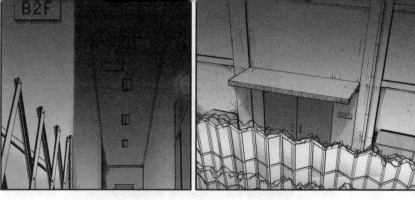

MURMUR

MURMUR

MURMUR

HUH?

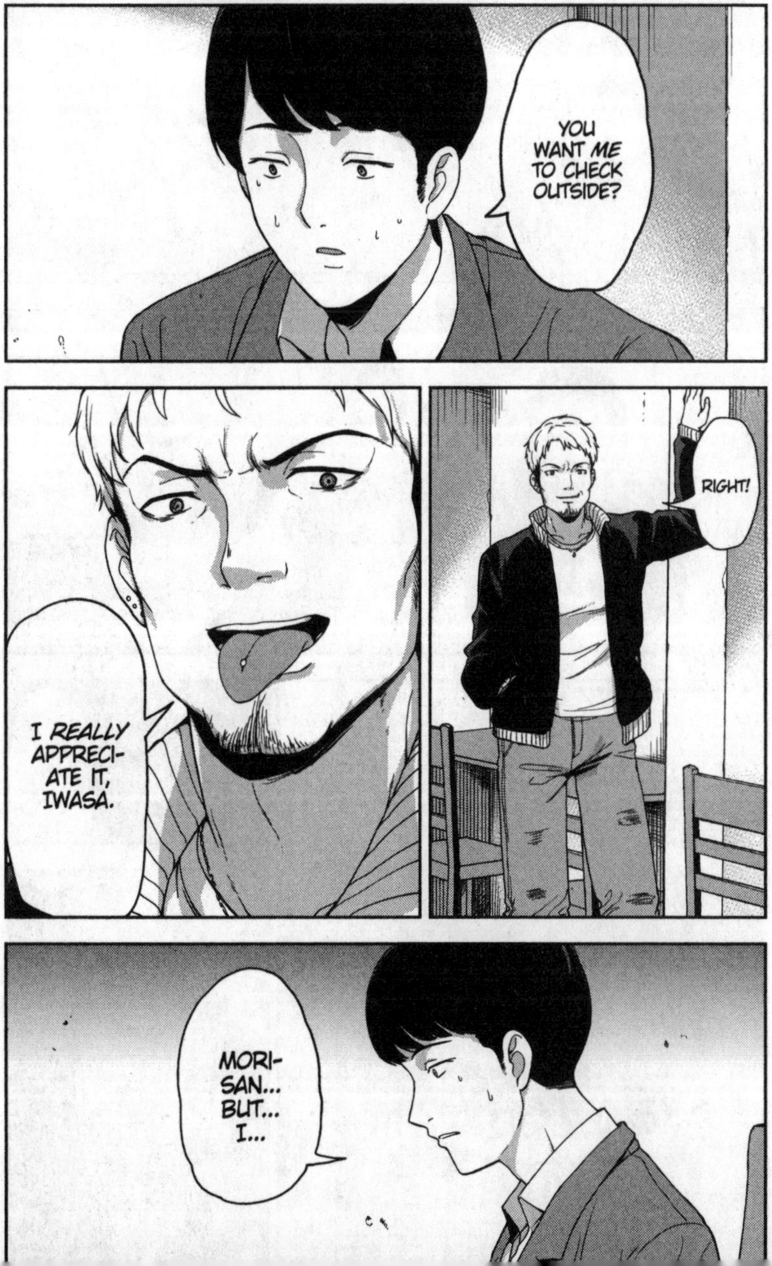
YOU WANT ME TO CHECK OUTSIDE?
RIGHT!
I REALLY APPRECIATE IT, IWASA.
MORI-SAN... BUT... I...

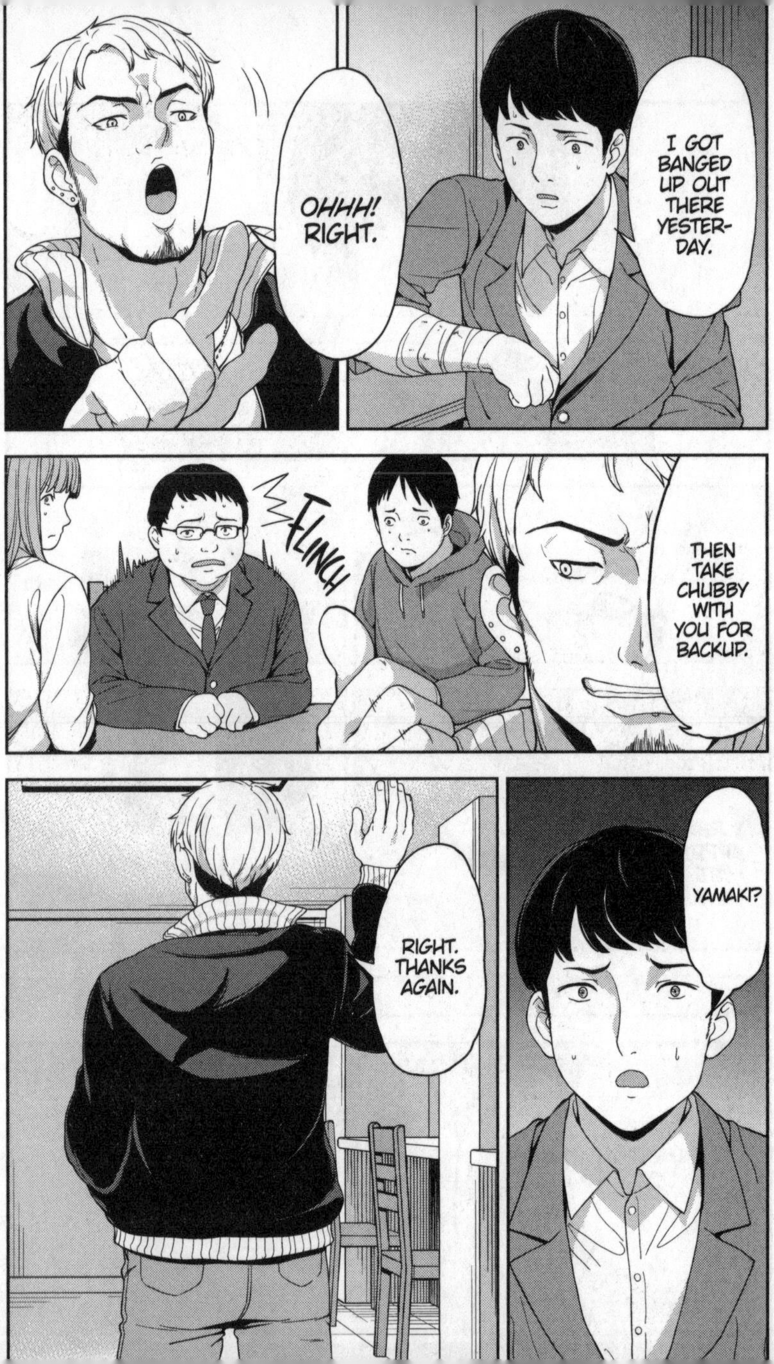
I GOT BANGED UP OUT THERE YESTER-DAY.
OHHH! RIGHT.
THEN TAKE CHUBBY WITH YOU FOR BACKUP.
FLINCH
YAMAKI?
RIGHT. THANKS AGAIN.

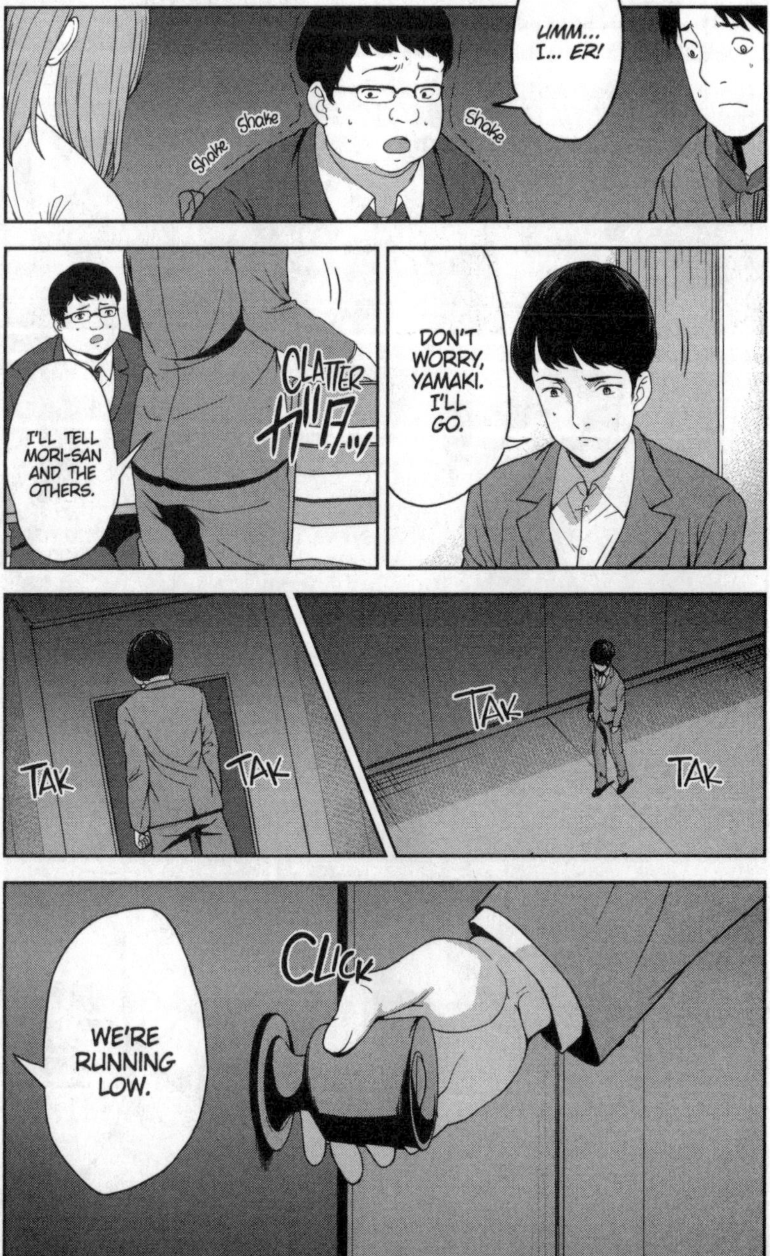
UMM... I... ER!
Shake
Shake
Shake
DON'T WORRY, YAMAKI. I'LL GO.
CLATTER
ガタッ
I'LL TELL MORI-SAN AND THE OTHERS.
TAK
TAK
TAK
TAK
CLICK
WE'RE RUNNING LOW.

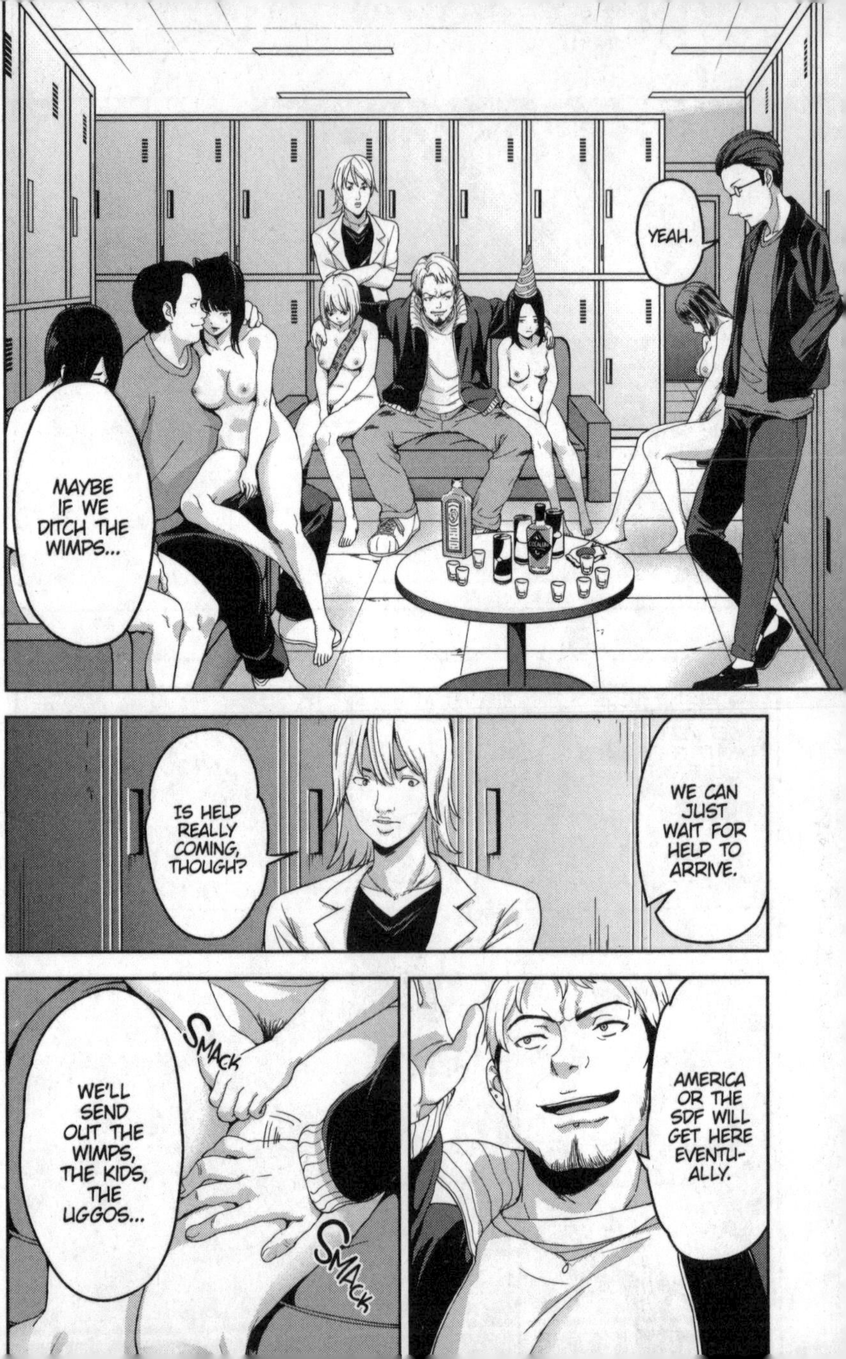
YEAH.
MAYBE IF WE DITCH THE WIMPS...
WE CAN JUST WAIT FOR HELP TO ARRIVE.
IS HELP REALLY COMING, THOUGH?
AMERICA OR THE SDF WILL GET HERE EVENTU-ALLY.
WE'LL SEND OUT THE WIMPS, THE KIDS, THE UGGOS...
SMACK
SMACK

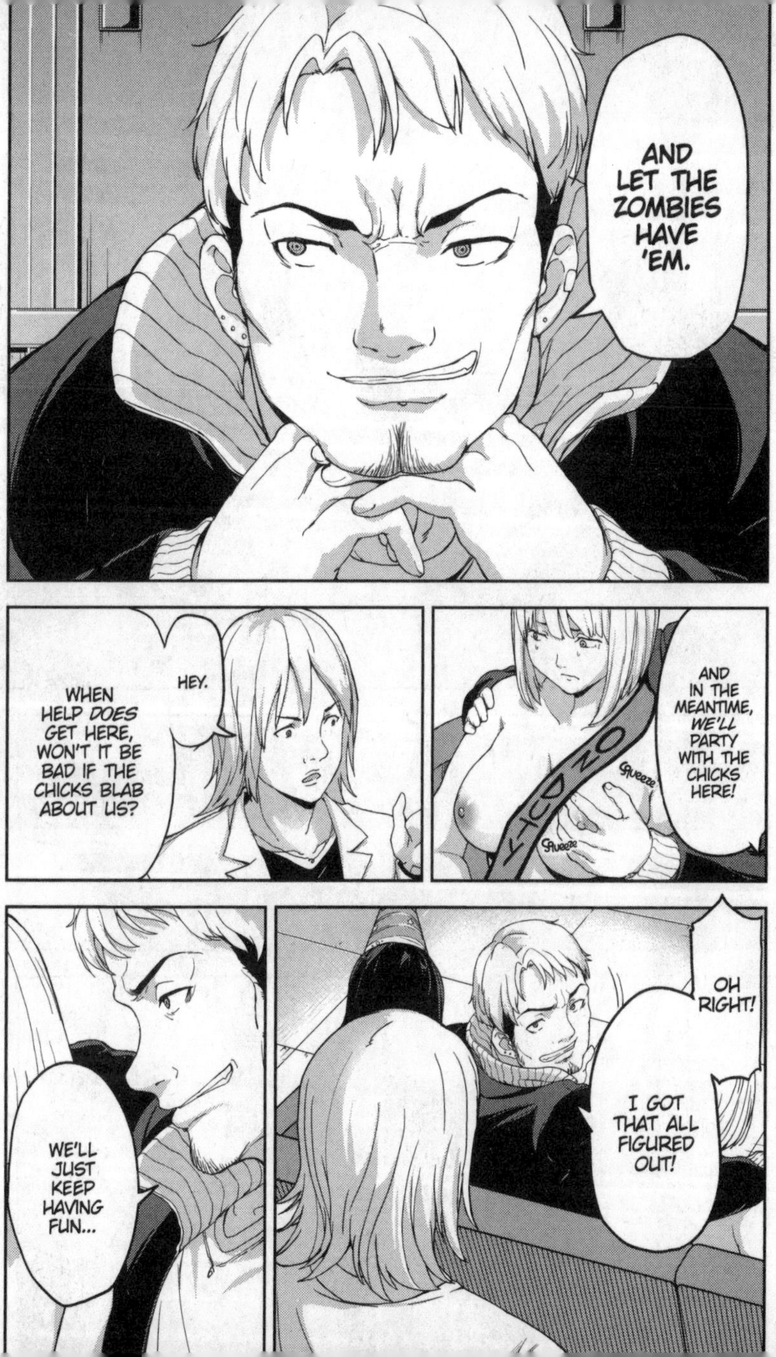
AND LET THE ZOMBIES HAVE 'EM.
AND IN THE MEANTIME, WE'LL PARTY WITH THE CHICKS HERE!
squeeze
squeeze
HEY.
WHEN HELP DOES GET HERE, WON'T IT BE BAD IF THE CHICKS BLAB ABOUT US?
OH RIGHT!
I GOT THAT ALL FIGURED OUT!
WE'LL JUST KEEP HAVING FUN...

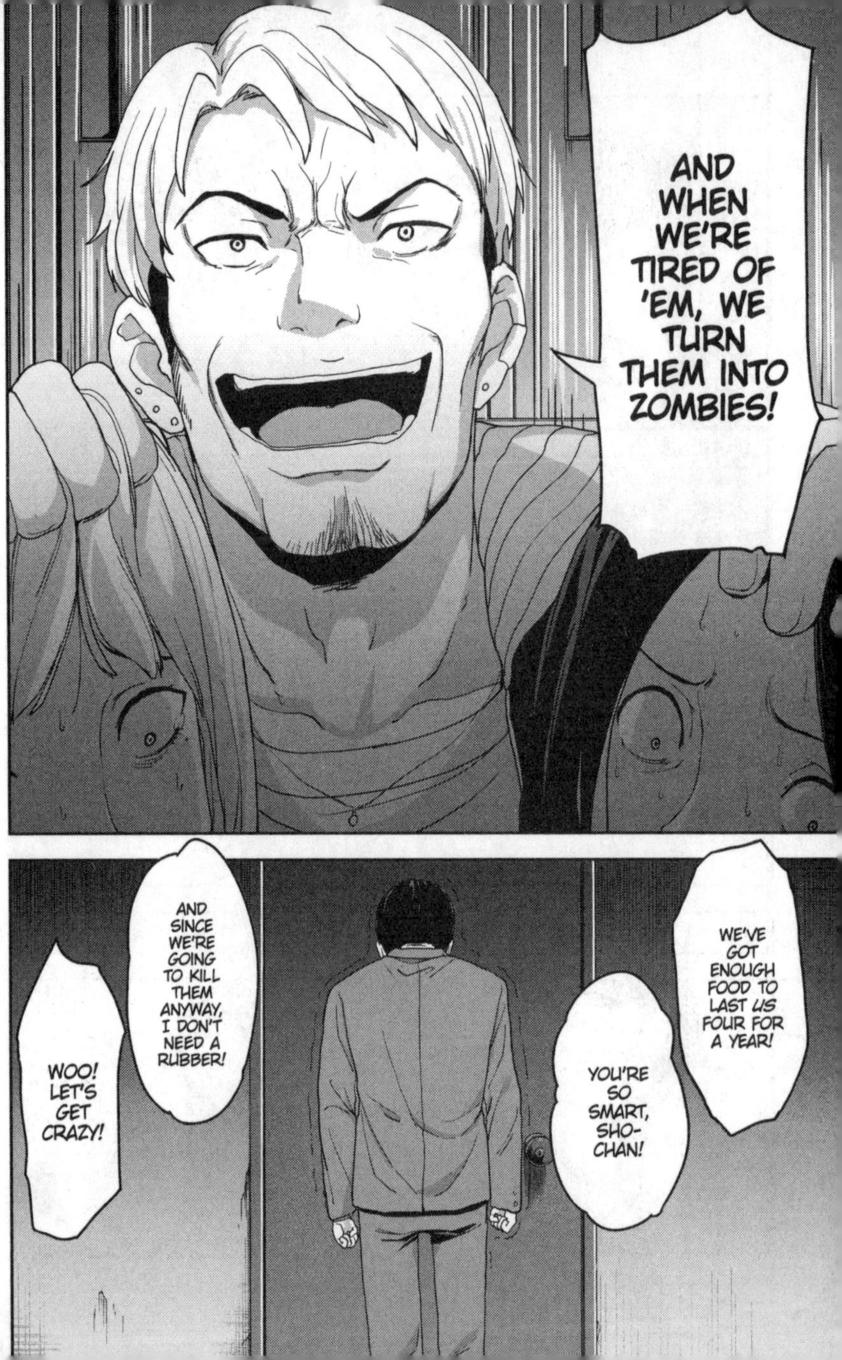
AND WHEN WE'RE TIRED OF 'EM, WE TURN THEM INTO ZOMBIES!
WE'VE GOT ENOUGH FOOD TO LAST US FOUR FOR A YEAR!
YOU'RE SO SMART, SHO-CHAN!
AND SINCE WE'RE GOING TO KILL THEM ANYWAY, I DON'T NEED A RUBBER!
WOO! LET'S GET CRAZY!

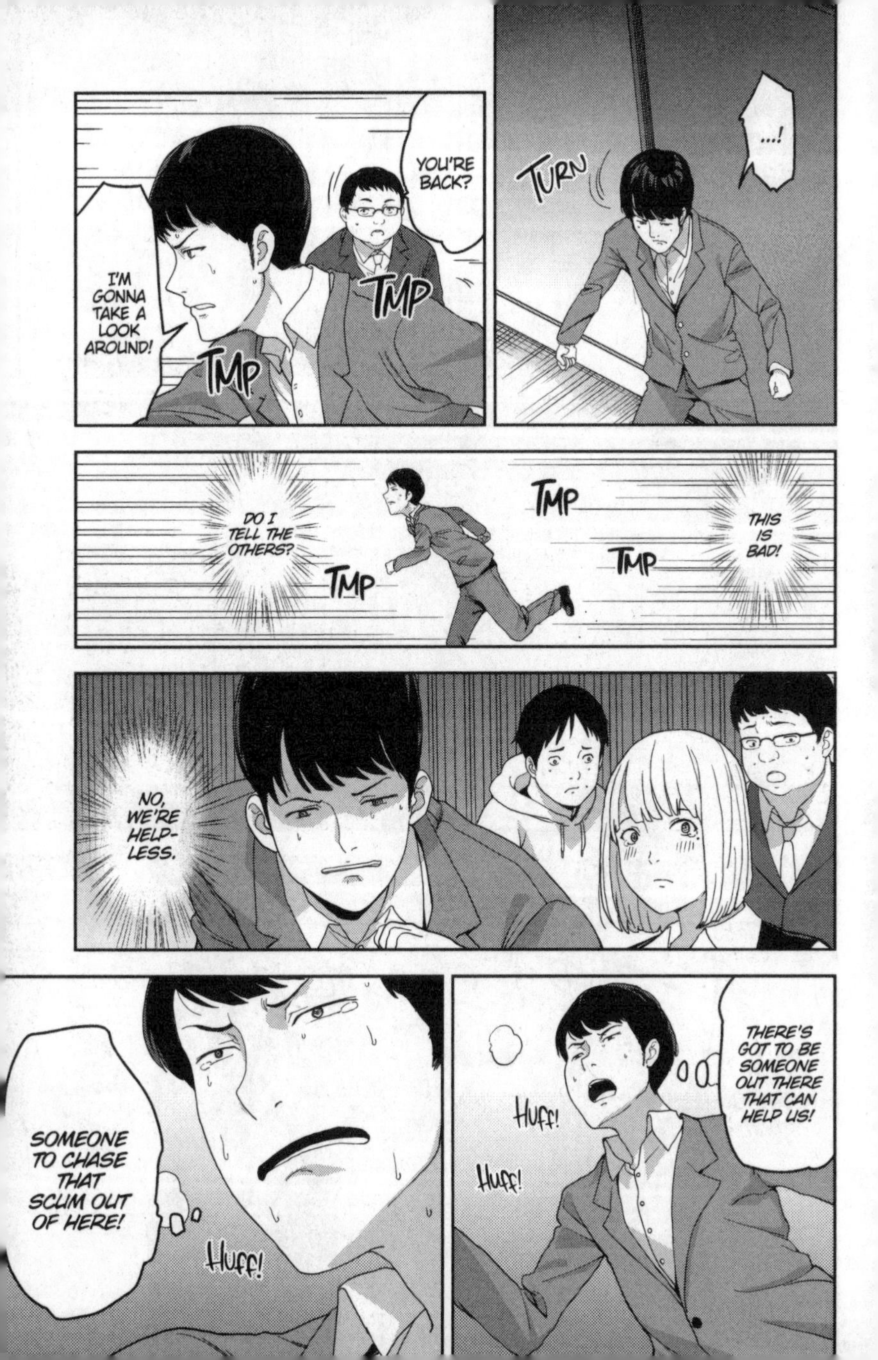
...!
TURN
YOU'RE BACK?
TMP
I'M GONNA TAKE A LOOK AROUND!
TMP
THIS IS BAD!
TMP
TMP
DO I TELL THE OTHERS?
TMP
NO, WE'RE HELPLESS.
THERE'S GOT TO BE SOMEONE OUT THERE THAT CAN HELP US!
Huff!
Huff!
SOMEONE TO CHASE THAT SCUM OUT OF HERE!
Huff!

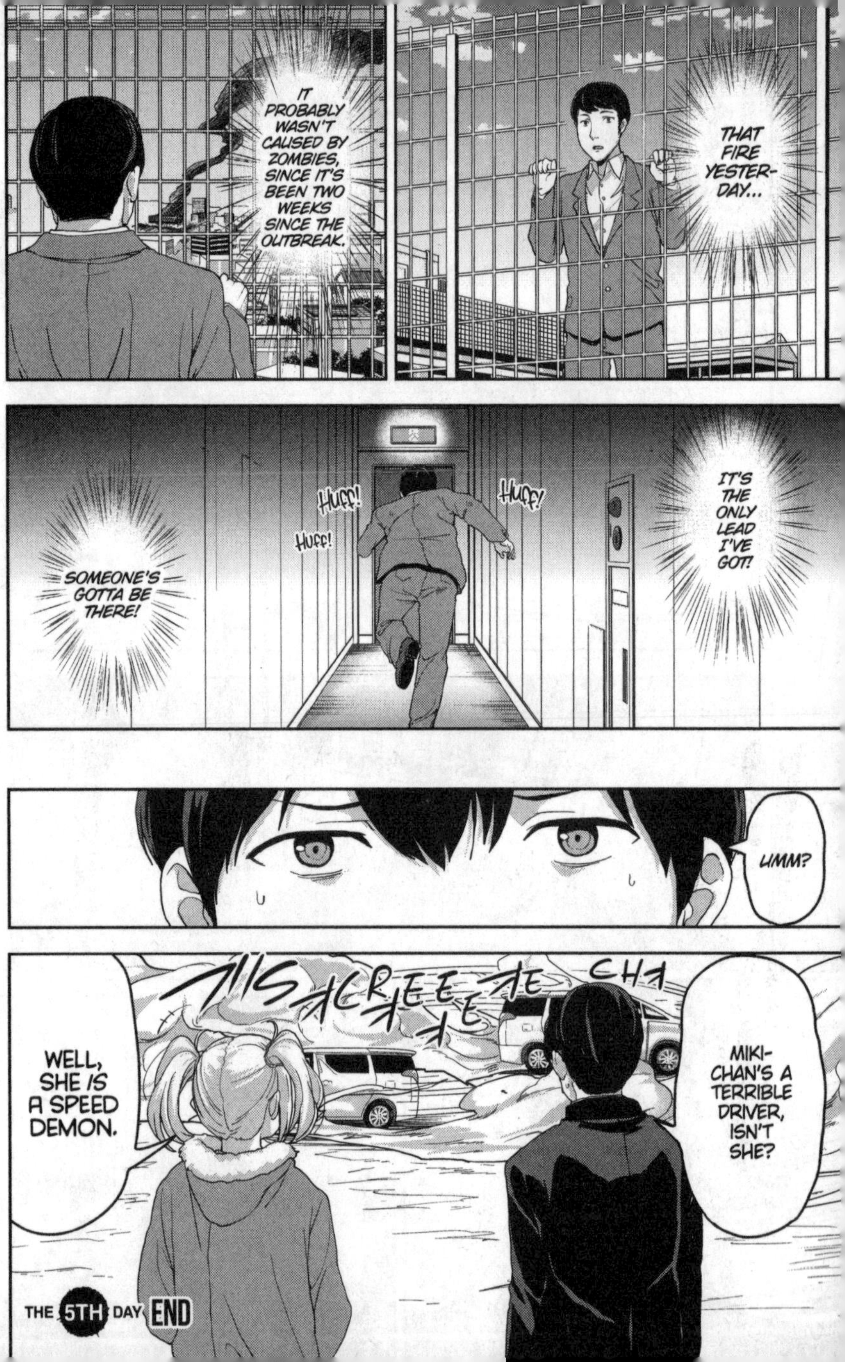
THAT FIRE YESTER-DAY...
IT PROBABLY WASN'T CAUSED BY ZOMBIES, SINCE IT'S BEEN TWO WEEKS SINCE THE OUTBREAK.
IT'S THE ONLY LEAD I'VE GOT!
Huff!
Huff!
Huff!
SOMEONE'S GOTTA BE THERE!
UMM?
MIKI-CHAN'S A TERRIBLE DRIVER, ISN'T SHE?
WELL, SHE IS A SPEED DEMON.
THE 5TH DAY END

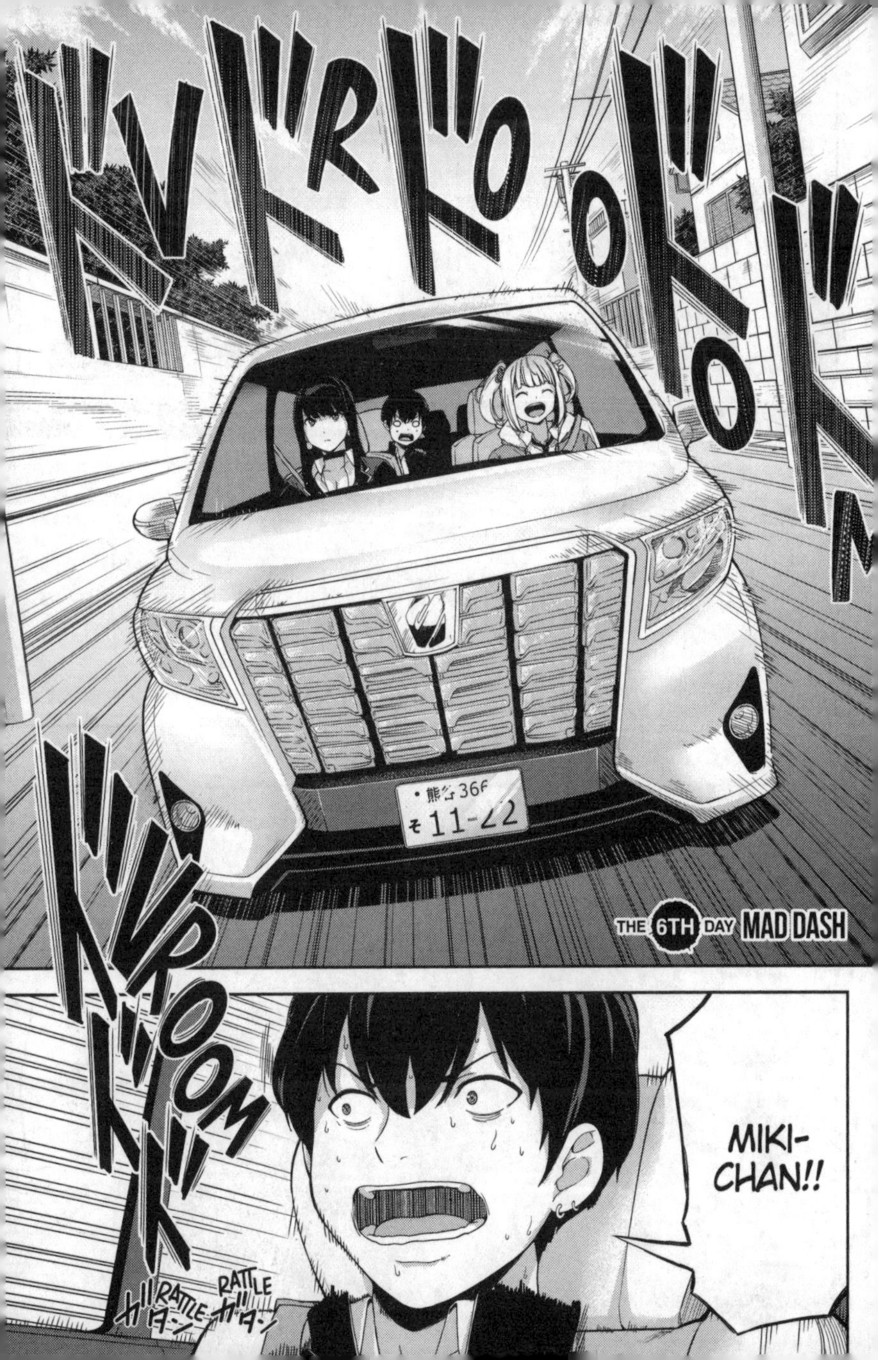
VROOON
THE 6TH DAY MAD DASH
MIKI-CHAN!!
VROOM
RATTLE
RATTLE

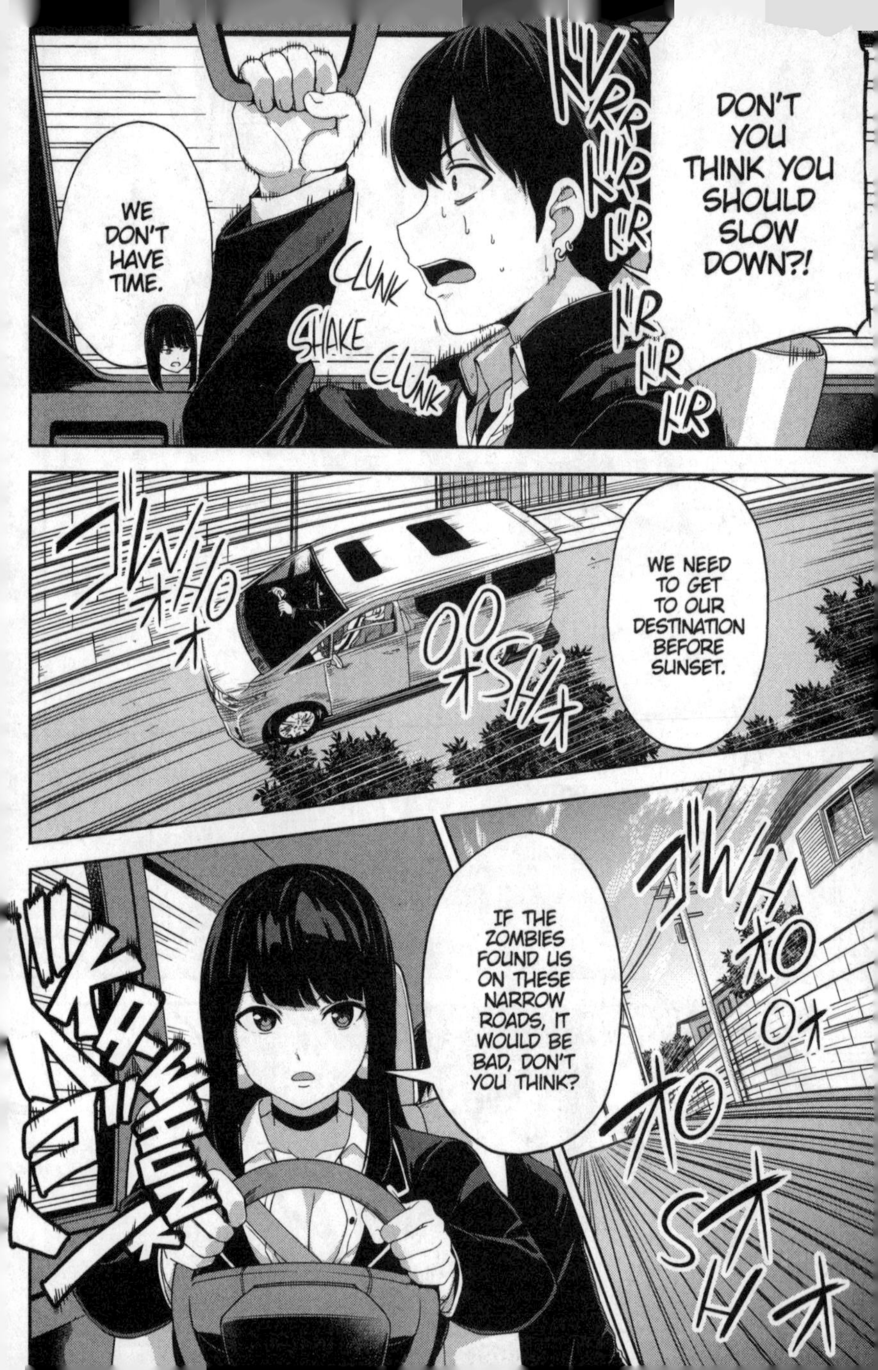
DON'T YOU THINK YOU SHOULD SLOW DOWN?!
CLUNK
SHAKE
CLUNK
WE DON'T HAVE TIME.
WE NEED TO GET TO OUR DESTINATION BEFORE SUNSET.
IF THE ZOMBIES FOUND US ON THESE NARROW ROADS, IT WOULD BE BAD, DON'T YOU THINK?

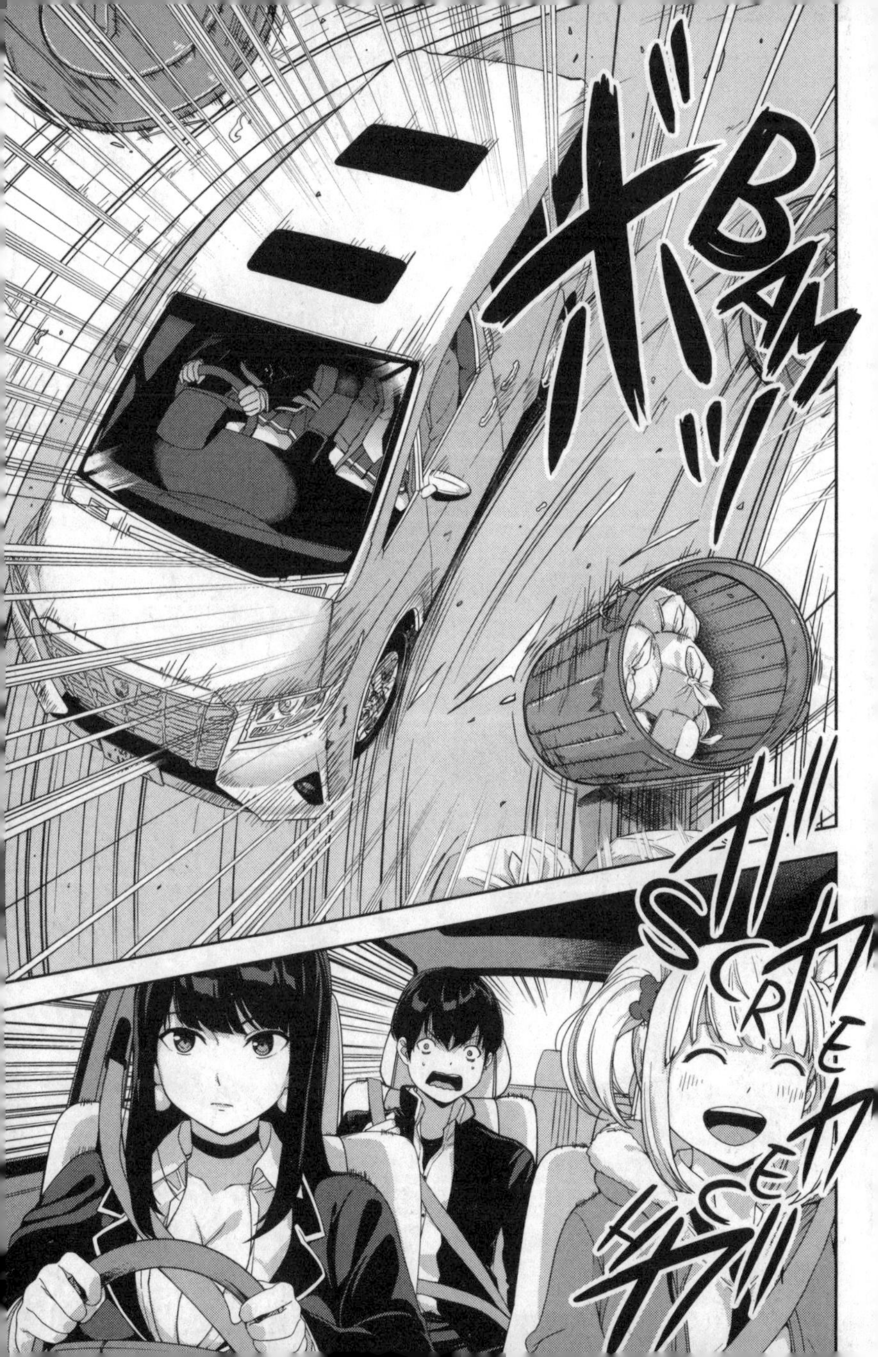
BAM!!
SCREECH

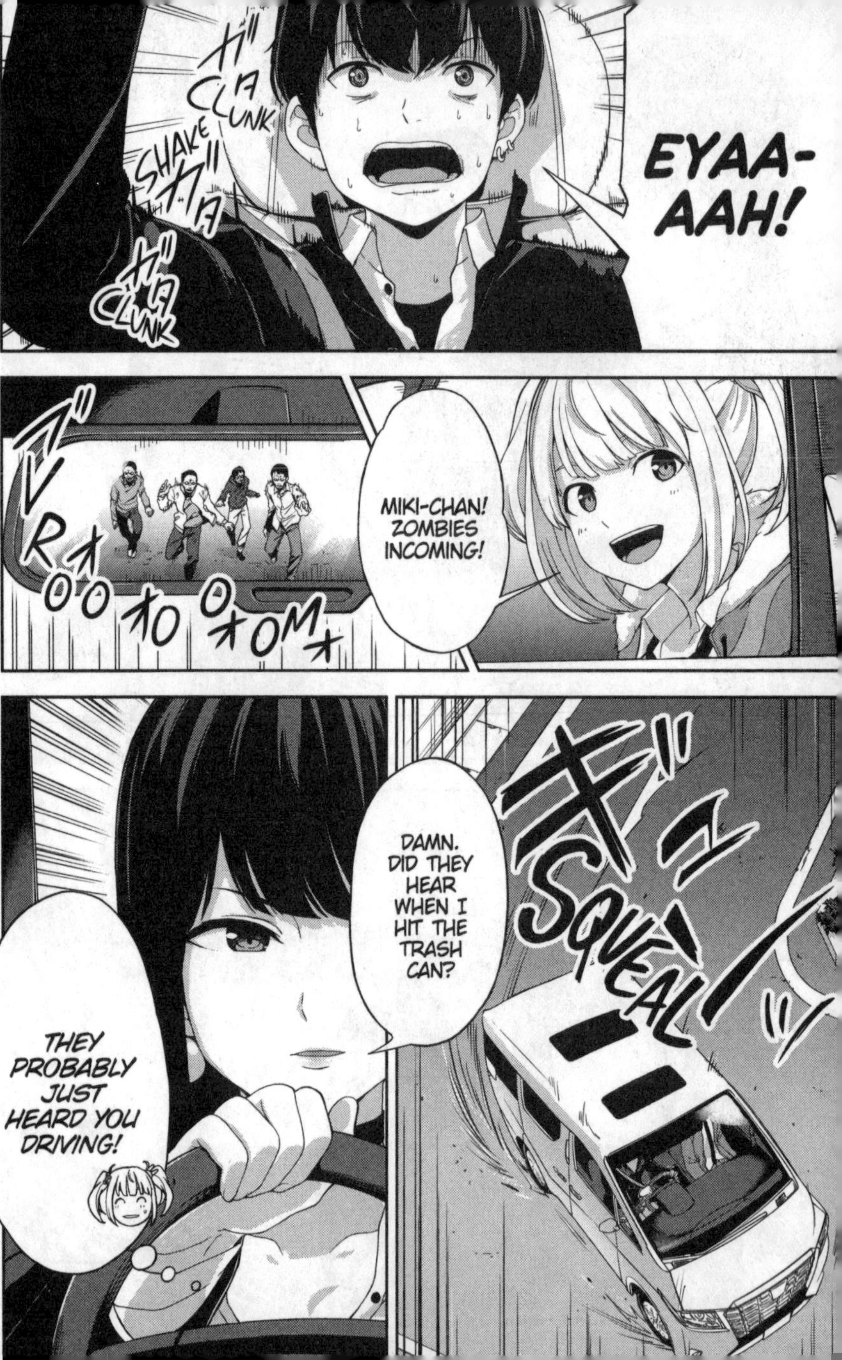
EYAA-AAH!
CLUNK
SHAKE
CLUNK
MIKI-CHAN! ZOMBIES INCOMING!
VROOOM
SQUEAL
DAMN. DID THEY HEAR WHEN I HIT THE TRASH CAN?
THEY PROBABLY JUST HEARD YOU DRIVING!

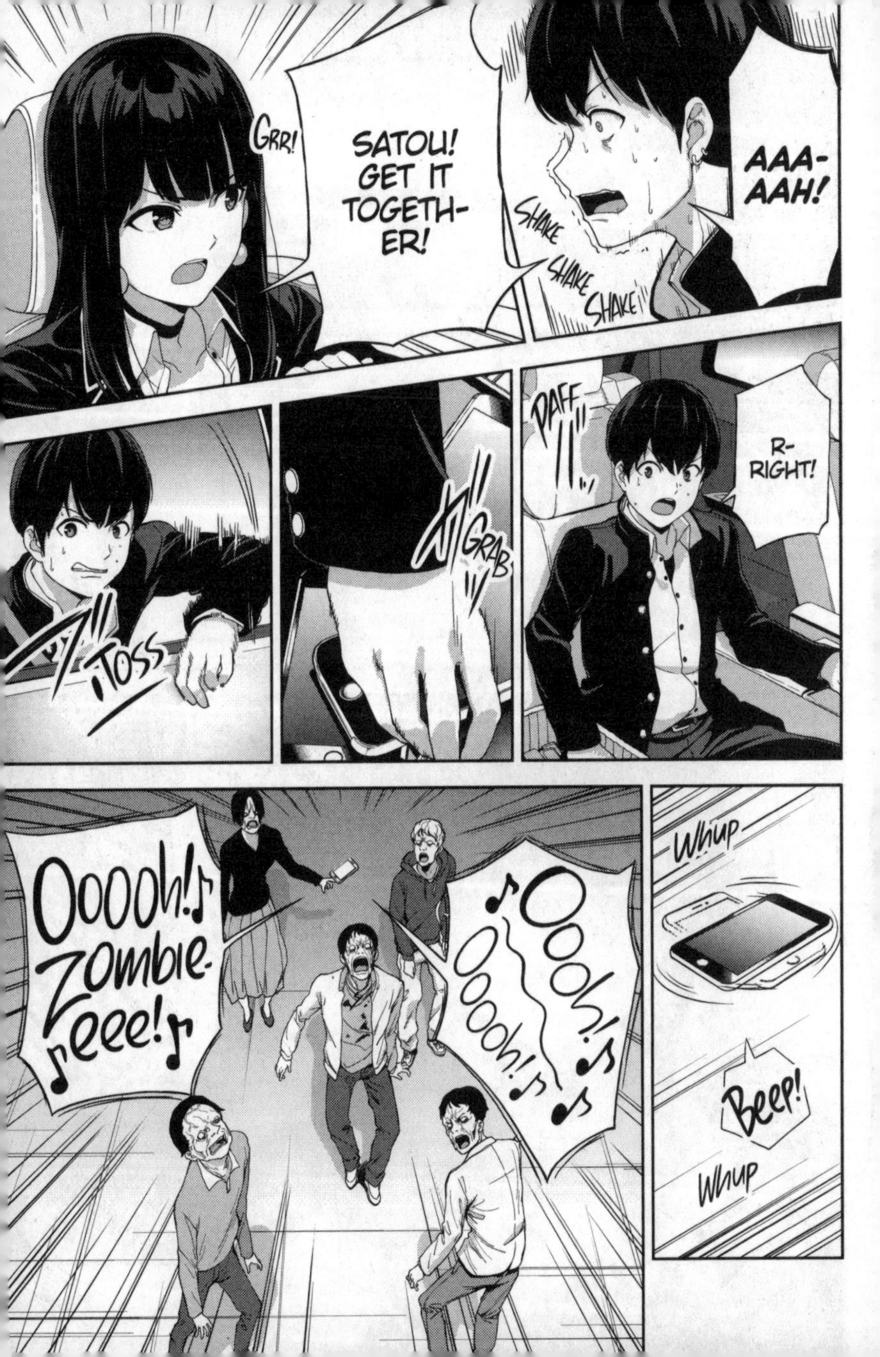
AAA-AAH!
SHAKE SHAKE SHAKE
SATOU! GET IT TOGETH-ER!
GRR!
R-RIGHT!
PAFF
GRAB
TOSS
Whup
Beep!
Whup
♪Oooh!♪ ~Ooooh!♪
Ooooh!♪ Zombie-eee!♪

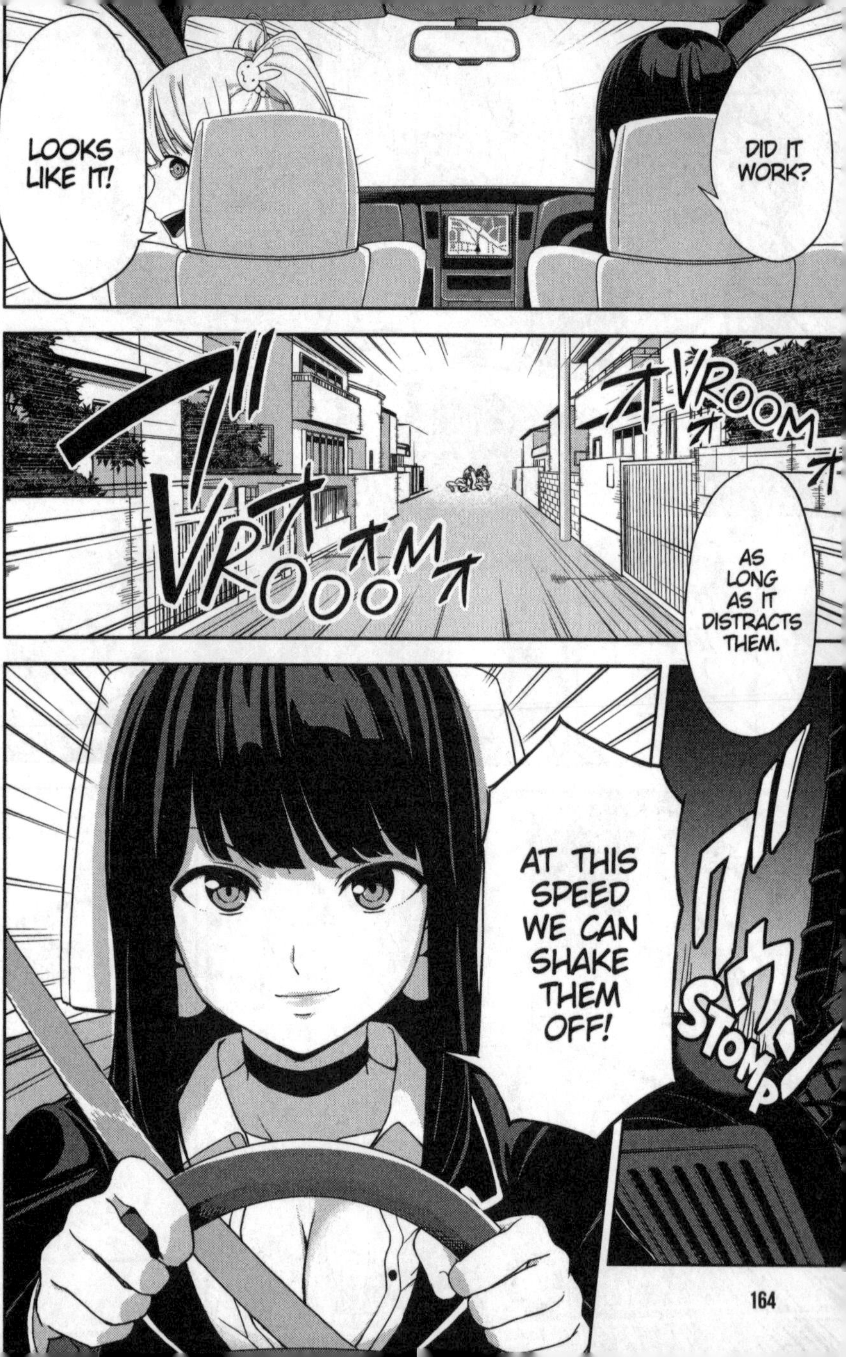
DID IT WORK?
LOOKS LIKE IT!
VROOM
VROOOM
AS LONG AS IT DISTRACTS THEM.
STOMP
AT THIS SPEED WE CAN SHAKE THEM OFF!

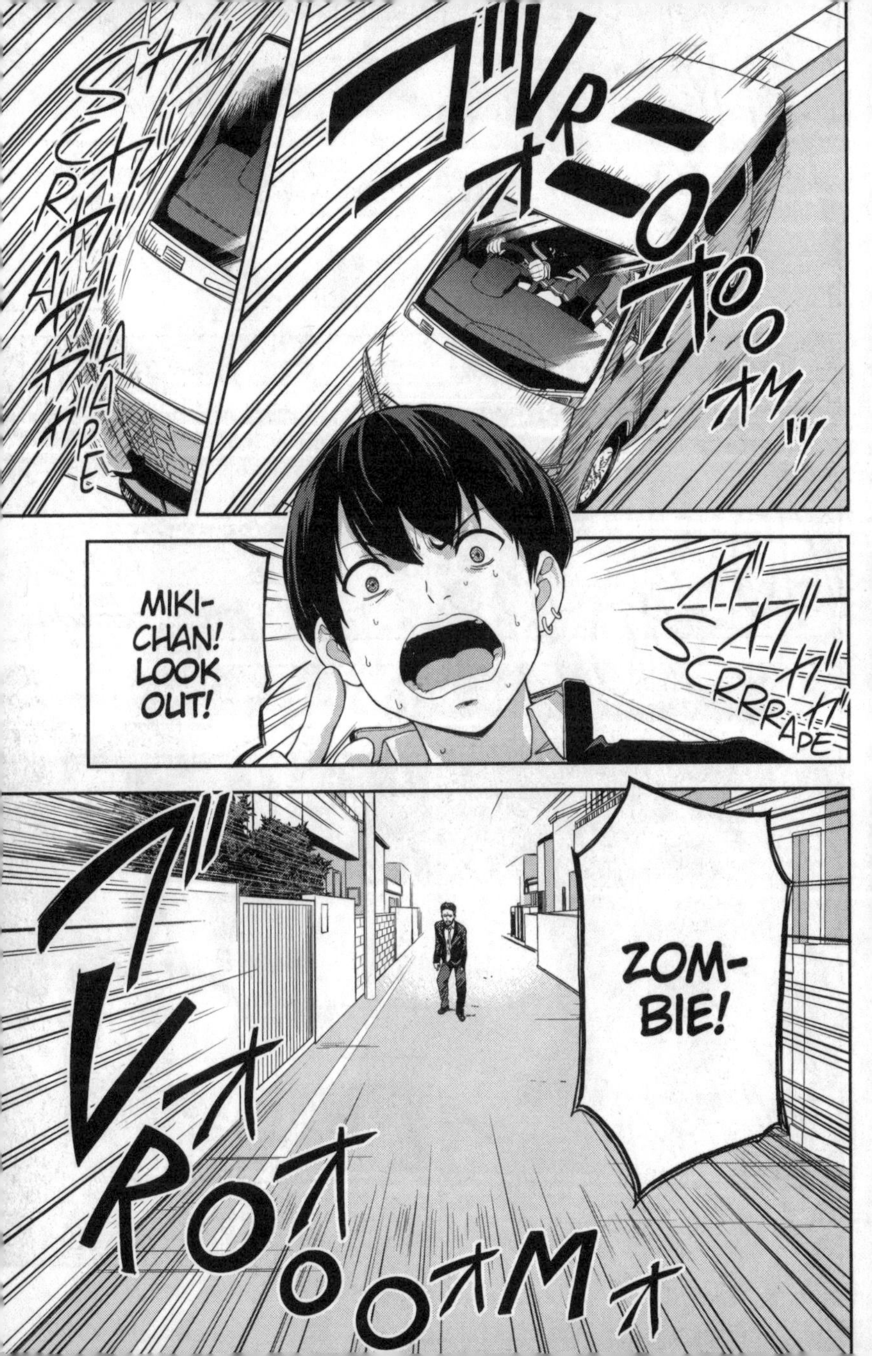
VROOOM
SCRAAAPE
MIKI-CHAN! LOOK OUT!
SCRRRAPE
ZOM-BIE!
VROOOM

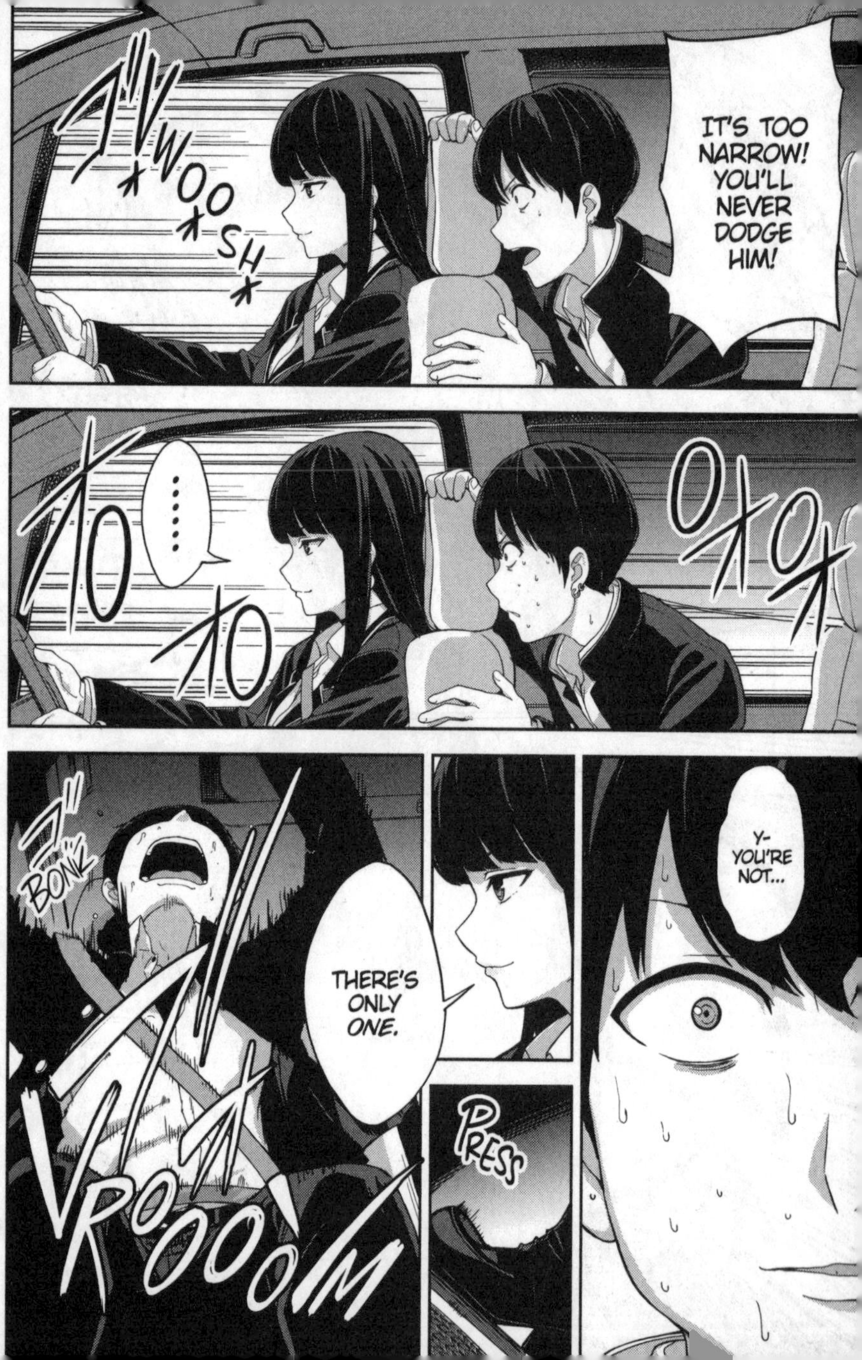

IT'S TOO NARROW! YOU'LL NEVER DODGE HIM!
WOOSH
......
Y- YOU'RE NOT...
THERE'S ONLY ONE.
PRESS
BONK
VROOOOM

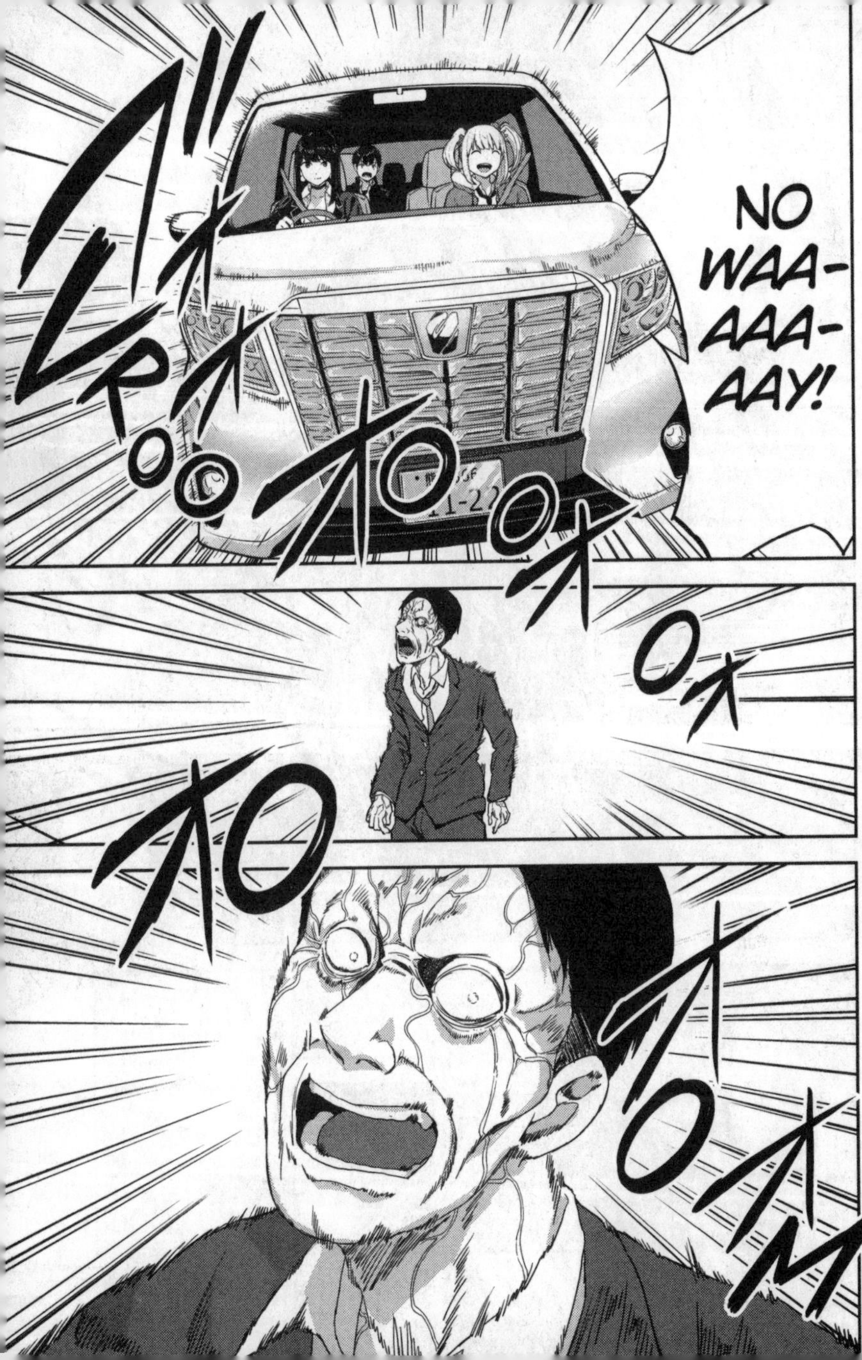
NO WAAA-AAA-AAY!

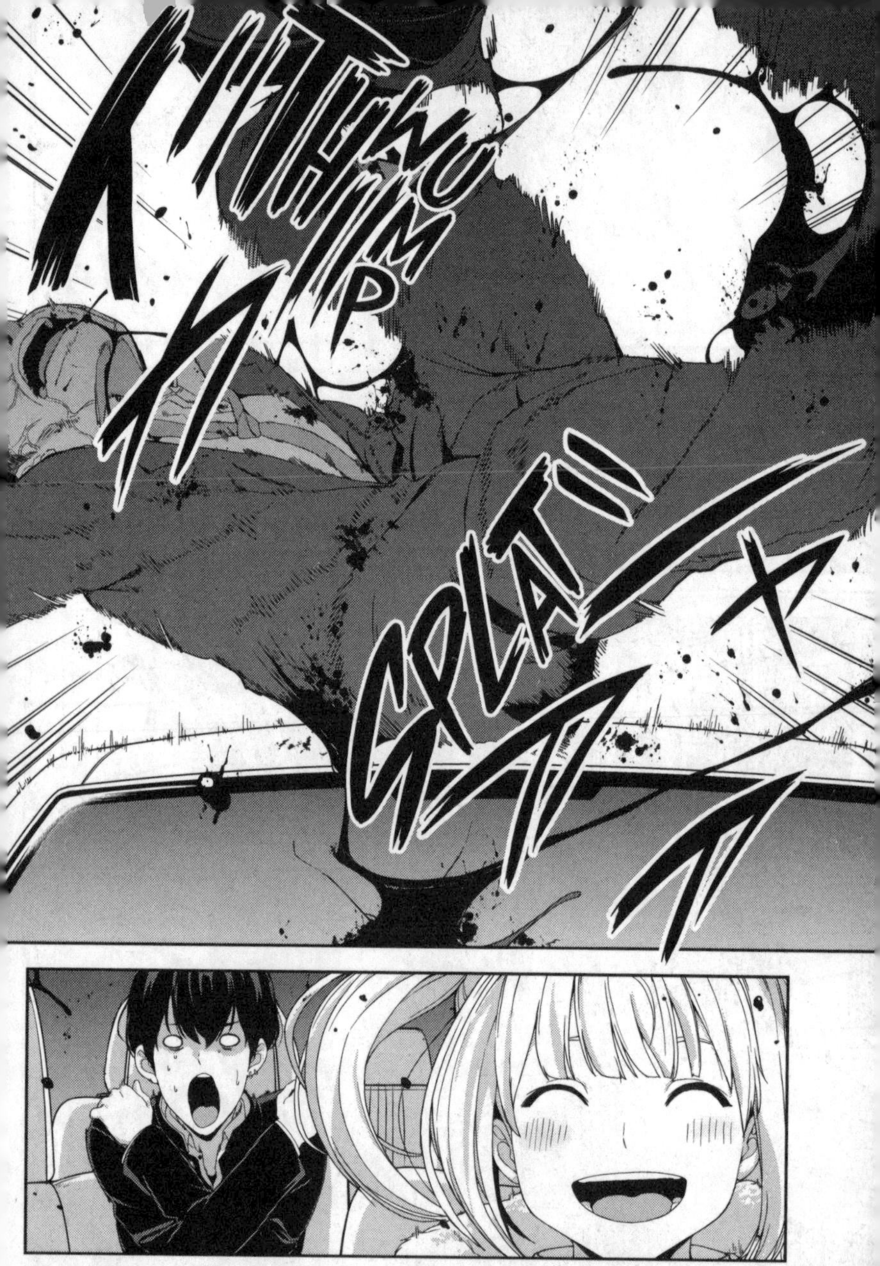
THUMP
SPLAT!!

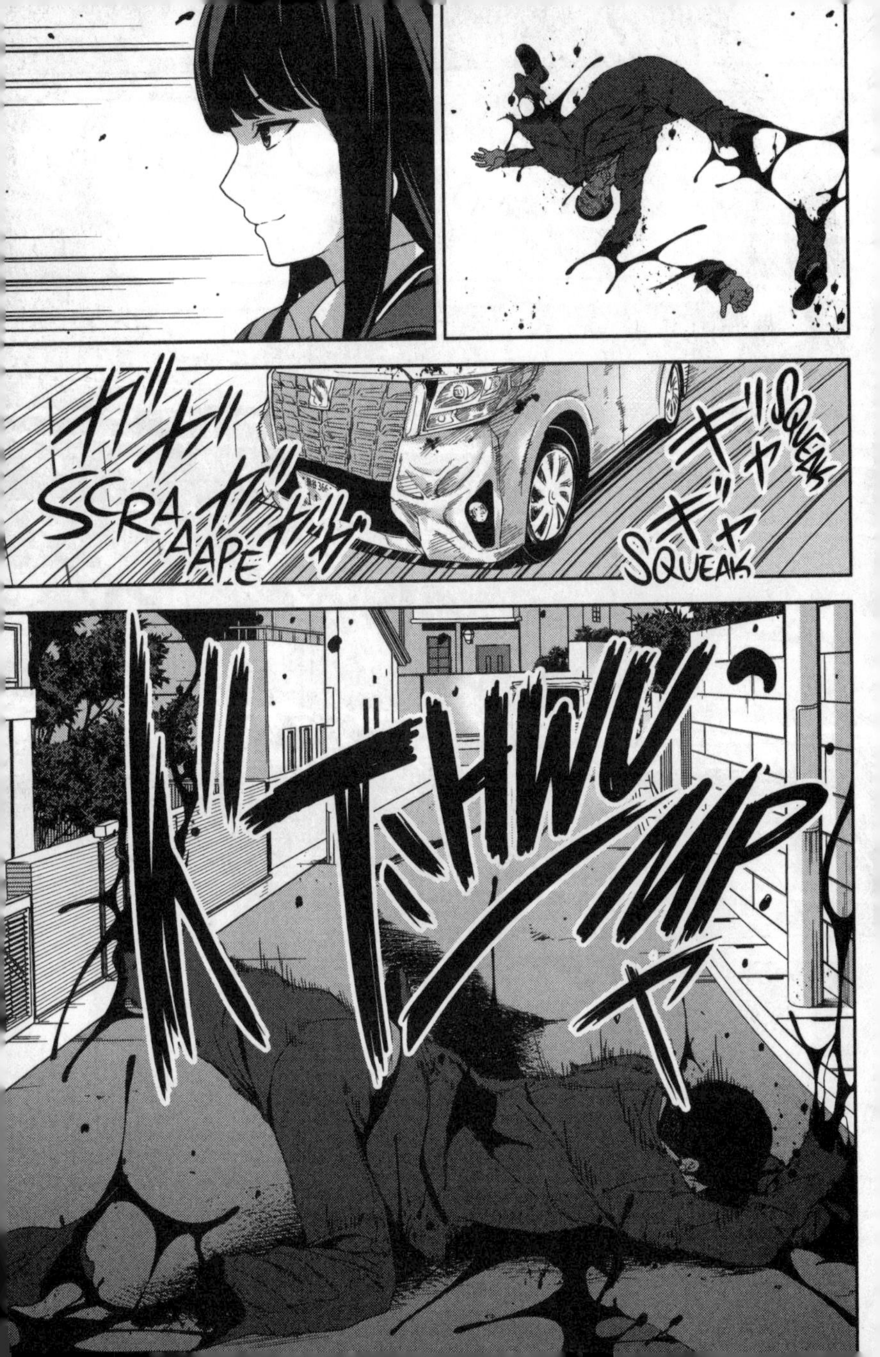
SQUEAK
SQUEAK
SCRAAPE
THWUMP

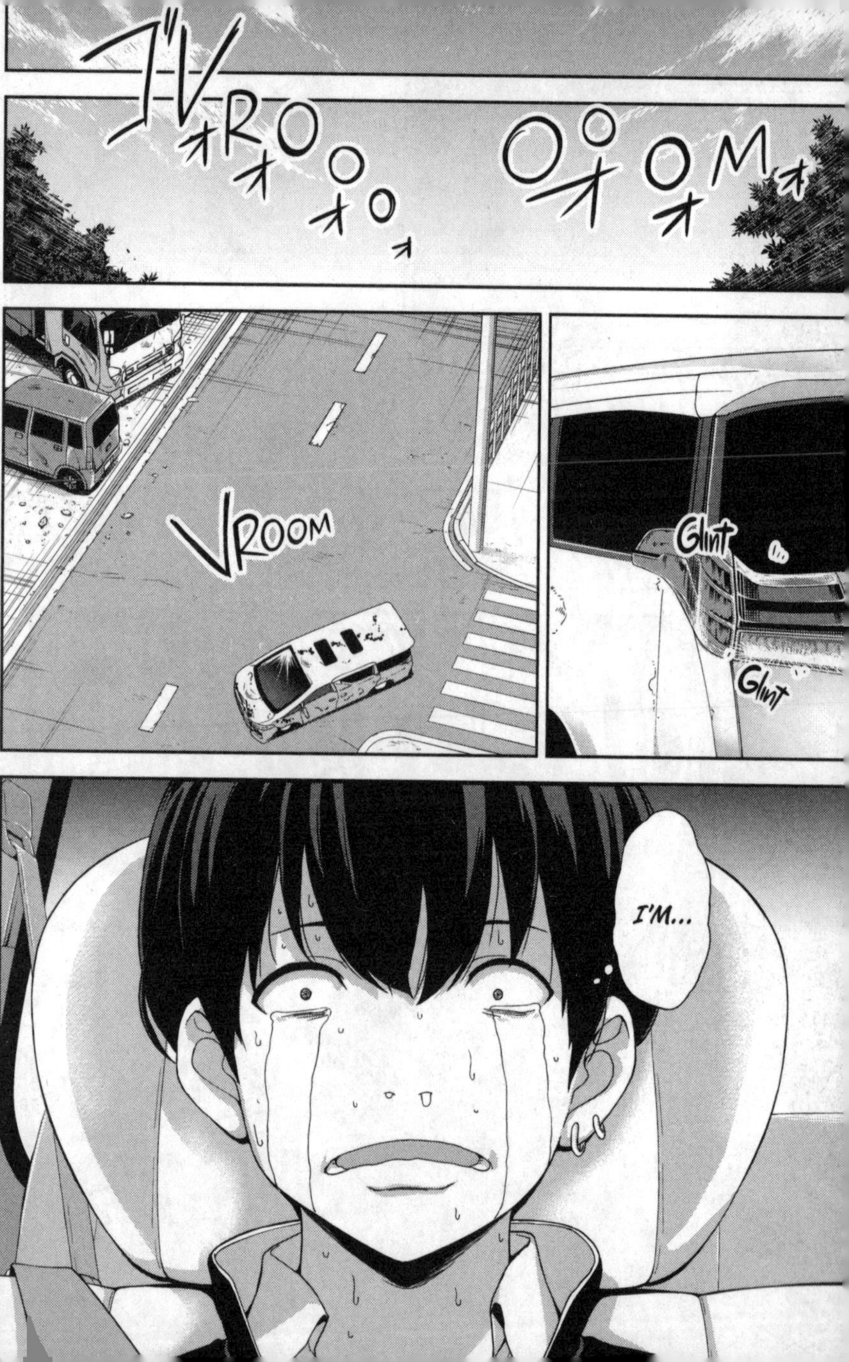
ROOOOOOM
Glint
Glint
VROOM
I'M...

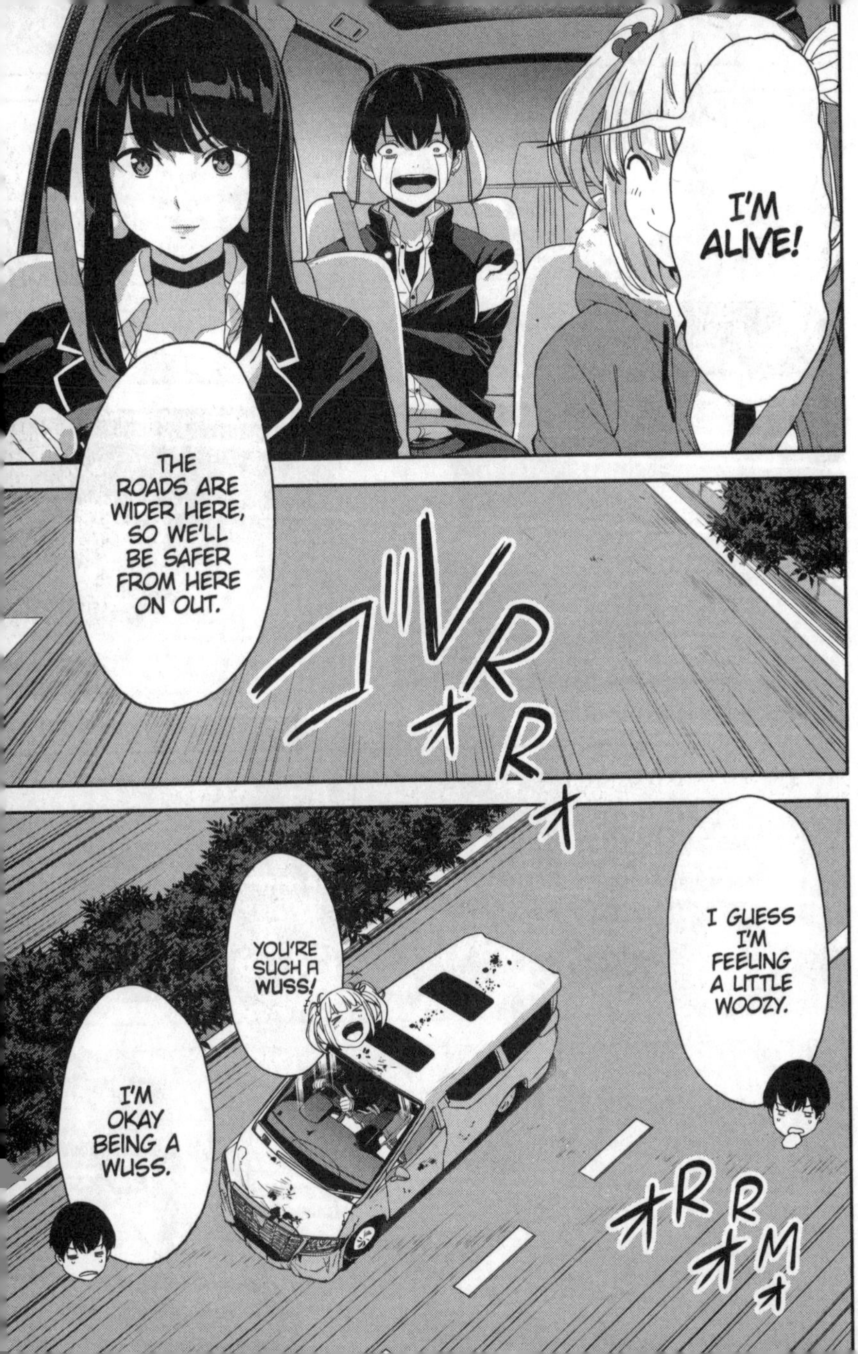
I'M ALIVE!
THE ROADS ARE WIDER HERE, SO WE'LL BE SAFER FROM HERE ON OUT.
VRR
I GUESS I'M FEELING A LITTLE WOOZY.
YOU'RE SUCH A WUSS!
I'M OKAY BEING A WUSS.
RRM

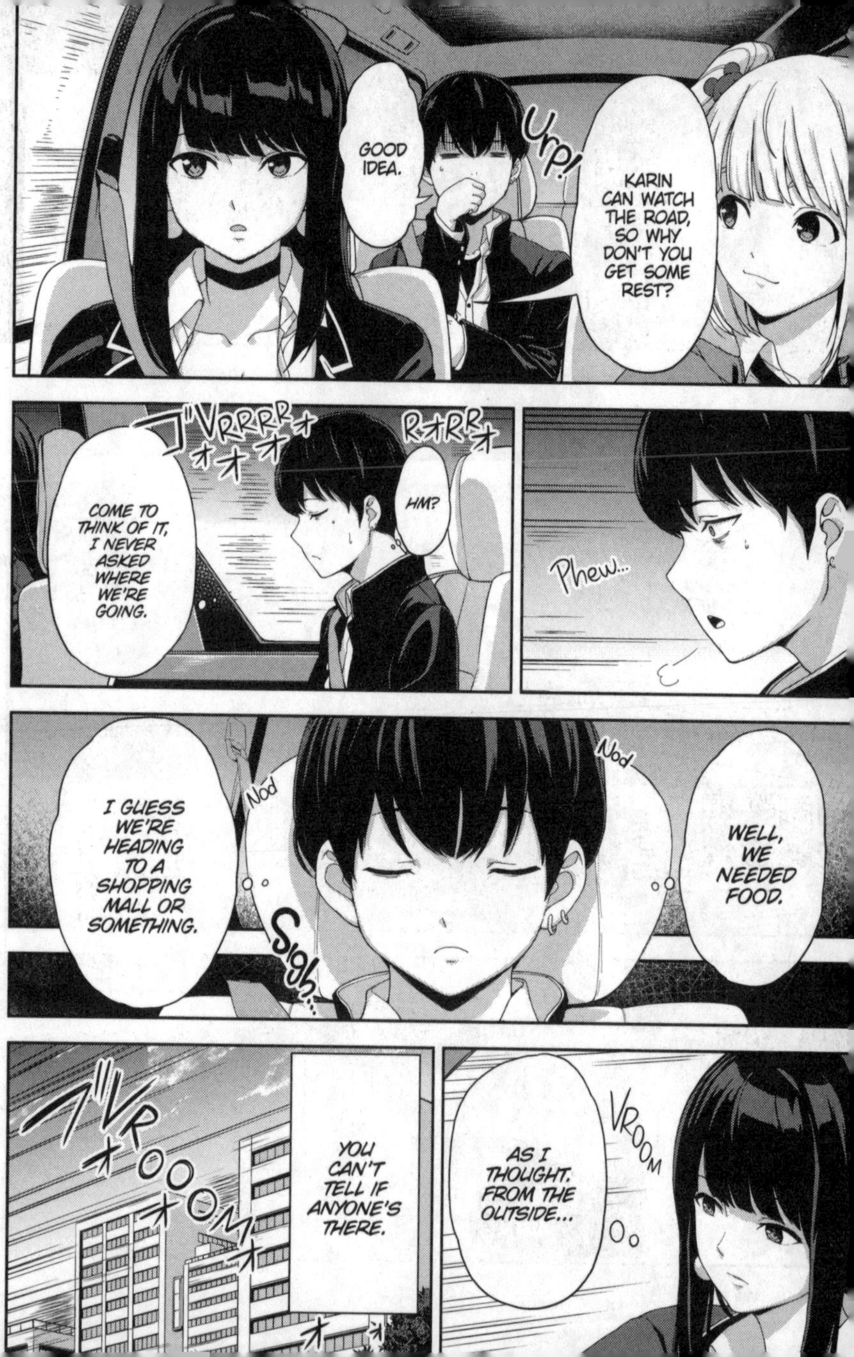
Urp!
KARIN CAN WATCH THE ROAD, SO WHY DON'T YOU GET SOME REST?
GOOD IDEA.
Phew...
RRRR
HM?
VRRRR
COME TO THINK OF IT, I NEVER ASKED WHERE WE'RE GOING.
Nod
WELL, WE NEEDED FOOD.
Nod
I GUESS WE'RE HEADING TO A SHOPPING MALL OR SOMETHING.
Sigh...
VROOM
AS I THOUGHT. FROM THE OUTSIDE...
YOU CAN'T TELL IF ANYONE'S THERE.
VROOOOM

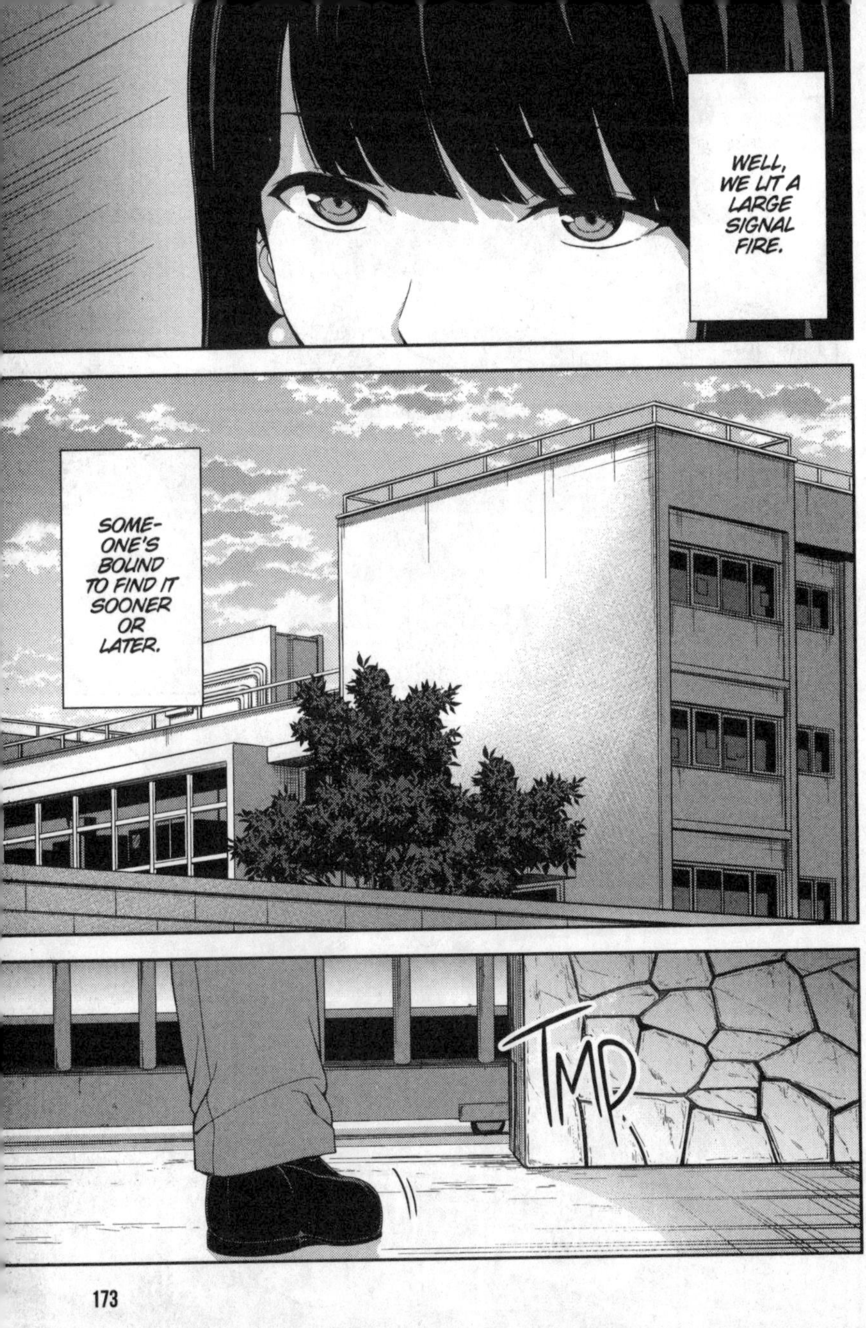
WELL, WE LIT A LARGE SIGNAL FIRE.
SOME-ONE'S BOUND TO FIND IT SOONER OR LATER.
TMP

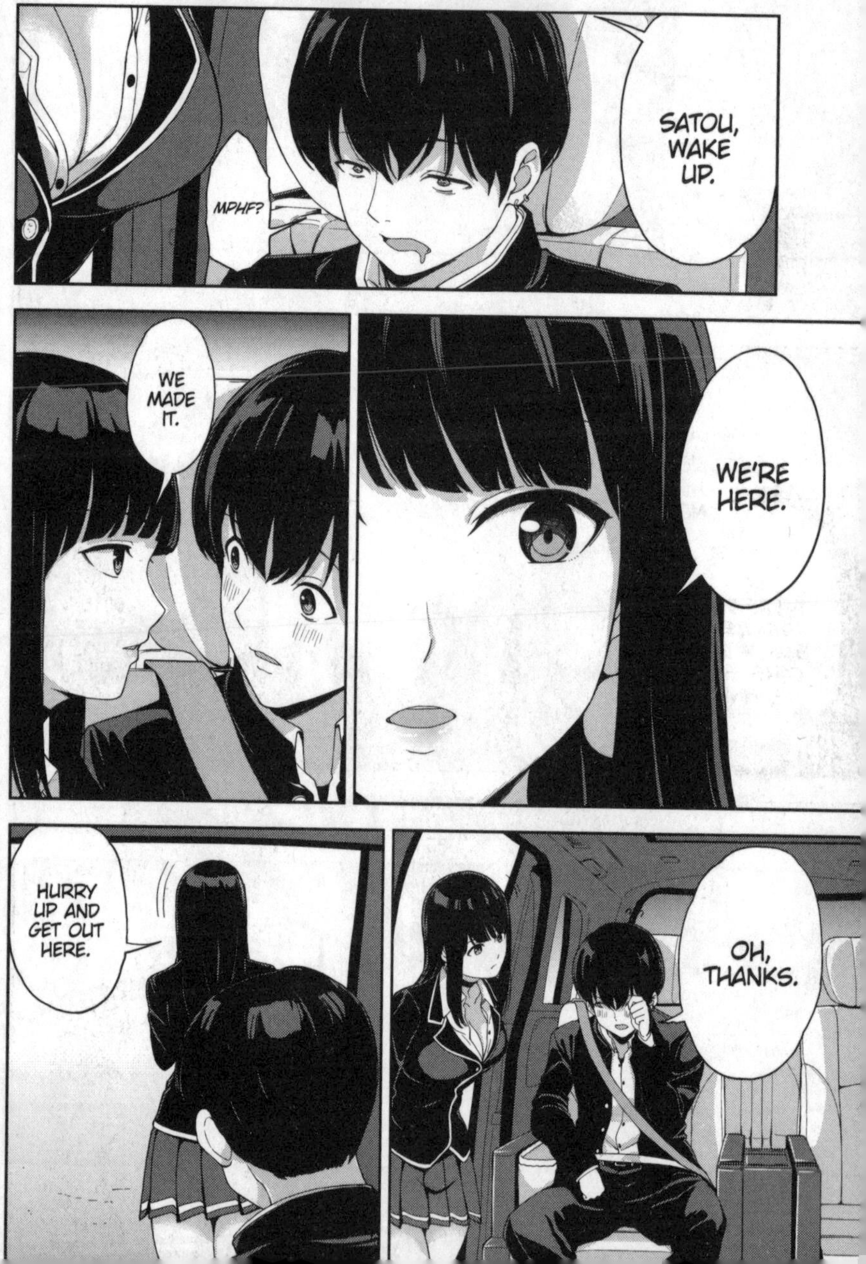
SATOU, WAKE UP.
MPHF?
WE'RE HERE.
WE MADE IT.
OH, THANKS.
HURRY UP AND GET OUT HERE.

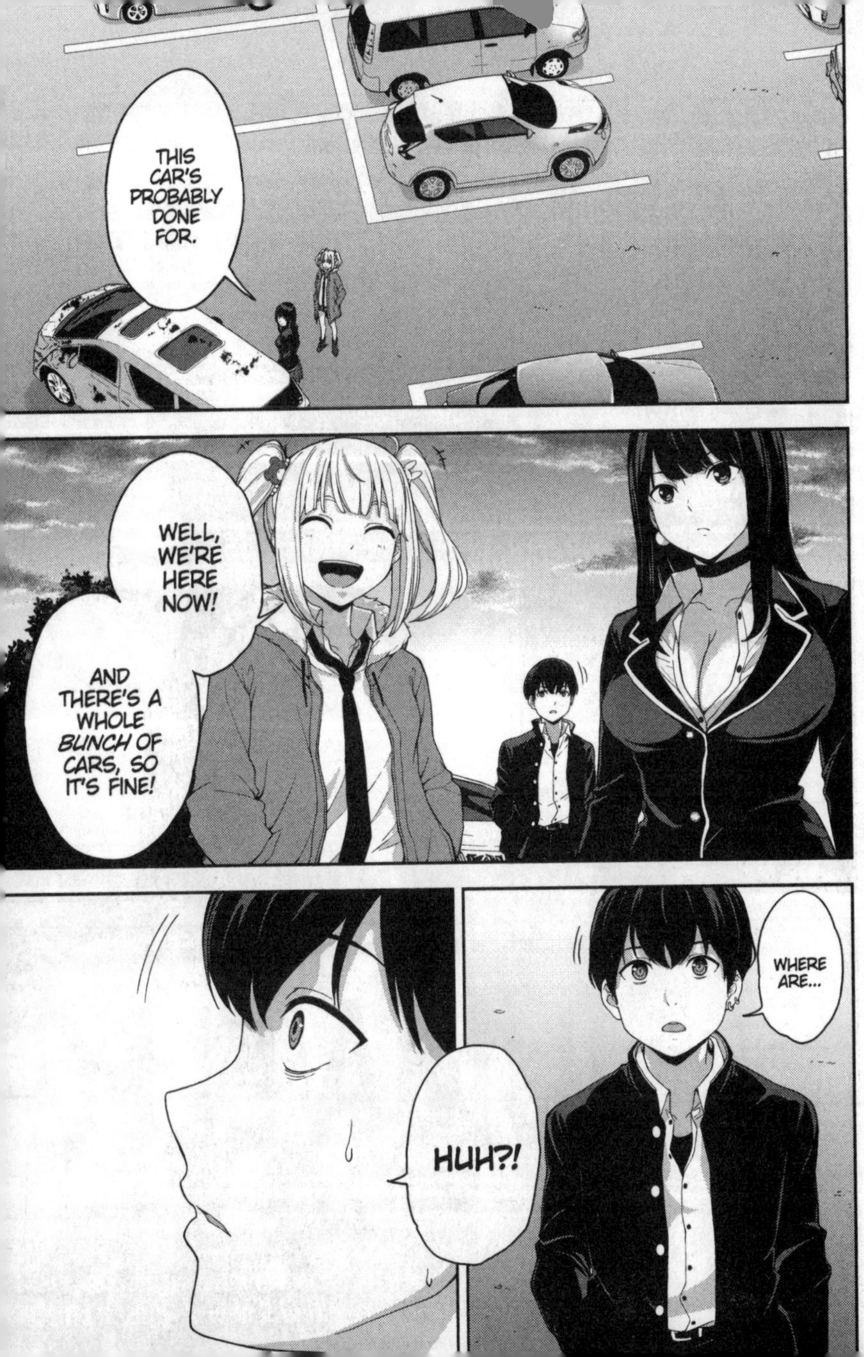
THIS CAR'S PROBABLY DONE FOR.
WELL, WE'RE HERE NOW!
AND THERE'S A WHOLE *BUNCH* OF CARS, SO IT'S FINE!
WHERE ARE...
HUH?!

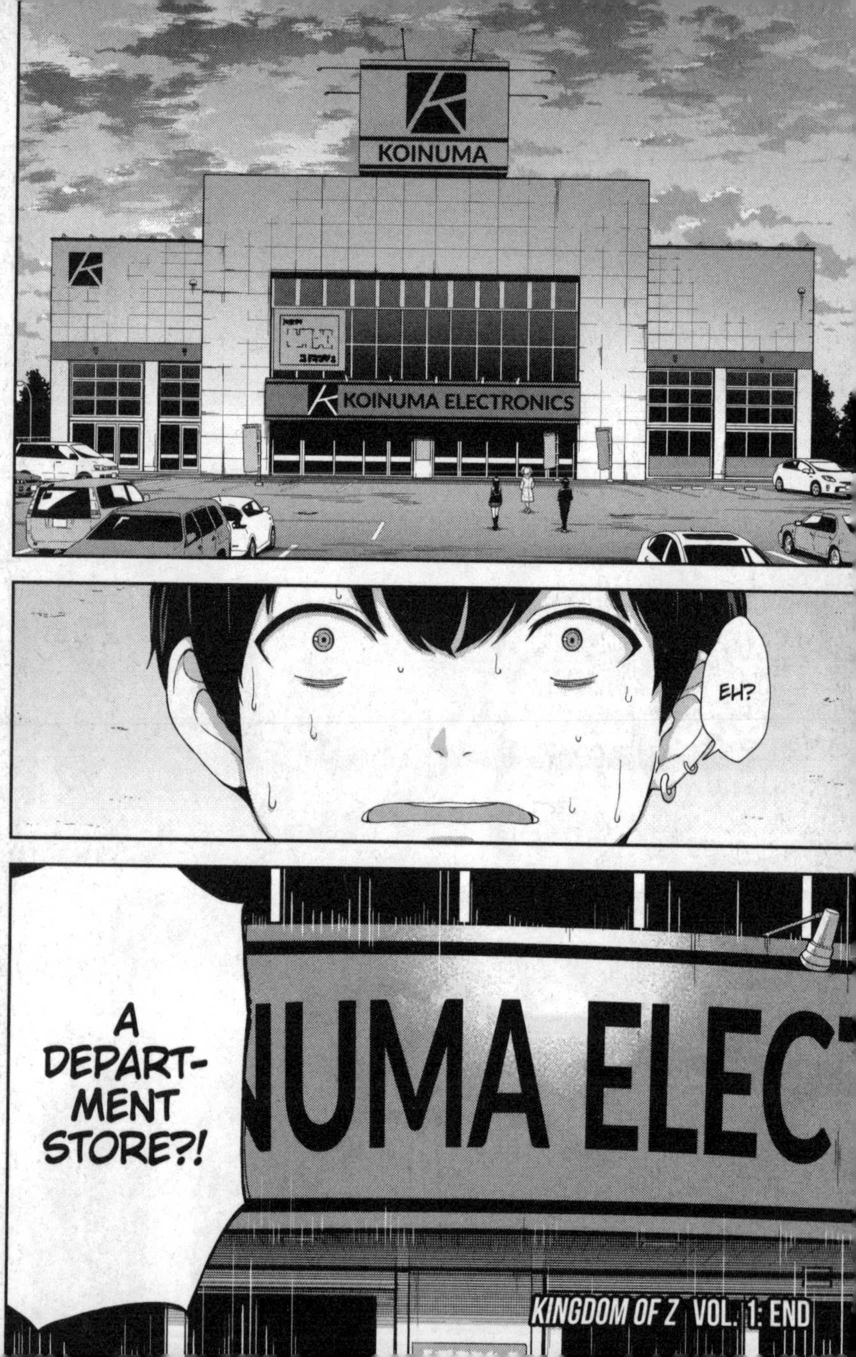
KOINUMA
KOINUMA ELECTRONICS
EH?
A DEPART-MENT STORE?!
NUMA ELEC
KINGDOM OF Z VOL. 1: END

SPOILS OF WAR
SUMMARIZED REPORT

- CITIZEN x1
- GYMNASIUM
- SHOWER ROOM
- CLUB ROOM BUILDING
- ZOMBIFIED JUDO CLUB
  MEMBERS x10
- INFORMATION ON
  OUTSIDE ENEMIES?

SEVEN SEAS ENTERTAINMENT PRESENTS

KINGDOM OF Z

story by **SAIZOU HARAWATA**   art by **LON WATANUKI**   **VOLUME 1**

TRANSLATION
Wesley Bridges

ADAPTATION
Largo Cygnus

LETTERING AND RETOUCH
Joseph Barr

COVER DESIGN
Nicky Lim

PROOFREADER
Kurestin Armada

EDITOR
Shannon Fay

PREPRESS TECHNICIAN
Rhiannon Rasmussen-Silverstein

PRODUCTION MANAGER
Lissa Pattillo

MANAGING EDITOR
Julie Davis

ASSOCIATE PUBLISHER
Adam Arnold

PUBLISHER
Jason DeAngelis

KINGDOM OF Z VOLUME 1
© Saizou Harawata, Lon Watanuki 2019
All rights reserved.
First published in Japan in 2019 by Kodansha Ltd., Tokyo.
Publication rights for this English edition arranged through Kodansha Ltd.,
Tokyo.

Seven Seas press and purchase enquiries can be sent to Marketing Manager
Lianne Sentar at press@gomanga.com. Information regarding the distribution
and purchase of digital editions is available from Digital Manager CK Russell
at digital@gomanga.com.

Seven Seas and the Seven Seas logo are trademarks of
Seven Seas Entertainment. All rights reserved.

ISBN: 978-1-64505-640-9

Printed in Canada

First Printing: July 2020

10 9 8 7 6 5 4 3 2 1

FOLLOW US ONLINE: *www.sevenseasentertainment.com*

READING DIRECTIONS

This book reads from *right to left*, Japanese style.
If this is your first time reading manga, you start
reading from the top right panel on each page and
take it from there. If you get lost, just follow the
numbered diagram here. It may seem backwards at
first, but you'll get the hang of it! Have fun!!

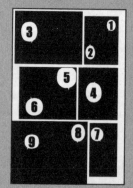